Inside the Mason Court Revolution

Inside the Mason Court Revolution

The High Court of Australia Transformed

Jason L. Pierce
University of Dayton

Carolina Academic Press
Durham, North Carolina

Library of Congress Cataloging-in-Publication Data
Pierce, Jason Louis.
  Inside the Mason Court revolution : the High Court of Australia
transformed / by Jason Louis Pierce.
    p. cm.
  Includes bibliographical references and index.
  ISBN 1-59460-061-9 (alk. paper)
  1. Australia. High Court--History. 2. Courts of last resort--
Australia--History. 3. Political questions and judicial power--
Australia--History. I. Title.

  KU3466.P54 2006
  347.94'035--dc22

                                        2006015834

Carolina Academic Press
700 Kent Street
Durham, North Carolina 27701
Telephone (919) 489-7486
Fax (919) 493-5668
www.cap-press.com

Printed in the United States of America

To Emily and Daniel Ewing

CONTENTS

ACKNOWLEDGMENTS

Preliminary fieldwork for this book began in 1997, when I spent a few months as a research intern at the Australian Parliament and the Australian National University in Canberra. Over the ensuing years, an ever-growing number of individuals have assisted me along the way. This book would have been impossible without the help and encouragement of many.

The book draws heavily upon eighty-plus in-depth interviews that I conducted with Australia's most senior appellate judges from 1997 to 2000. These interviews were conducted under conditions of anonymity, meaning that I draw quotations from the interviews, but nowhere disclose who made particular comments. My informants agreed, however, to have their names listed as participants, which I have done in Appendix A. First and foremost, then, I thank those judges who took time out of their hectic schedules to talk about their judiciary and the profound changes that beset it in the 1990s. They showed remarkable generosity, forthrightness, and patience with this political scientist. Collectively they provided a richly contoured mosaic of High Court history that scholars would be hard pressed to glean from other sources. I hope this work does justice to their thoughtful remarks and to this historic period of High Court history.

The fieldwork would not have been possible without generous financial support from the Fulbright I.I.E. Program, the Australian-American Fulbright Association, the Edward A. Clark Center for Australian and New Zealand Studies at The University of Texas at Austin, and the University of Dayton Research Institute. Nor would it have been as professionally profitable and personally rewarding without the kind hand of many Australian academics and government officials: Christopher Doogan, the High Court's Chief Executive and Principal Registrar, Senator Nick Bolkus, former Commonwealth Shadow Attorney-General, Simon Banks, Patrick Keyzer, George Williams, Fiona Wheeler, Adrienne Stone, Graeme Hill, and Tony Blackshield. I extend a special thanks to Professor Michael Coper, Dean of the Australian National University Faculty of Law, who supported this project in word and deed over many years, providing ample office space and institutional support, and welcoming me into his faculty's vibrant intellectual community. Absent my home base at the A.N.U., this project would not have come together.

The finishing touches were put on this book after I joined the faculty at the University of Dayton. With the university's financial assistance, I completed a final round of fieldwork in Australia in 2003, this time with the able assistance of four university honors students: Amy Batchman, Michelle Berry, Jim McFarland, and Jackie O'Brien. They toiled through the stacks at the National Library of Australia with great aplomb and patience, exemplifying what faculty-student collaboration can produce. I also thank my faculty friends who made this collaboration possible: Steve Dandaneau, Roger Crum, and Christopher Duncan.

Several individuals read the manuscript and provided valuable feedback, including Gary Freeman, Sanford Levinson, and David Anderson. Special thanks go to John Higley and H.W. Perry for their steady guidance, wisdom, and tireless commitment to me and this project. Their tutelage was indispensable. I consider myself fortunate to have worked with such professional political scientists. Any errors or omissions that remain in the manuscript are mine. I also extend my thanks to Keith Sipe, Tim Colton and others at Carolina Academic Press for their excellent work on this book.

On a more personal note, I want to mention several individuals who made this journey in Austin, Australia, and Dayton, Ohio all the more meaningful: the McTaggarts, the Freudenbergers, Aaron and Cathy Kennedy, and Joseph Santamaria and his family. My parents, Dan and Susan Pierce, and my in-laws, Kay and Ewing Werlein, Jr., deserve special mention for their constant support and encouragement over the years.

I dedicate this book to Emily, my best friend, life-partner, and greatest blessing, and to Daniel Ewing, who entered our lives with great joy as this book went to press.

Inside the Mason Court Revolution

1

Introduction

That court was "hyperactive," "adventurous," "incomparably activist," "composed of judicial legislators," and "controlled by Jacobins." The Justices were "under the influence of left-wing theorists," "deciding cases as Marx or Freud would have," "defying common sense," "moving the goal posts instead of just deciding if a goal had been scored," and "overcome with delusions of grandeur." Americans might think such disparaging remarks (or perhaps endearing, depending upon one's judicial politics) are the exclusive domain of the U.S. Supreme Court and its justices. But in fact, each of these tart descriptions came when I asked Australian appellate judges to describe their country's final appellate court, the High Court of Australia.

Students of American courts may not bat an eye at such characterizations. We are long accustomed to the U.S. Supreme Court deciding controversial issues that divide the country and engender these sorts of criticisms. This banter, however, is not only foreign but heretical to accepted conventions about how Australians talk about their judges. During the last fifteen years, the High Court has captured time and again the attention of the Australian public and politicians in unprecedented ways. Great controversy has surrounded it. Legal and constitutional questions have leapt from the dusty pages of casebooks to the front pages of newspapers. Conversations about the High Court and its judges have echoed in the corridors of the state and national parliaments, if not the courthouses. Many of the Court's decisions in the last fifteen years have occupied state and national governments like few other issues. A single 1996 decision concerning land rights for Australia's indigenous people nearly precipitated, for example, a double dissolution election in the federal parliament, something that has occurred only six times in Australia's history, whereby both houses of the national parliament are dissolved and new elections held.

What occurred Down Under to generate these reactions? What could solicit these characterizations of the judges on Australia's highest court? This book makes the case that from the mid-1980s to the mid-1990s a group of High Court judges embarked on a concerted effort to redefine substantively their institution's role within the political system. These judges introduced a new vision for the Court's role that stood in sharp contrast to a well-entrenched vision that had dominated the Court and the broader judicial and political cultures for much of the twentieth century. While the Court's history is punctuated with politically contentious decisions, these judges moved the Court from operating on the margins of Australian politics to its storm center. The Court shifted its institutional focus away from simply resolving legal disputes to making policy that addressed some of the country's most controversial issues. Fairness, not certainty, became the Court's watchword, and as a result, it employed new, controversial modes of legal reasoning. A sense emerged in the legal community that the High Court was about the task of crafting a distinctly Australian vision of justice and the judiciary's role—nationalizing Australian law. To an unprecedented extent, these High Court judges viewed their decision-making powers as a mechanism to address shortcomings and stalemates in the political system and their institution as a legitimate source for reforms. The cumulative result was a more activist, more controversial, and much more politicized High Court.

The emergence of this new institutional role coincided roughly with the tenure of Anthony Mason as High Court Chief Justice from 1987 to 1995. While Americans are quick to label eras of Supreme Court history in terms of the chief justice at the time, e.g., the Marshall Court or the Warren Court, Australian legal scholars and judges show greater reticence toward this nomenclature. This watershed point is best understood, however, as the Mason Court era. "Watershed" is an apt label. The Mason Court brought profound changes to numerous areas of public and private law. Some of these legal reforms were readily apparent to average Australians and others known only to the legal fraternity. Yet the judges' reform efforts transcended substantive law. The Mason Court also marked a turning point as it supplanted long-established norms and expectations about the Court's role with a new vision—a *nueve raison d'être*. This book contends that the changes to substantive law, the Court's formal rules and powers, as well as its informal norms constituted a transformation in the High Court's role in the legal and political systems, a phenomenon that may be described as a *judicial role transformation*. This transformation, from what was an *orthodox judicial role* to a new *politicized judicial role* represents one of the most significant developments—some might say the most significant—in the Court's history. The political firestorm that surrounded this transformation was on par, by way of comparison, with any period of U.S. Supreme Court history and explains the vitriol quoted above.

By saying that the Mason Court supplanted an orthodox judicial role I mean several things. First and foremost, it signifies that for most of the twentieth century a widely held set of normative claims were shared by members of the judiciary and broader political community about the Court's functions and purposes. There was general agreement about what the Court should and should not do and a pattern of behavior over the decades where High Court judges comported with those expectations. This orthodoxy's multi-layered set of prescriptive expectations addressed a number of jurisprudential and political issues. Chapter 3 explores this in detail. Briefly, the orthodox judicial role conceived of law's purpose as providing certainty. In other words, the law should give clear direction and guidance to those raising and deciding legal disputes. Appellate litigation followed a private model, meaning that it was understood first and foremost as a venue for resolving disputes between parties rather than promulgating broad social policy. Non-party interventions by interveners and amici curiae, therefore, were discouraged. Judges were not thought to make law, but as apolitical decision-makers they simply discovered the law. Legal reasoning was declaratory in nature, such that the judge's responsibility was to find the one correct answer for each case. The orthodox role also placed great weight on stare decisis and law developing interstitially. Finally, Australia's Commonwealth Constitution was seen as a document that distributed political power among the federal branches of government and between the federal, state, and territory governments, and said little about the country's enduring political values or civil and political rights. As a consequence, textualism and structuralism were the dominant interpretive approaches. Second, this judicial role was "orthodox" in the sense that judges infrequently violated its prescriptions. This set of normative ideas did not guide every judge in every case—one can point to instances where judges contravened it—but it operated in the judicial culture as a powerful meta-narrative about the High Court's function. Finally, it was "orthodox" because those few judges who persistently challenged or violated these ideas were castigated as rabble-rousers who refused to play by the rules.

The politicized judicial role is distinguished from the orthodoxy in several ways. Under this alternative, law's primary purpose is to secure individual justice and promote fairness rather than certainty. Litigation is conceived as a legal and political enterprise where broad social policy may be established. Given this directive, non-party intervention in appellate litigation is more acceptable. Although it may sound naïve or antiquated, the politicized role is also notable for its admission that judges make law and exercise discretion. A number of changes occur to legal reasoning as well. The identification of overarching principles is encouraged, the constitution is understood to contain certain unarticulated rights and freedoms that are judicially discoverable, and the tradition of stare decisis is weaker. In short, judges are less constrained and the Court plays an increasingly prominent role in policymaking.

Let me state explicitly what I intend to convey (and not convey) in saying that the High Court underwent a *transformation*. I employ the term foremost to capture the profundity and uniqueness of the events and decisions that attended the Mason Court, but I do not intend its use to imply that the Mason Court's reforms were immutable—that post-Mason Court judges have never backed away or retreated. Indeed, quite the opposite has occurred. Beginning in the late 1990s a majority of the Court abandoned—for reasons addressed in chapter 7—some of the most notable jurisprudence and legal reasoning that had secured footings just a few years earlier. Nor do I intend to imply, by describing these changes as a transformation, that one finds unanimous support or a consensus today over its merits. Australia's judicial and political communities remain divided over what role the High Court should play in Australian politics and they certainly remain divided over the Mason Court reforms. Finally, this transformation did not have a definitive beginning and ending. I will indicate in the coming chapters those events and decisions that roughly signposted the transformation's beginning and denouement, but this was not a transformation marked by a single causal event or discrete dates. This transformation was attenuated, the cumulative result from a set of actions and decisions made over several years by many different judicial and political actors.

Having offered these provisos, let me say what I do mean by transformation. First, a transformation occurred in the sense that the Court from the mid-1980s to the mid-1990s assumed an institutional role in the legal and political systems that differed from its predecessors in profoundly significant ways. Second, the events that transpired during these years transformed the way in which politicians and judges perceive the High Court. Whereas before the mid-1980s the Court was seen as somewhat removed and separate from the political world, it has since become politicized to unprecedented levels. The High Court is now nearly universally conceived as both a legal and political institution, meaning that judges and politicians see the Court as another forum for political contestation, not unlike other branches of government. Moreover, its judges are seen today as active participants in the governing process, to a degree that was previously not the case. Finally, these changes to substantive law and judicial norms are transformative in that they are now indelibly part of Australia's legal discourse and politics. Even if future Courts retract or consolidate these reforms, the new vision that the Mason Court ushered in cannot be erased. The Court permanently altered Australian law and politics, in so far as judges, litigants, and politicians must at the very least reckon with the new ideas about the Court's role. The genie is out of the bottle.

Before diving headlong into describing this genie and why it appeared, some key concepts must be defined. First, this project is premised on the idea that individual judges hold conceptions about their institution's purposes and the methods by which those purposes should be fulfilled. Court scholars refer to these as *judicial role conceptions* (see Becker 1964; 1966; Berry 1974). J. Woodford Howard defined these as "normative expectations shared by judges and related actors regarding how a given judicial office should be performed (1977, 916)." James Gibson succinctly characterized them as what judges "think they ought to do (1983, 9)." Drawing from more recent scholarship, judicial role conceptions constitute "bundles of ideas and motivations," institutional statements of "mission" (Gillman 1999, 78), or "rationalities of action" regarding the judiciary (Skowronek 1995, 94). They provide judges with what Rogers Smith calls "distinctively institutional perspectives" or "senses of purpose and principle" and "conceptions of duty (1988, 95)." A judicial role conception answers a number of questions: What functions should a final appellate court perform and not perform? What are the purposes of law and aims of litigation? What sort of institutional relationships should courts have with other branches of government? What are acceptable modes of legal reasoning and interpretation?

Judicial role conceptions are both descriptive (what *is* the court doing?) and normative (what *should* the court be doing?). They also are highly contextualized within particular political settings and judicial cultures, such that judges in one country likely conceive their institution's function differently from judges in other countries. Role conceptions are also institutionally specific, meaning that judges at different hierarchical positions within a judiciary think differently about courts. One naturally would expect trial court judges to perceive their functions differently from appellate judges.

A judicial role conception—those "bundles of ideas" that individual judges hold about their institution's purposes—is distinct from the functions that a court actually fulfills, something I have referred to in these opening pages as a *judicial role*. One would anticipate overlap between a court's *judicial role* and the *role conceptions* that those judges who comprise the court hold. Distinguishing these two concepts is necessary to be clear about what this book accomplishes. At its core, it explores the transformation that occurred in the High Court's *judicial role*. To understand why it occurred, how it occurred, and what consequences it portends for Australian law and politics, it draws upon interview data that provide an assemblage of individual judges' *role conceptions*. Its priority, however, is to explain the institutional change. This research obviously assumes, then, that one can identify and describe a judicial role—those functions that a specific court fulfills at a given time—and assess if and how that role changes over time. This book also is premised on the idea that judicial roles may vary cross-nationally as well as longitudinally in single courts. It focuses on the role changes that occurred over time at the High Court and on the circumstances that made that possible. This change in institutional function across time is technically what I mean by a *judicial role transformation*.

The idea that people think in terms of "roles" is hardly new to social science. Role theory has a long and rich history in sociology, psychology, and anthropology, and has been used to study an array of human phenomena (see Gross 1958; Wahlke 1962; Biddle and Thomas 1966; Biddle 1979). Role theory seeks to explain human behavior as a product of individuals and their values interacting within particular environments (Gibson 1983). Political scientists first applied role theory to judicial bodies in the 1970s. At that time, role theory seemed to offer a promising approach to studying judicial behavior. One scholar boldly claimed that what judges thought their role should be was "the major independent variable in the judicial equation (Becker 1964, 13)," while another said it was "the most significant single factor in the whole decisional process (Dolbeare 1967, 69)." Despite these hopeful pronouncements, the use of role theory to study judicial behavior waned in the early 1980s.

This literature from the 1960s to the 1980s tended to pursue two aims. First, some scholars tried to explain why judges develop different role conceptions. Social background characteristics such as education, religion, class, and career history (Wold 1974), political ideologies (Howard 1977; Glick and Vines 1969), professional norms, and institutional resources (Gibson 1981) were correlated to particular judicial role conceptions. A second line of research tried to categorize and classify judges' role conceptions based on survey data and close analysis of written opinions (Scheb, Ungs et al. 1989; Baas 1971). A panoply of typologies soon emerged that described different judicial role conceptions. Judges were classified as activists and restraintists (Scheb and Ungs 1987); law interpreters and lawmakers (Wold 1974); ritualists, adjudicators, policy makers, and administrators (Glick and Vines 1969); and law appliers, law extenders, and mediators (Flango et al. 1975).

This book employs the judicial role concept to achieve somewhat different aims. First, it goes beyond simply labeling individual judges' outlooks, trying to isolate those factors that explain why judges have different role conceptions, or utilizing role theory to understand judicial behavior. My unit of analysis is the High Court as an institution, rather than the individual judges who comprise it. I seek to explain institutional development—the transformation in the High Court's institutional role within the legal and political systems—and not judicial behavior. To focus on this means that I do not conceive the Court as a *tabula rasa*, through which unconstrained judges pursue their policy preferences. The events surrounding the High Court's transformation affirm the influence of formal and informal institutional structures on what judges can and cannot accomplish. If a judicial role is understood in the institutional sense, as "an identifiable purpose or shared normative goal that, at a particular historical moment in a particular context, becomes routinized within an identifiable corporate form (Gillman 1999, 78)," then this book explores a case where those shared normative goals radically changed. While focusing on the institutional change, I do not intend to dismiss the individual judges who participated in and observed the transformation. As Rogers Smith reminded us, "The Lord Baltimore Hotel is a kind of institution. The Social Science History Association is a kind of institution. The State Department is a kind of institution. But none of these institutions will function for a second if there aren't a whole lot of human beings with ideas in their heads defining their roles in relation to those institutions. It is their purposes, their projects that make those institutions go and work (1995, 136)." Individuals animate institutions.

PLACING THE HIGH COURT'S TRANSFORMATION IN COMPARATIVE CONTEXT

Discerning the relative influence that individuals have on an institution's role, vis-à-vis other factors, is tricky. The corollary question that it poses is just what functions can a supreme court assume? Political scientists have identified a number of potential purposes or roles that supreme courts play within democratic political systems. Some argue that supreme courts should function as "representation reinforcing" institutions by eliminating structural or procedural obstacles that prevent minority segments of society from accessing and participating fully in the political process (Ely 1980). Removed from the hurly burly of politics, supreme courts are also capable of reminding a polity of its enduring political values (Bickel 1986) or handling distinctly moral questions (Perry 1982; Dworkin 1996). Others think that the courts should discern and promulgate the intent of those who penned a political system's constitutive documents (Meese 1985; Powell 1985). Still others claim that courts of final appeal are uniquely equipped to protect numeric minorities from majority tyranny (Abraham 1997; Lane 1996; Davenport 1996; Stepan and Skach 1993; Elster and Slagstad 1988), to circumscribe majority preferences (Weaver and Rockman 1993; Lijphart and Waisman 1996; Baaklini and Desfosses 1997; Diamond 1997), to legitimize the present political regime (North, Weingast et al. 1989; Weingast 1993; Olson 1993), or to sustain policies implemented by governing majorities that have since lost power (Ramseyer 1994). Supreme courts can also alleviate executive branches of the need to constantly monitor bureaucratic compliance (McCubbins and Schwartz 1984), they can break institutional deadlocks in political systems (Hand 1958), and may provide additional veto and access points for interest groups (Kirchheimer 1980; Weaver and Rockman 1993).

While scholars point to empirical examples of supreme courts fulfilling these and other functions, courts of final appeal in numerous countries and at the international level have assumed greater power and political salience in recent years. The scholarship tracking this global expansion of judicial power is extensive (see Waltman and Holland 1988; Holland 1991; Jackson and Tate 1992; Tate and Vallinder 1995; Stone Sweet 2000; Shapiro and Stone Sweet 2002). Supreme courts in many Anglo-derived, common law judiciaries have formed the vanguard for this expansion. Several have undergone their own transformations in the last twenty years, including courts in Canada, New Zealand, and the United Kingdom, all in response to newly ascribed powers to protect civil liberties and human rights. The Australian High Court's role transformation occurred, then, in a period when courts were assuming new powers and duties across the globe, and courts in several Anglo-derived judiciaries were undergoing or had undergone their own transformations. Consider briefly three cases.

Canada's Charter of Rights and Freedoms, enacted in 1982, constitutionally protects a litany of rights and has fundamentally altered the Supreme Court's role in Canadian politics (Manfredi 2001). Its constitutional caseload has shifted from straightforward federalism disputes to abortion rights, immigration policy, indigenous people's land rights, language politics, equality, religious rights, hate-speech, and prostitution.[1] Former Chief Justice Lamer declared on the Charter's tenth anniversary that it brought "a revolution on the scale of the introduction of the metric system, the great medical discoveries of Louis Pasteur, and the invention of penicillin and the laser (Lamer 1992)." Jurisprudential developments since that anniversary require the Chief Justice to qualify his assessment, but the Charter undeniably transformed the Supreme Court's role in Canadian politics.[2]

---

1. For example, on abortion see *R v. Morgentaler and Smoling* [1988] 1 SCR 30; on immigration see *Singh v. Minister for Employment and Immigration* [1985] 1 SCR 177; on indigenous land rights see *R v. Delgamuukw* [1998] 1 CNLR 14 (S.C.C.); on language politics see *Ford v. A.G. Quebec* [1988] 2 SCR 712; on equality see *Andrews v. Law Society of British Columbia* [1989] 1 SCR 143; *Tetrault-Gaboury v. Canada* [1992] 2 SCR 679; *Schacter v. Canada* [1992] 2 SCR 679; on religious rights see *R v. Big M. Drug Mart Ltd.* [1985] 1 SCR 295; on hate speech speech *R v. Keegstra* [1990] 3 SCR 697; and on prostitution see *Edwards Books and Art Ltd. v. R* [1986] 2 SCR 713.

2. The scope and timing of the Supreme Court's transformation is heavily debated. Morton, Russell and Riddell (1994) found that during the first two years when the Court heard Charter appeals, rights claimants won 64 percent of the time. This success rate lev-

New Zealand's parliament enacted a rights-protecting measure in 1990 similar to the Canadian Charter: the *Bill of Rights Act* (*BORA*).[3] It catalogs a number of rights and freedoms concerning life and security of person, democratic and civil rights, non-discrimination and minority rights, and criminal procedure protections. Unlike the Charter, which trumps statutory law by virtue of its constitutional status, New Zealand's bill of rights is a statutory instrument, meaning that a simple majority in Parliament can repeal or amend it at any time. The courts are not authorized under the Act to void legislation or issue declarations of incompatiblity, as is the case in the Canadian and British regimes, respectively.[4] *BORA* has had its greatest impact not in the courts but in Parliament, where debates now occur over whether proposed legislation comports with *BORA*. The statute also has equipped litigants with rights-based arguments previously unavailable, and consequently transformed the Court of Appeal's (recently renamed the Supreme Court of New Zealand) role.[5] *BORA* has been used to advance arguments regarding Maori land claims,[6] immigration policy and gay marriage,[7] religious freedoms,[8] and criminal procedure.[9] As a result, the Court has assumed a more prominent position on many political issues. *BORA*'s impact on the Court's institutional role is well illustrated in its 1999 *Moonen* decision.[10] In this case, the Court reserved to itself the right to notify Parliament when a proposed statute violated *BORA*, a power nowhere provided to the Court in the statute. Some scholars anticipate *Moonen* will encourage litigants to request that the Court declare certain statutes incompatible with *BORA* (Butler 2000). To the extent the

---

eled off in the 1980s and some think the Court's activism subsided in the 1990s (Kelly 1999). Others hold the view that the Court has assumed a moderately activist approach since the Charter's adoption (Russell 1992; Vallinder 1994), although see Kelly (2005) who argues that the Charter has made all branches of government more sensitive to rights, including the Court. All agree, however, that the Charter profoundly impacted the Supreme Court's institutional role in Canadian politics.

3. *Bill of Rights Act 1990 (BORA)*, New Zealand Stat., No. 109.

4. For a comparison of New Zealand's statutory bill of rights and Canada's Charter, see Principe (1993). On an institutional note, appeals from New Zealand's Court of Appeal to the Privy Council ended in January 2004, when New Zealand's parliament created a new final appellate court, the Supreme Court of New Zealand.

5. See Richardson (1995); Rishworth (1997), (2003); Joseph (1996).

6. *New Zealand Maori Council v. Attorney General* [1987] 1 NZLR 641.

7. *Quilter v. Attorney General* [1996] NZFLR 481.

8. *Re J (An Infant)* [1996] 2 NZLR 134.

9. *R v. Jefferies* [1994] 1 NZLR 290; *R v. A* [1994] 1 NZLR 429; and *R v. Laugalis* (1993) 10 CRNZ 350.

10. *G.A. Moonen v. Film & Literature Board of Review* [2000] 2 NZLR 9 (CA).

Court entertains these invitations, it would enmesh itself deeper in political, value-laden disputes.

In the last several years, reforms in the United Kingdom have laid a foundation for far reaching changes to its judiciary's role. Tony Blair's New Labor Party was ushered into power in 1996, in part, on a legislative platform that promised several significant constitutional and judicial reforms. On November 9, 1998 the Blair Government received royal assent to one such reform, the *Human Rights Act* (*HRA*), which incorporated the *European Convention on Human Rights* (*ECHR*) into domestic law. Prior to the *HRA*, the only avenue for British citizens to pursue human rights claims was through the European Court of Human Rights in Strasbourg. The *HRA* incorporates the European convention rights into British law, providing a domestic alternative to the Strasbourg system by vesting British courts with the power to hear convention claims (Zander 1997; Hoffman & Rowe 2003).

Several aspects of the *HRA* raise the specter of profound change in British courts. First, it introduced the first modern catalog of human rights. Before the *HRA*, rights were protected through a hodgepodge of common law and statutory law assembled over the centuries. Absent a single statement of rights, the legal system provided primarily "negative rights," meaning that a person had a right to do whatever was not prohibited. With the *HRA*, British citizens can point to positive rights guaranteed in law. Second, the *HRA* empowers select courts to issue "declarations of incompatibility" when judges confront legislation that infringes the ECHR.[11] British judges have exercised judicial review over administrative decisions since 1982, but not until the *HRA* were they equipped to review the substance of parliamentary statutes.[12] The power to issue such declarations, which has occurred only ten times since the *HRA* took effect, nonetheless represents a new arrow in the judiciary's quiver.[13] Third, the *HRA* enables British judges to rely upon Strasbourg's case law to decide domestic human rights cases. The *HRA* took effect only in October 2000 and the scholarship to date points to some areas where its impact is great and oth-

---

11. *Human Rights Act 1998*, §4(6). The Judicial Committee of the Privy Council, the Appellate Committee of the House of Lords, the Court of Appeal, and the High Court exercise this power.

12. For general discussions of judicial review in Britain, see Sterett (1993) and Sunkin (1994).

13. A declaration of incompatibility does not impact a law's validity, operation, or enforcement, but it enables the judges to second-guess Parliament's wisdom. It falls, however, to Parliament to correct any instances of incompatibility. The Department of Constitutional Affairs tracks these data. See http://www.humanrights.gov.uk/decihm.htm (last consulted January 2, 2006).

ers where it remains an unknown potentiality (see Jackson 1997; Ashcroft, Gibson et al. 1999; Betten 1999; Cheney 1999; F. Butler 2000; Clayton and Tomlinson 2001). One organization monitoring *HRA* litigation reports that the Act impacted the outcome, reasoning, or procedure in 315 out of 428 cases that raised *HRA* claims decided between October 2, 2000 and April 30, 2002 (O'Brien & Arkinstall 2002).

These three examples of appellate court transformations share a common characteristic: the source of change lay outside the judiciary. Supreme courts in Canada and New Zealand have undergone profound change, and the British appellate courts appear poised to follow suit. These transformations became possible only after the legislature in each country adopted new rights-protecting measures. In each case, extra-judicial authorities vested the courts with new responsibilities and new roles. Sufficient time has passed in the Canadian and New Zealand cases to conclude that lasting changes have occurred. Indications point to similar lasting changes coming to British courts.

The Australian High Court's transformation, by contrast, appears to have been more internally driven. Extra-judicial authorities did not grant any substantively new powers to the Court. No bill of rights or legislation expanding judicial review powers precipitated the role change. Rather, a group of entrepreneurial High Court judges embarked, on their own volition, to redefine their institution's mission. This makes the Australian case particularly intriguing because it provides a unique vantage point to explore the dynamic between political actors and political institutions. It raises a number of compelling questions: To what extent can individual political actors shape or influence the political institutions they occupy? What conditions within political institutions enable or discourage individual political actors from shaping their institution's role? These are admittedly broad questions that do not lend themselves to straightforward or simple answers. One could imagine any number of influential factors: the institution's size, the assignment or distribution of power within the institution, and individuals' responsibilities or potential responsibilities to that institution to name just a few.

The question about an individual political actor's capacity to influence their institution's role is particularly apt with justices and supreme courts. Institutional membership is usually small—so small that individual justices can influence the court's trajectory. Although a supreme court's powers and procedures are laid out in formal rules and informal conventions, its members often exercise discretion over what cases they review, when and how work is distributed, and how they articulate decisions. Moreover, in many judicial systems the court's decisions are not reviewable. In the Anglo-derived judicial systems mentioned above, the justices are not directly accountable to voters and have longer tenure than other political actors. Australian High Court justices may serve until age 70, Canadian Supreme Court judges may serve until age 75, while their U.S., British, and New Zealand counterparts enjoy lifetime appointments. These institutional features theoretically provide opportunities for individual judges to shape their institution's role in the political system. The transformations that came to British, Canadian, and New Zealand courts owed much to the reordering of institutional power from without. The High Court's largely internal transformation raises then a question that these other cases do not: Under what conditions can individual judges, working on their own or collectively, utilize existing institutional powers and their own discretion to transform their institution's role? Later chapters will demonstrate that the Mason Court's transformation succeeded in the short run but sputtered over the longer term. If judges can precipitate a role transformation, a secondary question is what it takes for them to sustain the transformation over the long term?

Focusing on the Australian case and the efforts of Chief Justice Mason and his colleagues will not provide definitive answers to these inherently complex questions about institutional change, but this book will explain the Court's transformation. It will provide an additional point of comparison and raise hypotheses for future research.

The radical changes that occurred during the Mason Court did not go unnoticed by Australian scholars.[14] Much of the scholarship, however, has been piecemeal and addresses micro-level issues. That is, it focuses on individual High Court decisions or doctrinal developments within single areas of law, rather than studying the Court's changing roles as a larger dynamic. Legal academics unsurprisingly have generated most of this valuable research, while political scientists are, for the most part, surprisingly silent on the Court. Legal scholars tend to ask certain types of questions and not others and approach this scholarship with certain suppositions and methodologies. One consequence is that the scholarship has inadequately placed the High Court and its decisions within broader political contexts. In saying so, I do not mean to suggest that existing research fails to appreciate the politically charged environment in which the Court's decisions are reached or the political fallout those decisions frequently create. Legal scholars have not neglected these issues. Likewise, I do not intend to suggest that the legal academy fails to appreciate how courts serve as venues for political contests as easily as legisla-

---

14. For an introduction to this literature see Mason & Saunders (1996); Williams & Stone (2000); and Patapan (2000).

tures. What I mean to suggest is that the legal academy generally tends to focus on the Court's end product—the decisions and doctrines. The scholarship treats decisions as atomized outputs and sometimes underestimates or underplays the extent to which decisions in different areas of law may be interconnected and may evidence larger trends. Aside from a few superficial assessments and passing comments, most legal scholarship has treated the Mason Court reforms as a series of discrete, albeit significant, phenomena. Insufficient efforts have been made to synthesize these developments and assess their impact on the High Court as an institution operating at the apex of a judiciary and within a broader political system.

One can point to several possible reasons for this dearth of scholarship. First, those scholars who might be more inclined to contextualize the Court in a broader political system—Australian political scientists—have historically left the study of courts to legal academics. As one Australian political scientist admitted, "[P]olitical scientists have left the study of the High Court and judicial review to constitutional lawyers. Emerging as a separate discipline only in the postwar period in Australia, political science has been mainly concerned with political parties, elections, bureaucracies, interest groups and voting (Galligan 1987, 3)." It might be the case that these other topics are far more compelling to political scientists than the Court, its judges, and their decision-making. Alternatively, it could be a simple division of labor, where questions about law and the courts remain in the lawyers' domain and the explicitly political world falls to political scientists' purview. A third reason may be that while the Court has reached its fair share of politically controversial decisions, it has not played—not until the mid-1980s—as public or pivotal a role in shaping Australian politics and public policy as the U.S. Supreme Court has played in American politics. This tendency to leave the High Court to the lawyers may explain why the *Australian Journal of Political Science*, the country's flagship political science journal, published only eight articles and three book reviews concerning the High Court from 1975 to 2003. Moreover, all were published after 1992, four from a single author.[15]

---

15. The eight substantive articles are Haig Patapan (2003) "High Court Review 2002: The Least Dangerous Branch," *Australian Journal of Political Science* 38(2): 299–311; Haig Patapan (2002) "High Court Review 2001: Legalism and the Gleeson Court," *Australian Journal of Political Science* 37(2): 241–53; Russell Smyth (2002) "Historical Consensual Norms in the High Court," *Australian Journal of Political Science* 37(2): 255–66; Jason L. Pierce (2002) "Interviewing Australia's Senior Judiciary," *Australian Journal of Political Science* 37(1): 131–42; R. Smyth (2000) "The 'Haves' and the 'Have Nots': An Empirical Study of the Rational Actor and Party Capability Hypotheses in the High Court 1948–99," *Aus-*

If Australian political scientists consciously or unconsciously leave the Court to legal academics, it is unsurprising that existing legal scholarship fails to contextualize the Court within the political system. Why is that the case? Australia's legal academy exhibits immunity from two intellectual developments that profoundly shaped twentieth-century American judicial scholarship: legal realism and behavioralism. American academics have long abandoned debates over whether judges make law and no one argues that the law alone dictates decision-making. As the adage goes, we're all legal realists now. Similarly, American legal scholarship was not immune from the behavioral revolution that occurred in the social sciences over the last fifty years. Neither appears to have permeated Australian legal scholarship to the same extent. The intellectual milieu in Australia's legal academy is quite different. Much of it is pre-legal realist and pre-behavioral, which partially explains the lack of scholarship that treats the Court as a political institution and its members as actors in the political process. To illustrate the point, the first book that explicitly treated the Court as a political institution appeared only in 1987 (*Politics of the High Court*[16]) and came from an Australian political scientist, Brian Galligan, who completed his Ph.D. in politics at a Canadian university.

Another reason for the dearth in political science scholarship on the High Court is that those who study it lack the comprehensive, publicly available data sets that for U.S. political scientists enable rigorous quantitative analyses on the U.S. Supreme Court, such as the *U.S. Supreme Court Database: 1953–1997 Terms*, compiled by Harold Spaeth and distributed by Inter-University Consortium for Political and Social Research. The High Court itself publishes some workload data in its annual reports, but there are no comprehensive, public data sets on decisions, outcomes, voting patterns, the

---

tralian Journal of Political Science 35(2): 255–74; Haig Patapan (1999) "Separation of Powers in Australia," Australian Journal of Political Science 34(3): 391–405; Haig Patapan (1996) "Rewriting Australian Liberalism: The High Court's Jurisprudence of Rights," Australian Journal of Political Science 31(2): 225–42; and James Warden (1992) "Federalism and the Design of the Australian Constitution," Australian Journal of Political Science 27(Special Issue): 143–58. The three book reviews are Tom Round (2003) "The Australian Federal Judicial System by Brian Opeskin and Fiona Wheeler (eds.)," Australian Journal of Political Science 38(1): 153–54; John Doyle (2001) "Judging Democracy: The New Politics of the High Court of Australia by Patapan," Australian Journal of Political Science 36(2): 389–90; and Peter Russell (2000) "The Political High Court: How the High Court Shapes Politics by David Solomon," Australian Journal Of Political Science 35(3): 542.

16. Brian Galligan (1987) *Politics of the High Court: A Study of the Judicial Branch of Government in Australia*. St. Lucia; New York: University of Queensland Press.

judges' backgrounds, intervener or amici participation, or caseload trends—all topics that receive wide coverage in U.S. Supreme Court databases. Only a handful of articles have ever taken a behavioral approach to the High Court. Most were written in the 1960s and 1970s, and not by political scientists but by a constitutional lawyer.[17] These flash in the pan articles were dismissed in Australian academic circles, marking a premature end to behavioral research into High Court decision-making. Even data sets that would enable scholars to study very basic institutional trends are few in number, not comprehensive, and publicly unavailable, as in the U.S.[18] This book, for example, presents in chapter 4 statistical data concerning basic questions that have not been gathered previously, such as how many constitutional cases the Court has decided over its history or what sections of the constitution have been most litigated?

Two exceptions to this dearth are noteworthy. Mentioned above, Brian Galligan's *Politics of the High Court* (1987) was the first book to treat the Court explicitly as a political institution. Galligan explores the historical development of the Court's judicial review powers by placing its decisions within a broader political context. He pays particular attention to the historic tensions between the High Court and Labor Governments that consistently stretched the boundaries of their constitutional powers—something he characterizes as "Labor versus the Constitution" (Galligan 1987, 118–83). Galligan is to be commended for recognizing the Court's many political facets: the institution within a broader political system, the politics surrounding its membership, and the political consequences and fallout that come from its decisions.

A second notable exception, *Judging Democracy: The New Politics of the High Court of Australia* (2000), surveys several jurisprudential developments that occurred in the late 1980s and 1990s before concluding that what marks the contemporary High Court is its heightened tendency (as the title indicates) "to judge" Australian democracy. Its author, Haig Patapan, presents the first and only attempt, as far as I am aware, to synthesize the many reforms that occurred since the mid-1980s. This book is valuable in constructing a meta-

17. Glendon Shubert (1969), a doyen of American judicial behavior research, compared U.S. and Australian judges. The best known judicial behavior work in Australia is an article by Tony Blackshield, a constitutional lawyer, published in the 1970s (Blackshield 1978), although also see Douglas (1969).

18. Russell Smyth and Mita Bhattacharya, economists at Monash University, have published a number of quantitative articles on the High Court in the last several years. See Smyth (2003; 2002; 2001; 2000) as well as Smyth and Bhattacharya (2001). Their scholarship is needed and welcomed, but underscores the point that political scientists remain largely silent on the Court.

narrative for the changes that occurred: that today's Court is more than a boundary-enforcer in federalism disputes, but is instead "prepared to adjudicate constitutive questions—matters that go to the very make-up of the regime (Patapan 2000, 178)." Patapan argues that the Court is putting into place its own comprehensive vision of Australian democracy. After identifying various institutional impediments and competing democratic visions among judges, he questions the comprehensiveness of this vision and the Court's capacity to realize it.

Both books offer important and insightful analyses, but the fact that they are the only two monographs from political scientists also speaks to the inchoate state of the research. This book seeks to build upon their worthy contributions. I will draw from both books in later chapters, but at this stage let me mention how this book differs from Galligan's and Patapan's works. Both authors are right to treat the Court as a political institution, but they often marshal the same sort of evidence that legal historians would to build their arguments: published judicial opinions, speeches, and other historical records. These sources are valuable—my research relies on them—but inadequate for tackling the important questions that this book poses. This book not only describes the nature of the role transformation and the High Court decisions that signaled it. It also explores the causes and consequences of the transformation by evaluating the judges' motivations and perceptions—those on the High Court and lower appellate courts. What were the motivations of those judges who initiated the transformation? How did they and their colleagues perceive what was happening?

This book presents an argument regarding these motivations and perceptions, something no other work has done to date. It accomplishes this by analyzing in-depth interview data collected from Australia's High Court and appellate judges. It also assembles other empirical data to test the interview data's accuracy. Bringing the judges' fresh, direct voice to the judicial role transformation distinguishes this research. This book also seeks to test the explanatory power of competing theories for when and how courts of final appeal undergo institutional role change. These theories emerge from scholarship on the U.S. Supreme Court. Exporting these theories is reasonable in this instance, given the many similarities between the U.S. and Australian judiciaries and the extent to which Australia's constitutional framers borrowed from the U.S. document to draft their 1901 Constitution. How then have American political scientists theorized about changes to the judicial role? One could survey this extensive literature in any number of ways. For my purposes, I divide the scholarship into four broad categories—those that adopt a legal, individual, institutional, or political system explanation for judicial change.

Popularized in the writings of Justice Felix Frankfurter and extrapolated by several twentieth-century legal luminaries (Bickel 1986; Fuller 1978; Hart and Sacks 1958; Jaffe 1965; Wechsler 1959; Freund 1961), the legal model sees judicial decision-making as a professional enterprise. In other words, there is something unique about how judges reach decisions vis-à-vis how legislators or bureaucrats reach decisions. Court decisions are products of judges applying a set of *a priori* canons, rules, and principles to cases. Fundamental to the legal model is its expectation that judges abide by stare decisis, the practice whereby previously decided cases guide judges in future analogous cases. To understand how judges reach decisions, the legal model emphasizes legal reasoning, judicial technique, and precedent. It would hold, therefore, that a judicial role—the functions and purposes that a court fulfills—is dictated less by judges and more by the powers formally ascribed to the courts and by accepted interpretative techniques. A court's role is found, according to the legal model, in the formal grants of power in constitutions, statutes, and other promulgated rules. Change to a court's role would come from some alteration to these formal grants of power.

In kindred spirit with legal realists and behavioralists, some U.S. political scientists in the 1960s began to challenge the legal model's veracity. As an alternative, they theorized that decision-making was better explained by studying individual judges, specifically their policy preferences (Spaeth 1961; Rohde and Spaeth 1976). This individual-based approach is commonly referred to as the attitudinal model. Championed most exhaustively in Jeff Segal's and Harold Spaeth's *The Supreme Court and the Attitudinal Model* (1993), this approach finds the legal model providing limited explanatory power. Rather than legal reasoning and precedent guiding decision-making, attitudinalists argue that personal policy preferences are far more determinative. Segal and Spaeth concluded, "The Supreme Court decides disputes in light of the facts of the case vis-à-vis the ideological attitudes and values of the justices. Simply put, Rehnquist votes the way he does because he is extremely conservative; Marshall voted the way he did because he [was] extremely liberal (65)."

The attitudinal model borrows from economic theory to assert that judges are rational preference maximizers and that their decisions reflect their attitudes toward the policy questions underlying cases. The individual—not the institution or the broader political system—is the determinative independent variable in decision-making. The attitudinal model would see a court's role as a simple by-product of individual judges pursuing their policy preferences, an aggregation of individual actions. Changes to a court's role, then, would come from judges pursuing different policy preferences, but because the attitudinal model conceives those preferences in static terms, changes to the institution's role follow the appointment of new judges who bring new policy preferences.

An extensive and disparate collection of studies could be assembled that adopts institutional approaches to studying politics. In an earlier era, institutional scholars tended to study brick-and-mortar institutions and formal power structures and procedures (Corwin 1936; 1940; Haines and Sherwood 1944). As political scientists have turned increasingly to institutional questions (March and Olsen 1989; Koelble 1995), what exactly counts as an institutional approach is itself debatable. Today it could just as easily mean studying mores, norms, culture, and ideas (Brigham 1987). Whether focusing on brick-and-mortar or mores, institutional approaches work from the premise that factors outside individuals are critical to understanding the political world. Rather than focusing on how individuals shape institutions, this approach explores the inverse relationship. Judicial decision-making and the judicial role, therefore, are determined by more than judges' idiosyncratic policy preferences. Substantive law, judicial norms, legal reasoning, constitutive documents, formal powers and informal conventions all shape the judicial mind.

Under the institutional tent, one can point to a variety of extra-judicial factors that impact a court's role. The "strategic approach," building upon Walter Murphy's path-breaking work, *The Elements of Judicial Strategy* (1964), shares with the attitudinal approach a conception of judges as preference maximizers. Unlike the attitudinalists, however, the strategic approach claims that judges are constrained in promoting their preferences by surrounding institutional and political contexts. Judges reach decisions in a strategic manner, "realiz[ing] that their ability to achieve their goals depends on a consideration of the preferences of others, of the choices they expect others to make, and of the institutional contexts in which they act (Epstein and Knight 1997)." To advance their preferences, judges must make strategic calculations about the views of other colleagues on the bench, legislators, administrators, and what the law might allow. They must understand the consequences of their own actions and anticipate the responses of others (Maltzman et al. 1999). The strategic approach sees a judicial role as an aggregation of individual judges' preferences, conditioned by relevant institutional contexts that impact the capacity to advance those preferences. Changes to a judicial role could occur, therefore, from judges bringing new preferences to a court or institutional contexts changing a court's responsibilities.

The "historical-interpretive" institutional approach takes a less behavioral tack by rejecting the notion that judges are, first and foremost, preference maximizers. Instead, these scholars leave room for the possibility that institutions may actually inform or shape judges' behavior. Decision-making then is "not merely structured by institutions but is also constituted by them in the sense that the goals and values associated with particular political arrangements give energy and direction to political actors (Clayton and Gillman 1999, 6)." In other words, what judges do (and the roles their institutions assume) is not simply a reflection of policy preference or a strategic calculation of what can be accomplished given the parameters of choice. Instead, the "historical-interpretive" approach explains judicial decision-making "as a process in which judicial values and attitudes are shaped by judges' distinct professional roles, their sense of obligation, and salient institutional perspectives (Ibid., 32)." In order to study changes to the judicial role, these scholars would focus on how these institutional perspectives and habits of action change over time (see Burgess 1993; Gillman 1993; Smith 1985).

A final approach to studying courts points to the influence of extra-judicial factors in the political system. Scholars who occupy this "political system" camp share a presumption that developments outside of the court exert a significant influence on what happens in it. Robert Dahl's article, "Decision-Making in a Democracy: The Supreme Court as a National Policy-Maker," is a classic example of political system analysis. There Dahl addressed concerns over the Supreme Court functioning in a counter-majoritarian manner by demonstrating that the Court's policy views were historically never long out of line with the policy views of the lawmaking majorities (1957, 285). Dahl argued that U.S. politics is characterized by a relatively stable alliance of interests that exerts a substantial amount of control over the Court through the appointment process. A court's role, then, is more likely determined by the politics of lawmaking majorities than individual judges' policy preferences or their strategic decisions. Changes in this alliance are likely to produce, with time, changes in that role.

Later scholars have reached similar conclusions. Some have pointed out how the Court's decisions generally track major party realignments and shifts in governing majorities, albeit with some delay given the justices' lifetime appointments (Funston 1975; Lasser 1985). Others point to still broader social forces and groups impacting the court's role (Goldman 1982; Schubert 1974). All of these scholars would see these broad, extra-judicial developments and conditions of politics profoundly influencing a court.

THE ARGUMENT

Having sketched the comparative context in which the High Court's transformation occurred and the competing theories that could explain it, what is this book's argument? It begins by describing the nature and scope of the High Court's role transformation. It illustrates how the High Court from the mid-1980s to the mid-1990s coupled landmark changes to substantive areas of private and public law with equally profound changes to its institutional role. It describes how an entrepreneurial coterie of High Court judges supplanted an orthodox judicial role with a significantly different vision. This transformation in the Court's role touched a number of normative claims about jurisprudential and political issues: the purposes of law; the aim of appellate litigation; the relationship the justices maintain to the law, the political world, and their community; the vision of what makes a good High Court judge; accepted modes of legal reasoning; and how law is understood to develop.

The book then explores the transformation's causes and consequences, tackling two distinct questions: First, what precipitated the transformation? Second, why did these changes occur when they did? Many of the reforms that came to the High Court in the 1990s occurred in the U.S. and other Anglo-derived systems decades earlier, but they remained somehow at bay in Australia. I make the case that to understand role transformations that are largely judge-driven one must consider the judges' motivations and perceptions, as well as the particular political and historical circumstances in which they operated. In other words, the attitudinal model's reliance on rationality and preference maximization does not wholly account for judicial motivation and behavior.

For this reason, this book relies heavily upon Australian judges themselves to describe the High Court's transformation. In addition to utilizing historical, legal, and statistical data, I draw upon more than eighty in-depth interviews with Australia's most senior appellate judges, comprising sixty percent of the total appellate bench. Participants included a majority of the current and retired High Court Justices, a majority of supreme court judges in the six states and two territories, and a sample of Federal Court judges. I also interviewed a dozen leading barristers, attorneys-general, and solicitors-general (state and Commonwealth) who regularly appear before the High Court. In short, nearly all protagonists in the High Court's transformation participated in my research. These in-depth interviews were conducted over the course of several years, beginning in 1997 and the bulk occurring from September 1999 to April 2000. The Mason Court, thus, was fresh in their minds. The interview data provide a behind-the-scenes perspective and enable me to analyze the perceptions and motivations of the High Court judges involved in the transformation and those appellate judges who closely observed it. My informants were well informed and eager to discuss the High Court's transformation, although few had participated in social science research. Appendices A and B list the participants, describe how the interviews were arranged and conducted, and discuss how the interview data were systematically analyzed.

A measure of forbearance is required, however, given the data's nature. To convey the transformation's revolutionary scope and significance, I quote my informants extensively. Fortunately for readers, Australians have a knack for turning phrases, which makes, I hope, the frequent use of quotations (some lengthy) more palatable, and dare I hope stimulating? The quotations come from a colorful cadre of jurists. By way of example, I am reminded of a Sydney-based judge whose office was filled with enough museum-quality sculptures, busts, and *objets d'art* to open his own gallery; indeed, his collection spilled out to much of the common space on his floor. Also coming to mind is a judge whose office sported an unexpectedly large poster of a high performance motorcycle. Upon my inquiry, he explained that his obsession with motorcycles began when in graduate school. He completed his Ph.D. thesis in nine months and used the remaining two years of scholarship funds to race motorcycles. And it is hard to forget the judge who photographs each visitor to his office and maintains an extensive album of "who's who" visitors. A colorful group indeed.

This book advances the following thesis regarding the High Court's judicial role transformation. First, the best account for the changes cannot come from a single explanatory variable. One legal, individual, institutional, or political variable alone cannot account for the transformation's emergence and timing. Instead, the interplay of factors was responsible. Multiple factors produced the role transformation. To say that it was a complex phenomenon may be stating the obvious. However, some court scholars have been advancing the opposite argument; that the judicial process is reducible to a single explanatory variable. Often in a quest for theoretical parsimony, they turn blind-eyes toward the complex interactions of legal, individual, institutional, and political variables that go into judicial decision-making and changes to the judicial role. The up-close examination offered here is intended, in part, to illustrate the rich complexity of Australia's judicial revolution.

In advancing the interplay thesis for why the transformation occurred, I do not mean to imply that all factors—legal, individual, institutional, and political—were equally in play at all times. That certainly was not the case. Some factors proved more critical to advancing reforms than others. For example, this book partially affirms the attitudinal and strategic voting models' emphases on individual judges forging a court's role. The interview data make a convincing case for what many attitudinalists merely assert: namely, that judges do think strategically about their decision-making and institution's role and draw upon this vision when deciding cases. The High Court's transformation would not have occurred without individual judges advancing their normative visions for the Court.

Yet this book should bring pause to those who think that individual preferences alone dictate a judicial role or changes to that role. The High Court's transformation illustrates time and again the limitations and constraints that individual judges confront in advancing their preferences. Favorable institutional and political conditions must exist for a judicial role transformation to survive beyond the short-term.

The book then explores what happened to the transformation after the Mason Court. The answer is that the Court retreated from the politicized role back toward the orthodoxy. As with the transformation's genesis, its rollback is best explained through the interplay of legal, individual, institutional, and political factors. Given this retrenchment, the book then considers the longer-term viability of the politicized role in Australia's legal and political systems.

Does the High Court's transformation tell us anything generalizable about how courts initiate and sustain changes to their institutional roles? In other words, when are courts more effective at changing the roles they play in political systems? One must be cautious about drawing broad conclusions from single cases; however, the Australian case demonstrates that individual judges do have the capacity, at least in the short-term, to reform their institution's role to comport with their own normative visions, as attitudinalists claim. A certain threshold of agreement must be reached and maintained among the judges for this reform to occur from within, but they have the power to instigate a role transformation. However, the transformation's long-term viability is dependent upon institutional and political contexts that are at least amenable to the reforms, if not supportive. The Australian case confirms how favorable institutional structures and support from other political branches can enable and legitimize transformations. It also confirms that hostile or even benign institutional and political arrangements can incapacitate a judicial role transformation.

Outline of the Book

Before proceeding, let me outline the book's chapters. The next chapter orients readers to Australia's legal history, constitutional framework, judicial structure, and High Court. It highlights the many legal legacies that Australia's High Court inherited from the British and American systems, including formal laws and structures and informal judicial practices and norms, and then explains how these legacies encouraged the development of a judicial orthodoxy in Australia.

Drawing upon High Court judgments and interview data, chapter 3 advances the argument that an orthodox judicial culture dominated the High

Court (and its jurisprudence) for much of the twentieth century. It delves into the orthodoxy's core normative and prescriptive claims about law, appellate litigation, the constitution, legal reasoning and judicial decision-making, and the High Court's interaction with other branches of government.

Chapters 4 and 5 make the case that the High Court's institutional role in the political and legal systems underwent a profound transformation in the 1990s. Both chapters closely analyze the Mason Court's actions and motivations and explore how other appellate judges perceived and reacted to its innovations. The Mason Court supplanted the inherited orthodoxy with a more activist, political (and therefore controversial) role. Chapter 4 studies the normative claims that the Mason Court advanced, including a commitment to justice and fairness over legal stability, a heightened attention to rights-related constitutional disputes, a recognition that appellate litigation is a political enterprise as much as a legal enterprise, and a willingness to tackle politically explosive issues.

Chapter 5 analyzes how the Mason Court altered the accepted modes of legal reasoning. Its thesis is that the Court ushered legal realism into a judicial culture long-steeped in formalism. This new ethic acknowledges the choice and discretion inherent in decision-making and judgment writing, a weakened commitment to stare decisis and textualism, and a willingness to articulate extra-legal values that often inform decisions. The causes and timing of the High Court's transformation are addressed in Chapter 6. Drawing upon statistical, historical, legal, and interview data, the chapter demonstrates that the transformation was highly contextual and involved an array of political, individual, and institutional factors. Central to the Mason Court's successes, however, were the presence of justices willing to reform their institution's role from within—rather than in response to some external prompting—and institutional and political contexts that accommodated the politicized judicial role, at least in the short-term.

Since Chief Justice Mason's retirement in 1995, the Court gradually has rolled back many Mason Court reforms. Chapter 7 begins by describing areas of substantive law where consolidation has occurred. It then considers how Mason's successors have moved away from the activist, politicized role toward the orthodoxy. I argue this is best explained through the interplay of political, institutional, and individual factors. Australia's judicial role transformation failed to outlive the Mason Court itself because of lackluster support in the broader judicial community, an inadequate constitutional infrastructure to support them, and reticence among Mason Court successors about losing institutional legitimacy.

Chapter 8 situates the High Court's transformation in the wider context of similar changes that occurred in other common law judicial systems during recent decades, especially the U.S., the U.K., and Canada. The High Court's transformation stands out for the extent to which it was internally driven and not precipitated by a new external grant of power. It concludes that the High Court's internally driven role transformation was viable in the short-term, but susceptible to collapse without formal and informal institutional support. The chapter concludes by assessing the Mason Court's legacy and analyzing if, when, and how a Mason-like High Court may reemerge.

2

A Sketch of Australia's
Legal History and Judiciary

Before exploring the High Court's transformation at the end of the twentieth century, it is necessary to trace briefly the development of Australia's legal system from the first settlements in the late 1700s through federation in 1901. After outlining this history, the chapter describes key features to Australia's constitutional framework and judiciary.

Although Captain James Cook and his HMS *Endeavor* landed on the shores of Botany Bay in April 1770 and claimed the continent for Britain, it was not until after the American Revolution that the British seriously turned their colonizing eyes toward the fatal shore. Prisons and prison ships in England were overflowing in the late eighteenth century and the loss of the thirteen American colonies closed off what had been a popular place for Britain to send its convicts. When no suitable place was found for a penal colony in Africa, Botany Bay was selected in 1786. The First Fleet, composed of roughly 850 convicts and the requisite military guards and officers under the command of Governor Arthur Phillip, arrived on the shores of what became New South Wales in January 1788. The first free settlers arrived some five years later. From the First Fleet's arrival to 1824, New South Wales operated as a military settlement and penal colony. Ultimate authority over the colony theoretically rested with the British Crown and Imperial Parliament in London, where the Crown delegated authority to appointed Governors through Royal Commissions. The Crown and Parliament could not escape, however, what Geoffrey Blainey called the "tyranny of distance" (1968). New South Wales, a colony that encompassed half the continent in 1788, was some 20,000 kilometers from Britain. It took eight months for British ships to complete the voyage to Australia. Telegram service between Australia and Britain did not come until 1872. This tyranny of distance meant that until a colonial legislature was established in 1823, the governor exercised near dictatorial power.

Although New South Wales was established as a penal colony, all statutory and common laws of England that were applicable to settlement conditions came into force with the First Fleet's landing. To help enforce this law, the British Parliament created the colony's first criminal court in 1787. The act charged judges to decide cases "according to the known and established laws of England."[1] Civil jurisdiction was extended shortly thereafter. The first equity jurisdiction was extended in 1814. Most colonial judges were members of the armed services and lacked training in non-military law.

The first significant constitutional development in the new settlement occurred in 1823 when New South Wales became a full British colony and its governmental institutions were statutorily defined in the *New South Wales Act*.[2] The Imperial Parliament recognized the need for a local lawmaking body in the colony, but it claimed that there was insufficient time to put together a representative assembly. Instead, the act enabled the Crown to appoint residents to a Legislative Council. The Council's powers were rather anemic. It was prohibited from enacting laws that violated or contravened the laws of England, a legal concept known as the repugnancy doctrine. Only the Governor had the power to put bills before the Council for consideration. Moreover, before any bill took effect the Chief Justice of the Supreme Court was required to review and certify that it was not inconsistent with the laws of England. On the judicial front, the 1823 Act established a new Supreme Court that exercised civil and criminal jurisdictions, and it provided for the appointment of court officers and admission of lawyers.

The Imperial Parliament passed an act in 1828 that replaced the 1823 *New South Wales Act*. This act, the *Australian Courts Act*,[3] changed the Legislative Council's procedures and structures (increasing its size for instance) and formally promulgated that all laws of England (common law and statute) were in force in New South Wales as of 1828, so long as they were pertinent in the colony. Historians have noted that Governors and Legislative Councils frequently modified English law for local conditions (Campbell 1965).

The first half of the nineteenth century brought significant westerly settlement of the continent. Van Diemen's Land, later renamed Tasmania,[4] was established as a separate colony in 1825, Western Australia in 1829, and South Australia in 1834. Port Phillip District, later renamed Victoria, was established in 1836 as a settlement and became a separate colony in 1851. The 1840s and 1850s were also years in which governing authority within the colonies shifted somewhat from the governors to the legislatures. Representative government

---

1. *New South Wales Courts Act* (27 Geo. III, c.2).
2. *New South Wales Act* 1823 (4 Geo. IV, c.96).
3. 9 Geo. IV., c.83.
4. The colony's name changed from Van Diemen's Land to Tasmania in 1853.

came to New South Wales in 1842, with passage of the *Australian Constitutions Act* (No. 1).[5] This act provided for a thirty-six member legislative assembly, twelve of whom were appointed by the Crown and the rest elected. The assembly exercised legislative powers, but the Governor retained the veto and ministers were not drawn from the assembly. In the years to come, constitutional reforms established representative legislative assemblies in the other colonies: Victoria (1851), Tasmania (1854), South Australia (1856), and Queensland (1859). By the end of the 1850s, five of the six colonies exercised their own legislative powers, which provided some newfound autonomy, at least in theory (Lumb 1977, 1–44).

That autonomy was derivative, however, because the colonial courts and legislative assembles were products of British statutes. As the colonies began to assert greater autonomy in the mid-nineteenth century, the question emerged over the appropriate relationship between colonial laws and the laws of England. To what extent could the two diverge? Could colonial legislatures limit the application of British law in the colonies or enact laws that knowingly differed from British law? The dilemma, of course, was that the Imperial Parliament had not legislated specifically on these questions, so it remained a point of debate especially in the colonial courts. A single judge on the Supreme Court of South Australia, Justice Benjamin Boothby, appointed by the British government in 1853, was a notable protagonist in these debates. Boothby frequently hamstrung the South Australian government in the early 1860s. He argued in judgments spanning a decade that the colonial government consistently exceeded the power vested to it and enacted laws that were repugnant to British law. A second judge on the three-judge Supreme Court often joined Boothby to strike down local laws, frustrating the South Australian government and causing much controversy (Castles 1971, 155–57).

London finally addressed this issue in the 1865 *Colonial Laws Validity Act*,[6] which was applicable in nearly all British colonies. The Act set clear parameters for colonial power. The colonial parliaments were subject to their own constitutions and the Imperial Parliament retained the right and capacity to legislate for the colonies. The repugnancy doctrine was also kept in place, meaning that colonial parliaments could not enact laws that went against any British laws directed at the colonies. They were also prohibited from enacting laws that had any effect beyond their borders, a concept known as extra-territoriality. Finally, the Act retained the requirement that all laws receive the

---

5. 5 & 6 Vic. c.76.
6. 28 & 29 Vict., c.63.

Crown's assent. While these features limited colonial power, the Act was seen at the time to expand the colonies' independence. Colonial parliaments were freed from having their legislation struck down in London, unless it violated the repugnancy or extra-territoriality doctrines. In addition, the colonies could amend or repeal the general mass of British law that had not been made operative in the colonies by statute. This included British statutes and other laws that had been received under common law principles. Moreover, they could amend statutes that previous colonial legislatures had enacted. The notion that the *Colonial Laws Validity Act* furthered colonial independence would be upended in the early decades of the twentieth century as it came to be seen as hampering independence (Castles 1963).

THE ROAD TO FEDERATION

The next major constitutional development centered around the protracted effort to join the colonies in some union. Although the first legislation calling for a union of the colonies was introduced in 1850, it would take some fifty years before the colonies formed the Commonwealth of Australia. Historians have identified two reasons for the lengthy timetable. First, the union movement was conducted in a democratic fashion from the outset. What ultimately became the 1901 Commonwealth of Australia Constitution was drafted in a series of constitutional conventions and put before the citizens in two referenda. In addition, a majority in each colonial legislature had to ratify the document before it took effect. Democracy sometimes takes time. The second major reason for the attenuated federation movement was that it began in the 1850s when the colonies faced few external pressures or threats.

The fact that the colonies united in a federation was all the more remarkable given the limited incentives present. By the 1860s each colony was self-governing. There was little national identity to speak of, with citizens' loyalties tied more to their respective colony than some yet undefined continent-wide union. Moreover, the economies that had developed by mid-century often put the colonies in competition with each other. Each had erected tariff and duty schemes on goods from other colonies and abroad that did little to encourage unity. Attempts were made during various Inter-Colonial Conferences from 1863 to 1880 to establish a uniform tariff structure, but to no avail. The two colonial behemoths had competing policies. New South Wales tended to promote free trade, while Victoria insisted on protecting tariffs. Neither colony felt comfortable leaving important trade questions to some unknown federal government.

In the end, domestic economic factors alone were not enough to unite the colonies. The real stimuli came from abroad. The colonies had demonstrated little interest in foreign policy, even after British garrisons pulled out of Australia in 1870. Thereafter, geographic isolation and the British command of the seas were thought sufficient. Attitudes changed, however, as rumors spread of foreign powers establishing presences in the Pacific. Queensland was particularly concerned, for example, when the Germans set up trading posts in New Guinea in the 1870s. France began transporting prisoners to New Caledonia in 1864, which heightened concerns that escapees would wash up on Australia's shore. The colonists, whose anxious demands for greater protections fell on silent British ears, were advised that their petitions might be more successful if they spoke in a single voice. The need for national defense ultimately led to the first serious efforts at unification (Parkinson 1994, 148–55).

In 1885, the colonial legislatures and the Imperial Parliament enacted complementing legislation that created the Federal Council of Australasia. This Council met intermittently from 1886 to 1899 to make suggestions for common legislation on a range of issues. It proved a useful forum for inter-colonial discussion, but lack of funds and authority hamstrung the body from the start. For example, each colony reserved the right to secede from the Council. The Council's legislative sphere was kept purposefully small and it remained dependent upon the colonies for funding. It also lacked authority because New South Wales chose not to join. Political leadership in the "mother colony," especially Sir Henry Parkes, saw the Council's creation as an impediment to a more robust and, therefore, successful federation. Like the American colonies, Australia's first effort at unification failed. The Council disbanded after thirteen years.

Proponents of a stronger federation persevered under the Council's foibles until colonial leaders gathered in Melbourne in 1890 to take up the question anew. They concluded that the time was ripe and that a representative constitutional convention should convene—one fully authorized by all the colonies. The first of these conventions took place in Sydney in 1891, where delegates deliberated on the structures and powers of a new national government. The drafting fell to a small committee led by Queensland's Premier Sir Samuel Griffith. Whereas America's constitutional framers nailed shut the windows in Philadelphia's Independence Hall for privacy, Australia's framers took to the water. Griffith had traveled to the convention on Queensland's official yacht, the *Lucinda*. Final drafting was completed while it cruised the Hawkebury and Pittwater Rivers. The Sydney convention had at its disposal the American, Canadian, and Swiss constitutions, as well as the legislation that created the Federal Council. The two significant issues raised during this first convention would percolate throughout the federation debate: balancing small and large state interests and managing tariff policies. At its conclusion, the convention passed a draft constitution that was sent to the colonial legislatures for consideration.

The colonial legislatures failed to ratify this draft constitution. Some delayed considering it because of approaching elections or changes in government. Others found the federation issue inconsequential. An economic depression in the early 1890s directed attention temporarily away from the federation proposal to shoring up the economy. This downturn ironically underscored the colonies' economic interdependence and the costs of inter-colonial tariffs and duties. The federation movement was revived then in the mid-1890s, finding its strongest footing when it appealed to both security, pocketbook, and heart.

Premiers from each colony met in Hobart, Tasmania in 1895 and agreed that it was necessary to revisit federation in earnest. Each agreed to elect delegates to an 1897 convention in South Australia. Meeting in Adelaide, delegates to this convention produced another constitution that was again returned to the colonial legislatures for approval. Delegates met again that year in Sydney to take up the 286 amendments that the colonial legislatures proposed. An overlapping election in Victoria prevented the Sydney convention from making much progress on the amendments, so delegates reconvened in 1898 to hammer out a final version.

Public referenda then were held in New South Wales, Victoria, Tasmania, and South Australia in 1898 on the proposed constitution. Eligible voters approved it with the requisite margins in all colonies except New South Wales, where opposition to the constitution had been particularly vociferous. Without New South Wales on board, this second constitution faced certain demise. After concessions were made to New South Wales, most notably that the new capital would be located within its borders, a second round of referenda occurred in all colonies from April to September 1899. Approximately 600,000 Australians or 61 percent of eligible voters participated in the referenda. The proposed federal constitution secured the necessary majorities in each colony, with roughly seventy-two percent of all voters supporting federation. The proposed constitution then went to London for the Queen's assent. A delegation from Australia arrived in London in March 1900, anxious to secure the Crown's assent with few changes. London's only objection was to the constitution's nearly complete abolition of appeals from Australian courts to the Privy Council.

The issue of Privy Council review was featured prominently in the constitutional conventions. At the 1890 Australasia Federation Conference, a majority of delegates supported the idea of abolishing all appeals to the Privy Council

and creating a domestic court with final authority over all Australian cases. Andrew Inglis Clark abided the conference's preferences. His draft constitution, introduced to the delegates at the 1891 Sydney convention, prohibited appeals
from any state courts or federal courts to the Privy Council. The Sydney convention amended, in the end, Clark's draft to allow Privy Council review "in
any case in which the public interests of the Commonwealth, or of any State, or
any other part of the Queen's dominions are concerned (Beasley 1955, 401–3)."
The appeal clause underwent further revision at the Adelaide conference in 1897.
Inter-colonial business interests fought against restricting Privy Council review
at the third and final Melbourne convention in 1898, arguing that restrictions
on appeals would discourage British investment in Australia. In the end, the
Melbourne convention ratified a Privy Council clause (clause 74) that provided,
"No appeal shall be permitted to the Queen in Council in any matter involving
the interpretation of this Constitution or of the Constitution of a State, unless
the public interests of some part of Her Majesty's Dominions, other than the
Commonwealth or a State, are involved (Quick & Garran 1976, 748–50)."

The delegates expected little opposition to the language used in clause 74
because it mirrored the Privy Council provision in the British North America
Act. They were flummoxed when Colonial Secretary Joseph Chamberlain objected to clause 74. The negotiations that ensued between Australia's delegates
and Chamberlain are well told elsewhere and need not be repeated here (see
Deakin 1963). In short, Chamberlain thought Privy Council appeals should
remain to ensure uniformity of law throughout the Empire. The compromise
reached after much negotiation left constitutional cases involving Australian
interests in Australian courts. Cases with wider relevance were open to Privy
Council review. The new clause provided the following:

> No appeal shall be permitted to the Queen in Council from a deci-
> sion of the High Court upon any question, howsoever arising, as to
> the limits *inter se* of the Constitutional powers of the Commonwealth
> and those of any State or States, or as to the limits *inter se* of the Con-
> stitutional powers of any two or more States, unless the High Court
> shall certify that the question is one which ought to be determined by
> Her Majesty in Council.[7]

Both sides claimed partial victory. The Australian delegates pointed to the
fact that their High Court retained review over all constitutional matters and
only with the Court's consent could constitutional questions go before the

---

7. *Commonwealth of Australia Constitution Act*, 63 & 64 Vict., c.12, art. 74.

Privy Council. Chamberlain claimed victory in that all non-constitutional matters could be reviewed in London. On July 5, 1900 the British Parliament passed the proposed constitution, titled the *Commonwealth of Australia Constitution Act 1900* (U.K.).[8] Four days later Queen Victoria gave her Royal Assent. The Queen's Proclamation of the Commonwealth was held off until January 1, 1901, however, to give Western Australia adequate time to pass the constitution in a referendum and enact enabling legislation so it too could join the Commonwealth of Australia (Swinfen 1987, 54–87).

Australia's Constitutional Framework

The Commonwealth Constitution is a hybrid document that borrows heavily from the American and British constitutional traditions. While the framers reviewed the constitutional practices of Canada, the United States, Switzerland, and Britain, the influences of the U.S. constitutional system and the British political system loomed large. By this I mean that the Commonwealth Constitution reads very much like the American document, while politics operates more in line with the British system. Sir Owen Dixon, Australia's celebrated High Court Chief Justice (1952–1964), alluded to this hybrid quality in a 1942 speech before the American Bar Association. "The men who drew up the Australian Constitution had the American document before them; they studied it with care; they even read the standard books of the day which undertook to expound it.…Indeed it may be said that, roughly speaking, the Australian Constitution is a redraft of the American Constitution of 1787 with modifications found suitable for the more characteristic British institutions and for Australian conditions (Dixon 1965c, 101–2)." The U.S. Constitution was at the forefront of their minds, almost too much as Dixon lamented. "The framers of our own federal Commonwealth Constitution…could not escape from its fascination. Its contemplation dampened the smoldering fires of their originality (Dixon 1965a, 44)."

Several similarities exist between the American and Australian constitutions. The Australians drafted a written constitution that enumerates the national government's powers and duties, like the American document. Both are built upon federalist principles that divide power between state and national governments. Both Senates provide equal state representation and six year terms for senators. Each document promulgates those powers granted to the

---

8. 63 & 64 Vict., c.12.

national legislature, with all residual powers reserved to the states. Both also incorporate separation of powers principles at the national level, such that powers are divided between a legislature, an executive, and a judiciary. Australia's constitution draws this tripartition of powers in the British tradition, in that it retains the Queen of England as head of state. The legislature is composed of the Crown, the Senate, and the House of Representatives. The executive is composed of the Crown, a Governor-General who acts on the Crown's behalf, and Ministers of the Crown, including the Prime Minister. The judiciary is composed of the High Court and other courts that Parliament creates.

Retaining the British Crown as head of state is just one of many ways in which Australia's constitution exhibits its British heritage. Operating alongside the separation of powers system is the practice of responsible government. Responsible government places executive authority in a ministry whose members come from the legislature, blurring the line that separates legislative and executive power. All ministers are responsible to Parliament and the electorate. The executive can be dismissed after losing an election or losing a vote of confidence in the House of Representatives. The practice of responsible government operates in Australia by convention. The words "Cabinet" and "Prime Minister" appear nowhere in the constitution, nor are there provisions requiring the Prime Minister and Cabinet to be appointed from the party or coalition of parties commanding a majority in the House of Representatives. Section 64 is the only constitutional provision alluding to it, which requires ministers to be members of the Senate or House of Representatives.[9] Given that most delegates to the four constitutional conventions in the 1890s were colonial parliamentarians, whose governments operated for decades under responsible government traditions, it is not surprising that this convention was never explicitly mentioned in the constitution.

The constitution also exhibits its British heritage by containing no bill of rights. This absence was not due to oversight or ignorance. The framers were familiar with the U.S. Bill of Rights and the constitutional law that had developed around it by the end of the nineteenth century. Much of the scholarship on Australia's constitutional conventions intimates that the bill of rights option was fully aired and explored and that the framers explicitly rejected it (Hutley 1981). The convention records indicate, however, that delegates to the 1891 and 1897–1898 conventions never debated the merits of a bill of rights

---

9. A caveat regarding Section 64: the clause actually gives a three-month grace period for ministers to secure seats as senators or representatives. It states, "After the first general election no Minister of State shall hold office for a longer period than three months unless he is or becomes a senator or member of the House of Representatives."

per se. The limited debate that did occur revolved around a handful of rights-oriented provisions. Delegates seemed far more concerned about preserving states' rights than the rights of individuals (Zines 1986).

The few enumerated constitutional rights are there largely because of Andrew Inglis Clark, an early participant in the federation movement and delegate to the 1891 Sydney convention. Clark, an admirer of the U.S. constitutional system and friend to Oliver Wendell Holmes, Jr., prepared the draft constitution that served as a starting point for deliberation at the 1891 convention (Warden, Haward et al. 1995). Several components of Clark's draft survived the 1891 convention and those that followed. Key structural provisions and a handful of rights contained in Clark's draft survived in some form to appear in the 1901 Constitution. Clark also lobbied throughout the 1890s for the constitution to include some version of the U.S. Constitution's Fourteenth Amendment, specifically its due process and equal protection clauses. In the end, a convoluted, watered-down provision prohibiting discrimination based on state citizenship was enacted, but the phrases "due process," "equal protection," and "privileges and immunities" appear nowhere in the text (La Nauze 1972, 227–32).

Australia's constitution provides very few rights. Section 41 secures the right to vote in federal elections. Section 80 provides for jury trials in cases involving Commonwealth law. Section 92 guarantees freedom in interstate trade and Section 51(xxxi) guarantees payment on just terms for Commonwealth acquisition of property. Section 116 prohibits the Commonwealth from establishing a religion, imposing any religious observances, or passing laws that prohibit the free exercise of religion. Finally, Section 117 prohibits discrimination based on state residence.

Several reasons were at the heart of their opposition to an American-style statement of rights. First, they thought it unnecessary because the parliaments and the common law were thought adequate. Sir Own Dixon captured this sentiment when he wrote:

> The framers of the Australian Constitution were not prepared to place fetters upon legislative action, except and in so far as it might be necessary for the purpose of distributing between the States and the central government the full content of legislative power. The history of their country had not taught them the need of provisions directed to the control of the legislature itself. The workings of such provisions in [the U.S.] was conscientiously studied, but wonder as you may, it is a fact that the study fired no one with enthusiasm for the principle. With the probably unnecessary exception of the guarantee of re-

ligious freedom, our constitution makers refused to adopt any part of the Bill of Rights of 1791 and a fortiori they refused to adopt the Fourteenth Amendment (Dixon 1965b, 102).

If an unfettered parliament somehow offended these rights, the polling booth was the place for recourse, not the courts. However, a variety of drawbacks to this traditional approach has been identified (see Charlesworth 1994; Williams 1999). A second reason for rejecting a bill of rights was that it was not a priority for Australia's framers. In fact, many colonial delegates considered it an anathema because it could hamstring their legislatures from passing laws that preserve and manage the non-European labor market. Thus, Section 51(xxvi) originally vested the Commonwealth Parliament with power to enact laws with regard to "the people of any race, other than the Aboriginal race in any state, for whom it is deemed necessary to make special laws." One could read beneficence into this clause—protecting against racial discrimination—but its practical consequence was just the opposite. Australian industry at the time of federation was heavily dependent upon Chinese labor, and the framers did not want the constitution to shackle labor practices in nascent industries. Quick and Garran write that this section empowered the Commonwealth "to localize [Chinese laborers] within defined areas, to restrict their migration, to confine them to certain occupations, or to give them special promotion and secure their return after a certain period to the country whence they came (1976, 622)." Indeed, one of the first laws enacted in the new federal parliament was the *Immigration Restrictions Act 1901*, which prohibited anyone from immigrating into the country who was unable to write out a fifty word dictation in a European language (Palfreeman 1967). A third reason why Australia's framers rejected a bill of rights is that they were concerned about rights, but not for individuals. They were most intensely interested in what rights the colonies would retain in a federation. Given that bills of rights, at least in the American example before them, typically dealt with the vertical relationship between individuals and their governments, not between governments, it was not prioritized (Irving 1999; Williams 1999).

Given this mixture of British and American constitutional influences, scholars describe Australia as a "Washminster" system (Thompson 1980; Jaensch 1991).[10] It blends American and British practices: federalism, separation of powers, and a written constitution from the American system, and responsible party government with no entrenched bill of rights from the British system.

---

10. Yet see Thompson (2001).

AUSTRALIA'S JUDICIAL SYSTEM

The American influence is also seen in the constitutional provisions for a federal judiciary. Chapter III vests judicial power in the High Court, currently composed of seven justices, and other courts that Parliament creates or vests with federal jurisdiction. The High Court exercises both original and appellate jurisdictions, but unlike the U.S. Supreme Court, it also serves as the final appellate court for federal *and* state matters. Whereas a federal or constitutional question must arise for the U.S. Supreme Court to intervene, that is not the case for the High Court. It serves as the final arbiter for all state matters, including state constitutional law (Lumb 1977).

Much of the constitution's language concerning the High Court's original and appellate jurisdictions was borrowed from Article III of the U.S. Constitution. The Court's original jurisdiction extends to matters arising under treaties (Section 75(i)), affecting counsels or ambassadors (Section 75(ii)), where the Commonwealth is a party (Section 75(iii)), between the states (Section 75(iv)), and in which writs of mandamus or other injunctions are sought against officers of the Commonwealth (Section 75(v)). Parliament also has the authority under Section 76 to vest additional original jurisdiction in the High Court. Most original jurisdiction cases concern Sections 75(iii), (iv) and (v) (Jackson 1997). Together, Sections 75 and 76 define an extensive original jurisdiction, such that some scholars have voiced concern that it could distract the Court from fulfilling its appellate functions (Cowen and Zines 1978, 4). One mechanism for limiting the Court's original jurisdiction caseload is its power to remit cases to lower courts. In practical terms, proceedings commenced under the Court's original jurisdiction are normally remitted unless they raise constitutional questions.

The lion's share of the High Court's workload comes under its appellate jurisdiction. This jurisdiction extends to judgments of any justice or justices exercising the High Court's original jurisdiction (Section 73(i)), any other federal court, courts exercising federal jurisdiction, or state Supreme Courts (Section 73 (ii)). The High Court has mechanisms here too for controlling which cases it reviews. In this sense, the Court's appellate power is discretionary. Since reforms to the *Judiciary Act* in 1984, no appeal may proceed to the High Court without the Court first granting "leave to appeal" or "special leave to appeal."[11] The "leaves to appeal" are issued when the full High Court agrees to review decisions from single High Court judges or panels of High Court judges exercising original jurisdiction. On the other hand, "special

---

11. *Judiciary Amendment Act* (No. 2) 1984.

leaves to appeal" are issued for cases that come to the Court under its appellate jurisdiction. Both mechanisms filter out cases that the Court does not wish to review for various reasons.

What criteria are used to determine which cases are granted leave? The 1984 reforms state that the Court may consider any matter it thinks relevant, but it "shall have regard" to whether the case involves a question of law that is "of public importance... or [where] a decision of the High Court, as the final appellate court, is required to resolve differences of opinion between different courts, or within the one court, as to the state of the law (Mason 1996)."

Australia's constitutional framers enacted provisions enabling Parliament to create other federal courts in addition to the High Court, including federal trial courts. Not until 1977 did Parliament create the Federal Court of Australia, a national court of first instance composed of roughly fifty judges who sit throughout the country to hear matters of law and equity. The Federal Court possesses no general jurisdiction, but only that which Parliament assigns to it in over 120 statutes. While it operates as a court of first instance for many criminal and civil matters, it also functions as an intermediate appellate court for cases from single Federal Court judges, the Supreme Court of the Australian Capital Territory (ACT) and Norfolk Island, and decisions from state supreme courts concerning federal matters. This appellate variant, known as the Full Federal Court, consists of three Federal Court judges empaneled on an ad hoc basis. All Federal Court judges serve when needed on the Full Federal Court. The Federal Court's jurisdiction encompasses a bevy of civil and criminal matters, including trade and consumer protection, review of administrative decisions, migration and refugee issues, intellectual property (copyrights, patents, trademarks, and designs), maritime, bankruptcy, anti-discrimination, and corporate law to name a few (Opeskin and Wheeler 2000).

The court systems within Australia's six states and two territories vary in size and structure. All have courts of first instance and appellate courts. New South Wales, Victoria, and Queensland maintain separate courts of appeal within the state judicial systems. South Australia, Western Australia, and Tasmania do not have separate appellate courts. Instead, they empanel trial court judges to sit in appellate capacities when necessary. Figure 2.1 provides a hierarchical schematic of the Australian judiciary that ignores this state court variation. The shaded courts are those whose judges exercise some sort of appellate jurisdiction.

All state and federal judges in Australia are appointed. The Crown's representatives at the state and federal levels (state Governors and the Commonwealth Governor-General) technically make judicial appointments, but in practical terms this power falls to the state and federal Cabinets, on the advice of the Attorneys-

Figure 2.1 Structure of Australia's Judiciary and Appellate Routes

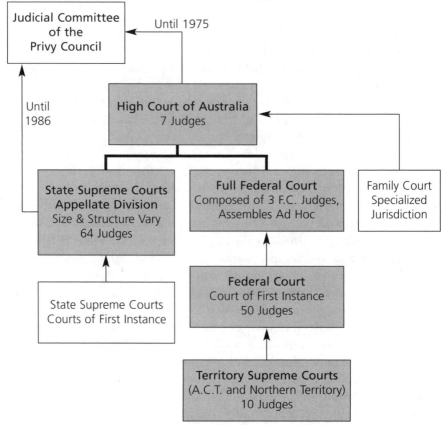

General. Filling vacancies on the High Court has required the Commonwealth to engage in some consultation with state governments since reforms in 1979, but much of the appointment process operates by convention. When such a vacancy occurs, the Commonwealth Attorney-General solicits recommendations from each state. The Attorney then distributes a list of names under consideration and consults with state and federal judges, as well as leaders in the legal community. Following this time for input, the Attorney makes a recommendation to Cabinet, which may or may not be followed, and reports the Cabinet's decision to the Governor-General. It is the Governor-General who formally commissions the judge. The Commonwealth Constitution does not provide guidelines or qualifications for appointment to the High Court or the Federal Court. All High Court judges had life tenure until a constitutional amendment in 1977 set a mandatory retirement age of 70 years. The amendment also enabled Parliament to set a similar requirement for other federal court judges.

3

The High Court's Orthodox Role

Chapter 2 provided a thumbnail sketch of Australia's judicial system and signposted notable constitutional developments since British settlement. It gave close attention to the strong and encompassing institutional linkages between the Australian and British political and judicial systems. These linkages, which were put in place during the colonial era and retained until the last quarter of the twentieth century, served many purposes. First, they enabled Australia's first settlers to bring with them a ready-made system of laws and institutions to the new land. Settlement presented its own uncertainties, but there were never any questions about what their source of law would be. These linkages not only helped the settlers organize themselves politically, but also appeased British investors who took comfort in knowing that British law operated in the distant settlement and that recourse to London's courts was possible should complications or disputes arise. These colonial linkages finally had the consequence of generating a judicial legacy for future generations of Australian lawyers and judges. This legacy included formal laws and legal structures, as well as informal legal practices and judicial norms. It contributed to the development of a judicial orthodoxy that governed how High Court judges conceptualized their individual roles and the proper functions and methods for their institution.

Components to this orthodoxy, which are described in this chapter, were present before federation in 1901, but much of the legal scholarship picks up on its presence in the early twentieth century and how it became more entrenched through the 1970s. Beginning in the mid-1980s Chief Justice Mason led his High Court colleagues in upending much of it. Drawing from the interview data, this chapter shows that today's appellate judges recognize that an orthodoxy had infused their judicial culture and that it significantly influenced what the people, politicians, and judges thought the courts could and could not do. It became apparent from my interviews that this orthodoxy influenced the judicial culture writ large and acutely shaped High Court judges.

Table 2.1: Tenures of Australian Chief Justices and
High Court Membership During the Mason Court Transformation

Chief Justice	Tenure	Natural Court
Sir Samuel Griffith	1903–1919	1–4
Sir Adrian Knox	1919–1930	5–7
Sir Isaac Isaacs	1930–1931	8
Sir Frank Gavan Duffy	1931–1935	9
Sir John Latham	1935–1952	10–14
Sir Owen Dixon	1952–1964	15–18
Sir Garfield Barwick	1964–1981	19–27
Sir Harry Gibbs	1981–1987	28–30
Sir Anthony Mason	1987–1995	31–32
Natural Court 31	1987–1989	
Sir Daryl Dawson		
Sir Ronald Wilson		
John Toohey		
Sir Gerard Brennan		
Sir William Deane		
Mary Gaudron		
Natural Court 32		
Sir Daryl Dawson	1989–1995	
Michael McHugh		
John Toohey		
Sir Gerard Brennan		
Sir William Deane		
Mary Gaudron		
Sir Gerard Brennan	1995–1998	33–36
Anthony Murray Gleeson	1998–Present	37–39

Australia's appellate judges tend to speak in "then and now" terms regarding the High Court, such that the "then" encompassed the years from federation to the mid-1980s, while the "now" meant the years since the mid-1980s. Whether this particular bifurcation of time is the most historically accurate or not is secondary to the fact that the appellate judges thought in these terms. It conveys how they make intellectual sense of their experiences. This division of High Court history was nearly universal among the judges and not contrived or encouraged by the wording of interview questions. The Mason Court was the fulcrum point for the judicial role transformation. In particular, informants identified 1987 to 1995 as the critical years for the transformation. This period encompasses two natural courts—that is, the time between appointments where there is stable court membership. Table 2.1

orients the Mason Court in High Court history and provides a roster of High Court Justices who served on the two key natural courts, #31 (1987–1989) and #32 (1989–1995). These names will occur frequently in the ensuing pages. That today's appellate judges speak in "then and now" terms does not belie the profound dissension that remains within the judiciary over the legitimacy of the Mason Court reforms. Indeed, my research uncovered deep divisions within the senior judiciary, including judges who sit on the same courts. Many appellate judges still adhere wholly or partly to the orthodox model and disapprove of the changes that came with the transformation. On the other hand, many judges support the Mason Court reforms. They see the politicized role as a necessary break from the past and as a way for the Court to further shape Australian law. In short, the Australian judiciary finds itself divided.

Just how divided and along what cleavages? Answering this question is difficult because I did not conduct the interviews with the goal of labeling each informant. I was more interested in getting the individual judge's assessment of the High Court and the reforms that came during the Mason era. Taking this tack naturally influenced how I conducted the interviews. Even if I wanted to assess each judge's individual role orientation, to impose a dichotomous label on each judge—orthodox or politicized —would have glossed over important nuances and qualifications that the judges offered during the interviews. Having said this, I can report that a clear minority (no more than 30 percent) of my informants unabashedly supported either the orthodox *or* politicized roles. This comes as little surprise. At the time I conducted the interviews, the fate of the High Court's transformation was unknown. Some consolidation had occurred under Chief Justice Mason's successors. An overwhelming majority of informants acknowledged, however, that 1) the Mason Court ushered in profound changes, 2) they were uneasy with what the politicized role may portend for the High Court and the broader judiciary, and 3) they were just as, if not more, uncomfortable with the orthodox role guiding the contemporary High Court. I can also report that those informants who supported the orthodoxy tended to be older and their numbers, already a minority in the judicial ranks, are likely to erode in the longer term. Later chapters have much more to say on this point.

The rest of this chapter describes this orthodoxy along six dimensions. It should be noted that this six-dimension categorization was not constructed prior to the interviews; rather, it emerged organically from the data. In other words, I did not impose the dimensions or labels. Many came directly from the judges. Not everyone used the same terms or language, but when judges from different courts located in different states consistently described characteristics of the historic or contemporary High Court I felt safe concluding that there was actually something to these individuals' perceptions. These dimensions best represent how appellate judges thought about the orthodox and politicized judicial roles. I was conscious at all times to ensure that generalizations or conclusions regarding the High Court as a whole or the judiciary writ large were supported by multiple interview sources and that no single source had a disproportionate influence. It must also be said that most quotations are representative of a larger body of opinion contained in the interview data. Space limitations and readers' patience require that I offer choice examples instead of quoting ad nauseam. Striking a balance between proving a point and exasperating the reader is my goal.

Relying on contemporary judges to describe the orthodoxy's contours and historical development can be hazardous. Good judges do not necessarily make good historians. Recounting history, particularly history in which one has participated, in the format here—narrative interviews—is an intrinsically personal and selective enterprise. Personal experiences no doubt colored my informants' conceptions of the High Court's role and how they perceive its history. However, I was not asking my informants to be good historians, though some are.[1] Rather, I wanted to know how today's judges conceptualize the Court's history, irrespective of their accuracy.

The senior judiciary is a small, tightly knit elite group with a strong collective memory. My informants' knowledge about the High Court's role comes from their firsthand experiences as law students, judges' associates (Australia's equivalent for clerks), solicitors and barristers, and judges. The relatively small number of appellate judges means that my informants are well acquainted with their colleagues and developments occurring within the judiciary. The federal appellate bench includes seven High Court Justices, about fifty Federal Court judges exercising general statutory jurisdiction, and other lower court judges exercising specialized jurisdictions in the Family Court and the Administrative Appeals Tribunal. At the time of my fieldwork, the number of judges exercising appellate jurisdiction in each of the six states were as follows: New South Wales (12), Victoria (10), Queensland (5), South Australia (14), Western Australia (16), Tasmania (7), the Australian Capital Territory (4), and the Northern Territory (6).[2] The elite network of High Court Justices is even

1. See, e.g., B. H. McPherson's (1989) *The Supreme Court of Queensland, 1859–1960: History, Jurisdiction, Procedure.* Sydney: Butterworths. Justice McPherson sits on the Queensland Court of Appeal.

2. This total—74 appellate judges—over represents the true number of appellate judges in the states and territories, given that only New South Wales, Victoria, and Queensland

smaller. Excluding its seven current members, only thirty-eight judges have been appointed to the High Court since its first sitting in 1903. Only thirty judicial appointments were made during the Court's first 75 years (1903–1977), with roughly 2.8 years elapsing, on average, between each appointment. A constitutional amendment in 1977 set the mandatory retirement age for High Court Justices at 70 years, changing what had been lifetime appointments. In the twenty-eight years since the retirement reform took effect (1978–2005), thirteen judges have been appointed, with an average of 2.1 years elapsing between appointments.

Much like the U.S. Supreme Court bar (see McGuire 1993), a small network of elite lawyers handles the lion's share of cases before the High Court. The New South Wales (NSW), Victoria, and Queensland legal professions are divided into solicitors and barristers, like Britain's. By contrast, South Australia, Tasmania, Western Australia, and the territories have amalgamated bars, in which lawyers operate as both solicitors and barristers (Weisbrot 1990). As the legal profession has developed in Australia, the classic distinctions between solicitors as "office lawyers" and barristers as "courtroom lawyers" are less and less true. In general terms, barristers are independent, solo practitioners who argue cases in court based on solicitors' instructions. Solicitors receive their instructions from clients. Barristers make up about ten percent of the bar. At the bar's apex is an elite group of barristers known as Queen's Counsels or "QCs," who in turn comprise about ten percent of all barristers (one percent of the entire profession), and who tend to handle the most significant litigation before state supreme courts and the High Court.[3] Governments typically draw from this top echelon of QCs for state supreme court and federal appointments. Nearly all of my informants were leading QCs or "silks," as they are known, in their respective bars before coming to the bench. Their earlier careers at the bar, where they appeared before an earlier generation of Australian judges, provide them with valuable perspectives as participants in this research. Moreover, their insights regarding the judicial orthodoxy are all the more perspicacious because they witnessed and experienced as judges the politicized role that the Mason Court introduced. The final proviso concerns the layout of this and the next two chapters. These chapters are designed collectively to describe how contemporary judges perceive and conceptualize the

---

maintain separate Courts of Appeal. The remaining states and territories empanel appellate benches on an ad hoc basis from their roster of Supreme Court judges.

3. Becoming a Queen's Counsel or "silk" is the capstone event for an Australian lawyer. When I asked the judges to provide a brief biographical sketch, most recalled the exact date that they became a QC or "took silk," as it is known.

pre- and post-Mason High Court. This chapter covers the orthodox, pre-Mason era and organizes itself around six categories or dimensions. The same dimensions will be used in the next two chapters to describe the politicized role. Therefore, this chapter should be read with an eye toward how the orthodoxy differs from the politicized role along these six dimensions. What, then, are the core features to the orthodoxy?

DIMENSIONS #1 & #2: THE PURPOSES OF LAW AND APPELLATE LITIGATION

The first dimension to the High Court's orthodoxy is one that addresses a question that transcends the Court as an institution and captures a foundational characteristic to the broader judicial culture. It is a perennial question for legal theorists and plays a central role in the transformation: What are the law's purposes? While my informants' normative views ran the gamut, a strong consensus emerged that the judicial orthodoxy places great weight on the law providing *certainty*. It requires the legal system to have precedents and rules in place, and judges who follow them, that enable lawyers to advise clients with reasonable confidence about what the law is in a given circumstance. A system valuing certainty does not envision the law providing *a priori* answers necessarily to every conceivable legal question, but it aspires to create predictable and stable legal outcomes. Australia's orthodoxy did not display the pragmatism of Holmes and the early legal realists. For judges, promoting certainty means that they do not haphazardly change the law or change it for transient reasons. The orthodoxy, therefore, dissuades judges from reaching decisions that foster uncertainty, however noble the reasons.

Informants tended to make two interconnected arguments about this dimension: the orthodox role placed a premium on certainty while the Mason Court often engendered less certainty, less predictability in law. Speaking broadly about the judiciary, a Federal Court judge commented, "Who was it that said, whilst the law must be stable it needn't stand still? One of your [American] judges probably. We all hold to that. It's a question of degree. If the reforms produce destabilization, then that's bad because no one knows how to advise their clients and no trial courts know how to judge cases (53:1030)."[4] Another Federal Court judge remarked, "You have to be cautious

---

4. Quotations from the interviews are cited using an interview number followed by a numeric line marker from the transcripts. When no marker is provided, the informant did not want the interview recorded, in which case the quotation is drawn directly from my

about taking [reform] too far, otherwise you really have no certainty. I know there is a view that certainty isn't the end all and be all.... It comes down to predictability too. You don't want to be moving the goal posts continually (113)."

The orthodoxy's concern about creating uncertainty—moving the goal posts too much—was well illustrated by one High Court Justice's observation about the legitimate sources for constitutional interpretation.

> The other argument against giving effect to contemporary values is that, in fact, it amounts to a retrospective alteration of the law. It's retrospective because it affects the litigants in the case in which the new rule is laid down. So that, Mr. Theophanous, the victim of the decision about freedom of speech, was deprived of a right that he previously had and which he couldn't reasonably expect to be deprived. In principle it's wrong. (94:900)

The reference here was to the Mason Court's 1994 *Theophanous v. Herald & Weekly Times Ltd.* decision.[5] Andrew Theophanous, a member of the Commonwealth Parliament, sued a Victoria newspaper for defamation following the publication of a letter to the editor. The Court concluded that a freedom of political speech implied in the constitution's text limited Theophanous's capacity to recover damages under Australian defamation law. The High Court Justice quoted above criticized this decision because it deprived Theophanous of defamation protections he theoretically possessed before the suit but lost as a result of it. The certainty that Theophanous and other public officials had regarding law's protection from defamatory remarks was lost with the Court's creation of implied political speech protections. Another judge remarked, "I have personal reservations about the implied rights cases because it creates a form of injustice when people go about their affairs and the Court changes its mind and implies a right (60:4545)." Compromising predictability in this way was problematic for these judges and emblematic of the orthodox approach to law's purposes.

Most informants agreed that Australia's law had greater certainty in the early twentieth century and during the decades leading up to the Mason

---

notes. A few quotes have no interview number to ensure even greater anonymity. Interview data were organized and content analyses conducted using Q.S.R.'s NUD.IST (Non-Numerical Unstructured Data Indexing Searching and Theorizing) software, version 4.0. This software program enables scholars to code and analyze large amounts of textual data, in my case interview transcripts.

5. (1994) 182 CLR 104.

Court. A state appellate judge said, "Although my legal education was not in Australia—it was in England—I was an associate in the High Court when Dixon was Chief Justice....[T]here was a certainty about law fifty years ago which most practitioners would tell you is now absent (34:2130)." The Mason Court (and to a lesser extent the Brennan Court that followed, 1995–1998), represented according to a Federal Court judge, "the first time that the Court made a concerted effort...not only to right social wrongs but to fix up any legal error they could find." He continued, "There was a conscious jettisoning of the notion that certainty is the object of the legal system, in favor of correcting absurd rules. I'm sure the theory was 'better to be right once than forever wrong' (85:1000)." In a similar vein, a South Australia supreme court judge observed: "The High Court itself has been very active in recent years... some would say overactive to the extent there has been an element of instability infused in some areas of the law which is perhaps felt to be undesirable. (12:700)." A Western Australia judge echoed these sentiments, admitting that some change in the law was "desirable." He cautioned against "taking it too far because then you have no certainty (8:745)." A Queensland appellate judge admitted that since the Mason Court's advent, "There is less certainty so it's harder for lawyers advising clients as to what's the likely outcome of cases." The judge continued, "Certainly that's the feeling here in Australia—that it's very difficult to say your chances of winning are good, because the feeling is that if you get to the High Court, the rules could change....Nowadays, everyone's on notice that things are in a state of flux and there are no definites anymore. The good side of it is that law can be used for positive change more than it has in the past (1:2700)." One clear implication of the orthodoxy's premium on certainty is that it discourages judges from embarking on significant political and legal change.

Holding certainty as the overarching goal for a legal system has a rippling effect on other dimensions. It impacts the litigation process, how the judiciary interacts with other branches, the factors that enter judicial decision-making, and how the community views judges. The orthodoxy's next dimension is clearly informed by its emphasis on certainty. It concerns how judges view the aims of appellate litigation.

Legal scholars have conceptualized appellate litigation in a variety of ways. One common distinction is between public and private litigation models. The private litigation model understands litigation first and foremost as resolving disputes between specific parties. Those parties directly involved bring their conflicts before courts, where judges function as passive umpires, reaching decisions specifically tailored to the disputes (Fuller 1978).[6] Litigation is foremost a *legal enterprise*. The public model conceives litigation in broader terms. Litigation still resolves specific disputes, but it has additional effects, including social control, lawmaking (in the sense that some legal rules are judge-created), promulgation and enforcement of public norms, and providing a venue for interest groups to pursue policy goals (Chayes 1976; Fiss 1982; Lawrence 1990; Olson 1990).

Australia's judicial orthodoxy conceives litigation mainly in terms of the private model, emphasizing judges' responsibility to limit themselves to resolving particular disputes. What takes place in a court, even an appellate court, is conceived first and foremost as a private affair between the immediate parties and the court. Shapiro's classic triadic description of a court captures this view, in that the judge umpires a dispute between two individuals (Shapiro 1981). For example, one Federal Court judge spoke about litigants "owning" litigation, such that it would be inappropriate for a judge, even a High Court judge, to "take the law forward" when the parties are asking the court simply to determine "what the law is (127)." A South Australia Supreme Court judge echoed the litigant-centered view of courts:

> [T]he legal system should never be used as an instrument for social or political change. That would be a misuse of the legal system and likely lead to anarchy. *I think judges have to keep constantly in mind that they're there to decide the cases. You're only deciding a particular case.* In the course of doing so, we may try to educate people in another sense—try to make it plain perhaps that a minority point of view has a right to be heard or freedom protected...or that everyone is equal before the law and it's wrong for moral majorities to attempt to impose their will on others....But I don't think we're there to change social attitudes except in making people more law abiding. We don't have an evangelical role in the community (18:1945) (emphasis added).

It is not surprising that judges in courts of first instance and intermediate courts, though to a lesser extent, describe their work along private litigation lines. Resolving the immediate dispute is their foremost task. The orthodoxy, however, conceives of litigation along these narrow grounds even at the High Court. Thus, one High Court Justice insisted that the Court's primary purpose was to "resolve the disputes that arise—the litigation that is put before

---

6. Although see Bone (1995) who questions distinctions between public and private litigation models.

it (63:2500)." The orthodox approach to litigation rests on the fact, as a Federal Court judge put it, "the High Court cannot create cases. They can only decide cases that come before them." For the Court to view litigation beyond the immediate parties "would lead to an inappropriate resolution of particular cases and could be unfair to the parties who brought the suit (28:2645.)" Reflecting on the High Court's approach to litigation, another Federal Court judge concluded:

> If a case is a test case—both sides are saying, "We want to go forward and the law doesn't definitively address this problem," then the judge has a mandate from the parties to say, "I can be a bit adventurous. I can tell you where I think the law will direct itself." *Mabo* was a test case, so it was perfectly legitimate for [Justice] Brennan to do what he did. The problem is that if you don't get a mandate from the parties, I don't think you can do it. It's their litigation and they're entitled to do with it what they want.... It's not as if a judge is considered a law reform commission. No judge can go in depth into policy making behind legislation. The best a judge can do is look at the common law or statute, hear the arguments of the parties, and *within the contests set up by the parties, take the law forward if asked by the parties.* I have real problems with judges who take the law forward when the parties say, "We don't want that. We want to know what the law is now (127:1200) (emphasis added)."

The orthodoxy's distrust of expanding litigation beyond what the immediate parties seek is illustrated by the comparatively anemic practice of third-party intervention and amici curiae participation in Australian courts. Amici curiae, or friends of the court, are not formal parties to a suit, but inform a court on points of fact or law; interveners join litigation because they typically have direct financial or other interests in the outcome and wish to participate formally as parties. A NSW appellate judge summarized the attitude of many of his colleagues regarding amici briefs: "I think you'll find there is a great deal of conservatism toward amicus briefs. They are considered to expand litigation beyond a point to which we think is appropriate (58:2845)." Both amici curiae and interveners appear before the High Court with relative infrequency. The Court traditionally limits participation to the immediate parties and views amici and interveners as unnecessary distractions. This is by convention given that there are no formal rules governing intervention. The Court's official rules provide no guidelines for interventions or criteria for evaluating requests for intervention. In fact, those seeking intervention are left to file motions under Order 51 of the *High Court Rules*, a catchall order that enables motions to be put before the Court for which "no other procedure is provided." With no formal rules governing intervention, dicta from a 1930 High Court decision guide the Court. Chief Justice Dixon laid down the standard:

> The discretion to permit appearances by counsel is a very wide one; but I think we would be wise to exercise it by allowing only those to be heard who wish to maintain some particular right, power or immunity in which they are concerned; and not merely to intervene to contend for what they consider to be a desirable state of the general law under the Constitution without regard to the diminution or enlargement of the powers which as States or as Commonwealth they may exercise.[7]

Dixon's cautious approach constituted the norm for much of the twentieth century.

In January 2005 a newly drafted set of High Court rules came into operation. The rewrite was designed, in part, to better enable the Court to handle the increasing number of special leave petitions filed under its appellate jurisdiction, most notably petitions coming from unrepresented litigants that often raise frivolous claims. The new rules significantly change the process by which the Court reviews these petitions. Instead of reviewing written briefs and then conducting oral arguments for each special leave application, the new rules enable the Court to consider special leave applications from unrepresented claimants first on the written submission. If the two judges reviewing the application agree that there is no merit, the claim is dismissed without oral argument and before the respondent files a reply. Furthermore, the rules enable the Court to determine any application for special leave, whether it is from a represented or unrepresented litigant, solely on the written briefs and without oral argument. These changes were thought to keep out frivolous cases, improve logistics, and heighten efficiency. It acknowledges that given the Court's finite resources, it must be selective in how it reviews special leave applications. By framing the rule in this manner, the Court is cognizant of its public responsibilities.

It would be wrong to conclude, however, that the new *High Court Rules* mark a fundamental shift toward the public litigation model. Indeed, many of the rules still reflect a private litigation model. Most notable in this regard is the absence of any new rule governing requests for intervention and ami-

---

7. *Australian Railways Union v. Victorian Railways Commissioners* (1930) 44 CLR 319, 331.

cus status. The Court could have written criteria and procedures for non-party interventions, but it did not. The fact that no clarifications came from this rewrite in an important area of High Court procedure is significant. The Court chose to keep the process as is—informal and ad hoc. It illustrates how the private model still has currency among some contemporary High Court justices.

Amendments in 1976 to the *Commonwealth Judiciary Act* heightened the opportunity for governmental intervention in High Court litigation. Section 78A created an automatic, non-discretionary right of intervention to the Commonwealth and state Attorneys-General, but only in cases that raise *constitutional* issues. The Attorneys-General regularly exercise this power, whereby they become formal parties to the proceedings. No similar right of intervention exists for Attorneys-General in non-constitutional matters.[8] In private or common law appeals that raise no constitutional questions, the Court retains the same discretion over governmental requests to intervene as private individuals or organizational requests.[9] In these instances, leave must be secured and the Court tends to abide by Dixon's dicta. Thus, while the Court has been more tolerant of state and Commonwealth participation in constitutional questions, it has granted a paltry number of discretionary interventions; that is, interventions not requested under Section 78A (Campbell 1998). One study reports that until the 1980s discretionary intervention (either interveners or amici curiae) was nearly nonexistent. Since the 1980s, the High Court has granted discretionary intervention in less than fifty cases (Williams 2000a).

Several appellate judges criticized the High Court's leeriness about discretionary intervention, particularly in high profile cases that raise broad social and economic issues. One such case was *Dietrich v. The Queen*.[10] In *Dietrich*, the question before the Court was whether the common law recognized for accused indigents a right to legal representation at public expense. Absent a bill of rights, statutory and common laws govern rights of the accused. The trial court had failed to stay a proceeding in which Dietrich, through no personal fault, was unable to obtain legal representation. The Court concluded that while there is no common law right to counsel at public expense, the accused has a right to a fair trial. If having no legal representation fosters an "unfair trial," then the proceeding must be stayed until counsel is provided.

---

8. *Judiciary Act 1903*, ss. 78A, B.
9. See *Corporate Affairs Commission v. Bradley* [1974] 1 NSWLR 391.
10. (1992) 177 CLR 292.

This decision was significant on legal grounds, but it raised equally weighty economic questions about the state governments' responsibility to fund legal aid. Many appellate judges objected to the fact that the Court decided *Dietrich* without discretionary interveners or amici curiae, despite its potential impact on state budgets and how legal aid offices allocate finite resources.

> Judge: The effect of *Dietrich* was that legal aid began to be almost totally confined to criminal cases....The greatest proportion of criminal cases involves crimes committed by men, and a goodly proportion of those involve crimes committed against women by way of domestic violence and sexual assault. These women needed to be able to bring domestic violence proceedings...or proceedings for child support or divorce and legal aid became virtually unavailable. It was provided to the defendants because the High Court would say, "Well applying *Dietrich*, this person is entitled to legal representation and his prosecution ought to be stayed until he's afforded it." The legal aid offices reacted to this by channeling funds in that direction. So, the High Court in an effort to protect one section of society severely affected the rights of another section of society. I wonder to this day whether any members of the High Court even thought about that.

> Q: I'm sure a woman's advocacy group would have advanced this argument if afforded an opportunity [to appear as amicus curiae]?

> Judge: That's exactly right. Whether the result would have been different is another matter. It may have made a difference to the structure of the judgment or to whether this was a matter that needed to be addressed by Government....My concern is always that [judges] don't always have the information (58:3815).

Another remarked,

> *Dietrich* was a decision that had profound consequences on governments and government funding because governments allocate an amount of money for legal aid....The point is that the High Court decided the case where the states weren't represented and without any opportunity, as would happen in the [U.S.] Supreme Court, for amicus briefs so that the consequences of the decision would be known. There have been significant financial consequences which have had a significant impact on taxpayers. That decision was made without any supporting material as to the effect of that impact....The High Court is reticent because of the practical difficulties (21:1045).

Another recent case that exposed the continued salience of the private litigation model in the judicial culture was the High Court's 1992 *Mabo v.
Queensland* decision.[11] In *Mabo*, the Court overturned the two-hundred-year-
old precedent that British settlement of Australia, which occurred absent any
treaty with indigenous Australians, was justified because the land at the time
of settlement lacked any owners—a doctrine known as *terra nullius*. The
Court concluded that the *terra nullius* doctrine was inapplicable throughout
the Australian continent based on litigation that questioned its applicability
only to a cluster of small islands off the Queensland coast, the Torres Strait
Islands. Extending the decision's scope angered many because it violated their
sense of what appellate litigation should accomplish: resolving private disputes. A Western Australia Supreme Court judge commented:

> You should only deal with a given set of facts. Courts always get into
> trouble when they try to legislate in relation to matters where there
> has been no evidence. We're all trained like that, to think like that.…
> You should only decide a case that has been fully factually investi-
> gated. One of the criticisms of *Mabo*…is that the Court went further
> than it ordinarily does by deciding on issues that were not ventilated
> properly before it.…The Court decided the issue for mainland Aus-
> tralia when mainland Australia was not an issue before it. Some of
> the members made factual findings about historical material which
> was not an issue before the trial court. Should the High Court deal
> with cases where the facts are not fully ventilated, their decisions are
> suspect. That's what all judges believe (106:2145).

Another judge concluded that the Court went "terribly wrong" in *Mabo*.

> The [Mason] Court invented a doctrine that didn't exist about native
> rights and in favor of someone who wasn't even party to the case—
> the Australian Abos. It started off with a dispute dealing with the
> rights of a small drift of people in the Torres Strait. There was a ques-
> tion of whether they were…*terra nullius*. *Terra nullius* doesn't mean
> there was no one else there, which is the way journalists translated it.
> *Terra nullius* means whether there was any legal system in place where
> there was some sort of hierarchy in place, where a chief can say, "You
> own that plot of land and somebody else owns that plot of land." As
> far as mainland Australia is concerned, the traditional view that there
> was *terra nullius* is perfectly correct because the Aborigines had no

---

11. *Mabo and Others v. Queensland* (No. 2) (1992) 175 CLR 1.

system of government at all. There was no chief or subchief, no concept of private ownership of property. Just men roaming around spearing kangaroos whenever they wanted to. There was no one to do a deal with, which was not the case with the Torres Strait Islanders. Each of them had little plots, so if you grew cabbages on your plot people with other plots couldn't invade them. So it's perfectly true that on the Torres Strait Islands there is no sensible doctrine of *terra nullius*. But how the High Court managed to extrapolate that fact to a general body of principles and applied it to Australia I simply can't imagine (3:2700).

High Court Justice Toohey, a member of the *Mabo* majority, anticipated this private litigation critique. He wrote in his *Mabo* judgment:

While this case concerns the Meriam people, the legal issues fall to be determined according to fundamental principles of common law and colonial constitutional law applicable throughout Australia. The Meriam people are in culturally significant ways different from the Aboriginal peoples of Australia, who in turn differ from each other. But, as will be seen, no basic distinction need be made, for the purposes of determining what interests exist in ancestral lands of indigenous peoples of Australia, between the Meriam people and those who occupied and occupy the Australian mainland. The relevant principles are the same.[12]

This excerpt demonstrates that Justice Toohey was cognizant of the fact that many, even within the judiciary's rank, would criticize *Mabo*'s broad sweeping conclusions. It is difficult to know whether these criticisms are grounded in concern over how the Court's decision transcended the immediate parties, over the significant political and economic fallout it brought, or both. What is significant is that many informants criticized *Mabo* using private litigation arguments. The fact that they couched their criticisms in "use of litigation" terms confirms the continued salience of the orthodox private litigation model today.

DIMENSION #3: JUDGES' RELATIONSHIPS TO LAW, POLITICS, AND COMMUNITY

It became apparent from my interviews that the orthodoxy says much about how judges should relate to the law, the political system, and community. Re-

---

12. *Mabo*, 179.

garding the first, the orthodoxy holds that "the law" exists separate from judges, distinct from what they do, say, write, or think. The judges maintain a caretaker relationship to law, tending to it as the high priests. In the orthodox view, the law not only exists independent of judges, it also subverts judges' wills. Judges can do all sorts of things, but they do not "make law" except interstitially under common law traditions. The American legal academy abandoned this claim decades ago, so it seems antiquarian and naïve, if not altogether untrue. It has been a cornerstone of Australia's orthodoxy, exhibiting a much longer half-life than in the U.S. Many appellate judges still adhere to it. A Federal Court judge concluded that the "mainstream view" among his colleagues is "still that courts declare law and don't make it." He continued, "It has been said for a long time, until recently, that in Australia the judiciary declares existing law. It is this common law theory of precedent, that [judges] declare the law, [judges] don't make the law. The High Court would say that the law is and always has been and that they find the law (85:1000)." Another remarked, "It has been said for years…that the judiciary doesn't make law, it simply declares what the existing common law is (117:1915)." Consider this circumscribed description from a High Court judge of the normative relationship between judges and the law: "Judges are required to develop and clarify the law, and in that sense, they make new law, but it's within limits. The judge inherits the corpus juris. That is what he clarifies. He holds the corpus juris on trust (78)."

Just as the orthodoxy separates law from judges, it similarly separates judges from politics. Many informants were quick to describe how their traditional judicial culture encourages judges to divorce themselves from the political system. An illustration of this expectation came during an interview with a South Australia judge. Reflecting upon his visit to a U.S. appellate court he observed:

> When I was in the United States, I sat for a period with the Fourth Circuit in Virginia. I spent a lot of time with the judges there. The thing that really struck me was how familiar they were with the politicians, senators, and members of the House of Representatives. They were so friendly and familiar with them. I'd be sitting in the chambers of a judge and he would phone up the senator and say, "Hey, look we need another several million dollars because our computer systems have broken down and you've got to lobby for us." And then the money would arrive. There was a mutual respect between the judiciary and politicians in the U.S. which doesn't exist here. That was one of the most remarkable things I found.

He continued:

When I actually asked a number of the judges about it they explained it by saying that so many of them had been in politics and had left politics to be a judge. That's a natural career path. They understand politics because they've been there. They respect politicians more than many judges here do. Many of the politicians had been lawyers and some had been judges. There is a much greater understanding of each other in the U.S. than there is here, where that's very rarely the case. Although the separation of powers is much stronger on paper in the U.S....in the ordinary currency of judicial work and political work they're very close and work together constructively. I really envied them. I thought that was wonderful....That's just a different culture. [The U.S.] system is based on knowledge. Ours is based on ignorance of each other and suspicion (106:2745).

The idea that judges should remain apart from politics is deeply engrained in the orthodoxy, so much that the above judge found it odd to see American judges hanging on their office walls pictures of themselves with members of Congress. The orthodoxy almost encourages a cloistered existence, cut off from political arenas. One High Court justice took great pride in this separation.

[T]he judiciary should have no day by day relationship with the other branches. When I was on the High Court, we were always very careful to have nothing whatever to do with the legislature. We didn't sit out in the gardens giving advice to the politicians, as apparently has happened in the U.S. We had really no contact with politicians although the move to Canberra...was regarded by some as likely to lead to that. I don't think the influence of the Federal Government is any greater after the move to Canberra than before....As far as the bureaucracy is concerned, we had really no contact at all. We were quite isolated from them. We had close links with the state courts, but those were the only links. It was within the judiciary (37:1730).

The division that the orthodoxy seeks between the judiciary and the other political branches is so clear that Chief Justice Sir Owen Dixon (High Court puisne judge 1929–1952 and chief justice 1952–1964) warned that previous work experience in politics would impugn a judge's ability to serve impartially on the bench. The "Earl Warrens" of Australian politics have no place in the judicial orthodoxy. An appellate judge recounted the speech in which Dixon made this claim:

Judge: Sir Owen Dixon, on the occasion of his retirement, gave a speech where he was reminded of how he observed that the law was good preparation for politics, but that the process once begun was ir-reversible. That engendered in Dixon's mind a view that if a lawyer chose to go into politics, he surrendered any right or asserted enti-tlement to be appointed a judge because that was an irreversible process.

Q: Do you think it is irreversible?

Judge: No, I don't but you have to acknowledge…that if you have persons with strong political histories preceding their appointment to a court, it's a pretty demanding thing to expect at that point the capacity to shake off any influence of that previous political experi-ence. There will always be a real risk that the political behavior of the past could influence, perhaps to a significant degree, some de-cisions in some cases. For example, the most recent and controver-sial appointment to the High Court would be Lionel Murphy, who, so the rumors suggest, was appointed to the High Court because the Prime Minister of the day no longer wanted him part of his cabinet. He, accepting the appointment, was seen by many to remain a politician, not shaking himself off politically. Locally we can in-stance a former chief justice of [the South Australia Supreme Court] who was an attorney general in a government not long before his first appointment to the court….He, having spent more time in par-liament and less time in the courts, might be seen in the eyes of some as less able to cease being a politician and becoming a judge. These things might seem foreign to you in light of the American sys-tem (25:1100).

Under the orthodoxy, politics is viral for anyone with aspirations for the bench. Once exposed, a politician-cum-judge is unlikely to shake it. Such a person would face an insufferable transition. It comes as little surprise then that the orthodoxy demands a similar relationship between the judiciary and the broader community. It sees a judge's published opinions as the chief method for communication. If a judge has something to say about a case or her decision, say it in the opinion itself. What if clarification is required? At the federal level, the historical convention was that the Commonwealth At-torney General—not individual justices or even the Chief Justice—explained High Court decisions to the public, if necessary, and defended the Court from criticism. This convention was the modus operandi until Daryl Williams, At-torney-General from 1996 to 2003, refused to follow it. He specifically demurred from defending the Court's 1996 *Wik Peoples v. Queensland*[13] decision (Edwards 1964; Plehwe 1980). Disputed in *Wik* was whether native title claims to government land (a right secured in *Mabo*) could coexist with pastoral leases that the government granted on that same land. The Court decided that native title and pastoral leases could coexist. This decision placed Attorney-General Williams, who was an elected member of the House of Representatives and Howard Government minister, in the awkward position of having to choose between adhering to the existing convention, such that he would defend the Court, or support his Government's general opposition to the decision. Williams found that the difference between endorsing the Court's decision and defending the Court as an institution amounted to a distinction without a political difference. He publicly bucked the convention, to the chagrin of many appellate judges who preferred the Attorney-General handle *Wik*'s potential fallout. That the judicial culture includes this convention in the first place confirms the orthodoxy's reservations about judges interacting with the community. As a High Court judge insisted, "What judges have to say they should say in their judgments and that's that (78)!"

The orthodox view also cloisters judges from the public, viewing them somewhat sacrosanct, aloof, and even slightly mysterious. A Federal Court judge observed that, "The status of the judiciary has changed quite considerably in the last decade. A generation ago, judges were respected, feared, enabled to do naughty things and get away with it. Naughty things like going home early and having mistresses....That's not a good example, the last one. But there was a hands-off attitude (13:10130)." A Melbourne judge offered a similar assessment:

> Courts are much less formal than when I started at the bar. It may be a function of age. Maybe to a twenty-five year old the courts looked formal and foreboding, but I suspect judges are more human now. It was widely believed twenty to thirty years ago that it was improper for a judge to go into a bar at a hotel. Judges were supposed to lead sheltered lives. They could only go to the Melbourne Club and such like places....Judges aren't so much on a pedestal as they used to be (102:4915).

Just how removed from the community should judges be under the orthodox model? One respondent went so far as to commend forbidding judges from voting in elections, fearing that doing so compromises the public's confidence in

---

13. (1996) 187 CLR 1.

the judiciary's independence. Orthodox judges are self-conscious about their separation from politics and the community and do not pretend that this separateness affords any vantage point to critique politics or use the bench as a bully pulpit. A High Court judge said:

> The [Mason Court] activists took the line that it's proper to give effect to contemporary values in framing the law. I disagree with that. Certainly contemporary values have to be given effect in applying the law, but the initial difficulty is to know what contemporary values are. If one gives effect to so-called contemporary values that really means that one gives effect to the values of the justices. The essence is that we live in a democracy and judges are not elected, fortunately. Their values are not necessarily the values of the community (94:900)."

In a rather self-conscious disclosure, a NSW appellate judge said that because the judiciary does not reflect a diverse cross-section of the community judges should stay out of politics as much as possible.

> [T]he problem is that judges are extremely ill-equipped to work out what the impact on society and the economy will be, and not well equipped to work out what community standards are.... The difficulty with community standards is: 1) What do we mean by them? 2) Having worked out what we mean by them, how do we find out what they are? If what we're talking about is general moral norms, I suppose you look into your own heart.... Politicians are elected to make these sorts of decisions. They see their constituents. They have a better understanding of what the people might want. They, through government commissions or the public service, are better equipped to work out what the economic and social impact will be than judges are. There's great danger in judges taking judicial notice of all sorts of things or thinking that just because they think it's a good idea it really will be a good idea.... The more conservative judges here and in England say, "There are some things we can adjust, amend, or qualify in an accretion way, but with a major matter, it's better for us to say we're not going to solve this problem. It must be solved by parliament (94:900)."

This orthodoxy encourages the separation of law from politics and endorses the private litigation model for courts, even appellate courts. But how does the orthodox role conceive of the relationship between the High Court and the other political branches? Are High Court justices to avoid institutional confrontation with parliamentarians, bureaucrats, and cabinet members? Here too deference to the elected branches is expected. Unlike the U.S. Supreme Court, the High Court still resolves a good number of common law cases in addition to its constitutional work. This bears significantly on how its judges conceive their institution's role. Based on the interview data, the orthodoxy perceives the High Court first as a court of common law appeals and only secondarily as a constitutional court. In other words, it is more a place where legal disputes are finally decided than a place for political battle. Hints of this ordering appeared in many interviews. A state appellate judge remarked, "My father [who also worked in law] would say that the High Court should be more like an intermediate court, but I disagree with that. Australian society is so conservative that it needs prodding occasionally (52:134)." A NSW appellate judge said, "The High Court's sole function is to mark out the boundaries of power. It is not concerned with the justice or wisdom of the exercises of power within those boundaries. Those are non-justiciable issues and I agree with that. That is the only way to go as a court under the separation of powers. Their job is to mark off the limits and then back off. If someone has a power, they can exercise it (99)."

The High Court is also conceived as passive, in the sense that it exercises little control over what cases comprise its docket. This too may seem naïve to American court scholars who speak of the U.S. Supreme Court "constructing its agenda" through the certiorari process without batting an eye. Not so under Australia's judicial orthodoxy. Consider this exchange with a former High Court Justice regarding the Court's workload:

Q: Are there instances when the Court should intervene in the democratic process?

Judge: No. The question so phrased seems to suggest that the Court itself has some initiative to undertake. I don't think there is an initiative for the Court to undertake. The Court's function is simply to resolve the question that arises from the litigation that is put before us. The Court has no agenda of its own.

Q: To what extent does the High Court have control over the cases that come to it?

Judge: Its control over major constitutional questions is extremely limited. First, it is open to a party that wishes to agitate a constitutional proceeding in the Court itself and the Court then has appellate jurisdiction that must be exercised to determine that question....In the case of litigation in other courts, not only is there the prospect of special leave to appeal, there is also the procedure by which the attorney general from the Commonwealth, any state, or territory can remove a matter to the High Court to have it determined. If there is a live question of some substance to the constitution, the High Court's practice has been to give a ruling on the point. The High Court does not abjure any opportunity to determine an important constitutional question.

When asked about the timing of the controversial native title decisions (*Mabo* and *Wik*), one judge responded, "The High Court had no role in bringing those issues to its doorstep. The issues were chosen by the litigants, but they may have thought they had a creative environment in which to argue those issues (11)." Another judge stated, albeit defensively:

Q: Are there areas of law or issues of governance that the judiciary should be tackling?

Judge: Are you assuming that there's a choice? Because there isn't. I responded that way because of this notion, which I think is correct, that courts don't have a choice. If someone brings up a dispute, they have to decide it.

If the orthodoxy calls for the High Court to take a passive, deferential approach toward the cases on its docket, it calls for a similar tact toward the federal and state parliaments. Its justification for deference is premised on the doctrine that sovereignty lies with parliament, a doctrine Australia inherited from Britain.

There is broad consensus among legal scholars that the *grundnorm* (if one follows Kelsen) or ultimate rule of recognition (if one follows Hart) of British constitutionalism, at least since 1688, is parliamentary sovereignty. This term has taken on innumerable meanings to different scholars at different times. A particular variant informs Australia's orthodoxy.

While much ink has been spilled in Britain and Australia over the meaning of "parliamentary sovereignty," no legal theorist has had more of an impact on how Australians incorporated this constitutional principle into the colonial and later federal systems than Albert V. Dicey, Oxford's Vinerian Professor of Law from 1882 to 1909. Dicey's *An Introduction to the Study of the Law of the Constitution* was to late nineteenth-century British constitutional law (and by extension Australian law) what Locke's *Second Treatise on Government* was to American constitutional law. Its prominence in the political and judicial cultures warrants close attention here.

Dicey's aim in writing his book, first published in 1885 and six times since, was primarily empirical. He sought to describe the contours and content of the English constitution and constitutional law as he saw them. Because

Britain lacks a single written constitution, Dicey sought to reduce the observable laws, legal rules, and conventions that comprised the late-Victorian constitutional regime to a few basic principles. He has been roundly criticized for his empirical shortcomings (some charge that his Whiggish political proclivities jaundiced his observations), yet he emphasized two defining features of the British system: the sovereignty of parliament and the rule of law.

To say that parliament is sovereign, according to Dicey, means that "Parliament...has the right to make or unmake any law whatever; and further, that no person or body is recognized by the law of England as having a right to override or set aside the legislation of Parliament" (1982, 3). Or as it is proverbially put in English legal circles, Parliament can do everything but make a woman a man, and a man a woman. But what exactly did he mean by this? First, parliament exercises unlimited legislative authority. Dicey noted, "There is no law which Parliament cannot change....Fundamental or so-called constitutional laws are under our constitution changed by the same body and in the same manner as other laws, by Parliament acting in its ordinary legislative character (37)." This had an important consequence for the hierarchy of laws. Dicey continued, "There is under the English constitution no marked or clear distinction between laws which are not fundamental or constitutional and laws which are fundamental and constitutional (Ibid.)."

The second component to Dicey's definition of parliamentary sovereignty is the absence of competing legislative authority or judicial authority that could overturn or repeal parliamentary acts. "There does not exist in any part of the British Empire any person or body of persons, executive, legislative or judicial, which can pronounce void any enactment passed by the British Parliament on the ground of such enactment being opposed to the constitution, or on any ground whatever, except, of course, its being repealed by Parliament (39)." Like many of his positivist predecessors, Dicey found it necessary to vest indivisible sovereignty in a single body: Parliament. It is important, however, to note how Dicey defined Parliament, which for him included the Crown, the House of Lords, and the House of Commons. In other words, Dicey defined Parliament as it operated in its classic age, before the electoral reforms that came about in the second half of the nineteenth century.

It finally should be noted that while Dicey vested legal sovereignty in Parliament, he recognized two limitations to its exercise. The first, an external limitation, is the need for Parliament (and parliamentarians) to secure and maintain the polity's support. Laws passed by a sovereign Parliament that proved repugnant to the people would be disobeyed. Sovereignty extends only as far as legitimacy. The second limitation, an internal one, is that members of Parliament are themselves products of the society they represent, so that "the permanent wishes of the representative portion of Parliament can hardly in the long run differ from the wishes of the English people (34)."

The Diceyan conception of parliamentary sovereignty is a cornerstone of Australia's judicial orthodoxy in that the courts are expected to defer to parliaments.

> [The High Court] is really responsible for saying to each of the parliaments, state and federal respectively, what their powers are and what powers they don't have. *Subject to that, it's always been our tradition that what parliament says must be applied, provided it says so with sufficient clarity. If it says white is black, that's it—nothing judges can do about it, unless it hasn't used sufficiently clear language* (70:1315) (emphasis added).

A NSW appellate judge said of Dicey:

> That's certainly what I was taught. All of the "with-it" professors say that it should be rejected, but I think it is an absurd view. After all it is encapsulated in the constitution itself. The constitution says that the sovereign power of the Commonwealth should be vested in the House of Representatives and the Senate—the legislative wing.
>
> Q: What is the judiciary's function within the Diceyan model?
>
> Judge: When the sovereign body speaks it's the end of the matter. Popular sovereignty—that's your [American] sort of grundnorm.... "We The People" is a really recent sort of concept. That's not our legal concept (3:1).

In the orthodox view, state and federal courts are subordinate to parliament's will. As one Federal Court judge said, "Ideally, what one would hope is that the judiciary is not entirely separate from Parliament in the sense that they are carrying out—in this court being a statutory court—what Parliament would wish, given the legislation of the day. The interrelationship between Parliament and the judiciary is very close—the judiciary are servants of Parliament (sic) (127:2720)."

The extent of the judicial deference was starkly illustrated in a 1995 High Court case originating in NSW. The case raised the question of whether the NSW Parliament could enact criminal legislation concerning a single individual, Gregory Kable. Kable killed his wife, was convicted of manslaughter, and sentenced to prison. After he threatened from prison those who cared for his children, the NSW legislature passed the *Community Protection Act 1994*, which enabled state judges to issue preventive sentences for anyone considered likely to injure another if released from prison. Kable argued, *inter alia*, that this act exceeded state legislative powers and violated the Commonwealth

Constitution. The NSW Court of Appeal concluded that the state parliament was acting within its prescribed powers and it was not the Court's duty to evaluate the act's merits. One judge wrote in the opinion:

> The principle that a sovereign and plenary legislature may enact private acts has long been recognised....Courts may, no doubt, reconsider the extent of the powers of legislative bodies or, at least, the form of their enactments in the light of modern views of the requirements of a democratic society. But for the courts to hold that a sovereign and plenary legislature may not now enact private acts would, in my respectful opinion, involve not a remoulding of the existing constitutional arrangements but the adoption or arrogation by the courts of a constitutional power of a kind fundamentally different from that which previously the constitutional arrangements have allocated to them.[14]

A NSW appellate judge who sat for that case admitted during my interview with him that, "None of us thought that was good legislation, using 'good' in a very broad sense." Despite this, he concluded, "I was firmly of the view that we were bound to accept the legislation—legislation which was directed to one particular person (34:3600)." A Western Australia Supreme Court judge agreed with his colleague:

> We [judges] firmly hold to the view that parliament has full authority to make the law and we're here to interpret and apply it. But we're also of the view that the executive government can't transgress or step beyond the authority that is given to it by the law. So if we see cases where ministers have done things that we don't believe a parliamentary act authorized them to do, we have no hesitation in telling them. And they accept it. *Given a law that is clear in its terms, it would never occur to me to write a judgment questioning parliament's authority to make the law or wisdom in doing so. That's for politicians not for judges. I don't say that view is unanimous in the judiciary* (53:2200) (emphasis added).

One may be less surprised that state appellate judges adhere to this principle. More surprising may be the extent to which it infuses High Court thinking. Judicial deference calls on judges to refrain from second guessing the merits of parliamentary acts. Similarly judges must not question inaction. One High Court Justice lamented, for example, that his institution usurped parliamen-

---

14. *Kable v. Director of Public Prosecutions* CA 40067 of 1995, NSW LEXIS 11355 at 38.

tary power over native title in *Mabo* and ignored the possibility that legislative inaction may have been a conscious choice by parliamentarians.

> *Mabo*…was a decision with which I profoundly disagree as a matter of principle. The legal question at the core of the matter, putting aside all of the emotion, was whether the law in Australia recognized native title. Of course it had been held in a number of cases—by single judges on the NSW Supreme Court and High Court—that it didn't. If a different view had been taken of course the legislatures would have dealt with the situation. They may have dealt with it fairly. They may have dealt with it unfairly, but they would have dealt with it without a doubt. So to change the law after 200 years was an irresponsible thing to do (94).

A third component to this judicial deference is the thought that judges should put greater faith in the elected branches than their own to promote justice. Consider this exchange with a High Court Justice regarding if and when courts should intervene in the political process:

> Q: The conventional story about the 1950s and 1960s in the U.S. was that the democratic process failed, in terms of civil rights, and the Supreme Court felt compelled to intervene.

> Judge: Well the court failed too, didn't it, for many years. So there's no point in putting your faith in the court as opposed to the democratic process. The democratic process that we've found in our tradition is very rich in history and tradition. We find, I think, it satisfactory. Liberties in Australia have never been less than they are in America, notwithstanding or because of the tradition in the democratic process. We would not have interned 14,000 Japanese citizens during the war, for instance. We would have never had slavery. I'm being quite blunt with you now. And one can hardly say that [your] court had a very proud record (78).

Although this judge ignored Australia's use of internment camps during the First and Second World Wars (see Fischer 1989; Saunders and Daniels 2000) and he got his figures wrong—approximately 120,000 Japanese-Americans were relocated to internment camps—he affirmed the orthodoxy's ironic distrust of courts and judicial power. Most proponents justified this on the grounds that judges are appointed, not elected. An appellate judge articulated the sentiment well:

> I know many judges are elected [in the U.S.]. Judges here are not elected, they're appointed. That's a real distinction. Once you have

elected judges, you have people answerable to the public for what they do and say. Judges being appointed here…aren't answerable to the electorate. In your system, I can understand an argument that runs, because judges are elected, they have some role to play in the political system in terms of looking after minorities and the like. Under the Westminster system in which we operate, I don't see that role as being equivalent (32:2115).

The orthodoxy's judicial role has been defined thus far in terms of what appellate judges should not do. To leave it in such terms would be misleading.

In *The Path of Law*, Oliver Wendell Holmes, Jr. wrote, "If you want to know the law and nothing else, you must look at it as a bad man, who cares only for the material consequence which knowledge enables him to predict (Holmes 1897)." In similar fashion, if you want to understand a judicial culture, look at its images of good judges. Australia's judicial orthodoxy advances a clear vision of the good appellate judge. In addition to calling for judges to hold the law on trust and separate themselves from politics and the community, the orthodox view has been that *good judging* is equivalent to *superb lawyering*. Good appellate judges are not legislators, policy makers, or philosophers, but they are excellent lawyers. The lawyer's craft is the judge's craft: determine the facts, find the law, and apply the latter to the former. This view can be discerned in words that several judges used to describe the judicial function. Consider this exchange with a High Court Justice regarding the famous Australian jurist, Sir Owen Dixon: "Dixon said he put his faith in utter and complete legalism, but he explained what he meant by legalism, that is a method which one employs— the *lawyer's technique* (78) (emphasis added)." It is not inconsequential that this judge described Dixon's judicial method as "the lawyer's technique." Language suggesting that good judges are simply superbly qualified lawyers emerged in several interviews. Consider also another informant's word choice when describing the present Court's ideological composition.

Judge: The composition of the judiciary has changed quite a bit.…I suspect the social values of the judiciary have become more radical. I don't mean we're all raving comrades, but compared to earlier times—when judges were morally and socially conservative—I suspect that's so. Judges are—to use the Americanism—more liberal as a class. I doubt that twenty years ago you would have a judge on the High Court saying he was openly gay.

Q: Besides Justice Kirby, what other judges typify this more liberal judiciary?

Judge: Almost the entire membership of the Federal Court. Take Mar-
cus Einfeld—a very strong advocate for civil rights outside the judicial context. You've got a very powerful *contingent of lawyers on the
Federal Court in Melbourne* that is strong on anti-discrimination and
the rights of refugees (104:10130) (emphasis added).

It is noteworthy that even this judge, who wholly supported the transformation that the Mason Court precipitated, employed the word "lawyers" instead of "judges" when describing Melbourne's liberally minded Federal
Court bench.

It is also evident that the orthodox model leaves little room for judges who
take on the airs of legislators. "[J]udges ought to stay out of legislating—I'm
very strong on that!" remarked a Western Australia Supreme Court judge.
"We should not try to legislate. I know when we give a decision the effect of
it might be to change the law. Once we start legislating we're in deep trou-
ble. We're not elected. We're supposed to interpret the law, which is made by
parliament and the common law.... When we're operating in the common
law areas we tend to unwittingly legislate, but the less of that the better
(43:2415)."

Nor does the orthodoxy encourage philosophizing judges who remind the
country when it fails to fulfill its moral and political commitments. Philo-
sophical tones are shunned. Consider this judge's reaction to *Mabo:* "Its practical consequence was felt throughout Australia, but the legal community was
particularly taken aback by the moralizing tone the majority judgments employed. The joint judgment from Justices Deane and Gaudron caught the most
ire." The section of the *Mabo* judgment to which this judge referred stated that,
"The acts and events by which [the legal theory of *terra nullius*] was carried
into practical effect constitute *the darkest aspect of the history of this nation.
The nation as a whole must remain diminished unless and until there is an acknowledgment of, and retreat from, those past injustices* (emphasis added)."[15]
Cognizant that this supercilious tone may offend the orthodox norms, Justices Deane and Gaudron later explained in their judgment:

[W]e are conscious of the fact that, in those parts of this judgment
which deal with the dispossession of Australian Aborigines, we have
used language and expressed conclusions which some may think to
be unusually emotive for a judgment in this Court. We have not done
that in order to trespass into the area of assessment or attribution of

---

15. *Mabo,* 175 CLR 1, 109.

moral guilt. As we have endeavoured to make clear, the reason which has led us to describe, and express conclusions about, the dispossession of Australian Aborigines in unrestrained language is that the full facts of that dispossession are of critical importance to the assessment of the legitimacy of the propositions that the continent was unoccupied for legal purposes and that the unqualified legal and beneficial ownership of all the lands of the continent vested in the Crown.[16]

These sentences angered many of my informants because Australian judges historically avoided writing in moralizing tones. Said one judge, "It was common in the 1990s among intermediate court judges to speak of the High Court judges as politicians...'those politicians from Canberra.' Their *Mabo* decision is the best example. That opening paragraph from Deane and Gaudron shocked the profession. It was over the top—way over. That wasn't logical thinking. It was anger, emotion. Judges don't write that way (7)!"

DIMENSION #4: LEGAL REASONING AND DECISION-MAKING

Australia's judicial orthodoxy has been equally clear in its normative rules about legal reasoning. Law is understood as a logical, self-contained set of rules with determinant meanings that support correct answers to legal problems. Law is seen as a science. The orthodoxy presented a "Victorian façade," according to one Federal Court judge, that "judging was a science...[and that] there was a right result and wrong result and judges basically got the right results (12:1545)." Legal reasoning is, therefore, declaratory in nature—an articulation of the single correct answer. A High Court justice claimed, "So long as the [declaratory theory of law] was in ascendance, as it was for most of this century in the High Court of Australia, the judge's function was assumed to be largely mechanical. Find the rule. Determine what the facts are. Apply the rule to the facts—result (11)." Another judge remarked, "Years ago there was a greater emphasis on strict rules. Apply the strict rule and bang that's your answer." Previous generations of judges were "more inclined to say that the law is the law and we'll define it for you lesser mortals," according to a Western Australia judge. Their mindset was that "We don't make it up. This is the law that has come down to us (10:1000)!" Another remarked, "There was this sense [under the orthodoxy] that once a barrister was appointed there was a

---

16. *Mabo*, 120.

metamorphosis into a type of infallibility—the sense that I'm applying the law and there is only one correct answer, without fully recognizing there is a range of answers and discretion (58:1145)."

It must also be noted that the orthodoxy conceives of judicial decision-making as wholly distinct and different from decision-making in other branches of government. "Some disputes in the community have to be resolved impartially, clinically, and with rigor to fact-finding and the application of legal principle," said one NSW judge. Indeed, the apparent absence of subjectivity in decision-making is the orthodoxy's hallmark. A High Court Justice remarked:

> A judge doesn't come to a conclusion and then seek to justify it. The reasoning process he goes through, particularly in constitutional law, more often than not, leads him to his conclusion. Far from obfuscating, what it does do is ensure an objectivity which of course…would not exist otherwise. That's what Dixon meant. You can use this method of reasoning to ensure that your own personal prejudices are less important than otherwise would be. Of course a judge has certain leanings, and he doesn't come to solving it with a completely blank mind. This process of *legal reasoning, logic, and high technique*, are what will direct you more nearly to an objective than anything else. I think the important thing is…that the judge who approaches a matter this way does assume there is a correct answer and an incorrect answer, not a matter of personal prejudice, and it's this technique which will lead you more nearly anyway to the correct answer (78) (emphasis added).

It follows that the orthodox model places high value on the reasoning process itself and that written judgments accurately convey reasoning processes. One High Court judge offered the following:

> [The judges] have a discussion immediately after the case is finished, and we do because we have to go up and down on the lift. But even then you get people to say, "Well I'd like to have a look at it." Sometimes when you sit down and write you—and this is exactly what I was saying about this notion that people have—the Jerome Frank idea that reasons only disguise the real prejudices of the judge. In fact, sometimes when you sit down to write…you change your mind, so what you said going up [on the lift] is not right.
>
> And I think that is the one thing that my associates learn about. The reasoning process is important. You reason to an end. You can't always see the end (78).

Moving from the general to the specific, how does the orthodoxy guide judges in constitutional interpretation? The constitution is conceived first and foremost as a power distribution document, one that enumerates and assigns the powers of government to different branches. It is a document for the political branches and those who occupy them. The orthodoxy does not see the constitution as a document that identifies and protects individual rights. This is a reasonable approach because the constitution lacks an entrenched bill of rights and its few rights-related provisions are comparatively modest.[17]

The constitution's focus on distributing power constrains how judges interpret it under the orthodox model. First, orthodox judges see the High Court's constitutional role as policing the boundaries of state and federal powers and not passing judgment on the substantive value or wisdom of state or federal law. A Victoria Supreme Court judge claimed, "The High Court's function is an arbiter of the powers of the Commonwealth Government and the state governments. So to that extent it performs a fairly unique function which is not dissimilar to the Supreme Court in your country (70:1315)." A High Court Justice affirmed: "The view that parliament, acting within its powers has complete authority to change the law as it sees fit is a proposition that has thus far not been doubted in Australia.... [T]he general view...is that no matter what the courts may say, if the parliament is acting within its powers...the constitution provides. It is for the parliament to be the ultimate arbiter of the law, subject to the constitution itself." Within the orthodox framework, the High Court's function is, according to the same High Court Justice, "to identify the rights, powers, privileges, liabilities, and duties that the law imposes and to see whether it's connected with one of the heads of power in the constitution." In plain terms, according to this Justice, "If the connection appears, then the law is valid. If it doesn't, then it's invalid. That's a fairly mechanistic approach (63:2215)."

Given that the High Court functions as a boundary enforcer and abstains from evaluating the merits of parliamentary acts, it is not surprising that the

---

17. See chapter 2. Australia's constitution provides for very few rights. Section 41 secures the right to vote in federal elections. Section 80 provides for a trial by jury in cases involving Commonwealth criminal law. Section 92 guarantees freedom in interstate trade and Section 51(xxxi) guarantees payment on just terms for Commonwealth acquisition of property. Section 116 prohibits the Commonwealth from establishing a religion, imposing any religious observances, or passing laws that prohibit the free exercise of religion. Finally, Section 117 prohibits the citizens of one state from being discriminated against in other states.

orthodoxy employs methods of constitutional interpretation that limit judicial discretion. Textualism is the paramount modality for constitutional interpretation. As a High Court Justice recounted:

> The constitution is a living document, in the sense that it has to be applied to modern times, but that doesn't mean that judges can alter it just because they think the times have changed. I don't think one can pick and choose. My attitude is always to look at the words of the constitution first and see what they mean. Then you see if you're constrained by decisions of the Court to hold that they mean something in particular. If so, you give effect to that. If there are no clear decisions or ideas what the founding fathers said about it…the real thing is to look at the constitution itself and the authorities (94:4600).

Textualism often goes hand in hand with other interpretive modalities that appear to limit judicial discretion, such as originalism. One might expect the orthodoxy to encourage this modality as well. In fact, it eschews arguments based upon the framers' intent. A Federal Court judge admitted, "[Ours] is an unhistorical way of looking at federation. Until recently, the High Court ignored the historic context of federation.… Until recently the Australian tradition has been textualist and not historical (102)." This may come as a surprise given that Australia's framers kept an official transcript of convention debates. Lawyers could use the constitution's earlier drafts as points of comparisons, but for much of its history, the Court refused arguments based on the transcripts. Reference to Quick & Garran's 1901 annotated constitutional commentary was also acceptable. Yet in its first term the Court decided that what delegates said during convention debates was inadmissible.[18] The Court affirmed this practice as late as 1975: "In case of ambiguity or lack of certainty, resort can be had to the history of the colonies, particularly in the period of and immediately preceding the development of the terms of the Constitution. But it is settled doctrine in Australia that the records of the discussions in the Conventions and in the legislatures of the colonies will not be used as an aid to the construction of the Constitution."[19] The underlying concern about resorting to the debates is that rather than clarifying intentions they would muddy them up. To avoid slogging through and trying to recon-

---

18. See *Tasmania v. Commonwealth of Australia & State of Victoria* (1904) 1 CLR 329.
19. *Attorney-General (Cth); Ex Rel McKinlay v. Commonwealth* (1975) 135 CLR 1, 17.

cile competing visions, the Court prefers to trust that the constitution's language best captures what the authors intended.

DIMENSION #5: TREATMENT OF PRECEDENT

A cornerstone to the Anglo-American common law systems is stare decisis, the practice whereby previous decisions guide analogous cases in the future. Scholars have concluded that these legal systems adhere to varying degrees to this practice (Brewer-Carias 1989). This dimension taps the orthodoxy's approach toward precedents. Informants suggested that Australia's orthodoxy encourages rigorous adherence to stare decisis. A Victoria appellate judge suggested that judges who adhered to the orthodox model were "more enthralled about the past." He continued, "It's recent to see judge-made law as a species of rulemaking instead of just working out logical implications of what has been laid down (65:1300)." A strong consensus emerged that under the orthodox model the longer a precedent had been in place, the less likely the High Court would overturn it, regardless of whether it originally was rightly or wrongly decided. "Previously, the High Court would have accepted that if there was a lot of established precedent [for a case] the precedent would stand. Now [with the Mason Court] the question is if there is a long established precedent, perhaps it's time to look at it again," said a South Australia judge (48:2215). A NSW appellate judge offered a similar assessment:

> The entire Australian judicial hierarchy was…much more settled. Single judges followed decisions of intermediate appellate courts and the High Court without question. They followed decisions of the Court of Appeal in England without question. Intermediate courts followed decisions of the High Court and English courts without question. So at least in theory there was a more rigid hierarchy. There was not much opportunity for judges to say what they thought the right result…was.…The High Court wasn't strictly bound by its earlier decisions, but they almost always followed them. It was very difficult to get leave from the High Court to have an earlier decision of the Court reargued. In the last fifteen years, it's become much more common for that to happen (103:245).

Stare decisis is so strong under the orthodoxy that judges may support precedent with which they disagree. One High Court Justice admitted:

There was a case in which I was constrained to give a decision against my better judgment. It was in *[Queensland v. The Commonwealth]*, the second territory case.[20] The question was whether the power to make laws with regard to the territories allowed the Commonwealth to create senators for the territories. In the first case it was held by a narrow majority that the Commonwealth did have this power. Then one member of the Court retired and was replaced by someone else. So the second territories case was brought in raising the same point, asking the Court to depart from the earlier decision. I took the view that the earlier decision was wrong but it was a reasonable decision. It had been acted upon. Senators had been appointed. There was no logical reason to depart from it. So in that case, I was constrained by precedent to depart from what I thought the constitution itself required (94:5315).

Another judge confirmed this long-established orthodox tradition: "If there is an incorrect principle which is going to work injustice, then prima facie there is no justification for saying, 'Well I should continue to perpetuate injustice because my brethren had done that before me.' That just doesn't seem to me to be a morally defensible judicial stance, *but I say that cautiously, having regard to the fact that generations of judges thought that it was the only morally defensible stance.* All I can say is that I don't agree with them (74:1530) (emphasis added)." Another offered, "The principle of stare decisis was when I grew up very strong, even to the point of the High Court saying in the [*Geelong Harbor Trust* case] that the preexisting law might be wrong but it has been applied for so long there is no point in changing it (81:430)." A High Court Justice put it this way: "The norm is the Dixonian approach. Find the principle from the decided cases so any good lawyer can see the possibilities (94:2030)." Another High Court Justice offered this comparison:

> Judge: My own view about U.S. lawyers is that if you ask them a question, they're likely to attempt to resolve it from their own jurisprudential kick bag. That's an exaggeration. But with an Australian or English lawyer their immediate reaction is to try and think of the closest judicial decision to the question at hand.
>
> Q: Straight to the [law reports]?
>
> Judge: That's right (17:2430).

---

20. (1977) 139 CLR 585.

THE HIGH COURT'S ORTHODOX ROLE   75

All precedent is important under the orthodox model, but not equally important. In earlier decades, the orthodox model favored English decisions from the House of Lords and Court of Appeal. A Western Australia judge recounted, "Our constitution is based on the American constitution but we've never followed America in criminal law. I can remember standing up and quoting American decisions down in that court and being told, 'We follow English law, not American law (43:900).'" Another judge described his predecessors as employing an "insular approach" when it came to investigating foreign case law. "You looked [under the orthodox model] to the House of Lords or the Court of Appeal and that was your search (85:1430)!" One could hardly fault Australian judges in the early twentieth century for looking to British courts for guidance. A NSW appellate judge explained why:

> In the 1920s, Australia was a new federation. We had fought the Boar War with the Brits. We had fought the First World War with the British. If Britain declared war, we declared war. So there was still really total absorption with the British viewpoint. The British viewpoint was very strongly colonial. Churchill's view of England's role in Africa and the subcontinent in particular, these days we would see as quite extraordinary. I suspect that it reflected the view of most—and I suspect there would still be a few people around even now—that England was the great socializer. That it gave these countries a system almost of perfection that they never would have been able to achieve of themselves (58:1615).

Churchill may not have seen his legal system socializing Australia in the same way he envisioned it socializing other parts of the Empire. Yes, convicts settled Australia, but many were *English* convicts! Australia was not Africa or Asia, but Australians in the early twentieth century were of the mindset that what was good for Britain was great for Australia, including precedents from British courts.

DIMENSION #6: DEVELOPMENT OF THE LAW

With the orthodoxy calling for judges to separate themselves from politics and the community, to employ textualism, and to adhere rigidly to precedents, the question that naturally follows is what does it say about when and how law develops, especially within courts? In short, the judiciary is equipped to develop the law under the orthodox model, but only interstitially. A High Court Justice explained: "Justice Holmes and Cardozo described it. Judges make law...by filling in the gaps. One can make law in a different way. The legislature—subject to constitutional considerations—is utterly unrestrained as to the laws that can be made. It can be totally unjust or erratic." Interstitial legal development occurs when judges extend an extant legal principle in a new way or situation. The change is gradual. The same High Court Justice continued, "Although the judge makes law when he, for example, decides the existing principle should be applied in a new way, that's certainly making law. But he's doing it by extending existing principles (94:3000)." A state appellate judge commented, "I don't believe judges should be moving goal posts. They should just decide if a goal has been scored. Yet, the law must progress. But it is not our job to move the goal posts. The law develops because the concepts are not precise—categories of indeterminate reference exist where judges can develop the law (99)." Another offered: "Lord Denning…developed the law, extended it to accommodate the changing social environment, but his extension was based on principles that had been established since the foundation of our common law. He didn't all of a sudden say, 'Well I think this is a good idea that this person should have such and such a remedy and I shall therefore say he has it.' That's for parliament to do (70:1315)."

This notion of interstitial legal development is the overarching principle for changing law. It is noteworthy how the orthodoxy justifies the Court developing and changing constitutional law. One might envision an institutional justification based on the fact that the High Court, like no other political institution, is charged with deciphering the constitution's meaning. Indeed, one could claim that the Court possesses unique institutional skills, procedures, and staff that better equip it for this task than other institutions. Chief Justice John Marshall taps this institutional justification when he declares in *Marbury v. Madison* that, "It is emphatically the province and duty of the judicial department to say what the law is." Yet the orthodoxy does not offer an institutional justification. Instead, it says that the Court should exercise its power in the constitutional realm because it also possesses it in the common law realm. High Court judges, in other words, do not develop constitutional law because they sit on the High Court. Their authority to make constitutional law is not derived from their institution; rather High Court judges make constitutional law because they make common law. Sir Owen Dixon spoke to this in a 1957 speech titled, "The Common Law as an Ultimate Constitutional Foundation." He observed that the Australian and American constitutional systems place juristic authority in different sources. "In America…the authority for the establishment of their constitution is ascribed to the will of the people and not to the operation of existing law.…[J]uristically, in the case of each State, and in truth, of the Union too, the first constitutional laws and the system of jurisprudence possessed an original and not a derivative authority (Dixon 1965c,

203)." Australia's constitutional system, on the other hand, contained "an anterior law providing the sources of juristic authority.... In Australia we begin with the common law." American judges act "from the authority of the organs of government of the State, statute law from the legislature, and unwritten law from the judiciary." Australian judges, on the other hand, "act every day on the unexpressed assumption that the one common law surrounds [Australians] and applies where it has not been superseded by statute (Ibid., 204–5)." Because the common law is anterior to the constitution, Australian judges derive their constitutional lawmaking powers from the common law. A State appellate judge explained:

> It's a bit difficult to suggest that the judiciary has a constitutional position where it can usurp any part of the democratic process. Its position is to protect the democratic process. I suppose if it's necessary to protect the democratic process by galvanizing the Executive to do something, then that's appropriate, but it can't arrogate to itself a role that is for the legislature or the executive, although it's got to be recognized that the judiciary at the highest level does make law. *It does because that's what the common law has always been about. It's been said for years until recently in Australia that the judiciary doesn't make law, that it simply declares what the existing common law is—that they're essentially the only ones who know what the existing common law is....* I suppose it does have to make law to make the democratic process work, but it's got to be careful not to step outside of the incremental decisions, which are associated with the common law decisions, to assume a place which would, if the courts lost their way, actually threaten the democratic process. It's the legislature's duty to make sure that the democratic process is retained (12:1915).

This common law justification for constitutional change means that interstitial change is expected on the constitutional front as well. Big leaps are eschewed. Australia's colonial past contributes in large measure to this. Those who settled Australia brought with them the British common law. This common law was in operation at the state level decades before the High Court reached its first constitutional decision. This legal inheritance also included the notion that Parliament is sovereign and naturally takes the lead in governing. What did not come with this legal inheritance were institutional justifications for the Court initiating constitutional change. This void may be chalked up, in part, to the absence of a written constitution in Britain, where courts only developed the common law. This became the orthodoxy's lone defense for constitutional law reform.

It is little wonder given this background that the U.S. and Australian supreme courts find their authority for constitutional change in different places. The clear severing of institutions that came via revolution provided the U.S. Constitution, according to Sir Owen Dixon, "an original and not a derivative authority" in the people. Forged from revolution and resting upon the consent of the governed, the U.S. Constitution became a foundational, first-principles document. This is not the case for Australia's constitution. Lacking a clear and decisive separation point, what unified the Australian colonies and established the Commonwealth's authority was the shared common law. Because of this, Australians are able, wrote Dixon, "to avail [themselves] of the common law as a jurisprudence antecedently existing into which our system came and in which it operates (Dixon 1965c, 202–204).

If Australia's constitutional system's authority is derived from an antecedent common law then it is reasonable to expect that the judges who interpret the constitution would do so employing common law techniques and justify constitutional development as an extension of the common law. One way in which the orthodoxy overcomes the tension inherent between British constitutionalism and the written Commonwealth Constitution is to justify constitutional change relying upon that augustly British creation, the common law. I surmise that this lingering tension also partially explains Australia's reluctance to adopt a bill of rights (even a statutory version a la New Zealand) and its failed effort to become a republic in 1999, when Australians rejected a referendum that would have replaced the Queen of England as Australia's head of state with an Australian.

A final component to this discussion concerns the issue of who is responsible for initiating constitutional reform. The orthodoxy envisions litigants and their attorneys as engines for legal change more so than judges. For instance, a Federal Court judge remarked, "It's what counsel puts up to the bench that results in the development of the law, rather than the bench itself going off on some adventurous streak (13:400)." A recent articulation of this position occurred in the High Court's *Coleman v. Power* (2004) case.[21] The case concerned whether a section of a state vagrancy law could criminalize insulting words directed at public officials. The answer to that question depended, first, on whether the law burdened political communication. The petitioners and respondents conceded that it did and asked the Court to address whether the law was justified, notwithstanding the burden. Some judges did not acknowledge that the law burdened speech and wrote judgments fully ex-

---

21. 220 CLR 1.

ploring this question, frustrating others on the bench. Justice McHugh chastised his colleagues for taking the case in a direction different from the parties' wishes. He wrote, "If parties do not wish to dispute a particular issue, that is their business. This court has no business in determining issues upon which the parties agree. It is no answer to that proposition to say that this court has a duty to lay down the law for Australia. Cases are only authorities for what they decide. If a point is not in dispute in a case, the decision lays down no legal rule concerning that issue."[22] McHugh's hesitancy illustrates the orthodoxy's emphasis on litigant-centered legal change.

The collective portrait that these dimensions to Australia's orthodoxy paint is of an apolitical judiciary exercising delimited powers and rather mechanical legal methods. Many appellate judges abide by these orthodox conceptions today and think that the High Court should follow them as well. While the appellate bench remains divided over the continued merits of these orthodox conceptions, there is an overwhelming agreement that their historic influence has been pervasive. Beginning in the 1990s, however, a cadre of entrepreneurial High Court Justices introduced an altogether new judicial role conception that upended much of the orthodoxy. It brought new understandings to the purposes of law, the aims of litigation, judges' relationships to law, the political branches, and the community, accepted modes of legal reasoning, use of precedent, and how law develops. The next chapter tackles this transformation.

---

22. McHugh, 44.

4

The Mason Court Supplants the Orthodoxy

The previous chapter established that an orthodox judicial culture dominated Australia's appellate courts for much of the twentieth century. It demonstrated that the dimensions of this orthodoxy portray an apolitical, deferential judiciary. In many respects, this vision comports with Australia's Westminster political tradition that locates the primary powers and responsibilities of government with Parliament. This chapter and the next present evidence that a profound transformation—an intellectual shift—occurred within the High Court in the late 1980s and 1990s that presented new ways of thinking about the Court's role within the political system and challenged much of the orthodoxy. Pinpointing when this intellectual shift started and what were the key markers in its development is susceptible to disagreement and debate. The phenomenon being studied is itself an abstraction: normative views about a political institution's *raison d'être*. Two broad visions for the High Court's role were in competition over the last twenty years—the orthodoxy having enjoyed widespread acceptance for much of the twentieth century and the politicized role battling for intellectual footholds. But unlike many battles waged between actual armies, the battle over the Court's role did not have a single, agreed upon start and it was not always clear who was on which side. In one case a High Court judge would advocate for aspects of the orthodox or politicized roles only later to back away. Although the object of study may be somewhat illusive, that does not mean we cannot understand it, we cannot identify its key features and core players, and mark its development. My informants roundly agree that in the late 1980s and early 1990s a group of High Court judges introduced a new vision for the High Court. This alternative to the orthodoxy gained the most ground under Chief Justice Anthony Mason's tenure (1987-1995) and involved numerous changes. This chapter will explore how the politicized role conceptualizes the purpose of law, the aim of appellate litigation, the normative relationships between judges and the law and between judges and the political system and community. How the politicized role conceives of legal reasoning, precedent, and the development of law are addressed in chapter 5.

DIMENSION #1: THE PURPOSE OF LAW

While Australia's judicial orthodoxy placed a premium on law providing certainty, it became evident from my informants that the politicized role eschews such a strong emphasis on certainty. It holds the values of fairness and individualized justice in higher regard. A legal system that places a premium on certainty stresses the importance of deciding cases according to promulgated norms and standards and following precedents. One emphasizing individualized justice strives for the fairest decision in each case, which may require judges to ignore or alter established norms and abandon precedents. If certainty and fairness occupy opposite ends of a spectrum, the shift that my informants described was not a wholesale move from one end to the other. The difference between the orthodox and politicized roles' perspectives on law's purposes is not that the former exclusively pursues certainty while the latter opts strictly for fairness. In truth, both roles balance law's duty to provide clear *a priori* answers to legal questions and to ensure sufficient flexibility for justice in individual cases. It becomes a matter of emphasis, as Dias and Michael wrote, "between distributive equality of treatment and corrective equality requiring redress in the individual case (1976, 279)." The shift that I discerned involved the Court striking a new balance between these two goals. The Mason Court brought not a paradigmatic reordering on this dimension, but a subtle change in mood that was nonetheless palpable to appellate judges.

This tension between courts providing legal certainty and individualized justice is a well-trodden area for legal theorists (see Pound 1959; Stone 1964; Dias and Michael 1976; Paterson 1982; Llewellyn 1996). The Mason Court moved this scholastic debate from the academic world to the real world. According to one judge, the Mason Court represented

> [t]he first time that the Court made a concerted effort … not only to right social wrongs but to fix up any legal error they could find. There was a conscious jettisoning of the notion that certainty is the object of the legal system, in favor of correcting absurd rules. … It's a view that I hold firmly to my heart, but about which you can do [nothing] unless you're in an appellate court or the High Court.

The judge continued:

It manifested itself in much wider areas than *Mabo*. We've had for a hundred-and-fifty years a distinction between error of law and error of fact in restitution cases. If you made a payment under mistake of fact, it's recoverable. If you made a payment under mistake of law, it's irrecoverable. The dichotomy is absurd. If you went to a fella in the street and asked, "Can you justify this?" they would look at you and say you're a lunatic. It's those sorts of rules that the High Court under Mason just got rid of.... If you've got a rule that every academic has criticized for time and immemorial, even if it's from the highest court in the land, why not fix it? ... Legal error was the storm center (85:1000).

Another judge perceived this shift occurring in contract law. "Take the law relating to privity of contract," he said. "I was brought up on the tradition that if you were not a party to a contract you couldn't enforce it.... The High Court has swept all this away some time ago by recourse to notions of justice and fairness.... That's another example of an approach that would have never been taken in the 1950s and 1960s (53:730)." A Commonwealth attorney claimed that the Mason Court was "adventuresome," "more concerned with the big picture." He continued, "This is actually part of a broader pattern where the Mason and Brennan Courts were more concerned with the big picture and ensuring that law was just (63)." A Mason Court judge circumspectly confessed the Court's preference for fairness over certainty: "It is possible that the judges who were on [the Mason Court] were more minded by social justice ... than their predecessors. Part of the appeal is providing a forum for those who don't have voices elsewhere in the political system. This power is more limited under the Australian constitution because we don't have a bill of rights, but you can get some of that here (17:3130)."

It was broadly held that the Mason Court's penchant for fairness introduced greater uncertainty into the legal system. The Mason Court "created a general air of uncertainty (94:1410)" said a High Court judge. Another remarked, "There is less certainty.... The feeling is that if you get to the High Court, the rules could change.... Nowadays, everyone's on notice that things are in state of flux and there are no definites anymore (105:2000)." A Victoria appellate judge commented:

There used to be a smug certainty about courts and the law. They were institutions staffed exclusively by ... men from a certain social stratum who held, for the most part, like views on social issues. I think that one thing that has happened over the last ten years or so is that there has been a[n] ... opening up of that. Courts don't reflect such a homogenous view and not such a smug certainty ... that their views should be preferred because of education, wealth and the like. The courts are, in a lot of ways, much less hidebound and more open to and receptive of ideas about institutional unfairness, which hitherto they might not have accepted or ever thought of. Nowadays they do think of them. We do consciously think of the ways in which minorities and even huge majorities—women—are affected by things in a way I don't think courts ever did before (65:5345).

The consensus in my interviews was that this change in posture, where certainty was more readily sacrificed for individualized justice, was a relatively recent phenomenon that made the practice of law—advising clients about what is the law and representing their interests—more challenging. "Apart from the traditional equity areas, it's relatively new that ... courts have been handed these enormous questions and told to do what you think is a fair thing (45:730)," said one judge. A South Australia Supreme Court judge offered:

The biggest criticism of the High Court is that it has tended to shift ground in a number of areas quite rapidly and on a fairly unpredictable basis, so it's very difficult for the profession to advise their clients with reasonable certainty as to what any decision of the High Court is likely to bring (117:700).

Some thought the challenge of providing sound legal advice in times of uncertainty discouraged litigation and may have even encouraged mediation among parties unwilling to shoulder the risks of taking cases to an apparently mercurial High Court.

The big development in mediation is interesting in Australia. That's really kicked on, particularly in Queensland.... One of the reasons it's been so successful is because of the feeling of uncertainty at the High Court level as to how things might go in the end—the unknown. It will depend on which judge you're before at trial, how things go on appeal, and at the end the High Court might change the rules anyway, so mediation has an attraction. Its popularity is connected to the new role of the High Court and the uncertainty of the law (1:5100).

Disagreements existed among informants over the normative merits of this shift. Some regretted the unpredictability it created. Others lamented the challenge it presented to intermediate appellate judges to keep abreast of the law. What was striking about this was that many appellate judges based their criticisms on conceptions of the High Court that failed to distinguish it institutionally from lower appellate courts. In other words, some critics thought High Court judges should operate under the same institutional and legal constraints as, for example, state appellate judges. Many informants, therefore, were unwilling to accept that as the High Court pursued individualized justice greater uncertainty in the law was an expected byproduct. The following remark is emblematic:

> You can't take [legal change] too far, otherwise you have no certainty. I know there is a view that certainty isn't the be all and end all—this is the point that Mason kept on making. It comes down, of course, to predictability. You don't want to be moving the goal posts continually. This was particularly so in the field of equity, which is Mason's and Deane's forte, where the unconscionability concept came in. What's unconscionable to one is not to another. It's very hard to tie it down. It's rather like the traditional unruly horse. There were great moves in [equity] … where everything depended on the unconscionability of the behavior and the consequences which flowed from that…. They were trying to get some principles in there that aren't always easy to detect (112:745).

Proponents of the Court favoring justice over certainty conceived law less as a conservative, constraining force and more as an active, enabling implement. The new concept of law, according to one judge, puts "into the equation thoughts about what are good and bad results (82:345)." A Queensland appellate judge remarked, "Chief Justices Mason and then Brennan were both adventurous, in that they were willing to adopt more progressive attitudes toward the development of law and the role of the Court. That was undoubtedly required and good (87:1245)."

The first dimension to the politicized role serves as a foundation for other normative commitments about the High Court and the judiciary. If the Mason Court placed greater weight on law securing justice in individual cases over legal certainty, it follows that the Court would adopt different commitments regarding the aim of appellate litigation, the High Court's relationship to other political branches and the community, and the types of cases to which the Court directs its attention. Each of these is discussed below.

DIMENSION #2: THE AIM OF APPELLATE LITIGATION

Whereas the orthodoxy understood appellate litigation first and foremost as a process for resolving private disputes, the politicized role envisages litigation in terms of a public model. Under a public model, appellate litigation is understood as both a *legal and political enterprise*. It is a legal enterprise in that judges resolve the specific disputes that come before them. It is a political enterprise in that resolution of these disputes often have profound consequences beyond the immediate litigants. Appellate litigation is also a political enterprise because determining what the law is or should be is itself contested. The courts become venues for political actors to advance their interests as they also do through other institutions, such as parliaments or executive agencies. Given the contested nature of law and the recognition that judicial decisions influence interests beyond the immediate parties, the public litigation model, as part of the politicized judicial role, encourages judges to consult sources and solicit information from non-party participants.

Many informants found the 1980s and 1990s as years in which the Court transitioned from the historically (and staunchly) private to a more public model of appellate litigation. A Federal Court judge remarked, "If you regard law as being a small-p political enterprise, which in my view it must be because it's about human relations and social organizations, I think that both the [Mason and Brennan Courts] had a reasonable sense that that's what it is all about (86:2430)." Another judge admitted:

> The High Court lives a different life from other appellate courts. There are some instances where it is very difficult for them to completely divorce themselves from an appearance of being involved in social or political issues, rather more so than appellate courts at other levels. It's something that I accept. It first became apparent during the period Sir Anthony Mason presided over the High Court (18:130).

This shift toward a public model evidenced itself in several ways, including how the justices managed litigation and wrote their judgments. The Mason Court favored laying down broad legal principles that transcended the cases at hand. In doing so, the Court recognized an obligation to lower court judges deciding cases, lawyers advising clients, and legislators drafting laws to use individual cases to formulate broadly applicable legal principles. The judges viewed an audience beyond the immediate litigants and wrote accordingly. In several areas of private and public law, the Mason Court appeared to be undertaking "justificatory ascent," to borrow Ronald Dworkin's term. Dworkin employs this term as a normative descriptor for judicial decision-making that strives to unify the law under an umbrella of meta-principles that define a particular legal and political system. He writes, "We must strive, so far as we can, not to apply one theory of liability to pharmaceutical companies and a different one to motorists, not to embrace one theory of free speech when we are worried about pornography and another when we are worried about flag burning." He encourages judges to "raise [their] eyes a bit from the particular cases ... and look at neighboring areas of the law, or maybe even raise [their] eyes quite a bit and look in general, say, to accident law more generally, or to constitutional law more generally, or to our assumptions about judicial competence or responsibility more generally," spiraling ever upward in "justificatory ascent." (1997, 356).

Several informants noted that a hallmark of the Mason Court was its penchant for just this justificatory ascent. As a Federal Court judge remarked, "The High Court tried to modernize, to rationalize the law. Identifying overarching principles was the big theory. The fault of the common law is that disparate rules can develop over hundreds of years that aren't cohesive.... The High Court was hell bent on trying to work out overarching principles (85:1000)." An ACT judge suggested:

> [T]here are six features to an adversarial system of justice: the ascertainment of truth, the establishment of principle, the sublimation of conflict, the establishment of procedural safeguards, and the value of the legal ritual (which is largely overlooked) in affirming important values. This is lost sight of—that courts not only have a role to get cases right. Jeremy Bentham had this idea that you evaluate legal proceedings just in terms of the most number of correct results.... The courts constantly affirm values of decency, fairness, justice and truth, which should be an important part of the community (74:10945).

Mason Court justices candidly acknowledged their drive to establish overarching principles and that this distinguished them from their predecessors. One assessed their approach as follows:

> In recent times, the articulation of particular propositions hasn't been mistaken for the underlying principle which informs an area of legal discourse. The emphasis has been on the identification of the basic principle, however it might be expressed. Earlier cases which contain a particular articulation have not been followed as though that articulation exhausted the whole concept. This means that there is a more realistic approach to the appreciation of precedent and also means, because one goes to the underlying principle, that it's more flexible and capable to cope with a variety of fact situations.... That flexibility and insistence on the underlying principle has been a major shift [in legal reasoning].

The High Court judge supported this shift "provided there is a continuous insistence on understanding ... that it's possible to regard [the underlying prin-

ciple] as a loose concept and molded to the judge's predilections (63:1230)."
Another Mason Court judge suggested that their drive for overarching principles occurred, in part, because British courts (once the most influential referents for Australian judges and once responsible for legal uniformity across the Empire and Commonwealth) were proving less adroit at it. The judge stated:

> This was the significant development of the Mason Court: The English had not for many decades attempted a principled response to legal problems. In large measure their decisions were, "Well, a chap knows what a chap should do, and a chap shouldn't do this." There had not been for many decades any serious attempt, I think, by the British to expose fundamental legal principles. The big change in the Mason Court … was the recognition that if the Australian common law was to develop in a coherent way and adapted to Australian conditions, then fundamental legal principles have to be exposed. *You had to reason from the principle to the result, rather than this "a chap knows what a chap should do" superior moral tone that the English had* (92:1945) (emphasis added).

A notable example of this trend toward exposing overarching legal principles—and again a shift toward the public model of appellate litigation—was the *Mabo* case. The core question that the litigants put before the Court was whether the *terra nullius* doctrine applied to the Murray Islands, a cluster of islands off the Queensland coast. The Court could have answered this specific question—addressing only its applicability to the Murray Islands—but chose instead to promulgate a legal principle for the entire continent. Criticism soon followed because it was thought that a more nuanced survey of Aboriginal land practices would have revealed that the *terra nullius* doctrine was appropriate to some, but not all, parts of Australia. But they did not take the nuanced approach, although cognizant of the diverse social and economic conditions within mainland Australia's aboriginal communities. It also was cognizant of the dissimilar social and economic conditions between mainland Aborigines and the Meriam people, the indigenous inhabitants of the Murray Islands. Yet the Court overturned the *terra nullius* doctrine for the whole of Australia based on a single case concerning the Murray Islands. Just as the British laid down a blanket categorization of "empty land" upon all Australia when they landed on its shores in the eighteenth-century, so too did the High Court in *Mabo* regarding native title.

Many appellate judges criticized this blanket approach to rewriting one central principle underpinning land law. Said one judge: "Eddie Mabo came from an island off the north-eastern coast of Queensland. The islanders had gardens, they cultivated things, and they had small farms. They had a totally different structure than most mainland Aboriginals.... [A]ll facts found [in *Mabo*] were about the islanders not about the mainlanders (103:10115)." As another inform- ant remarked, "Murray Islanders are not Aboriginal.... The High Court made a vast generalization about Aboriginal people (7)," while another said, "Murray Is- land people farmed five acre lots, but that's not like native title on the mainland (32:1715)." Even informants who supported *Mabo* on its merits questioned the Court's approach. A High Court judge concluded, "*Mabo* was a revision of the common law view about unoccupied land. It's a quite useful alteration of the doctrine. [It was] entirely suitable to the small island community they were deal- ing with, but the contention is that *Mabo* is not suitable for the mainland of Aus- tralia. (37:545)." The case clearly illustrated the difference between "the scope of the case versus the scope of the decision, (99)" as one judge pithily put it.

My informants also cited the law of estoppel as another private law area where the Mason Court promoted overarching principles that favored a pub- lic litigation model. Estoppel, in its basic formulation, recognizes that the law should provide remedies to persons who commit some act, ultimately to their detriment, upon assumptions induced by another person. Although no con- tractual relationship may exist between the parties, estoppel sees the violation of that assumption as an injustice. The law of estoppel developed in piecemeal fashion. Its central tenets were applied to different fact situations over the years, resulting in a number of variants. For example, estoppel by represen- tation (or estoppel *in pais*) covers unjust departures from assumptions con- cerning present facts but not future promises. To operate, the parties must be in some legal relationship. Promissory estoppel, on the other hand, was de- veloped for unjust departures from assumptions between legally bound par- ties, but unlike estoppel *in pais*, it extends to assumptions regarding future ac- tion. Yet another, known as proprietary estoppel, covers future conduct between parties that share no contractual relationship. Several other variants developed as well. The point is that each form of estoppel covered its own sub- ject matter and had its unique scope and operation (Cooke 2000).

In the late 1980s, the Mason Court sought to group these disparate doc- trines of estoppel under a single, unifying principle. A Federal Court judge described the effort as follows:

[In the law of] estoppel, we had proprietary estoppel, promissory estoppel, equitable estoppel, common assumption estoppel, and the rules were different for each, largely because we have theories that we take from history called "consideration." If you can't find consideration, how can you have a promise about the future? Things that are just nuts! So the [Mason] Court said, "We actually need to fix this. The only way we can fix it is to get rid of these 500 categories." Lord Denning had the "house of estoppel"—this room, that room, all with different principles and different chairs in them. The High Court said "We'll get rid of it. We'll rationalize it (85:1200)."

Another Federal Court judge suggested:

The change came with Sir Anthony Mason.... The Court then was composed of a group of judges who felt free to break out of the straight jacket that Barwick had set up. People like Deane and Mason were prepared to look outside ... the black-letter law of Barwick, and before him, Sir Owen Dixon. In the broad development of general law concepts, there was an explosion of ideas. In Mason's case, it always seemed to me that he wanted to rationalize the law—to do away with historical categories that had developed with good reason, but had no relevance any longer to Australian law. So he looked for overarching principles (113:1025).

The *Waltons Stores* and *Verwayen*[1] cases were the vehicles for this consolidation in estoppel. The *Waltons Stores* case concerned a negotiated lease on a piece of property, whereby the lessor had taken certain actions on the assumption that the lease would be executed; namely, the demolition of an existing structure on the property and partial construction of a new building. When forty percent of the new structure was completed but the lease had not yet been executed, the lessee (Waltons Stores) decided not to proceed with the contract. The Court concluded that it was unconscionable for the potential lessee to expose knowingly the lessor to detriment on the basis of a false assumption and that the lessee intended to execute the contract notwithstanding their delay in returning the signed copy to the lessor. The second case addressed whether the Commonwealth could raise certain defenses in an injury liability case. Verwayen had been injured at sea while serving the Australian Navy. In the earliest litigation, the Commonwealth Government never contested whether it was liable or owed a duty of care. As the litigation progressed, the Commonwealth attempted to introduce these defenses. Verwayen argued that the Commonwealth had waived such defenses and that it was estopped

---

1. *Waltons Stores (Interstate) Ltd. v. Maher* (1988) 76 ALR 513; *Commonwealth of Australia v. Verwayen* (1990) 95 ALR 321.

from relying on them. Here too the Court concluded that it would be an unconscionable departure for the Commonwealth to violate this assumption.[2]

What makes these cases significant for our purposes? First and foremost, the Mason Court scrapped the disparate forms of estoppel and advocated that they be coalesced into a single category. The Court concluded that in a modern judiciary it made no sense, promoted no principle, and reflected only the arbitrariness of case-by-case doctrinal development to retain the divisions.[3] Second, the Court advanced "unconscionability" as the unifying principle for estoppel.[4] A principle in equity law, unconscionability calls on the Court in good conscience to impose an obligation of fairness on a promisor even if no legal obligation has been undertaken. The Court may impose an obligation where it would be unconscionable for the promisor to insist strictly on his legal rights. Third, the Court did away with the doctrine that limited the situations in which estoppel may operate. No distinctions remained between present and future promises, whether the assumption concerned land or not, or if the parties shared a contractual relationship.

The Mason Court's focus on identifying overarching principles led informants to remark that the style and content of High Court judgments also changed. In other words, judgment writing changed with the transformation. Legal scholars and practitioners alike have noted in a growing body of empirical research that High Court judgments have become lengthier and more cumbersome in recent years.[5] Groves and Smyth (2004) looked at High Court judgments from 1903 to 2001. They concluded that the average length of judgments was relatively consistent from 1903 to 1990—about ten pages. Beginning in the 1990s, however, the average length jumped to 12 pages and peaked in 1996 at 14.4 pages (258). My informants acknowledged that the Mason Court ushered in lengthier judges. They also found the content changed. A Federal Court judge found that with Mason Court judgments, "[T]here was as much written about jurisprudence and jurisprudential theories as there was about what was decided in case A, case B, and case C." The rhetorical emphasis was expected because, "When a court is struggling to find doctrines to bring particular cases under, you'll write differently than if you're dog-tied to prece-

---

2. For a thoroughgoing analysis, see Spence (1999).

3. See *Verwayen*, Chief Justice Mason, 333; *Waltons Stores*, Justice Deane, 556.

4. All justices did not embrace the unified approach. In *Verwayen*, Justices McHugh and Dawson preserved the division between certain forms of estoppel. Justice Brennan did not address the topic in *Verwayen*.

5. See also Campbell (2003); Beaumont (1999); and Doyle (1999).

dent (85:3300)." Others agreed with this assessment, but they were less charitable toward this phenomenon.

> If you look at previous judgments [from the High Court] there was an application of principle to the facts. You applied it—bang. You can do it in a short, sharp, shiny manner. And the judgments were short, sharp and shiny compared to modern judgments.... Now you see with judges extending the boundaries of law, writing Ph.D. theses every time they sit down. So you get these long, over-footnoted articles. One wonders the extent to which the associates have just thrown everything in. Garfield Barwick once said that judges are there to decide cases, not write essays (81:915).

A state supreme court chief justice put it this way: "[The contemporary Court] writes too much. It thinks too much. Its judges are too often concerned with leaving a legal legacy. These are fair concerns (6:4430)." Another regretted, "Every [High Court] judgment becomes a discursive lecture. Not long ago judgments were not as long, even English cases last century were very brief. Pick up any High Court judgment today and you wade through fifty pages of the most complex verbiage that you care to encounter.... The law has run off the rails even though it's suppose to regulate the lives of everyday people. It should be in a form they understand (32:4345)."

Given that the Mason Court broadened its legal conclusions beyond the immediate parties and strove in several areas to identify overarching legal principles, it is not surprising that it also entertained a wider spectrum of authorities. It drew from more diverse foreign jurisdictions and from a wider array of non-legal sources. "I think the range of materials used in relation to this generation is probably greater than it was before—the range of views overtly. By that I mean references to academic articles and references to the laws in countries other than the U.K., which used to be the case (106:1000)," said a leading High Court barrister. An appellate judge and erstwhile Queen's Counsel who had a substantial High Court practice concurred: "We've gone from using dictionaries to a more open and detailed search into history, policy, and comparative law (123:300)." A Victoria appellate judge remarked:

> There has been a sea-change in judicial attitude. Thirty or forty years ago, appellate judges would go to textbooks, cases, and authorities to reach a solution. If a solution was at odds with [what that judge thought was the right result] then that was okay because that was the result. Today, judges think about what would be a good rule and de-

cide the case accordingly. They ask themselves, what makes sense today? We've got a dead hand of history (67).

Expanding the scope of authorities was justified, according to one Mason Court judge, because the purposes of appellate litigation had changed. The judge suggested:

> The real question is what changes in procedures and materials are appropriate and needed given the creative function of judges. When deciding from past analogous cases you only needed books. When judges have choices and you acknowledge that, then you need to change the procedures for considering a wider range of material and to be open-minded about that material. It may not be purely legal material. It might be economic or social in character. We're going belatedly down the track of the United States in the 1920s (116:300).

The public litigation model and politicized judicial role stress judicial decision-making that looks beyond the immediate litigants. Given this, the frequency with which non-parties participate in appellate litigation provides an indicator—though not exclusive—for the Court's fidelity to the public model. "Non-party" participants are those who join litigation by a court granting leave to appear as either formal interveners (who become official parties to proceedings and may adduce evidence, offer witnesses, cross-examine, etc.) or as amici curiae ("friends of the court" who offer advice on points of law but are not formal parties).

For much of the twentieth century, the High Court of Australia maintained a jaundiced view of non-party intervention, viewing amici curiae and interveners as unnecessary distractions from resolving disputes. Dixon's cautious approach loomed large for much of the twentieth century, and in fact, guides many appellate and High Court judges today.

The High Court exhibited an anemic record for non-party intervention during most of the last century, particularly compared to the U.S. and Canadian Supreme Courts. It allowed, for example, amici curiae participation in a scant fifteen cases from 1947 to 1997.[6] Only three of these cases involved

---

6. *Main v. Main* (1949) 78 CLR 636; *Blundell v. Musgrave* (1956) 96 CLR 73; *Armstrong v. The State Of Victoria (No. 2)* (1957) 99 CLR 28; *Russell v. Walters* (1957) 96 CLR 177; *Lamshed v. Lake* (1958) 99 CLR 132; *James v. Robinson* (1963) 109 CLR 593; *The Queen v. Public Vehicles Licensing Appeal Tribunal (Tas.); Ex Parte Australian National Airways Pty. Ltd.* (1964) 113 CLR 207; *The Queen v. Cook; Ex Parte Twigg* (1980) 147 CLR 15; *Victoria v. Australian Building Construction Employees' And Labourers' Federation (No. 2)* (1982) 152 CLR 179; *The Commonwealth of Australia v. Tasmania.* (The Tasmanian Dam Case) (1983) 158 CLR 1; *Wentworth v. New South Wales Bar Association* (1992) 176 CLR 239; *David*

non-governmental interest groups, organizations, or individuals. The Commonwealth or state solicitors-general were amici in the remaining twelve. This sharply contrasts with the U.S. Supreme Court, which allowed amici participation in 3,389 cases over the same period (Kearney and Merrill 2000). The Canadian Supreme Court has a practice of non-party intervention that falls somewhere between the Australian and U.S. courts. Scholars have noted that since passage of the 1982 Charter of Rights and Freedoms, intervener and amici participation has been more widespread in Canada (Epp 1998; Williams 2000a; Brodie 2002).

Over the last twenty years, however, the High Court took significant, albeit slow and inconsistent, steps toward the public model's acceptance of non-party intervention. Data gathered from published High Court judgments indicate that non-party intervention in High Court litigation has increased. Before presenting those data, a few provisos are required. First, the words "intervener" and "intervention" are used in this section generically for both formal interveners and amici participants, unless specified otherwise. Second, the data were assembled from full-text searches of all published High Court judgments available through Lexis-Nexis, for the years 1945 to 2001.[7] Data from earlier years were unavailable from Lexis-Nexis.

With those provisos in mind, Figure 4.1 plots by decade the mean number of annual High Court cases in which some sort of non-party intervention occurred. Again "non-party intervention" includes formal interveners and amici curiae participants. Figure 4.2 disaggregates the data in Figure 4.1 by individual year. Both charts show that since the 1980s, increasing numbers of High Court cases have involved non-party intervention.

In addition to more High Court cases having some form of non-party intervention, the raw number of interveners in litigation also has increased since the 1980s, as shown in Figure 4.3. The aggregate picture—more High Court

---

Grant And Co Pty Limited (Receiver Appointed) v. Westpac Banking Corporation (1995) 184 CLR 265; *David Russell Lange v. Australian Broadcasting Corporation* (1997) 189 CLR 520; *Laurence Nathan Levy v. The State Of Victoria & Ors* (1997) 146 ALR 248; *Project Blue Sky Inc. & Ors v. Australian Broadcasting Authority* (1998) 153 ALR 490.

7. For some unknown reason, Lexis-Nexis provides an incomplete set of High Court judgments for the years 1998-2001. Scaleplus was used to assemble data for these years. The years 1945 and 1946 saw no intervention, so the charts begin in 1947, the first year of this dataset with non-party intervention. Portions of the data and analyses that follow concerning non-party intervention were previously published in Jason Pierce (2003), "Nonparty intervention and the public litigation model in the High Court," *Alternative Law Journal* 28(2): 69-73.

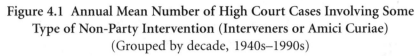

Figure 4.1 Annual Mean Number of High Court Cases Involving Some
Type of Non-Party Intervention (Interveners or Amici Curiae)
(Grouped by decade, 1940s–1990s)

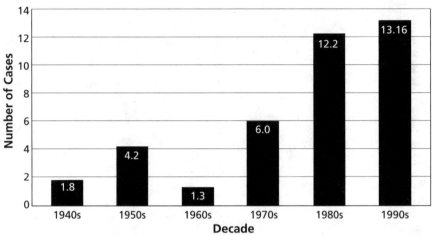

cases involving some sort of non-party intervention and greater numbers of
interveners—is that the Court has opened the litigation process in the last
twenty years.

These charts suggest movement toward the public model and confirm important changes in the composition and nature of High Court litigation. There
is little doubt the 1976 amendments to the *Judiciary Act* are partly responsible.[8]
Guaranteeing Attorneys-General the right to participate in constitutional litigation contributed substantially to the up-ticks charted in Figures 4.1–4.3. The vertical lines superimposed on these graphs mark that year of reform. Note that in
the years following the reform, the annual number of cases with intervention and
the number of interveners nearly doubled, demonstrating the reform's impact.

Just how much of this increase in non-party participation is owed to the
1976 reforms that enable Attorneys-General to intervene in constitutional
cases? To explore this further, Figure 4.4 contrasts the annual number of interventions by Attorneys-General versus private interveners.[9] State or Commonwealth Attorneys-General intervened far more frequently than private in-

8. *Judiciary Act 1903*, ss. 78A, B.
9. Included within this "private interveners" category are private organizations, individuals, and some governmental organizations, such as the Human Rights and Equal Opportunity Commission. I categorize these governmental organizations as "private interveners" because they do not possess the same intervention rights as Attorneys-General.

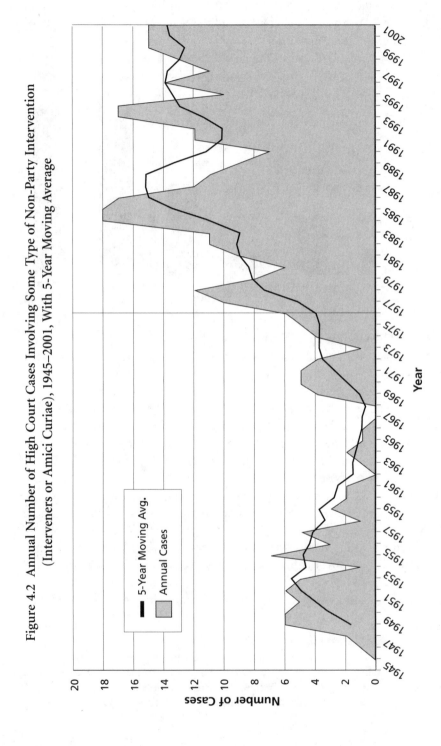

Figure 4.2 Annual Number of High Court Cases Involving Some Type of Non-Party Intervention (Interveners or Amici Curiae), 1945–2001, With 5-Year Moving Average

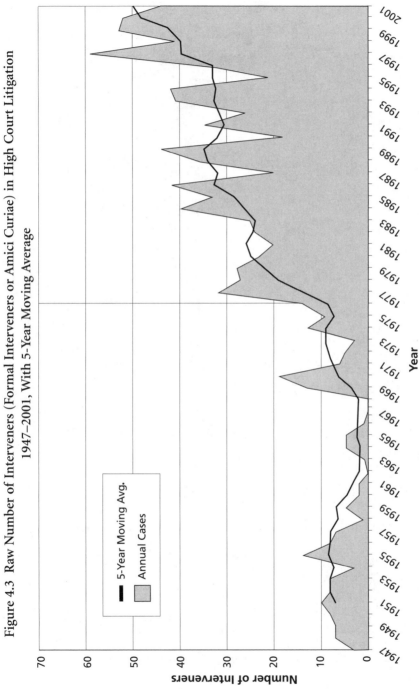

Figure 4.3 Raw Number of Interveners (Formal Interveners or Amici Curiae) in High Court Litigation 1947–2001, With 5-Year Moving Average

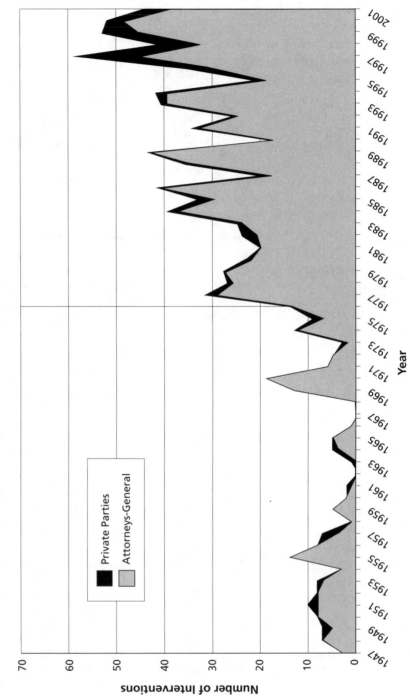

Figure 4.4 Annual Number of Interventions by Attorneys-General and Private Parties in High Court Litigation, 1947–2001

dividuals or groups since 1945. Figure 4.5 presents these data slightly differently, with the annual proportion of interventions from the two groups.

The fact that Attorneys-General accounted for a significant portion of non-
party interventions provides some evidence of a shift toward the public model,
in that non-party (governmental) perspectives were increasingly infused in
High Court litigation. This infusion occurred, however, not necessarily because the Court wanted or asked for it. At one level, by permitting governmental interventions the Court was simply discharging a statutory duty. A far
more convincing case for a shift to the public model could be made if data
showed the Court allowing more private intervention under its discretionary
powers. In such circumstances, the Court would be motivated not by duty,
but foresees private interveners improving the litigation process and its decision-making.[10] Discretionary intervention by private parties would occur because the Court presumably wants it. Figure 4.6 displays the annual number
of private interventions over this period. In fact, this figure convincingly illustrates that a second phenomenon was underway since the 1980s, separate
and apart from changes that came from the 1976 reforms: private interventions, which occurred wholly at the Court's discretion, also increased.

Finally, the growth in governmental and private interventions cannot be explained away as a byproduct of an ever-growing workload. Figure 4.7 weights the
annual intervention rates by workload, calculated by dividing the annual number of interventions by the number of decisions reported each year. The trend
could not be clearer. More interventions (governmental and private) occurred in
the last twenty years even when adjusted for increased workloads. These data provide, therefore, another compelling piece of evidence of the Court's increasing
adherence to a public model for appellate litigation. A court that adheres to the
public model welcomes these interventions because it recognizes the broader social, economic, legal, and political consequences to its decisions and the valuable
role that non-party, private interveners can play in exploring those consequences.

The High Court's intervention rate nonetheless pales in comparison to the
U.S. Supreme Court's rate. The Supreme Court also experienced burgeoning
non-party intervention in recent decades. The difference between the U.S. and
Australian courts is startling. A recent study reported that amici curiae briefs

---

10. Former U.S. Supreme Court Justice Sandra Day O'Connor's illustrated this point
in *Webster v. Reproductive Health Services*, 492 U.S. 490 (1989): "The willingness of courts
to listen to interveners is a reflection of the value that judges attach to people. Our commitment to a right to a hearing ... is derived not only from the belief that we improve the
accuracy of decisions when we allow people to present their side of the story, but also from
our sense that participation is necessary to preserve human dignity and self-respect (522)."

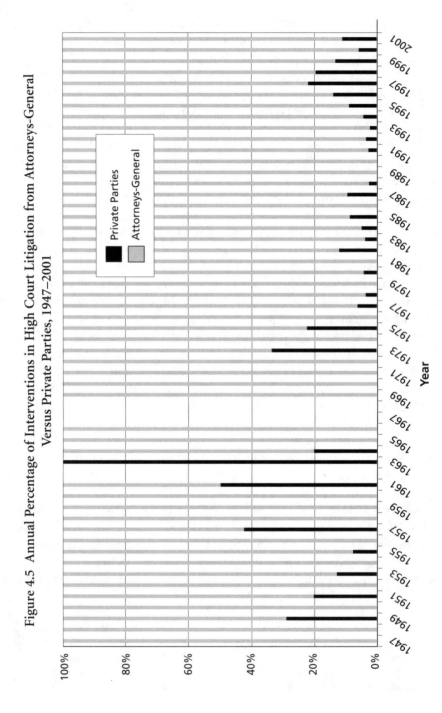

Figure 4.5 Annual Percentage of Interventions in High Court Litigation from Attorneys-General Versus Private Parties, 1947–2001

Figure 4.6 Annual Number of Private Party Interventions in High Court Litigation, 1947–2001, with 5-Year Moving Average

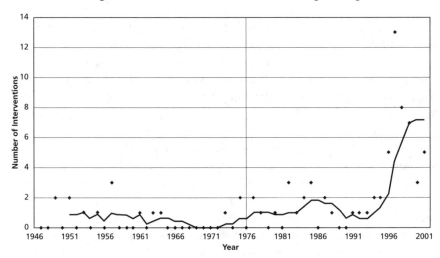

Figure 4.7 Annual Number of Interventions Weighted by Workload (Per Reported Decision), 1947–2001, with 5-Year Moving Average

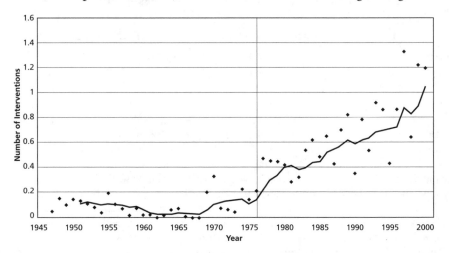

were filed in 85 percent of all Supreme Court cases decided from 1986 to 1995 and that the Court now averages 4.23 amici briefs per case (Kearney 2000). By comparison, the High Court averaged .005 amici participants per case over the same period. This comparison is made with some caution. As an indicator of the relative fidelity of both courts to the public litigation model, it confirms that the U.S. court far outpaces its Australian counterpart. The U.S. legal culture fosters non-party intervention and the Supreme Court accommodates it. This is less the case in Australia, for a number of potential reasons. One might speculate that the absence of a bill of rights partly explains the chasm between the two courts. Perhaps non-party intervention occurs more often because the volume of rights-based litigation simply brings out more groups wishing to push the Court's rights jurisprudence this way or that.[11] However stronger the Supreme Court's adherence to the public litigation model may be, the contrast should not conceal the significant changes that occurred in the High Court.

The contrast also suggests that Australia's appellate judges are apparently more wary of non-party intervention than their U.S. counterparts. This leeriness is evidenced in the fact that although single judges have articulated criteria for evaluating non-party intervention requests, the Court has promulgated no formal rules to govern such applications. As mentioned in previous chapters, the rules governing High Court procedure underwent a substantial rewrite in 2004. Changes were brought to many areas of High Court practice, but the Court did not see fit to promulgate any institutional criteria for evaluating non-party interventions. As one appellate judge concluded, "At the moment, the Court is struggling terribly with how to permit intervention by non-government bodies. They've got themselves into a terrible mess at the moment (123)."

The High Court's wariness and uncertainty were illustrated in two 1997 cases where private groups sought leave to intervene as amici: the *Lange* and *Levy* decisions.[12] Argued during a single hearing before the Court, the cases

---

11. For the U.S. Supreme Court figures, see Kearney (2000). One of the more politically charged cases in which the question of third-party participation emerged in the High Court was *CES v. Superclinics* (1995 NSW Court of Appeal). The case had all the makings for indicating, one way or another, the extent to which the transformation ushered in the public litigation model. It concerned a "wrongful birth" claim in which a woman sued her physician for failing to detect her pregnancy in time for her to have an abortion. The High Court, hearing an appeal from the NSW Court of Appeal, was to confront whether the woman could recover damages for delivering a healthy baby. The Australian Catholic Health Care Association and the Australian Catholic Bishops' Conference successfully argued for amici involvement. The Abortion Providers Federation of Australasia and its president also sought intervention, but the case settled before formal arguments.

12. *David Russell Lange v. Australian Broadcasting Corporation* (1997) 189 CLR 520; *Laurence Nathan Levy v. The State Of Victoria & Ors* (1997) 146 ALR 248.

addressed whether the constitution's implied freedom of political communication—a freedom the Court identified earlier in the 1990s—limited the grounds on which someone could recover damages for defamation. In other words, did the implied freedom protect speech that might otherwise be defamatory, save that the speech was political in nature? In both cases, a collection of newspaper and media companies were granted leave as formal interveners. Two organizations, the Media, Entertainment and Arts Alliance (MEAA) and the Australian Press Council were granted amici status, but not without hesitation. Their admission as "friends of the court" was granted after substantial debate during oral arguments. How the Court handled these intervention applications reveals the ongoing hesitancy and uncertainty about it and the standards used to evaluate such requests. At one point during oral argument, the judges questioned whether the MEAA, an association of 12,000 journalists and freelance writers, had sufficient interest in the defamation cases to warrant amicus status. I quote from the court transcript at some length.

Chief Justice Brennan: Mr. Catterns, you are seeking leave to intervene?

Mr. Catterns [MEAA's barrister]: Yes, your Honour, or, in the alternative, to appear as amicus.

Chief Justice Brennan: Yes. The basis of your application is not quite the same as that of [the media and newspaper litigants] who preceded you.

Mr. Catterns: That is so, your Honour.... Our interest is very much of the same class in that we are the journalists who write the material that our learned friends publish or broadcast. If anything, we would certainly submit that our interest is as close as our friends, perhaps closer.

Justice Dawson: Mr. Jackson says you do not ever have to pay [if a MEAA member is found guilty of defamation].

Mr. Catterns: That is so, your Honour, generally speaking....

Justice McHugh: No sensible plaintiff's counsel ever joins a journalist when you can sue the newspaper.

Mr. Catterns: Yes, your Honour, but our members include freelance writers and so on, and their modes of communication may not always be through what one might call the mainstream media, who our friends represent.

Chief Justice Brennan: But you are appearing not for the journalists but for their industrial association.

Mr. Catterns: Yes, your Honour, which in a sense represents their 12,000 journalist members....

Chief Justice Brennan: [W]hat is the interest of the industrial association as such?

Mr. Catterns: ... As an association per se it lobbies and undertakes other representative activities in relation to freedom of speech, defamation law and so on and it educates its members.... [B]ut it would be unreal, we would submit, to view the association as merely a disinterested conduit of whatever the current state of the defamation law is....

Justice Kirby: *But if we had every lobbyist in the Commonwealth who was interested in some way in an issue, the Court would be even more packed than it is.*

Mr. Catterns: *Your Honour ... that is a relevant discretionary consideration.... In the present case, although we have extensions to the Bar table, there is physical room and ... we certainly would not attempt to repeat matters that have not already been said....*

Chief Justice Brennan: You [Mr. Catterns] ... seek to raise an argument which has not been raised or not adumbrated by any other party or prospective intervener?

Mr. Catterns: ... [Y]es, to a limited extent. I am not saying that our colleagues have not thought of [our argument] and will not be referring to the same cases and have not got similar ideas, but that would be precisely the sort of matter that could be developed next Monday if we were granted leave in light of the arguments. It may be that the arguments would have been more than adequately covered in which case we would not seek merely to repeat matters....

Justice Toohey: Ordinarily an amicus appears on the basis that that person wishes to raise some issue that has not been raised by the parties, or has not been sufficiently canvassed for various reasons.

Mr. Catterns: Yes, your Honour.

Justice Toohey: Well then, you would hardly fit into that sort of category....

Chief Justice Brennan: The Court might be in a better position to consider the question of amici when we have heard what other parties have had to say. Thank you.... Professor Flint, you seek, as I understand it, to appear amicus, is that correct?

Mr. Flint: Yes, your Honour. I merely seek leave to appear and to have the amicus curiae brief filed with the Court....

Chief Justice Brennan: Professor Flint, whether or not it would be appropriate to receive and consider that written submission depends to some extent—perhaps to a large extent—on the course which the argument will take between now and the end of the day. The Court is prepared to consider the question whether it will take those into account at the end of the arguments (emphasis added).[13]

This exchange captures, in a telling way, the Court's continued leeriness about non-party intervention. It first questioned whether the MEAA had a genuine "interest" in the litigation. Clearly the MEAA and its members would have a general interest in any changes that might come to defamation law. The Court was pushing the argument here, however, that to become a non-party intervener the organization had to show an immediate and direct interest. Did the association have a stance on defamation law or serve simply as an information conduit for whatever that law might be? From a public litigation perspective, this line of questions is remarkable. It is akin to the U.S. Supreme Court questioning the National Rifle Association's interest in a Second Amendment case or the American Medical Association's capacity to speak for its members in a physician-assisted suicide case. Here the High Court defined having an "interest" in narrow terms. It is unclear whether Justice Kirby intended any hyperbole or sarcasm in his remarks, but his concern about the Court running out of physical space to accommodate the throngs of lawyers who would have a general interest in the case is nonetheless telling. The Court then expected the groups seeking amici status to present arguments that would otherwise not be put to the Court. Otherwise, there was no need for their participation. Finally, the Court conceived amici as true "friends of the court," meaning that the judges expected these groups to aid the Court in reaching decisions and not simply to submit their group's preferences.[14]

---

13. *Levy v. The State of Victoria and Ors,* M42/1995. Transcript of proceedings at Canberra on Monday, March 3, 1997 at 10:22 a.m.

14. This is evidenced further in *Kruger v. Commonwealth* (1997) 190 CLR 1. The case addressed the constitutionality of a government policy that operated until the late 1960s that removed indigenous children from their families and communities. A majority of the Court refused an application from the International Commission of Jurists to appear as amicus curiae. The Commission, according to the Court, failed to demonstrate that the

It is quite clear from this exchange and these cases that the Court is far from adopting an open door approach toward appellate litigation. Australia's High Court judges, even those who served during the Mason Court, are uncertain about non-party participants, particularly those with the expressed intent to influence the outcome. This is most evident with the Court's practice of considering non-party intervention requests only after the immediate parties fully argue the case. Only after observing where the arguments proceed with the immediate parties will the Court consider an amicus request. In sum, the Court's recent record confirms a shift toward the public litigation model, in terms of non-party intervention, but continued ambivalence about just how far to open up appellate litigation. This shift toward the public model is a central feature to the politicized judicial role.

Some of my informants supported the High Court endorsing more frequent non-party interventions, but not without worries over the risks. One judge justified more frequent intervention on these terms:

> Judge: With the High Court playing this role of making general observations ... there's a big argument for saying that if they're dealing with a case out of Tasmania ... that may have a significant impact on Western Australia and Western Australia should be heard. Some of the judges, particularly Kirby, will ask and require counsel to say what the position is in other states. He, of all of them, is the most explicitly aware of the general nature of his judgments and goes some way to accommodate different submissions. It is, I think, a problem for the High Court when it moves into this area. When it's more generalist, there is a corresponding obligation to open up the categories of people who may have an interest in the matter. If you're going to lay down general rules with general application ... then you need to hear from them, as indeed the Supreme Court in the U.S. The consequence, of course, is that they're overrun with paper.

> Q: My impression is that the High Court is reticent about opening the floodgates.

named parties were "unable or unwilling adequately to protect their own interests" and unlikely "to assist the court in arriving at a determination of the case" (See *Kruger v Commonwealth* (transcript, 12 February 1996). Also see *Brandy v. Human Rights and Equal Opportunity Commission* (1995) 183 CLR 245, where the Court refused leave to the Public Interest Advocacy Centre to appear as amicus curiae without reason and despite neither party objecting to its participation.

Judge: I can see why from a practical standpoint. I suspect that [in the U.S.] there is an awful lot more reading for judges that they really don't need to decide the controversy. But, if all you're about is deciding the particular controversy, then you don't need to go wider. I believe that the High Court, and maybe state appellate courts, if their job is to lay down general principle then that's the consequence (126:1045).

Another informant supported non-party intervention, but cautioned:

[O]nce you recognize ... a place for amicus briefs, it becomes very difficult to define the limits. Once you try to define the limits by saying "you can, but you can't" you are immediately imposing your own mindset upon what you allow in.... [O]nce you recognize the appropriateness of it, you have to have it in the American sense, provided that people have something to say. The limits come about probably by means of procedure—what you allow in terms of presentation of materials.

Q: Does the High Court have a different view of litigation?

Judge: Yes, it's a very micro approach to the result (58:3315).

Although these informants generally welcomed greater non-party intervention in High Court litigation, fully cognizant of the demands and challenges it brings, the High Court cannot expect much support for advancing a public litigation model. I discovered strong sentiment among intermediate appellate judges that even when a case goes to the High Court, it remains fundamentally a dispute between the named parties. My informants tended to discount the value of non-party participation. Indeed, discretionary intervention is nearly absent from intermediate appellate court litigation. A South Australia judge commented:

Amicus briefs are rarely used here. There has to be a real reason to need an amicus curiae. It might be a circumstance that the two parties were unable to put the argument as well as it ought to be put, and a third person is necessary to put it. The way we understand amicus in this court is a true amicus curiae—not a person there to represent either parties, but a person who's there to put the argument for the purpose of assisting the court.... You wouldn't see an amicus here often at all, except in circumstances where it is thought necessary.

Q: Have you had amicus participation in any cases you've handled?

Judge: I can't recall one. (117: 3515)

Other intermediate appellate judges had strong reservations about the High Court expanding litigation beyond the immediate parties, acknowledging the Court's finite abilities and resources. "Judges have to be a bit careful to remind themselves that they work in a micro world. They do single cases. It's not always possible for them to understand the ... ramifications of their decisions. It would be quite wrong for them to tailor decisions—either expansively or in a retracting sense—when the full ... picture is not before them," said a NSW appellate judge. Yet at the same time the judge admitted that, "It worries me greatly that we make judgments on social issues without social information. It's a real issue of how we can keep ourselves abreast, especially in a polyglot and polymorphous society. It really worries me that we keep ourselves up to date. I think the only true way to keep ourselves up to date is in that sense (58:2830)."

That intermediate appellate judges thought it inappropriate and generally unnecessary for non-party intervention in their own courts is not surprising. Their position in the judicial hierarchy does not provide the same opportunities for lawmaking and policy innovation that the High Court has. Given that the scope of their decisions is not as expansive, and that their decisions are reviewable, one might expect less appellate-level enthusiasm for non-party intervention. More surprising, however, was their dismissal of the idea that the High Court's unique constitutional responsibilities and position in the judiciary make non-party interventions more germane there than in lower appellate courts. There did not emerge from my interviews a clear sense that the High Court's unique institutional responsibilities might require practices different from those of intermediate appellate courts.

By way of summary, the second dimension to the politicized judicial role shows that the Mason Court transitioned from a private to a more public model of appellate litigation. This transition—evidenced by more frequent non-party, specifically non-governmental interventions—points to a Court increasingly aware of its legal and political powers.

Dimension #3: Judges' Relations to Law and the High Court's Relation to the Political Sytstem

Positivist assumptions about law underpinned Australia's orthodox conception of the judicial role. Law was understood as a nearly complete, pre-existing system of rules that judges consult to find the one correct answer to a legal question. Law was seen as separate and apart from judges. The interview data indicate that under the orthodoxy, judges were thought not to "make law," but rather to "discover" or "interpret" it. However fuzzy the difference may be between judges "making" versus "interpreting" or "discovering" law, the orthodoxy insisted on the distinction. Interpretation and discovery were inevitable byproducts of a common law heritage. Making law, however, was out of bounds. The conceptual relation between judges and law profoundly changed with the Mason Court. Rather than caretakers or stewards of a preexisting corpus of law, High Court judges were seen increasingly as "creators" or "makers" of law—active participants in its definition and development.

My research found near universal agreement among the appellate bench that the Mason Court replaced the judge-as-caretaker image with the judge-as-creator image. Informants divided deeply over the merits of this development, but nearly all agreed that it occurred. "The 1990s produced some remarkable things, like *Mabo* and *Wik*, but it was also a time when the High Court ... was prepared to make law, as some people say, rather than interpret the law.... There was more liberal lawmaking activity [in the Mason Court] (70:415)," said one judge. Another judge remarked, "The High Court makes law because that's what the common law has always been about. It was said for a long time, until recently in Australia, that judges declare the existing common law. The judiciary now more realistically says that it makes law. It does have to make law to make the democratic process work (117:1915)." An informant sympathetic to the politicized judicial role asserted, "I think the High Court should be prepared to take risks. Otherwise it's in a straightjacket. Judges make laws. Parliaments make law. We keep ourselves in straight jackets unless the High Court is prepared to take some risks (52:715)." In a critique of *Mabo*, one judge said: "The High Court exceeded its constraints in *Mabo*. That's why judges should stick to the law rather than make the law (81:3045)." A High Court justice remarked, "Judges now acknowledge that there are occasions when they frankly make the law. That is inevitable. I think, though, that judges are conscious that they are ill-equipped to make some of the broader choices and social decisions that have to be made. [Those choices] are better made perhaps by legislatures (100:200)."

Those informants who welcomed judge-made law criticized the orthodoxy's simpleton notion that judges only discover the law. Judges who admitted that they made law showed contempt for their colleagues who held fast to the idea that judges simply find or discover it. They agreed with John Austin's contempt for that "childish fiction employed by our judges, that common law is not made by them, but is a miraculous something made by nobody, existing, I suppose, from eternity, and merely declared from time to time by the judges

(Austin 1885, 634)." It was striking, however, that informants who welcomed judges making law spoke as if this admission was just recently accepted in the judicial culture and articulating it would place a judge on the vanguard of progressive legal thought in Australia. It was as though they were doing their part to slay a fanciful intellectual myth that had survived far too long in the judicial culture. Yet they treated this myth with a certain respect, not for its intellectual rigor or empirical veracity but because of its interminable dominance in the judicial mindset. By way of example, a Mason Court judge offered: "Equity lawyers never believed that common law judges found the law from analogous cases. Where else does the common law come from than the judges? Where did Lord Halsbury's encyclopedia of law come from but from judges (11)?"

Others held that appellate judges always have made law, but only recently with the transformation have they been forthright about it. A Western Australia judge remarked that the Mason Court was "frankly writing law, defining the law and legal concepts in ways that previous generations of lawyers on the High Court would not have admitted to doing, even if they did from time to time take that approach. They would have been more inclined to say, 'We don't make it up. This is the law that has come down to us.' There's no pretense of that kind today (10:1000)." A NSW appellate judge echoed this perception: "A significant development during [the Mason Court] was the open recognition that the judges were lawmakers. It's almost getting to sound trite just a short time later, in the year 2000, but there was a great reticence to accept that judges are lawmakers (58:1145)." Another concurred: "The idea that the common law is capable of change—we now enunciate that. It's always existed, but under Mason that fairytale was exploded—the idea that judges are guardians of the common law, not just in the sense of handling it but keeping it in shape. There is a new openness to mold the law.... That's a profound change (123:1500)."

Those who opposed the Mason Court's heightened tendency to "make law" did so because, in part, they were convinced that the judicial function should remain one of discovery and interpretation, not creation. They frequently responded to my questions about the normative merits of certain Mason Court decisions by exclaiming, "But we don't make the law, we interpret it!"

The politicized role's provision for judge-made law is well illustrated in the comments from a South Australia appellate judge regarding former Chief Justice John Bray, who headed that state's judiciary from 1967 to 1978:

> Judge: [Chief Justice] Bray was an outstanding lawyer. He was able to
> achieve results by molding the law without appearing to overthrow

previous precedent. He was sufficiently able to mold the law without causing offense to established precedent. I think that's a tremendous quality to bring about.

Q: Do you think the [Mason Court] lacked that subtlety and nuance—that the subtlety is no longer there?

Judge: It's not there. They are the High Court. They recognize they have the power, that they have the ability to, in effect, *legislate judicially*. I don't think you'll get much disagreement with that statement. The High Court has taken a very active role lately as judicial legislators. No question about that.... Sir Anthony Mason, as Chief Justice, led the charge (48:2500) (emphasis added)."

Critics genuinely perceived a difference between *interpreting law* and *making law*. Their criticisms that the Mason Court wantonly blurred this supposedly discernable line were not merely rhetorical or verbal subterfuges for conservative political leanings. Interpreting the law involves small, case-driven change, where novel fact situations—disputes for which existing precedent do not quite fit—require the application of extant legal rules in new ways. All informants accepted that interstitial development of the law is part of the judicial function. Making law, on the other hand, entails more rapid, substantial legal change. The politicized judicial role allowed for that sort of change and recognized that judges propel it when they envision that law creation is part of their job.

Australia's inherited political tradition of parliamentary sovereignty and its Westminster political structures and conventions fostered an orthodox judicial role whereby courts were separate and apart from the political system. This was true for the High Court and other appellate courts, as much as for trial courts. The orthodoxy's image of law as a self-contained system was mirrored institutionally in its vision of the High Court functioning in isolation from politics. In the politicized conception of the judicial role, by contrast, the High Court occupies a more visible, powerful, and therefore controversial place in the political system. Its stake in the governing process is much larger, which is anathema to the old orthodoxy.

This section will make the case that the transformation brought the High Court to the center stage of politics. It should be noted at the outset, however, that my informants were quick to note that the High Court historically has not burked contentious cases with profound political ramifications. The Communist Party case and bank nationalization case, both decided mid-century, were mentioned most often to support this claim.[15] For instance, a NSW appellate judge remarked, "There have been some major cases in the [last twenty years], which have been more obviously connected with political events than in previous years. Although back in the 1950s ... there was the Communist Party case. That was as political as you could ever get.... The political currents running through that case were just as strong (24:1030)."

The Court decided the Communist Party case in 1951, a year after the Liberal Government under Prime Minister Robert Menzies enacted the *Communist Party Dissolution Act 1950*. As its name indicates, this act banned the Australian Communist Party and other related organizations and gave the Governor-General discretionary power to declare certain organizations "communist," a label that would bring them under the act's purview. The Government justified the legislation under Parliament's defense power (Section 51(vi)) and Australia's constitutional equivalent of the elastic clause (Section 51(xxxix)). The Communist Party had grown in popularity through the 1940s, particularly within trade unions, such that by 1945, it controlled one-third of votes in the Australian Council of Trade Unions Congress. Conservative segments of the Australian Labor Party supported Menzies' bill, most notably B.A. Santamaria and his Catholic Social Studies Movement. In a 6-1 decision, the Court found the act unconstitutional on the ground, *inter alia*, that Parliament had provided insufficient evidence that the Communist Party posed a national emergency, and therefore could not justify banning it under its defense powers. The Court also raised concerns about the substantial powers the Act afforded the Governor-General. Failing in the High Court, Menzies tried to secure through constitutional referendum what the High Court would not grant. Australian voters went to the polls in 1951 to vote on a proposed constitutional amendment that would ban the Communist Party. Constitutional amendments require super-majorities to pass—a majority in both chambers of Parliament, a popular majority nationwide, and a majority within four of the six states. This hurdle proved too high to overturn the Court's decision. The referendum failed in the nationwide count and carried only three of the six states.

My informants also saw the 1948 bank nationalization case as another prime example of the Court grappling with politically contentious issues. The Labor Governments from 1942 to 1949 had dedicated much attention to the powers of the central bank and banking regulation generally. After the High Court found sections of the 1945 *Commonwealth Bank Act* unconstitutional

---

15. See *Bank of NSW et al. v. Commonwealth* (1948) 76 CLR 1 and *Australian Communist Party v. Commonwealth* (1951) 83 CLR 1.

and with other provisions appearing likely to fall on the Court's sword, Prime Minister Ben Chifley and his Labor Government promoted legislation that nationalized the entire banking system. Enacted in 1947, this legislation gave monopolistic banking powers to the Commonwealth Bank of Australia by calling for the dissolution of fourteen private banks. The High Court concluded in *Bank of NSW v. The Commonwealth* (1948) that this legislation was beyond Parliament's enumerated powers, specifically its power to regulate interstate commerce, a decision later upheld in the Privy Council.

There was much agreement among my informants that the Communist Party case and bank nationalization case illustrated that the Court was able and willing to reach politically controversial decisions. "The High Court has always been in the center of the political system," said a High Court barrister. "It was in the Communist Party case. It was in the bank nationalization case. It was in the tax scheme cases in the 1970s where [Chief Justice] Barwick happily rubberstamped all of the elaborate tax schemes on the basis of black letter approaches. The Court has never been a stranger to controversy (59:3035)." A judge concurred, "The High Court has throughout its history been significant in terms of politics in Australia.... It has on a number of occasions been close to the center of the Australian political scene, and curiously enough, I doubt anyone could name three justices on the High Court (34: 630)." A High Court judge recalled, "I was only a child and can't remember it too well. But there was a sense that the Communist Party was the devil incarnate and the High Court said you've got to live with the devil (92:20145)!"

Although not adverse to political controversy, the Court entered uncharted political waters in the 1980s and 1990s. For many, the Court's *Mabo* decision eclipsed the bank nationalization and Communist Party cases in disputatiousness. A Tasmanian Supreme Court judge remarked, "The Communist Party and bank nationalization cases put the Court in the storm center back then, but I'm not sure it didn't lose its virginity or came of age in the 1990s (35)." Another commented, "Our High Court has for nearly 100 years now been active in judicial review of government. I suppose *until Mabo* the high water mark was the Communist Party case (81:3045) (emphasis added)." A Queensland appellate judge agreed, "There have been, if you look back, some exciting constitutional cases in Australia—the Communist Party case, the banks case is another. But ... [the High Court] does seem to have become a more activist court in the 90s than in the past (1:1930)." A Federal Court judge distinguished the contemporary era in this way:

No doubt the High Court came in for a level of scrutiny and criticism that it hadn't been subjected to for quite some time. Even if you go

back to things like the Communist Party case and the bank nationalization case in the 1950s, there wasn't the same level of outrage from
those whose interests were not served by the decisions as there was
about *Mabo*. It may be because *Mabo* affected something more fundamental than the other cases in terms of our sense of Australian history, our relationship with indigenous people, and a sudden shift
from a position where indigenous people were the recipients of grace
and favor ... to a position where they now were the holders of rights
which could be recognized and given effect to by the courts. That did
mean a major shift in psychology, not just for individual interests,
but state governments who had seen land management as their constitutional bailiwick.... I think the scrutiny and criticism that *Mabo*
generated led to a wider debate about the role of the High Court
(89:300).

The combination of politically contentious cases and controversial legal reasoning distinguished the Mason Court from its predecessors for many informants. One judge confessed:

I've got vivid memories of Menzies enacting the [*Communist Party
Dissolution Act*] and the High Court challenge and ... [t]he bank nationalization case.... Both were decided according to terms of the
constitution. *Mabo* was different because it involved so many interests.... But all the interest groups weren't consulted and hence we've
had this political minefield ever since. I'm not saying *Mabo* is wrong.
There are constraints on what judges should do and I think they exceeded them in that case (81:3045).

Another judge explained the tempered reactions in the 1950s because "the Communist Party and bank nationalization cases came out of straight law because
the law was applied by studying principles of nineteenth-century liberalism (35)."
It was also suggested that while future generations of lawyers and judges will be
relying upon Mason Court judgments as precedent, the controversial cases from
the 1950s have lost relevance. "Curiously enough," said one judge about the bank
case, "no one seems to quote it much nowadays. Subsequent generations don't
seem to have taken it to establish any significant principle (3:2500)."

Finally, the judges frequently distinguished the Mason Court from its predecessors by the extent to which the criticism was ad hominem.

[Mason] Court judges were directly criticized for the views they
held.... I can't remember a similar occasion, but my history is limited
to my 50 years. In the famous Communist Party dissolution case ... I

don't know what sort of political fallout that had at the time or to what extent the Court was criticized.... [I]t's said by those who've surveyed that the direct attack on the judges was different.... But, *Mabo* was the biggest blip that I've experienced in my legal life (12).

The aggregate picture from the interview data is that the native title cases in the 1990s were more politically contentious and exposed the Court to more criticism than any other decisions in its history.

Mabo illustrates the Mason Court's willingness to assume a more politicized role, one that invites judges to construct theories not only about statutory and constitutional interpretation but normative political theories as well. A Mason Court judge disclosed:

> It does seem to me that it is very difficult for a court to shape principles of public law without having some idea, if not vision, of how the democratic process is to work. I'm not merely speaking about the constitution. The constitution has its own signposts and everything. If you haven't got a constitutional provision, it's the responsibility of the courts to shape public law. Take the United Kingdom courts. They don't have these signposts and they have to shape principles of law that enable the democratic process to work. It doesn't strike me that you do that by just letting the politicians shape the kind of process that they want, that happen to suit them. I don't know how courts shape the principles of public law unless they have in their mind some form of democratic governance with a structure and doctrines that are relevant to it.
>
> Q: In other words, you can't have a judicial philosophy without a theory of democracy?
>
> Judge: No, I don't think so (122:11210).

An appellate judge offered a similar account, stressing the inevitability of contemporary appellate judges crafting their own legal and political philosophies: "Judges are faced with cases ... that raise novel ideas or problems or try to develop ideas that they have not considered before. Now judges cannot escape from developing philosophies about things. Maybe 100 or fifty years ago you just applied the law, but more and more decisions involve discretion, and with discretion you intrude on judicial philosophies (34:1500)."

These responses contrast sharply with the orthodoxy's insistent separation of law from politics and judges from the political system. In suggesting that judges should construct their own coherent democratic theories and that these theories should inform decision-making, these judges exemplify the politi-cized role. Because High Court judges do more than resolve particularized dis-putes and because their decisions may bring far-reaching political, economic, and social consequences, a conception of how the democratic process works (and should work) is necessary. The politicized role accommodates neither a High Court separated from politics nor cloistered judges thinking only about legal matters. By contrast, the orthodoxy either denies that judges have polit-ical philosophies, or if it admits they have them, it discourages them from bringing those philosophies to bear when deciding cases.

This more expansive vision of the High Court's role also accepts that judges, as participants in the governing process, may speak publicly on political and legal matters. By way of example, in November 1999, Australians voted in a referendum that proposed changing Australia's constitutional structure from one where the Queen of England is technically head of state to a republic model with a president appointed by two-thirds of the Commonwealth Par-liament. Australian voters tend to be strangely skeptical of constitutional re-forms. Of the forty-two referenda that had previously been put before voters, only eight had passed.[16] The republic referendum failed to secure enough sup-port for passage, but the public debates leading up to the vote, in which sup-porters and opponents paraded an endless cadre of experts, were intense and well covered in the media. In the contemporary judicial culture, in which judges are regarded as participants in the broader political system, it was no surprise that a number of retired High Court justices spoke out publicly on the republic referendum.[17] My informants suggested that this public expres-sion of opinion on a politically charged, albeit legal issue, would not have oc-curred under the orthodoxy. Its occurrence signaled that times had changed. For example, a NSW appellate judge remarked:

> Mason and Brennan both came out publicly in favor of a "Yes" [vote
> for the republic]. I think they expected that their opinions would be
> deferred to in a way in which they weren't. This is part of the prob-
> lem with an activist court. It loses a lot of legitimacy.... So, some of

16. The eight constitutional referenda that passed covered issues such as concurrent elections for the House of Representatives and Senate, enabling the Commonwealth to take over state debts, giving the Commonwealth power to provide social services, allowing ter-ritory residents to vote, and requiring federal judges to retire at age 70, among others.

17. Former Chief Justices Anthony Mason and Gerard Brennan, as well as former vice regal representative Zelman Cowen wrote publicly in support of the republic. See "Justices Support Yes Case," *The Daily Telegraph*, October 8, 1999, p. 18; "Top Silk Throws Weight Behind Republic," *The Australian*, August 16, 1999, p. 2.

their judicial hubris has carried over into the non-judicial sphere of "political" campaigning—political in inverted commas. It was not party political. I suspect in an earlier generation chances that a former CJ [Chief Justice] would have done this at all were much less. At the same time, if a former CJ had come out, much more attention would have been paid to what he said.... I suspect that unless the issue was seen to be strictly legal, Dixon would not have bought into any referendum controversy. If there had been a legal issue in that controversy ... and he made a statement, it would have been treated with immense respect across the board. The guns would have fallen silent. Ex-CJ has spoken, end of question (99:800).

This component of the politicized role does not enjoy universal support among contemporary High Court and senior appellate judges. Disagreement exists over its merit. Mason Court judges acknowledged this break from convention, but proponents tended to think that public debate is enriched, if not improved, when judges weigh in. "I feel obliged to participate in the social dialogue," said one High Court judge. The judge continued:

Confining myself to just my judicial work goes against my intellect and is a waste of a valuable resource. It has to be done and I am willing to do it. My mind is stimulated to think about these things. Once judges ... admit that they face choices, they should be informed by something better than what you learned in Sunday school. It is the duty of High Court judges to be informed and knowledgeable about things beyond law books. Australia should tolerate Posner-like judges (116:2500).

Another High Court justice concluded, "I don't think ... there are any drawbacks at all. I think it helps to stimulate debate and stimulate minds. I think one has to realize that one shouldn't enter into debate on issues that are before the Court or likely to come before the Court (78)." An even more cavalier approach come from a Federal Court judge: "Appellate judges are more outspoken now than used to be the case. We've abandoned the protocol of not opening our mouths except in judgments.... That's good. We should be seen out in the community having views. If articulating those views lead to disqualifications in cases, then so be it. There are plenty of us (36:3545)."

If Australia has or someday produces a Judge Posner, he or she can bank on tepid support from intermediate appellate judges who think public comment should only come through written opinions. As a Federal Court judge claimed, "Most Australian judges are conscious of not speaking out on controversial issues. Our judgments are the place for explaining decisions, not outside (97)." This was echoed in comments from a High Court judge: "In general, anything is unhealthy except through the chief justices. Chief Justice Mason thought chief justices should make public statements. I don't think that's helpful or informative despite the good intentions because you can't reduce the complexities of cases. Our only speaking should be through our judgments. You can't reduce your reasoning to a seven second sound bite (100)."

Current High Court Justice Kirby came under particularly acute criticism from my informants for his proclivity for public pronouncements on legal, political, and myriad other issues. One judge remarked, "I have great concerns about the extent to which judges should [speak in public].... I'm not saying it should not be done. I think judges do have a role to perform in certain kinds of speech making—an educative role in the sense of ordinary, non-controversial instruction.... But when one gets into futurology—Justice Kirby is very naughty about getting into futurology—it demeans the status of him as a judge and the High Court (81:2445)." A Victoria judge quipped, "Justice Kirby talks about everything from breast feeding to basket weaving. That's wrong (69)." His intellectual wanderlust surfaced in another interview with a Federal Court judge. "There is a story—I don't know if it's apocrypha or not—that [Kirby] went to Africa and he addressed a meeting on breast feeding in the third world. Somebody expressed some surprise that he would be speaking on that topic. He said that when he was invited he misunderstood the phone call and later learned it was on *press freedom* in the third world.... Judges lecturing and hectoring society is not uniformly appreciated (102:4545)."

Beyond participation in public dialogue on topics legal and not, it also emerged that High Court judges under the politicized role have a greater obligation to speak beyond the immediate litigants in a case. Sometimes this educative function simply means that judges use more accessible language in their judgments. Other times it entails they speak through judgments to controversies or debates underway in the broader community. Underpinning this educative function is a belief in the efficacy of what judges say.

While the High Court may play an educative role, there was broad recognition that appellate courts, even the High Court, have few opportunities for this. Most judgments address particular legal disputes and garner no attention beyond the immediate litigants. One judge offered:

> Because the High Court is the ultimate appeals court and because it receives cases before it on principles that are more fundamental than we ordinary working-day judges, it probably has a greater role to

speak to the world at large than other judges. You can pick High Court decisions in the *Commonwealth Law Reports*. Ninety-seven percent of them will be speaking only to the litigants and lawyers. Three percent will be speaking to the public at large (32:3845).

Another judge remarked, "Most of our judgments are not read by the general public, but there are controversial cases where you have an opportunity to do that (1:3600)." The capacity to influence public opinion is nugatory, according to one judge, "unless the media pick up something a judge said in court and run with it. The problem is ... that there is no other way for the community to find out what judges think." The judge continued, "In cases involving constitutional law ... there might be more occasions for judges speaking to the community. If you look at the cases, 95 percent of them are of no great public interest. They are between the parties and the judgments must be written for the parties (121:3400)." An ACT judge asserted, "The role of the courts in shaping social opinion is overstated.... There are certainly individual cases—*Mabo* is one—where the case will capture the public's imagination and commentary about the case will move public opinion. But I suspect the percentage of Australians who have read Sir Gerard's words [in *Mabo*] would be miniscule (74:5845)."

Several informants considered the Mason and Brennan Courts particularly effective speaking beyond the immediate parties and educating the country about controversial decisions or legal reasoning, such as their indigenous land rights decisions. Said one NSW appellate judge, "Brennan, Deane, and Gaudron in *Mabo*—they ultimately changed the nature of the debate. [The ultimate effect] of their judgments may not be good because of the backlash and the creation of *Wik* and so on.... Yes, I think that what the courts say about law or the reason why the law should be so in some new case can have a big influence on public opinion, though it's not very common (103:5800)." Another responded about Brennan's *Wik* judgment:

Obviously Brennan was [speaking to all Australians] and I think he did a terrific job too. By expressing those thoughts at the time, which were held by a minority—he knew that a majority did not hold those views—they became mainstream views. That it's all right to recognize the Aborigines' cultural and spiritual identity with the land and the rights that arise out of that. It might take awhile, but gradually they'll become mainstream. What he did was very clever, but obviously you can't do it in every case. You have to pick the appropriate forum. Yes, opportunities arise and I would do it if the opportunity arose. If you did it too often you'd lose the effectiveness of it. You'd sound like a preacher (1:3600).

High Court Justices I interviewed divided over whether the Court can or should engage actively in societal debates by writing beyond the immediate litigants. Some envisaged a more passive institutional role.

> It's the function of the Court to expound its reasoning in terms that can be widely understood, when the circumstances of the case permit. It's not possible, for example, when one is dealing with technical concepts like obviousness or novelty in intellectual property. It is possible when dealing with problems of the kind raised in *Mabo*. I don't think it's the case of educating, in the sense of leading the community to a viewpoint which is one that the Court thinks the community should be led to. It is, however, the case of explaining the reasons why the Court has been led to a conclusion. If that means, as it was in *Mabo*, that the common conception of what the law was is being displaced in favor of what the law is for reasons which are explicable, it is incumbent upon the justices to make that explanation in terms which can be appreciated as widely as possible (63:830).

Another High Court Justice offered an equally benign view of the Court's educative function:

> Q: Do you think your court has a capacity to shape social opinion?
>
> Judge: It has a part but it ought not to be a major motivation. We do not have an agenda when we go into determining a case. On the other hand, you look at the *Mabo* case, I think the Court's proceedings in that case helped change Australian opinion on Aboriginal rights. That was a consequence of the decision, not a motivation of the decision. The Court on human rights or discrimination questions may outpace the average citizen but that is part of the symbiosis between institutions. We have democratic elements—the legislature and executive—and permanent elements—the judiciary, Crown, and public service. It's wrong to say that the High Court has an agenda to change social opinion but it could be a consequence (116:1500).

Modesty may have compelled these High Court Justices to speak in such diminished terms about their abilities as civic educators. Having said that, some informants endorsed the politicized role's view of the bench as a launch pad for societal education and reform. One informant admitted that he became a judge because he was unable to realize the legal reforms he wanted to advance as a barrister. "One ... reason I decided to leave the bar and become a judge was because ... it was no longer possible to go to the High Court and argue that the law should develop in these ways with any prospect of success. It was just a waste of time. The Court had changed dramatically in terms of personnel. So the sorts of arguments I could put on one day came to an end very suddenly. That motivated me (85:2100)." In response to a question whether tensions should exist in a separation of powers system between the elected branches and the judiciary, one judge responded, "Absolutely. The majoritarian autocracy is only itself a form of dictatorship as far as minorities and individuals are concerned. There has to be within the constitutional structures bodies which check and balance each other (87:3615)." Rest assured the judiciary was just the institutional body he had in mind. A NSW appellate judge offered the following answer to a question about the judiciary outpacing public opinion: "I believe that it is [acceptable] in some situations. *Brown* [*v. Board*] would be an example where the court got out ahead and ... the verdict of history was yes it is painful. But we now say it was a good thing.... [Y]es there are clearly situations where the court should go ahead.... There are areas where the courts can and should say this law is bad and we change it (123)." In a telling comment about reform mindedness, a member of the Mason Court offered the following:

> Conservative judges might be saying, "The courts shouldn't be doing these things. Once the courts do these sorts of things they're getting into the political area."... Other judges will say, "It's permissible for the courts to do this, because really there is a community consensus. What the courts do in this area will be accepted even though there will be criticism. Nonetheless, it will ultimately be accepted." The American experience is very useful because it shows that in the days of the Warren Court activism was acceptable. There were vociferous critics but whatever history has to say about the legal propriety of what the Warren Court did, there is no doubt that the ultimate judgment will be favorable in terms of the process that the Warren Court set in place (122:5400).

These reform minded judges were clearly at odds with the orthodoxy's expectations about how appellate courts should (or should not) interact with the community. They also took issue with the normative relationship between the High Court and other government branches. Australia's Westminster political tradition calls, under the orthodoxy, for a level of High Court deference that the politicized role does not accept. One way in which this deference is demonstrated is a wariness about the judiciary warring too often with parliaments or executives. Even the most conservative judges recognized that some tension was inevitable given the High Court's constitutional mandate to police the parliaments' exercises of power. The orthodoxy eschewed, however, too frequent conflict.

Under the politicized role, tension between the judiciary and other branches is seen as inevitable, desirable, and on the rise. A Western Australia judge offered the following response to a question on institutional tension: "I don't know whether this is a new development. One was never conscious of it a few decades ago, but it's become rather common. It really came to a head with *Mabo* (112:1100)." Whereas the orthodox judges justify their deference because of Australia's Westminster traditions, the proponents of the politicized role justify institutional tensions under separation of powers principles animating the constitution. "I certainly think that [tension] is inevitable," said a judge. "You can't have elected members of parliament and judges who come to issues with totally coextensive expectations.... There are cases that the Government will bring that it ardently wants to win, and it will lose. Courts will establish principles that governments don't agree with and find politically difficult. I don't think there is any way around that (74:5215)." Another judge explained:

> You might get a tension between the judiciary and legislature because it's the judiciary that is called upon to determine what the legislature meant, and the legislature finds that a bit difficult when they know what they meant, but the judiciary says otherwise. That's a healthy tension because someone has to ... umpire that. There will always be a tension between the judiciary and the executive because it's the judiciary's responsibility to keep the executive within power.... Again that's a healthy tension because without [it] the executive power would be boundless.... Someone has to stand between the citizen and the state and that's the job of the bench (117:1400).

Institutional tension is justified not only on the ground that it is inherent to a separation of powers system. The politicized role also condones it because of how politics operates in practice. The constitution provides formally for a tripartition of powers between an executive, legislature, and judiciary, but politics at the Commonwealth and state levels tends to operate along a bifurcated line. What Bagehot called Britain's "little secret" is also Australia's: a fusion, for all practical purposes, of executive and legislative power. While the Commonwealth Parliament theoretically checks the executive and its ministers—in a classic parliamentary system the executive is drawn from and answerable to the legislature—the two branches operate as one. A government attorney concluded, "Separation for us is really not separation for three but two. You have parliament and executive on one side and the High Court on the other.

THE MASON COURT SUPPLANTS THE ORTHODOXY   123

As you know, the executive entirely dominates the parliamentary arm, except for short-term problems about majorities in the Senate (94:3700)." One judge responded, "The judiciary plays an important part in maintaining a balance. It's the only branch that controls the executive and to a limited extent the legislature.... Without it you've got the executive running the country the way it wants (77)." A High Court judge agreed with the idea that fused legislative and executive branches demand a stronger judicial role.

> If you take the view that the political process is increasingly, in a sense, an elected dictatorship softened by spin doctors and alienated from the people, then there may be a case for an expansion of the judicial role.... What's happened is instead of parliament controlling the executive, we have a situation in which the executive controls parliament. In Australia, that's subject to a very big qualification: the executive doesn't control the upper house.... [There] the electorate is endeavoring to put a brake on the executive in Australia by voting differently in the Senate than in the House (122:122435).

The previous two quotations allude to the important institutional check that Australia's upper chamber, the Senate, historically provides. The Senate's powers are anathema to a purely responsible party system, given that it exercises equal legislative powers as the House. The one exception is that the Senate cannot introduce spending bills, but may amend or reject spending bills that originate in the House. The Senate was originally designed to provide institutional protection for the less populated states. Conventions require the Government of the day to retain control of the House, but not the Senate, to stay in power. The Government of the day for the last forty years usually has not controlled a majority of Senate seats. This is due, in part, to election reforms. Prior to 1948, Australia's first-past-the-post and preferential voting system meant that a single party often won all Senate seats for a given state. A proportional representation system was instituted for Senate elections in 1948. Under this system, each state retains equal representation in the Senate, but each state's seats are assigned on a proportional basis according to how the parties fared within the state. Consequently, smaller parties and independents have gained significant representation in the Senate, often requiring the Government to solicit support from non-Government Senators to secure passage of legislation (Jaensch 1986; Uhr 1998). The 2004 federal election produced an exception to this rule. The Howard Government's Liberal Party secured a majority in the seventy-six seat chamber, marking the first time since 1981 that a Government controlled both legislative chambers. Notwithstanding the Senate's capacity to check the executive, my informants insisted on the need for judicial checks as well. No one, for example, thought the Senate provides such an effective check on power that the courts are absolved of this duty.

Informants held strong views that parliamentarians and ministers at all levels of government were largely oblivious to arguments favoring institutional tension: first, that the federal constitution entrenches a separation of powers principle that calls on the High Court to police parliamentary powers and executive actions; and second, that the practical fusion of executive and legislative power demands a stronger role for courts. The following assessment came from a federal government attorney:

> [Former Victoria State Premier Jeff] Kennett has no real comprehension of separation of powers. Until recently, most people would be barely aware that we had a High Court [and] ... that we even have a constitution.... [U]ntil the 1980s, the High Court didn't even have a home. It was peripatetic and went around almost on a horse, so that there is an absence of an appreciation of the position. Now as far as the Government is concerned, I think it is distressingly true that by and large Governments are very neglectful of appreciating the position of the Court.... [It doesn't] enter into the cognizance of Government. It's very rare that we have a high profile conflagration such as we're having over native title, where one creates the unfortunate attitude of hostility, which at the moment seems to be escalating (127).

A South Australia appellate judge suggested, "I think [institutional tension] is very important in our parliamentary system of government. A lot of politicians tend to forget it—people at the state level especially—and they need a lot of educating. I don't think they understand the constitution and the origins of the systems. Many of them go as far to say that the courts should be [their] instruments of government.... Courts tend to be seen as just another department (60:3045)." These judicial sentiments about politicians' views of the judiciary are affirmed regularly in the popular presses. Particularly in the last decade or so High Court judges have come under heightened criticism from politicians for overstepping their supposed powers. In late 2004, for example, Justice Kirby gave a number of public speeches where he commented on a number of Howard Government policies. Attorney General Philip Ruddock rebuked Justice Kirby in diplomatic speak: "Judges, I think, need to be careful in the way in which they speak because it often invokes comment.... It is important that the separation of powers which we have where the legislature makes laws and the courts adjudicate be protected."[18] Ruddock later went so far as to say that the courts are intended to back up parliament. "There is in Australia respective roles for the legislature and the judiciary, and I would anticipate any judge in any proceedings would uphold the law of Australia."[19]

It also was widely believed that ministers fail to see the courts as serving a special role in protecting citizens from the state. "The executive would usually like to go about its objectives without being troubled by such things as resistance from citizens claiming their rights are being infringed," said an ACT Supreme Court judge. The judge continued, "Most executive members think, 'We're acting in the best interests of the country. We're elected to do this.'... All ministers are elected members of the legislature, so each of them thinks they have the sacred duty to do whatever they please (104:2130)." What some informants describe as parliamentary arrogance, others thought to be institutional ignorance. Said one informant, "Any sophisticated lawyer ought to recognize that tension is normal. But in Australia ... not all politicians are sophisticated. For instance, we had a minister from Queensland who entered a beer-belly, dwarf throwing competition (83:1230)."

Other judges with whom I spoke recognized that the High Court is prone to institutional conflicts with the federal and state governments because it is charged, unlike British appellate courts, with resolving federalism disputes. "The judiciary has a special importance in Australia because of the way the federal structure is put up. The Commonwealth's powers are only that which are given to it by the constitution.... In Australia, it's got that additional responsibility than in the U.K., where the judiciary stands between the executive and the citizen. The judiciary also umpires disputes between the states and the Commonwealth (117:1700)."

Another component to the politicized role is a recognition that the Court may legitimately tackle issues at which the other branches balk. Mark Graber (1993) wrote about occasions in U.S. history when the Supreme Court tackled issues that were too controversial or too divisive for the popularly elected bodies to handle. He sought to qualify claims of a counter-majoritarian Supreme Court by pointing to the fact that on occasion the elected branches purposively abdicate authority to the Court to decide issues that are too controversial for democratic politics or pose too much risk for politicians. Graber's "hot potato thesis" explains some of the controversy that surrounded the Mason Court. Several informants saw the Mason era not as a time when the Court ceaselessly grabbed power, but one where it attended to certain is-

---

18. "Fed: Ruddock says Kirby needs to be careful in comments," *AAP Newsfeed*, Oct. 24, 2004.

19. "Ruddock takes swipe at judge," *The Australian*, November 25, 2004, p. 1.

sues that other branches were unable or unwilling to address, such as native title. A Queensland judge remarked:

> From the mid-1980s to the mid-1990s, the High Court played a pivotal role in assisting Australia's progress as a nation, perhaps in part because of substantial deficiencies in our political process and constitutional arrangements. Our constitutional arrangements are deficient because they really are little more than a set of governing principles between the Commonwealth and the states.... Much of our constitutional law has been focused on the respective legislative powers. We haven't had any healthy development of an analysis of the relationship between the citizen and the body politic.... At the time our constitution was made ... [that relationship] wasn't seen as focal to the way government operated. That's of course changed significantly now.... The Australian judiciary has always been and continues to be ... extraordinarily conservative. The judges' role has traditionally been seen in terms of black letter law ... rather than a wider range of principles that takes into account core values.... *When the Mason Court was at its most active, there became an awareness that the political process couldn't really solve some of the social problems because they were politically too difficult* (87:445) (emphasis added).

This last assertion was echoed in several other interviews. "*Mabo* ... broke a tension which the politicians were quite unable to break," said one judge. "If the High Court had not ruled against the idea of *terra nullius* that would have been a political problem that we would not have been able to resolve through the ordinary democratic processes (34:1215)." A Federal Court judge thought, "[W]ith the two houses of Parliament and the difficulty of the Government actually commanding a majority ... it really does give courts the power to move where the legislature can't. Isn't that what you saw with the implied rights cases ... and native title as well? It's an invidious position in which to put judges ... when parliament gets jammed up (12:1100)." A Federal Court judge offered the following assessment regarding Parliament's capacity to bring about native title reform. "[Parliament] can't easily legislate on this. That's the whole problem. It's never been able to agree on a national land rights regime. They wimped out on that.... The whole issue is too divisive so it falls to the Court to fill in (89:5430)." A colleague concluded:

> In the last twenty years ... there is much decision-making that governments don't take on, for one reason or another. It's too hard. It's

too complicated. They're too worried about the political effects. That means ... that if the law isn't to remain totally static then it puts a lot of pressure on courts to make the changes.... Governments don't govern in some areas. *Mabo* ... is the great example. If you were in government and had half a brain, you could have seen it coming for twenty or thirty years some litigation involving Aboriginal rights (45:400).

Finally, a member of the Mason Court assessed this hot-potato argument:

Yes there was [legislative] inaction, but that wasn't the Court's motivation. The Court had to decide the question where there was no binding authority.... The case appeared before the High Court so it was forced to find a legal solution.... It was a case where the political process left it to the court to resolve. This was also the case in *Wik*, where Parliament could have intervened, but they made a deliberate decision not to introduce legislation [on native title] before it was decided. Two reasons for this: first the difficulty getting the legislation through the Senate, and second, Parliament thought that the High Court would decide against the [native title] claimants (17:4030).

A Victoria appellate judge was of the opinion that this heightened role was necessary in order for Australian politics to advance.

I think that there is room for the Court to be more adventurous.... I don't think the country can move forward, having regard to the structures that we've got, unless the High Court is prepared to take risks.... The highest judicial authority, which makes the law for the country ultimately, should be prepared to take some risks. Otherwise it's in a straightjacket if it interprets its functions too literally. As you know, judges make law, parliaments make law.... It's the ultimate arbiter, for instance, of common law rights. [The Court] has the capacity to stretch those rights for the betterment of the community as a whole. If they're prepared to take risks and stretch them and go outside the bounds of precedent ... I think it's better in the long run for the country. It takes parliaments a hell of a long time to make laws reflecting community feelings. The parliaments of Australia tend to follow the lead given to them by the High Court (52:700).

What was legitimate stretching to some, however, appeared overtly political to others. A High Court Justice told me, "One thing I don't like is people making implications in the constitution because they're impatient with what they regard as the slow pace of the legislature on a given subject.... That's not an appropriate function of the judiciary. The judiciary may not know why parliament is not moving on a particular subject or they think they know and might be wrong (96:3940)." A Victoria appellate judge found it "sad if the legislatures are not dealing with the real problems that society encounters." The judge suggested, "It's a consequence of that ill-fortune that courts themselves get dragged into it as surrogate legislatures. I don't think they are or should be. My own view is that courts should not respond to what they perceive as legislative shortcomings by taking the reins of power (65:2400)."

My interviews with Mason Court judges reveal, however, that the shortcomings they perceived in the political system motivated them to act. For example, the pre-Mason Court had dedicated significant docket space exploring the constitution's distribution of power between the state and Commonwealth governments. It had said relatively little about individuals' rights and duties to each other and to the government. Several Mason Court judges saw this as a shortcoming. The question confronting them was how to respond? Should the Court do nothing and remain complicit or abandon institutional conventions and respond in newfangled ways? I offer two extended quotations from Mason Court judges to illustrate their discontent and desire to correct this perceived problem. One High Court justice remarked, "Judges are essentially reactive people, except those who have been academics. Those who have been academics have had more time to think about things.... I think with many Australian judges who come from the ranks of the practicing profession, they don't really come to the Court with a fully developed or articulated judicial philosophy of their own. They develop it as time passes (122:11409)." The judge continued:

> The judicial function is a constantly evolving function. It may be static at periods of time but then it may move forward by perceptible steps. You take the rights revolution. That's changed the dynamic of what courts and judges do. Despite what the critics say in this country, it focuses the judicial mind on justice—according justice to individuals. The expression used by [Bagehot] was "an elected dictatorship." I think it really goes too far to talk about a dictatorship. What's happened is instead of Parliament controlling the executive, we now have a situation in which the executive controls the Parliament. In Australia that's subject to a very big qualification, of course. The executive doesn't control the upper house.... One has to attrib-

ute some sophistication to the electorate. The electorate is endeavoring to put a brake on executive power in Australia by voting differently for the Senate than they vote in the House (122:122435) (emphasis added).

Another Mason Court judge confided,

> In my youth, I opposed a bill of rights on the basis that it would be too narrowly construed by the High Court and at the same time absolve politicians of responsibility.... One thing I have long since come to respect is the sheer cowardice of politicians. For all the time sit-on-your-hands do nothing cowardice they cannot be faulted.... I think ultimately it is the party political system that we borrowed from [the U.S.], which we've allowed to develop in parallel to yours. I think it's got lots of problems.... I have no expectations of politicians. I have no expectations that there are any rules of the game [with regard to their interactions with the courts] or that they will observe them. Ultimately in this country, and I suspect it's the same in yours, there is clear research indicating that ... people have got a lot more respect and faith in the courts than they have in the political processes (92:4600).

These quotations from Mason Court judges reveal a distrust for the elected branches. They both have a clear skepticism about Australia's political system. One stresses the danger posed to human rights given the limited checks on executive power. He lauds the electorate's sophistication in checking executive power through split-ticket voting and intimates that the High Court should provide a similar check. The other judge expects politicians' behavior to reflect their desire for reelection. If that requires politicians to do nothing or sit on their hands, then that is what they will do. This judge clearly sees the High Court possessing a public legitimacy that the other branches lack, sustained not by judges removing themselves from the governing process (as advocated under the orthodoxy) but through full engagement.

The last several pages have outlined key components to the politicized role's conception of the High Court's relationship to the political system and community. In short, the Mason Court created an institutional role that is increasingly at odds with Australia's Westminster political traditions. The politicized role encourages the Court to tackle politically controversial issues, using equally controversial legal methods. This exposed the Court to unprecedented criticisms. It also calls on the judges to speak out beyond their judgments on political and legal matters, serve an educative role, and shape public opinion where necessary. The politicized role also accepts that institutional tensions will exist—indeed should exist—between the Court and other branches of government.

The Changing Agenda Under the Mason Court

My informants perceived that the role transformation can be marked by changes in the Mason Court's workload from its predecessors. The overall character of the Court's cases evolved. Under the orthodoxy, the Court was thought to exercise little discretion over which cases it handled. It emphasized private law disputes over public law disputes, and what few constitutional cases arose tended to deal with federal-state matters. The transformation brought several profound changes to the Court's workload. First, the Mason Court seemed as concerned about public law questions as private law questions. Second, in constitutional disputes, the relationship between individuals and their governments—not just federalism disputes—took on added salience.

The Mason Court, according to one Federal Court judge, "Signaled those matters that interested it: a preoccupation with human rights, which when unpacked, means controlling the exercise of power between states and citizens and between citizens themselves. [It has been] referred to as the Court protecting the vulnerable (86:1000)." Another judge described the change this way: "What's been more marked in the last twenty years is that the constitution is now concerned with more social matters, whereas in Dixon's time is was concerned with Section 92 matters and the relationships of the states with each other and perhaps the states with the Commonwealth. The constitutional law is now more concerned about people and citizens' positions in society—different things to look at because it's a different age (117:545)." A Commonwealth attorney suggested, "The *Tasmanian Dam* case was the last big federalism battle. Once that was over, the High Court turned its attention to the individual, and that's still today. By the 1980s, federal versus state issues had been resolved so the High Court turned its attention to other constitutional questions, such as the relationship between individual citizens and the executive (66)."

Does the empirical record bear out this shift from private to more public law cases? To examine this question, I assembled a data set consisting of all High Court cases reported in the *Commonwealth Law Reports* (CLRs) from 1903 - 2000.[20] Utilizing published opinions as a measure for tracking changes

---

20. Although one finds High Court decisions published in other reporters (e.g., the *Australian Law Reports*), the CLRs are the High Court's official reporter. Every decision is not published, but every important decision is. The CLRs provide, therefore, a reliable data source to evaluate changes in the Court's agenda.

in a court's agenda is a well-established practice in public law scholarship (see Pacelle 1991). By "agenda" I mean only the body of cases a court decides from year to year. One way to look for a shift from private to public law matters is to assess if and when the Court dedicated less attention to non-constitutional matters and more attention to constitutional cases. To determine the number of constitutional cases the Court decided each year, I assembled frequency tables using the keywords provided in each case's head note.[21] The Court decided 647 constitutional cases over this ninety-seven year period. Figure 4.8 plots the data since the Court's first term in 1903. The five-year moving average indicates that as the century progressed the Court handled increasing numbers of constitutional cases, except for the 1980s. The trend line for this decade swings more intently upward and then settles down by the mid-1990s.

A more salient issue is whether the Court dedicated increasing proportions of its annual agenda to constitutional disputes. Were constitutional cases occupying more of its attention vis-à-vis other types of cases annually? Perhaps the increase in constitutional cases illustrated in Figure 4.8 may be the corollary of an ever-growing workload. To address this issue, an antecedent question must be answered: What happened to the Court's overall workload throughout the century? Figure 4.9 plots the number of High Court cases decided each year and reported in the CLRs from 1903 to 2000. The data indicate a tri-modal distribution, with peaks in the 1910s, 1930s, and 1950s. Following the Second World War, the number of decisions shot back to pre-war levels, only to taper off consistently since the mid-1970s. The last twenty-five years have witnessed a precipitous and consistent drop in the Court's workload by this measure.[22] Why this decline occurred is an important historical question, but it can only be discussed cursorily here. Two critical institutional reforms bear much responsibility: first, a reform in how the Court handles appeals, and second, the creation of federal courts of first instance.

As with the U.S. Supreme Court, the vast majority of High Court cases come through its appellate jurisdiction rather than original jurisdiction. Until the 1980s, the Court was required to decide any and all cases that came before it under its appellate jurisdiction. No filtering mechanism was available, such as the U.S. Supreme Court's certiorari process, until statutory reforms were made

21. Cases were coded according to the content of the keyword section reported at the beginning of each case. The CLR's editors compose the content for the keyword sections. Because cases can raise a multiplicity of issues I coded a case as dealing with "constitutional law" if somewhere in the keyword section the words "constitutional law" appeared.

22. Annual workload is measured here as the number of cases reported in the CLRs for a given year.

Figure 4.8 Annual Number of Constitutional Law Cases Reported in the
Commonwealth Law Reports, 1904–2000, with 5-Year Moving Average

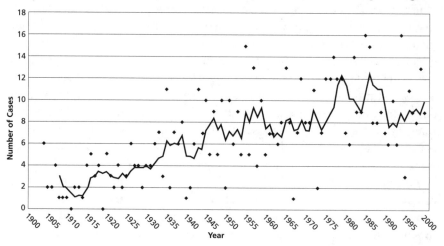

Figure 4.9 Annual Number of Cases Reported in the Commonwealth Law
Reports, 1904–2000, with 5-Year Moving Average

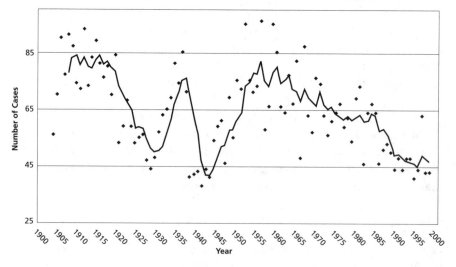

in 1984. That year, Parliament amended the *Judiciary Act of 1903* to require that any appeal from the state supreme courts, the Federal Court, and the Family Court proceed only upon the High Court granting special leave to appeal. Akin to a writ of certiorari, special leave to appeal may be granted, according to the amended act, if the case involves a question of law that raises an issue of public importance or requires the Court to resolve disagreements between lower courts on points of law.[23] Implementing the special leave requirement was premised on the idea that every litigant had an absolute right to at least one appeal, but not two (Mason 1996). The High Court no longer guarantees automatic review, enabling it to be more selective and discerning. I assert that the special leave requirement contributes substantially to the case load's drop illustrated in Figure 4.9.

The second institutional reform that no doubt contributed to the decline in the number of annual High Court cases was the creation of the Federal Court of Australia in 1976. Until then, no general court of first instance existed within the federal judicial hierarchy. Parliament had created a few specialized federal courts (e.g., the Industrial Court in various forms and the Federal Court of Bankruptcy), but nothing akin to U.S. district courts. The Federal Court of Australia (composed of roughly fifty judges who sit in courts of first instance) serves this role. Most of its jurisdiction is ascribed through 120 parliamentary statutes. The Federal Court also serves as an appellate court for territory supreme courts and state supreme courts under certain conditions. No separately staffed intermediate appellate court exists in the federal judiciary. To operate in appellate capacity, three-member panels of Federal Court judges are assembled ad hoc to form the Full Federal Court of Australia. Creation of a federal court of first instance represented a significant transfer of original jurisdiction (and cases) away from the High Court and alleviated it from an otherwise taxing appellate caseload (Crawford 1982).

Coupled, these reforms shaped the type of cases appearing before the Court. The special leave requirement required petitioners' cases meet a higher threshold of significance while the Federal Court reform transferred away jurisdictional responsibilities best handled in courts of first instance. The High Court could more fully function as Australia's constitutional court. Given that the Court tended to decide more constitutional cases from an ever-shrinking pool over the last twenty years, one would anticipate that the proportion of annual agenda space dedicated to constitutional disputes would have increased. Indeed, that is the case. Figure 4.10 plots the annual percentage of cases concerning constitutional matters.

---

23. *Judiciary Act 1903*, Sections 35 and 35(A).

Figure 4.10 Annual Percentage of CLR Cases That Raise Constitutional
Questions, 1904–2000, with 5-Year Moving Average

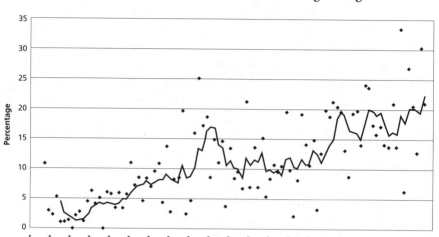

To what extent did this "constitutionalization" vary by chief justice? Figure 4.11 reports the mean number of constitutional cases decided per year during each chief justice's term, regardless of length. Figure 4.12 presents the annual percentage of cases that raise constitutional questions by chief justice. Figure 4.13 presents the high, low, and mean percentages of annual agenda space dedicated to constitutional cases during each chief justice's tenure. These last two figures demonstrate that Sir Anthony Mason's tenure was clearly correlated with a heightened attention to constitutional matters. The highest proportion of annual agenda space ever dedicated to constitutional matters occurred under his watch (1994, 33 percent). Statistically, however, the Gibbs Court dedicated more attention to constitutional matters (mean = 18 percent each year) than the Mason Court (mean = 16.8 percent each year). Indeed, it appears that Gibbs' tenure (1981–1987) marks the point where the Court's constitutional agenda permanently migrated up from the 10–15 percent range, where it had been since 1950, to hover between 15 and 20 percent. Furthermore, the data in Figure 4.12 seem to indicate that 1974 was a critical year. Since 1974 the Court has never dedicated less than 5 percent of its annual caseload to constitutional cases and only twice (1981 and 1995) would it dedicate less than 10 percent. The trend line offers strong evidence that the Court has shifted in the last twenty years from private to public law disputes.

Figure 4.11 Average Number of Constitutional Cases Decided Per Year
Grouped by Chief Justice, 1903–1999

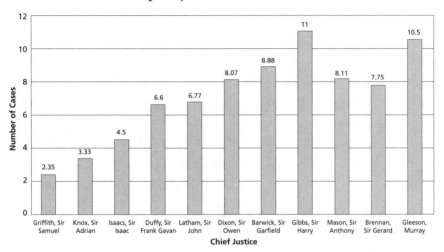

Figure 4.12 Annual Percentage of CLR Cases That Raise Constitutional
Questions, Grouped by Chief Justice, 1904–2000, with 5-Year Moving Average

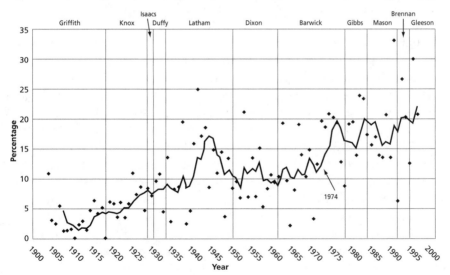

Figure 4.13 Amount of Agenda Space Dedicated to Constitutional Law Cases Grouped by Chief Justice with High, Low, and Mean Marks

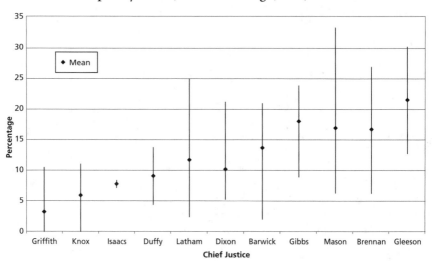

It does not follow automatically that this shift illustrates my thesis about a High Court transformation. In *The Transformation of the Supreme Court's Agenda*, Richard Pacelle studies the development of the U.S. Supreme Court's agenda space from the 1930s through the 1980s. He reports that in certain years the Court dedicated an unprecedented amount of attention, or what he calls "agenda space," to certain legal issues, such as free speech, criminal procedure, or civil rights cases. He coins these breakout years as *recrudescent agenda years*. Australia's High Court appears to have experienced a series of recrudescent agenda years with regard to constitutional disputes that coincides roughly with the role transformation. Just what threshold makes for a breakout year is subjective and therefore debatable. Pacelle does not offer a hard and fast standard, and he uses the "recrudescent agenda year" label loosely. In the end, it must be determined by having regard to the particular court's history and context. If in the Australian case, for example, the threshold for a recrudescent agenda year is set at any time the High Court issued fourteen or more constitutional law decisions in a year, then only six years qualify (1955, 1977, 1982, 1985, 1986, and 1996) or about six percent of agenda space over the century. Figure 4.14 charts those years. It is important to note that five of the six recrudescent agenda years occurred after 1977.

Moving from the raw number of constitutional cases decided each year to the proportionate agenda data, a similar picture emerges. Using a similar

Figure 4.14 Recrudescent Agenda Years in Constitutional Matters
Based on Raw Number of Annual Constitutional Cases, 1904–2000
(When Threshold = 14 Cases per Year)

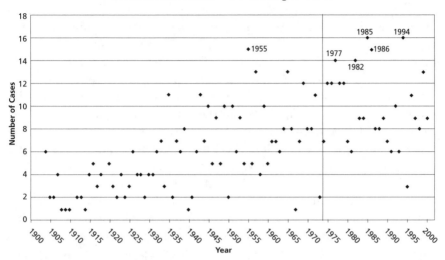

Figure 4.15 Recrudescent Agenda Years in Constitutional Matters Based on
Percentage of Agenda Space, 1904–2000, With 5-Year Moving Average
(When threshold ≥ 20 Percent)

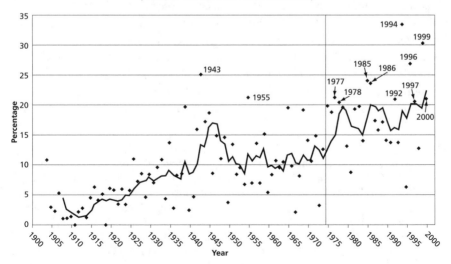

standard for the data concerning the proportion of the Court's annual agenda dedicated to constitutional matters—if recrudescent agenda years are ones where 20 percent or more of the annual agenda went to constitutional matters—then twelve years qualify. *Ten of the twelve recrudescent agenda years were after 1977 and eight occurred during or after the Mason Court, which further confirms a shift from private to public law matters.* When looking at the constitutional cases decided in these twelve years, it appears that in some years the Court issued a cluster of judgments concerning a single clause or provision in the constitution. In 1977, for example, inconsistencies between Commonwealth and state laws were particularly germane. That next year freedom of interstate trade was prominent. Recrudescent agenda years in the early 1990s reflect the Court deciding clusters of cases concerning Commonwealth powers, in particular the scope of Parliament's legislative powers.[24] In 1999 and 2000, the Court appeared to shift its attention to constitutional cases concerning judicial power and federal jurisdiction questions.[25] Illustrative here is the *Re Wakim* (1999) decision, where the Court concluded that cross-vesting schemes that many states had enacted, where state parliaments confer state jurisdictional powers on federal courts, was an unconstitutional exercise of power. Similarly the *Sue v. Hill* (1999) case put before the Court whether a Queensland senator, Heather Hill, elected to the Commonwealth parliament satisfied the constitution's prohibition of electing a "citizen of a foreign power" because at the time of her election she held dual citizenship with Australia and the U.K. The Court concluded that while the U.K. could not be considered "a foreign power" when Australia federated in 1901, it gradually became so through a number of twentieth-century legal developments. This constitutional separation was fully realized before Hill's election, rendering her a citizen of a foreign power and therefore ineligible to hold office. Explaining why these case clusters emerged when they did is a complicated matter—one that is beyond my purpose here. What should be noted, however, is that constitutional law gained a heightened salience during the past twenty years.

---

24. For example, relevant cases decided in 1994 include *Svikart v. Steward* (1994) 125 ALR 554; *Wallis v. Downard-Pickford (North Queensland) Pty Ltd.* (1994) 120 ALR 440; *P v. P* (1994) 120 ALR 545; *Re Alcan Australia Ltd. And Others; Ex Parte Federation of Industrial, Manufacturing And Engineering Employees* (1994) 123 ALR 193; *Health Insurance Commission v. Peverill* (1994) 119 ALR 675.

25. See *Abebe v. Commonwealth* (1999) 55 ALR 1; *Re Wakim and Others* (1999) 163 ALR 270; *Yanner v. Eaton* (1999) 166 ALR 258; *Sue v. Hill* (1999) 163 ALR 648; *Attorney-General (Cth) v. Breckler & Others* (1999) 163 ALR 576.

What made this period such a watershed? The institutional reforms mentioned above—enactment of the special leave requirement and establishment of the Federal Court of Australia—decreased the High Court's workload and enhanced its constitutional litigation. These two reforms together enabled the Court to select cases it wanted to decide and to filter out those that would have it operate as a first-tier appellate court or a court of first instance. One should not be surprised, therefore, that with these reforms more agenda space became available for cases that were of true national importance that required attention from a final appellate court. The Court all along served as the final arbiter in constitutional conflicts, but the reforms served to concentrate the agenda on constitutional questions. In sum, the "constitutionalized agenda" provides solid support for my informants' claims that the Mason Court brought a shift in focus from private to public law.

Not only did constitutional cases take on heightened salience, according to informants, but the nature of constitutional disputes changed with the transformation. Federalism questions (state-versus-state and state-versus-Commonwealth) under the old orthodoxy gave way to more individual, rights-oriented disputes. Appellate judges I spoke with widely agreed that the Mason Court promoted the idea that the constitution has much to say about relationships between individuals and government. A Commonwealth Solicitor-General reflected:

> When I took office, it was still the case that the constitutional litigation was basically an issue of governmental power—the question of limitations of Commonwealth and state power. Those issues still exist.... [B]ut increasingly ... these issues of the relationship between the government and those governed have emerged as the creative area where the High Court has been prepared to expound new and previously non-existent doctrine (127).

A NSW appellate judge concurred: "Constitutional issues changed dramatically in the last decade from being primarily federalist issues to primarily human rights issues. I'll use that as a label. But as a state solicitor-general, at the beginning of the ten years, nearly all the cases were states against federal. By the end of the ten years, in more and more of the cases the solicitors-general were all lining up on one side against the subjects, the citizens, and the individual (123)." Another judge described it this way: "What's more marked in the last twenty years is that the constitution is now concerned with social matters. In Dixon's time it was concerned with Section 92 matters and relationships between the states and the Commonwealth. Constitutional law is now concerned more about people and citizens' positions within society (117:830)." This is not to suggest that federalism disputes no longer concern the Court. What occurred during the Mason Court, however, was that the broad tenor of constitutional disputes dealt more with individuals' interactions with government, at whatever level, than disputes between the state and national governments.

To assess this claim, I examined tables published in each CLR volume (for years 1941 to 2002)[26] that report what sections of the constitution the Court "considered" in the cases reported in that volume. The tables also indicate how many cases reported in that CLR volume dealt with each clause of the constitution. When a CLR volume reports that the Court "considered" a section of the constitution, that means simply that at least one case in the volume dealt with or addressed the cited constitutional section. It does not mean necessarily that the case brought new meaning to the section or that the section was necessarily the locus of the litigation. Frequency tables were constructed for each of the constitution's 128 sections across the fifty-nine years, which provide a longitudinal map for what sections were litigated and when. The assumption is that not all sections were litigated or "considered" equally all the time; some provisions of the constitution were afforded greater attention at certain points in High Court history than others. The factors that may lead to certain emphases and not others are variegated, complex, and beyond the scope of this section. But what I intend to demonstrate, using this longitudinal map, is that the nature of constitutional litigation changed during the century.

It is first valuable to assemble a macro-picture of constitutional litigation for the years in question. Which constitutional sections, for instance, garnered the most attention? Figure 4.16 charts the cumulative frequency with which the Court considered each section. The most litigated constitutional sections from 1941 to 2002 were Section 51 (Parliament's powers), Section 92 (interstate trade regulation), Section 109 (requiring consistency between state and national laws), and Sections 75 and 76 (concerning High Court jurisdiction). It should come as little surprise that a handful of sections garnered most of the Court's attention, and that Section 51 was at the top of the list. Akin to Article II, Section 8 of the U.S. Constitution, Section 51 enumerates powers granted to the Commonwealth Parliament. These enumerations are more numerous and detailed than in the U.S. document. Section 51 begins, "The

---

26. The data are reported and plotted by CLR volume number. A single volume of the CLRs may report cases decided in more than one year, so the X-axis reports CLR volume numbers, but the year labels are rough estimates. The CLR tables do not disaggregate the "clause considered" data by year. I began with CLR volume 65 (1941) and ended with CLR volume 208 (2002).

Figure 4.16 Cumulative Frequency That High Court "Considered" Each Section of the Constitution, 1941–2002

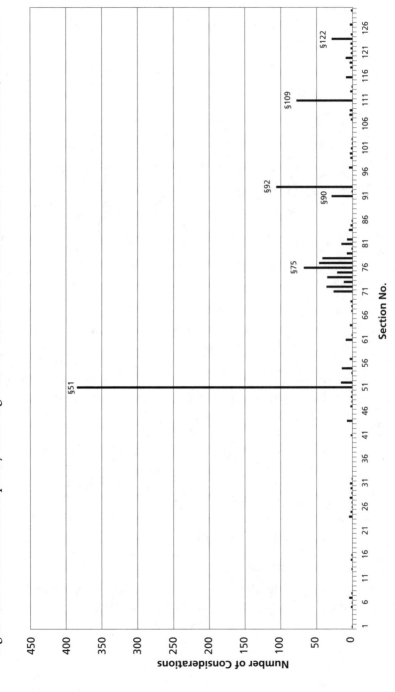

**Figure 4.17 Diachronic Display of High Court Considerations
of Section 51 Grouped by CLR Volume, 1941–2002**

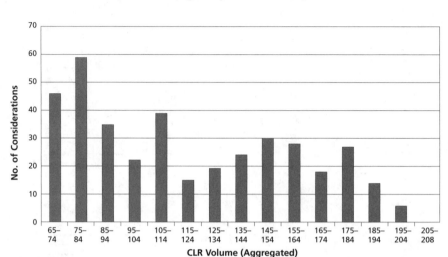

Parliament shall ... have power to make laws for the peace, order, and good government of the Commonwealth *with respect to ...*" and proceeds to enumerate thirty-nine powers. These include the power to regulate trade, the economy, and industry, to defend the country, to give effect to international treaties and conventions, to tax, and so on. Much of the litigation on this section has addressed whether particular federal statutes were enacted *with respect to* an enumerated power. Making this determination is a two-step process for the Court: first, determine the meaning and scope of the enumerated power (an exercise in constitutional interpretation), and then determine whether the statute falls within the ambit of the enumerated power. This second step, known in legalese as "characterization," requires the Court to give consideration also to Australia's necessary and proper clause, Section 51(xxxix). It provides Parliament with the power to legislate in "matters incidental to the execution of any power vested by this Constitution." This is not the place to explore Section 51 jurisprudence or approaches the Court has taken toward characterization.[27] Much change has occurred in how the Court understands this section, but Figure 4.17 demonstrates that the Court dedicated consistent attention to Section 51 over the years.

---

27. See Zines (1996), chapters 4, 5, 13, and 14.

Section 92 was the second most litigated clause—the constitutional requirement that interstate trade remain "absolutely free." A labyrinth of conflicting decisions came from the Court as the century unfolded, whipsawing the clause's meaning and scope. Some conceived it as an individual rights clause. Others saw it establishing free trade relations between the states. The High Court recently wrote of this Gordian knot: "No provision of the Constitution has been the source of greater judicial concern or the subject of greater judicial effort than Section 92. That notwithstanding, judicial exegesis of the section has yielded neither clarity of meaning nor certainty of operation."[28] This dictum came in *Cole v. Whitfield* (1988), where the Mason Court cast aside over one hundred contradictory and confusing precedents with a unanimous judgment that brought much clarity to Section 92. The Court lamented that the section "had not achieved a settled or accepted interpretation at any time since federation" and found this "unacceptable."[29] Looking to the framers' intent, the Court concluded that the clause was supposed to create "a free trade area throughout the Commonwealth" and deny the Commonwealth or states power to prevent "the free movement of people, goods, and communication across state lines."[30] The Court then articulated a new principle to guide lower courts. Section 92 was to provide a freedom from "discriminatory burdens of a protectionist kind." Testing whether a law violates Section 92 in this way must begin with the question of whether the law applies to both interstate and intrastate trade. If so, it is "less likely to be protectionist," and therefore less likely to offend Section 92. If, on the other hand, the law discriminates against interstate trade "on its face" or "in the factual operation" then it violates Section 92.[31] The Court will look at form and substance in evaluating a law's impact on interstate trade. That is, does it discriminate against interstate trade on its face? Second, does it discriminate against interstate trade in its operation? The Mason Court broke with earlier precedent in asking this second question on the law's substantive impact. Earlier courts only looked at laws on face value and not how they operated in the real world. The statute under question in *Cole*, which set minimum standards for crayfish harvesting in Tasmania, was deemed discriminatory neither in form nor effect. An intended consequence of *Cole* was that it brought such clarity to Section 92 that interstate trade litigation dropped precipitously since

---

28. 165 CLR 360, 383.
29. Ibid., 383-384.
30. Ibid., 391.
31. *Cole v. Whitfield And Another* (1988) 78 ALR 42.

**Figure 4.18 Diachronic Display of High Court Considerations
of Section 92 Grouped by CLR Volume, 1941–2002**

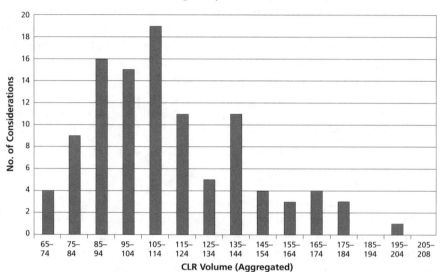

1988. Trade disputes still arise, but with *Cole's* "form and substance" test, lower courts are able to resolve them. Figure 4.18 maps the frequency with which the Court handled Section 92 cases. It confirms my informants' perspectives that interstate commerce questions had occupied the Court like few issues since the 1940s, but that *Cole* nearly evanesced this litigation.

Cole cleared the constitutional decks of Section 92 disputes, which according to some judges, provided the Mason Court with newfound space to explore other constitutional issues. An appellate judge remarked, "For many years, one of the most notorious sections of the constitution was Section 92, which was concerned with free trade. That attracted a large amount of work to the High Court.... [I]t reached a point that the activities of individuals, if it could be said they involved interstate trade, were virtually uncontrollable. [*Cole*] brought that all to an end.... [T]here was a total revision (34:630)." A High Court judge confirmed the Court's concerted desire to clean up and clarify Section 92: "[In] *Cole v. Whitfield* ... a unanimous judgment was assembled in order to promote clarity and coherence and guide interpretation and understanding of the constitutional text (63:2930)." Another High Court judge agreed that the historical treatment of Section 92 vacillated significantly, but with *Cole* "the Court came up with a decision that has been generally, if not universally accepted, and in effect terminated the never-ending litigation of this section of the constitution (122:10615)." Closing off this persistent litigation enabled the Mason Court to focus on issues it found more pressing.

SUMMARY

The Mason Court profoundly departed from the older orthodox understanding of the High Court's role in the legal and political systems. This chapter categorized these changes along four dimensions. The first (and foundational) dimension concerned the Mason Court's shifting stance toward the purposes of law. Rather than law providing certainty, informants and Mason Court judges alike said that questions of fairness and justice took priority during the 1980s and 1990s. This shift in first principles was reflected in the other three dimensions. For instance, the aim of appellate litigation moved from emphasizing dispute resolution toward a public model, in which High Court litigation is conceived as both a legal and political exercise. Given this, the politicized role encourages judges to take fuller stock of the broad issues that particular cases raise and explore materials that may better inform their decision-making. This tendency was apparent in the quest for overarching principles and more frequent reliance on non-British authorities and arguments. It also was evident in the Court considering more fully the consequences of its decisions and in soliciting governmental and private interventions in litigation. Give this revised conception of appellate litigation, it is not surprising that the politicized role acknowledges forthrightly that judges are more than mere interpreters or discoverers of law, but in fact creators of it.

Wider recognition that High Court judges make law leads to a corresponding alteration in how the judges interact with the legal and political systems. It became readily apparent from my interview data that the 1980s and 1990s were the most pivotal years in High Court history. Notwithstanding politically explosive decisions during the 1950s, the Mason Court came under unprecedented criticism, in part because of how it redefined the Court's interactions with the public and the political system. The politicized role it asserted accommodates judges speaking out in public on legal and political issues. It sees judges as civic educators and accepts that the Court inevitably comes into conflict with Parliament. The politicized role does not recoil from such institutional conflict. Indeed, the fusion of legislative and executive power, as well as legislative gridlock on controversial issues, exposed the Court to added controversy.

The final dimension involves changes that occurred to the High Court's workload under the politicized role conception. During the Mason Court, constitutional cases came to the forefront to an unprecedented extent. I argued that a significant number of "recrudescent agenda years" occurred during the Mason Court in constitutional law. In addition to the Court paying greater attention to constitutional matters, the chapter also discussed how the nature of those disputes has changed. Issues that had occupied the Court like few others (Section 92 interstate trade for example) were supplanted by a heightened interest in protecting the individual from the state. This next chapter takes up the ways in which legal reasoning itself changed with the Mason Court.

5

LEGAL REASONING IN THE MASON COURT

Just as the Mason Court reoriented its relationship to law, its normative aims in appellate litigation, and its interactions with the broader political system, so too it challenged several orthodox tenets regarding legal reasoning and constitutional interpretation. As discussed in chapter 3, legal formalism dominated the Court for much of the twentieth century. It placed a high premium on logic, deduction, textual and structural modalities to constitutional interpretation, and a robust commitment to stare decisis. My informants spoke with great assurance about formalism's dominance under the orthodox tradition. I confronted equal certainty among my informants about the reforms that came with the Mason Court. This chapter presents evidence that the judicial role transformation cemented a new rhetoric, if not a new judicial ethic, about how judges reach and articulate decisions. As with other aspects of the judicial role transformation, I did not find universal endorsement of the changes, though nearly all agreed that they occurred. This chapter begins by describing several general changes to legal reasoning. It then focuses on reforms in constitutional interpretation, norms regarding stare decisis and legal tests, and finally, conceptions of how and why law changes. The judges had much to say about these dimensions—so much so that they could fill a separate monograph on these topics alone. In the interest of space and this book's larger aim, I will provide illustrative evidence of the changes that my informants saw to legal reasoning during the Mason era.

If one described in a single sentence the changes that the Mason Court brought to legal reasoning it would be this: Legal realism secured a footing in a judicial culture where formalism long dominated. Changes came in a number of areas, but the mosaic that forms when one fuses these changes depicts a judiciary moving from a pre-legal realist stage to a realist stage, from a judicial role that sees legal reasoning in mechanistic terms to one that recognizes discretion and choice. Australia's judicial culture is still grappling with the meaning, scope, and consequences of the new realist understanding of judicial decision-making. Judges have not moved, as yet, to what might be labeled post-legal realist jurisprudence, typified in the U.S., for instance, by the critical legal studies movement, critical race theory, law and economics scholarship, or feminist and postmodern jurisprudence. This does not mean that Australian academics are not writing from these perspectives. Many scholars are.[1] Rather, the judges themselves have yet to imbibe post-legal realist theories or have yet to manifest these influences in their decisions. However, consensus emerged among my informants around four changes that the Mason Court brought to legal reasoning, constitutional interpretation, the use of precedent, and approaches toward constructing legal tests. These areas coincide with dimensions 4, 5, and 6 of the orthodoxy discussed in chapter 3.

DIMENSION #4: ACKNOWLEDGING THE DISCRETION IN LEGAL REASONING

The reader will recall from chapter 3 that the orthodoxy promoted a mechanical notion of legal reasoning, in which a judge's quest was to find the one correct answer for each case. The politicized role, on the other hand, accepts that judicial decision-making involves choice. Appellate judges exercise discretion when deciding cases. The Mason Court was less beholden to the idea that legal reasoning is a completely logical, deductive enterprise; decision-making is not simply a process of pulling legal levers to get the correct answer. Rather, the Court forthrightly acknowledged that sometimes more than one plausible interpretation can be given to a statute, constitutional provision, or legal rule. What distinguished the Mason Court from its predecessors (and the politicized role from the orthodoxy) was its admission that choice and discretion are part of decision-making. Informants described this change in a variety of ways: a simple "difference in approach (122:104)," "a radical change from black letter law and strict legalism (83)," and "a complete wind change (86)." The Chief Justice of a state supreme court spoke for many colleagues when he stated:

> There is less literalism now than there once was....I think there has been a shift...toward a reasoning that acknowledges that the choices being made aren't simply matters of deduction or induction....The change is most clear at the High Court level, where rightly the High Court has acknowledged that, particularly in the common law, language is such that previous precedents do present you with choices

---

1. See Davies (1996) for entrée to this literature.

and those choices can't be made just with logical deduction or in-
duction, and have to be made with reference to values (82:345).

Another judge concurred, "There has been much of a departure from a legalistic approach and much more of a readiness to apply accepted doctrines in
either novel ways or extended ways....The sea change might be in this area
where courts acknowledge that they create the law. Formerly that wasn't the
case, although in practice it's been accepted that the common law is moved
by accretions on a case by case basis (10:1615)."

The politicized role also involves an outright skepticism about the orthodoxy's claim that legal reasoning is mechanistic. It questions the veracity of how Dixon described the reasoning process (even his own) as "strict
and complete legalism." Several informants believed that legalism itself veiled
the policy preferences and discretion that earlier generations of appellate
judges no doubt confronted and often acted upon. A Mason Court judge remarked:

> I think a [shift] in legal reasoning has occurred in form if not in sub-
> stance. The notion of strict and complete legalism, which was re-
> garded as the hallmark of Dixonian legal thought, masked the enor-
> mous capacity of Sir Owen Dixon and other judges to articulate
> concepts which were significantly different from those articulated in
> earlier judgments. I have in mind cases in which doctrines of res ju-
> dicata and estoppel were raised....Now these were cases which though
> they were said to come under the rubric of strict and complete legal-
> ism, in fact used the words to conflate concepts with great and per-
> haps radical significance (63:1230).

A Federal Court judge said that the legalism label, used to describe the Dixonian period, really marks a different style of expressing conclusions. This judge
suggested:

> There has been a change in how legal reasoning is expressed. I don't
> believe there has been a fundamental change in how judges approach
> cases....I don't believe judges came to views any differently then.
> Judges are moved by the arguments—they don't change in hundred
> year slabs....Different techniques are used to get to what the judge
> thinks is the right result. The categorization of present times as lib-
> eral, non-literal as compared to earlier times of literalist is to create
> a distinction where there isn't one. Saying that requires you to pene-
> trate beyond the façade of the law reports and analyze how judges
> think about cases and get to decisions. That's the important thing.

That's the decisive thing. How it's dressed up might change as a matter of fashion (12:1245).

Another offered, "When some of us talk about a golden age of legalism...and
a wild, unruly modern era, I'm just not sure there's too much difference....
Judges at the top level have frequently been capable of achieving what many
might regard as radical results. There has to be a perspective kept on the labels used....The tools of the black letter lawyer and a radical activist may not
be that different (83)." A Federal Court judge challenged the claim that earlier
generations of judges were true Dixon devotees. "Rarely do you find cases
where judges decide cases contrary to their sense of right because of black letter requirements. It doesn't work that way. Judges are too intelligent and independent and always have been (12:1545)." A barrister who had frequent appearances before the High Court agreed: "Dixonian legalism...[required] as
many value judgments as there are today (2)." Another barrister quipped, "Legalism is a self-deception (68:500)." How then could orthodox judges operate
for so long under what many contemporary judges see as false pretense? A
South Australia judge, for example, concluded that previous generations of
judges "weren't knowingly deceiving the public" when they claimed that logic
and deduction drove their decision-making. He continued:

> They believed it....What it brings home to you is the force on your own
> mind of a professional culture that tells you this is how it is....Gener-
> ations of judges didn't fully understand what they were doing and
> thought they were reasoning by logic and analogy of a kind that was
> value-free. Now we see that there are choices that are value-laden and
> made by reference to intuitive views not set out in judgments (82:715).

Others made more individualistic assessments. "Judges like the feeling of
self-delusion that they are deciding the law in accordance with strict precedent
and logic. Judges don't like to think about deciding cases in accordance with
their set of values. But that's what we all do (77)." According to a Federal Court
judge, "'Dixon' became a dirty word....For my generation, he was someone
you were anxious to take apart and prove was wrong." When asked why Dixon
had become such a pariah, the judge said, "There were two aspects. The first
was simple rebellion against any one person dictating what Australian law
should be. The second was the very opaqueness of Dixon. Some people would
say clever....But you could never really understand what he meant. There were
too many qualifications, caveats, escape routes....That lack of transparency...
made one basically want to kick him, to kick against it (113:1930)." This sentiment was echoed by another judge who clerked in the High Court when

Dixon was Chief Justice. "As the years have gone by, my admiration for [Dixon] remains....He was truly a giant....That idea of strict legalism was an idea that he propounded, but it ultimately led the Court...down a dead end from which there was no way to go except back....My own view is that it's too rigid and one has to be more flexible (34:2130)." Whatever the motivation for advancing legalism as a convenient label, if not a practical mode of legal reasoning, I found broad consensus that members of the Mason Court sought to distance themselves from Dixon and acknowledge the choices that confronted them.

Another change that the Mason Court brought to legal reasoning was a greater acceptance that decision-making may require judges to draw from community values. In a sense, community values animate the law when the law is enacted through democratic means. A community values life, so its laws condemn murder. It values the possession and enjoyment of property, so its laws condemn theft. Australia's orthodoxy tells judges that they give expression to community values by following the black letter of the law. The orthodoxy's expectation that judges separate themselves from the political system carries with it the belief that judges are incapable of identifying what "the community" thinks about a particular matter, save for whatever is said in the written law. As a Federal Court judge offered, "It's dangerous to speculate on what the majority will is. The only safe guide is to regard the majority will as what's expressed in Commonwealth legislation." To the orthodox judge then, a statute requiring mandatory sentencing for criminal defendants convicted of certain crimes articulates a community value. In this view, an immigration minister following administrative guidelines for evaluating asylum seekers is also following the community's desires as promulgated in the law.

The Mason Court took a quite different approach to the role of community values in decision-making. It assigned judges greater leeway in tapping community values. My informants suggested that under the Mason Court, the judges made assessments and conclusions of what the community's values were on particular matters, regardless of whether Parliament had enacted legislation on those matters. Their legal reasoning allowed them to explore and rely upon the community's mores and norms in their decisions.

The best example of the Mason Court's willingness to draw upon community values is *Mabo*. In striking down the *terra nullius* doctrine, part of its justification was that the doctrine was at odds with contemporary community values. Justice Brennan, who wrote the lead opinion, said

> Whatever the justification advanced in earlier days for refusing to recognize the rights and interests in land of the indigenous inhabitants of settled colonies, an unjust and discriminatory doctrine of that kind

can no longer be accepted. *The expectations of the international community accord in this respect with the contemporary values of the Australian people....It is contrary both to international standards and to the fundamental values of our own common law to entrench a discriminatory rule* (emphasis added).[2]

In the end, the majority overturned *terra nullius* and recognized native title based on an examination of contemporary Australian moral standards and precedent from the International Court of Justice.[3]

Another example where the Mason Court appealed to community values was the 1992 *Dietrich* decision. Here the Court concluded that a criminal defendant's lack of counsel during a trial may demand a stay if it created an unfair proceeding. The Court again relied upon an appeal to community values to justify its decision:

> The genius of the common law system consists in the ability of the courts to mould the law to correspond with the contemporary values of society. Had the courts not kept the common law in serviceable condition...its rules would now be regarded as remnants of history which had escaped the shipwreck of time....The reluctance of the Courts in earlier times to acknowledge that function was due in part to the theory that it was the exclusive function of the legislature.... But legislatures have disappointed the theorists and the Courts have been left with a substantial part of the responsibility for keeping the law in a serviceable state, a function which calls for consideration of the contemporary values of the community.[4]

Brennan then acknowledged his institution's competency for identifying community values: "[J]udicial experience in the practical application of legal principles and the coincidence of judicial opinions in appellate courts provide some assurance that those values are correctly perceived."[5] In other words, being a judge provides a set of experiences and demands certain thought processes that enable judges to identify what the community's will is in a particular circumstance.

This new approach to community values engendered mixed responses among High Court and other appellate court judges. Critics of this approach

---

2. *Mabo*, 42.

3. Specifically, J. Brennan refers to the International Court of Justice's Advisory Opinion in *Western Sahara* (1975) 62 ICJR at 39. There the Court decided that continued use of the theory of *terra nullius* requires that the land truly be unoccupied.

4. *Dietrich v. The Queen* (1992) 177 CLR 292, 319.

5. Ibid.

claim that High Court judges are not positioned to make such determinations. Judges certainly confront issues that the community cares about and has interests in, but there are drawbacks to courts relying on perceived community values. First, judicial proceedings may not provide a reliable venue to identify and explore just what the community thinks. Second, the notion that a community ascribes to certain values is "a very slippery concept," as one judge remarked (89:2130). Another judge cautioned, "I don't know if judges always know what those community values are. Judges still come from a narrow field of society and reflect a narrow view, so we should not be too bold (77)." A Federal Court judge worried, "It's very dangerous if a judge starts to arrogate to himself a function of identifying majority will or community standards.... [I]t's dangerous because of judges' limited experience and exposure (28:2315)." This democratic legitimacy critique of the Court identifying community values emerged in several interviews. It was simply put and put often, "The legislature reflects the community. The judges don't reflect the community really (70:1630)."

If critics worried about judges being too far removed from a community to really assess its values, those who endorsed it tended to hold skeptical views about the democratic institutions acting any better upon such values. They were jaundiced toward the political process fully vetting community opinion because of reelection concerns. Removed from such pressures, judges could better tap community perspectives. A NSW appellate judge observed: "Politics is convenient and the judiciary should not be convenient. Politics usually reacts to a set of circumstances and acts to get a result and stay in power. The judiciary should not be like that. There should be steadfastness about the judiciary.... We have to be closer to the community and [have] a close understanding of trends, ways of thinking, [and] social circumstances in the community (58:11830)." A Mason Court judge provided the following rejoinder to the argument that judges are inept surveyors of community values:

> [Legal reasoning] does involve the application of community values.... The difficulty is...how do you determine community values? Are judges any better at determining [them] than others?... Once judges replaced juries, judges had to apply community standards in a whole range of issues....I don't think there is much force in the view that it's difficult to determine community values. It's a part of a judge's function. The other thing about judges is this: it's not as if they're ivory tower people. They're hearing cases day by day and in... listening to evidence they're in a much better position to know how the community responds, acts, [and] behaves than the vast majority

of people. They're not ill-equipped to determine what community values are (122:1800).

A fourth broad change that came with the role transformation was an acknowledgement that appellate judges should be forthright in articulating the reasons that truly underpin their decisions. Whereas orthodox reasoning may have veiled the genuine choices that judges confront, the politicized role encourages appellate judges to be honest about the range of factors that they consider. In other words, if an appeal to community values or consideration of economic or social consequences influences a judge's decision, then those factors should be articulated. A Western Australia Supreme Court judge commented, "I'm not at all convinced that the difference isn't just that courts today are just more frank about the process. I think the sea change might be in that area." This assertion seemed affirmed when a High Court Justice claimed, "There has been a shift toward greater realism and candor [in recent years]." Reflecting on his own reasoning, the judge admitted:

> Certainly in my own writing, I strive to be honest about the choices and to acknowledge that whether it's in constitutional interpretation, statutory interpretation, or finding a common law rule it's not a mechanical function. It's an evaluative function and in that evaluation there are frequently powerful reasons and counter reasons. The judge's function is not to find the only solution but to find the preferable solution (116:400).

A Victoria appellate judge thought that the last twenty years had brought more "honesty about the judicial process." He continued, "Things that the High Court did in the past were social engineering, but it was done in a secretive way. Barwick's interpretation of income tax legislation was social engineering—that's acknowledged. When it comes to duty of care in negligence and notions of proximity, the Court is being honest and frank in the extent to which they are responding to community needs (65:1100)." A Federal Court judge remarked, "Our judges, as they express themselves, are more inclined to open up the values behind their reasoning and the merits than judges were earlier....I think if you went back forty years ago, the judges were coming to similar outcomes and had a similar approach, but didn't express it so openly (57:2730)." Another judge said, "It's desirable that [judges] should say where they are in fact stretching, extending, or changing things [and] what they're doing, rather than saying it's inherent and I'm articulating what's already there—articulating what's unarticulated. The world deserves more honesty (65:1300)."

A barrister with an extensive High Court practice found that, "[Mason Court] judges are just more frank to articulate the underlying values that drive decisions. Values always drive decisions. The difference is that legalism had an element of pretense for conservative values. An inactive court is just as value-laden as an active—they just are not articulated (106:2000)." Finally, a Federal Court judge offered the following analogy about this judicial honesty: "You see parallels in the sexual revolution where in Victorian times woman wore long skirts and discussion of sex was not on the menu. These days sex is discussed openly....There's a frankness, an honesty, an openness where it's regarded as proper to get to the heart of things—not to skirt around and mythologize (12:1715)."

A handful of informants thought no change occurred at all. "I wouldn't think there has been any change. There may be particular instances, but generally there is still a fairly rigorous examination of precedent, a consideration of the consequences of deciding a dispute one way or another. I think if you go back and read the old judgments of Dixon and Latham it was differently expressed but the reasoning is as rigorous now as it was then (95:2000)." While I discovered wide agreement that the transformation ushered in a period of greater High Court candor, skeptics were not hard to find either. Many lamented it. My exchange with a NSW appellate judge provides a colorful illustration:

> Judge: I think [the High Court] has drifted towards a form of socio-political reasoning. It essentially has nothing to do with law at all.
>
> Q: What cases come to mind when you make that statement?
>
> Judge: All the recent constitutional cases on implied rights come within that. If, for example, they were going to say that the Constitution guarantees free speech, the Dixonian lawyer would say, "We have to look at the document and say where is it? Is it expressed? Is it here by implication?" What the smart, new people do is no go to any of that. They say, "Is free speech a good thing? Would our founding fathers have liked it if they had seen it?" Then we'll pretend it's there even though it's not. Seems to me to be extraordinary reasoning.
>
> Q: What precipitated this shift in legal reasoning?
>
> Judge: Incessant left-wing consumerism that people have been bellowing out for years. It eventually just all happened.
>
> Q: Could you unpack that for me?

Judge: People have been saying that it doesn't matter what the law says. You must make it what the people want. It doesn't matter what the law says, you must make certain it doesn't upset the feminists. If you get any legal journal, you'll find that there is almost no space left to struggle with legal concepts. No one I find reports on the assignability of bills for exchange, for example, but you'll find millions of articles on "women's lib" or gender language or some such. It's just the climate of the day I think. I think it's a reflex of what popular thinking…is all about these days, just as totalitarianism was popular thinking in the thirties (3:1).

Another judge offered a psychological explanation for the changes that came to legal reasoning.

Judge: Yes, a shift has occurred. It's part of a more grass roots phenomenon that it's okay to express feelings.…Tell it as it is and say how you feel. If you let that go to an extreme you get to barbarism, but at the moment it is regarded philosophically and morally at the highest level. Instead of being hidebound by precedent, convention, statute, you say the law as you feel it is and that's good! It's a cathartic experience, like going to a psychologist to have analysis, telling the psychologist how you really feel about life.

Q: Justices Mason and Kirby were just getting in touch with their feelings?

Judge: That's right, although I didn't mean that exactly. You can't isolate these currents from what's happening in western society generally where the power and merit of the individual have been taken to another stage—that expressing innermost feelings is really good. It is a way of living life in a good way and therefore laying down the law in accordance with your own moral code is good.…You let it out (105:1130)!

These two exchanges nicely capture the notion that the appellate judge should tell what she thinks the law should be, express what factors really enter into her decisions, give credence to community values, and recognize the discretion that the decision-making process affords. Against this backdrop of broad changes to legal reasoning, the next section describes the Mason Court's reforms to constitutional interpretation.

CONSTITUTIONAL INTERPRETATION

Informants were not short on opinions about what changes the Mason Court introduced regarding constitutional interpretation. The reader will recall from chapter 3 that the orthodox conception of the Commonwealth Constitution was to view it as a power distribution document. Containing few expressed rights and no bill of rights, the constitution and the litigation surrounding it for most of the twentieth century focused on the proper distribution of powers between the federal and state governments. Its framers have been criticized for borrowing so heavily from the U.S. Constitution those power distribution provisions, but little else. They borrowed from the U.S. document at a "secondary machinery level" but adopoted none of its spirit. As one scholar put it, the framers drew "on its most conservative, least inspiring features—jettisoning the rest (McLachlan 1989)." This allegedly produced a constitutionally "frozen continent" (Sawer 1967). The High Court's orthodox role in constitutional litigation historically, therefore, was as an institutional boundary enforcer. It did not look to the constitution as embodying the polity's enduring values and principles. It comes as little surprise, then, that the orthodoxy's approach toward constitutional interpretation was not too dissimilar from its rules for statutory interpretation: textualism and structuralism were the preferred modalities. In chapter 4 we saw how constitutional issues have become more salient over the last twenty years and how the nature of constitutional disputes has increasingly addressed individuals' relationships to government. This section considers how the accepted modes of constitutional interpretation evolved during the Mason Court. Three such developments emerged from my interview data.

The Implied Rights Jurisprudence

The first was the Mason Court's concerted effort to identify and promote values that infuse the constitutional regime but remain unarticulated in the constitution itself. Just as the Mason Court searched for overarching principles in several areas of private law, it similarly sought unarticulated first principles in constitutional law. "The U.S. Constitution, though older, is so much more sophisticated than ours," said a Queensland appellate judge, "because it recognizes that the majority are not entitled to give effect to their will against fundamental values. The thing that the Mason Court did so effectively was that at a critical time in this move toward national maturity, it found legally legitimate, albeit progressive, methods of trying to build some of those fundamental values into our system (87:2300)." The moniker given to these cases was "the implied rights cases."

The genesis of the implied rights jurisprudence in the 1990s may be regarded as the most consequential development in Australian constitutional interpretation during the last half century. In capsule form, the Mason Court abandoned the orthodox understanding that the constitution contains only those rights expressly stated in it. Beginning in the early 1990s, the Court held in a series of cases that the constitution contains fundamental rights and freedoms that are *implied* in the document and that operate as judicially enforceable limits on Parliament's power. That is, the constitution's text carries certain consequences that are not expressly stated. One must be cautious not to hyperbolize this development—the High Court's scope of implied protections pales in comparison to rights protected under the U.S. Bill of Rights, the Canadian Charter, and even New Zealand's Bill of Rights. Nonetheless, one must underscore the significance of the implied rights cases for the profound change they wrought in constitutional interpretation.

The effort began with the 1992 *Nationwide News v. Wills*[6] and *Australian Capital Television v. Commonwealth*[7] cases. The High Court concluded in these cases that Sections 7 and 24 of the constitution that call for "representative government" imply a right to free political discussion. The question raised in the *Nationwide News* case was whether a newspaper that had published an article challenging the integrity of the Australian Industrial Relations Commission, could be prosecuted under a Commonwealth statute that prohibited persons from speaking or writing in a manner that brought the Commission "into disrepute."[8] The Court unanimously invalidated this section of the Act, with three justices basing their decisions on a constitutionally implied freedom of political speech. Chief Justice Brennan well summarized the logic:

> To sustain a representative democracy embodying the principles prescribed by the Constitution, freedom of public discussion of political and economic matters is essential.... [It] would be a parody of democracy to confer on the people a power to choose their Parliament but to deny the freedom of public discussion....Freedom of public discussion...is inherent in the idea of a representative democracy.[9]

The *Australian Capital Television* case involved a challenge to the *Political Broadcasts and Political Disclosures Act 1991* that banned certain types of po-

---

6. (1992) 177 CLR 1.
7. (1992) 177 CLR 106.
8. *Commonwealth Industrial Relations Act*, sec. 299(1)(d)(ii).
9. *Nationwide News*, 47–48.

litical broadcasting and advertising leading up to elections. A broadcaster claimed that the ban infringed a fundamental implied right of political discussion. Here, too, the majority held that the principle of representative democracy was the basis for the implied freedom, and that the provision was invalid because it infringed on this freedom.[10]

The Court extended this freedom several years later in the *Theophanous* (1994) case, where the justices considered whether it protects someone who makes untrue or defamatory statements. A defamation suit was brought against *The Herald & Weekly Times* for publishing a letter that referred to a parliamentarian as an "idiot" and someone who "stood for most things that most Australians are against."[11] This was the Court's first occasion to explore the interchange between this newly created constitutional freedom and the common law of defamation. Four of seven judges concluded that the constitutionally implied right should override the common law of defamation. The majority drew upon *ACTV* and *Nationwide News* to create a positive protection against defamation liability. The Court was careful not to create a general constitutional freedom of speech, but protected instead a more limited freedom centered on "political discussion" or "political discourse."[12] According to *Theophanous*, a publisher is immune from defamation actions if the following conditions are met: 1) the publisher was unaware of the material's falsity, 2) it did not publish the material recklessly, and 3) the publication was reasonable given the circumstances. Like the U.S. Supreme Court's decision in *New York Times v. Sullivan*,[13] *Theophanous* provided a constitutional defense against defamation liability. The Court concluded: "Because the system of representative government depends for its efficacy on the free flow of information and ideas... the freedom extends to all those who participate in political discussion.... [This implied right] better equips the elected to make decisions and the electors to make choices."[14] *Theophanous* departed from *Sullivan* in that it placed the burden of proof (and a higher one at that) on the defendant publisher rather than on the plaintiff. The publisher would be liable unless it could be shown they were unaware of the falsity, that they did not publish it recklessly, and that the publication was reasonable in the circumstances. To meet this third prong, the publisher must show that some steps were taken to check the material's veracity or show that it was other-

---

10. *ACTV*, 133–46.
11. *Theophanous v. Herald & Weekly Times Ltd.* (1994) 182 CLR 104, 105–6.
12. Ibid.
13. 376 U.S. 254 (1964).
14. *Theophanous*, 122.

wise justified. Moreover, the protection afforded a publisher is weaker under *Theophanous*. To lose this protection under *Sullivan*, publishers must have demonstrated "actual malice" in publishing false defamatory material, whereas the Australian standard simply required that publishers acted "unreasonably" given the context.

Stephens v. West Australian Newspaper Ltd. (1994),[15] a companion defamation suit, arose from articles published in Western Australia about members of that state's legislative assembly. The newspapers sought protection from liability using the implied constitutional freedom. Again in a 4-3 split, the Court affirmed the implied freedom and concluded that it extended to discussion concerning political matters at the state level. This extension was justified on two grounds: first that the implied freedom in the Commonwealth Constitution covered all forms of political speech, including that which concerned state politics; and second, that Western Australia's constitution itself contained this implied freedom because it too mandated representative, parliamentary government.

Theophanous and *Stephens* are noteworthy because of the positive constitutional right the Court created that restricts legislative and executive power and delimits the capacity to recover under Australia's defamation laws. Inferring this freedom demanded a departure from orthodox constitutional interpretation. In his *Theophanous* dissent, Justice McHugh criticized the Court for abandoning firmly rooted traditional interpretive modalities. He wrote:

> Since...the *Engineers'* Case (1920)...this Court has consistently held that it is not legitimate to construe the Constitution by reference to political principles or theories that find no support in the text of the Constitution. The theory of constitutional interpretation that has prevailed since [then] is that one starts with the text and not with some theory of federalism, politics or political economy....It is the text and the implications to be drawn from the text and structure that contain the meaning of the Constitution.[16]

McHugh's dissent hit a chord because the doctrine developed no further after *Theophanous*. Although there was some hesitation on the Court about this methodology from its beginning (the Court rejected in 1992, for example, the argument that one may infer a general right of equality from the Constitution[17]), the Court refused, in earnest, to extend the doctrine by the mid-1990s.

---

15. 182 CLR 211.
16. *Theophanous*, 192.
17. *Leeth v. Commonwealth* (1992) 174 CLR 455.

Two cases decided in 1996 illustrate this consolidation. In *Langer v. Commonwealth*,[18] the Court considered the constitutionality of provisions in the *Commonwealth Electoral Act 1918*. Section 240 of the Act requires voters to cast preferential ballots in elections for the federal House of Representatives, meaning that voters express sequential preference for every candidate on the ballot from first to last, i.e. 1, 2, 3, 4. Another provision, Section 329A, prohibits anyone from printing, publishing, or distributing material that encourages voters to cast anything but legitimate ballots. Albert Langer in 1993 urged electors to cast ballots listing their preferences as 1, 2, 3, 3, such that the two major parties were equally ranked last. Langer argued that Section 240's requirement for sequential ranking violated the constitution's implied freedom of political speech. The Court rejected this argument, upholding both sections of the *Electoral Act* and thus trimming the scope of the implied freedom. Judges in the majority concluded that Parliament had a legitimate legislative purpose in Section 240, namely to minimize the number of inaccurate or illegitimate ballots. The limitations placed on Langer were not intended to dampen his speech, but to protect the voting process. The Court concluded that the law requiring sequential voting actual enhances the democratic process, just as the implied right of political communication does.[19]

A second case in 1996, *McGinty v. Western Australia*,[20] presented the Court with an opportunity to infer a new freedom in the constitution. Sections 7 and 24 of the constitution require that Senators and House members be "directly chosen by the people." The plaintiffs in this case argued, *inter alia*, that Western Australia's district boundaries violated this provision because of population differences between districts. They charged that the district boundaries created uneven and disproportionately sized districts, such that voters' ballots did not have equal weight in election outcomes. However, four of the six judges (Justice Deane did not hear the case as he was soon to leave the Court to become Governor-General) rejected the idea that the constitution implied voter equality in this manner. Instead, the Court held to a narrow view of what may be implied from Sections 7 and 24. To the majority, the implied freedom extended solely to communications concerning electoral matters and not to second order implications, such as voter equality.

My informants saw the implied rights cases as one of the most significant jurisprudential developments in the last fifty years. Whereas the native title cases fanned public criticism of the Court, the implied rights cases fueled con-

---

18. (1996) 186 CLR 302.
19. Ibid., 317–34.
20. (1996) 136 CLR 140.

troversy largely within legal circles. The cases received comparatively little attention in the popular press and public. One can certainly appreciate why. Nothing tangible was at stake, such as property rights, for most Australians with the implied rights cases. Some may have appreciated the small steps the Court took to further protect speech, but most Australians, had they known about the cases at all, would have thought the Court was further protecting a right they already had. The issue of how best to protect rights in Australia had been publicly debated, particularly after Canada and New Zealand adopted rights protecting documents of their own. Australians had bantered around for several decades the question of whether a bill of rights was necessary, so the issue was not altogether foreign. But the subtle tweaks in defamation law and the Court's identification of this narrow implied freedom were lost on the general public.

My informants recognized, however, the implied rights cases as important for jurisprudential reasons. Many were more passionate during interviews about the Court inferring this narrow freedom than about it capsizing property law in *Mabo* and *Wik*. As with other dimensions of the politicized role, the appellate bench divided deeply over 1) the rights that were inferred, 2) the Court's methods for doing so, and 3) the Court sticking its neck out in this fashion. Critics outnumbered supporters two to one.

Several judges thought that identifying new constitutionally protected rights was beyond the High Court's role—that it had effectively usurped Parliament's power. These informants saw a role for the Court in *protecting* rights, but it was Parliament that should take the lead in *identifying* which rights to protect. A High Court justice articulated this view:

> Every time the High Court holds that the constitution implies something, it cuts down the legislative power of the Parliament....That's a touch undemocratic. When unelected judges declare...there is a limitation on the lawmaking powers of parliament, elected representatives...say there better be a good explanation for that....My view is that whilst of course implication is an important aspect of constitutional interpretation, judges have to be cautious in cutting down the lawmaking power of Parliament to an extent greater than is necessary from the structure of the constitution or language of the constitution....[T]o say you're implying a right of free speech sounds good until someone points out that...you're implying a limitation on the power of parliament to make laws on the subject of free speech (96:3530).

Another High Court justice remarked, "My view about rights is that the best way to protect them is through detailed legislation," and not by the Court "inventing rights that weren't there (94: 10200)." The reservations that these High Court judges voiced echoed among their appellate court colleagues. A Victoria judge found it "dangerous" for the Court to "add to the constitution things that are not there." The judge continued:

> What I disagree with is the notion that the courts themselves are the source of these improvements....It's dangerous in that it makes a particular High Court with a particular cast of nine with the ability...to alter the political landscape by changing the constitution.... I'm not saying watch out because the conservatives will use this technique to throttle freedom or even the socialists will use this technique to put forward their ideas. Whoever happens to come along might find this device. It might be used. That's the danger....The notion that there are areas where the legislature cannot go and legislative areas where the courts can tread I just don't agree with that (65:1745).

A Federal Court judge stated, "I'm not a proponent of trusting judges to map out for the community the extent to which particular freedoms...are appropriate and when and how they should be qualified. I don't think judges are well equipped to engage in that legislative-type process. I'd feel more comfortable with at least a core of instructions available to judges as to what the key values are and how to go about weighing those values (44)." Another critic was "skeptical of judges' abilities to fulfill the role of politicians or parliament (57:1000)." Several judges were concerned that the High Court was behaving more like the U.S. or Canadian Supreme Courts. "I'm troubled by the methods of the implied rights case," said one judge, "and the politicization of the U.S. Supreme Court and controversy directed at the Canadian Supreme Court since they had the Charter. It makes me nervous to see social and economic issues decided by judges. It's preferable to have parliament decide these things (128:1500)."

Other judges voiced concerns not about the Court treading on Parliament's power, but whether the challenges and institutional costs the Court confronted when implying constitutional rights were too great. A number of judges were wary about the permanency of constitutional rights. A High Court justice said, "In principle, it would be preferable to have an expressed bill of rights with the authority of the people than judges develop implied rights, given that it is very difficult once a right is found to 'un-find' it (116:1015)." Another cautioned, "The High Court must be careful about making leaps that are too big....It's very difficult to unwind the clock, you know. Once you make the leap, you're stuck with it (32:3400)." A Queensland judge concurred:

You can suck anything out of anything if you want to. If you can't see it there, you're in a difficult position justifying the decision. What bothers me more than anything…is how do you abolish a right that isn't in the constitution, but is implied there? If you vote in a referendum here, they give you a piece of paper that…shows how the constitution will be after the change. Cross out this word. Put in that. How do you do that when it's an implied right? You have to say, "Assume it's in there and cross it out (2:2630)."

Others voiced this concern in terms of institutional legitimacy. "There is a danger in courts stretching things," said one judge. "At the bottom of the effectiveness of the courts is public acceptance of their decisions.…By and large people accept a court's decision simply because a court said it.…There's a danger in that being lessened or harmed by stretching. That has been seen with some of the extreme reactions to the High Court's judgments (95:3815)."

While much criticism was directed at the Court reaching decisions properly left to Parliament, a few judges criticized the implied rights decisions because they did too little to advance rights protection. "As an ordinary Joe, I had no difficulty with the concept. But as a legal process it struck me as being duplicitous," said one Western Australia judge. He continued, "It was a case where the judges found arguments supporting the result rather than applying the law to produce whatever results came. It's the cart before the horse.…The danger is that the High Court creates substantive law which is in response to the individual idiosyncrasies of High Court judges.…Palm tree justice makes me uncomfortable. I'd rather see it addressed honestly in a bill of rights (10:5500)." Another judge objected to its ad hoc nature. "The real problem is that we don't have a bill of rights and we should have one. The High Court thought it was necessary to get those rights. But the difficulty with the judiciary doing it is that it can't do it in a comprehensive way. Just bits and pieces and you'll leave holes and room for error.…The judiciary can't imply rights in a comprehensive way (77:1500)." Another judge objected to the Court's willingness to mold the common law using the constitution. Here the objection was to paring back defamation law using the constitutionally protected implied freedom of speech.

[The cases] created confusion for an end which is probably not necessary to be achieved.…I understand the concept of the implied right for ensuring an informed electorate. But it seems unnecessary for the government to use the constitution for the purpose of molding the common law to ensure those ends. It's a dangerous way of doing it. If it appeared to the High Court that the law of defamation was a real

threat to free speech or a threat to an informed electorate, it would
have been easy enough to mold the common law to achieve their end
without using the constitution as the lever and it would have been less
controversial (117:2700).

There were also strong objections to the Court's methodology. Many informants dismissed any suggestion that one could infer a right to political
speech from the constitution. "The judges were making it up! It's nowhere in
the text (44)." Another said:

> To a black letter lawyer, there is no implied freedom of political com-
> munication in the constitution. You've got to look for words that
> aren't there because the constitution says nothing about it. The judges
> in the implied rights cases would tend to say it's there and find ex-
> cruciating ways of distorting words to put it there. But it's not there.
> It's using creativity to develop a theme which doesn't exist in the writ-
> ten document....To a black letter lawyer, it's not there and it's simply
> a creative piece of legislation by the High Court (32:2900).

Variants on this "nowhere-in-the-text" critique abounded: "There just seems
to me something odd about discovering almost 100 years after federation fundamental rights which generations of lawyers, judges, activists, and politicians
overlooked. It's a very unhistorical way of looking at federation (102:530)." A
Federal Court judge elaborated the point:

> Justice Scalia came [to Australia] in the early 1990s. He was a speaker
> [at an event] and said, "You've got a very interesting approach to
> amendments. In my country, we have to pass them by referendum,
> but you just imply these terms without any referendum." It's...wrong
> for the Court to change the constitution simply to bring about the
> goals it wants to achieve. It does look comical when five or so judges
> say there's an implied constitutional right and then three years later
> the dissenters and a few new judges say there really isn't any such right
> at all. It makes it look if you have a plane crash, you'll get a new body
> of law (103:1045).

The judge continued, "You can't have seismic shifts in constitutional doctrine...without the process becoming debased in the eyes of the public
(103:5000)." The plane crash remark was not made in jest or without historical referents. Australia has its share of strange mishaps befalling its politicians.
For example, a place crash in 1941 at the Canberra airport killed the chief of
the general staff and three cabinet members. Prime Minister Harold Holt

(1966-1967) disappeared mysteriously when swimming on the coast. Conspiracy theories abound, including a shark attack, a faked death, and even Soviet or Chinese agents abducting Holt in a submarine.

I recorded a seemingly endless variety of disparaging characterizations of the implied rights cases. "What [the Court] was engaged in was constitutional amendment not constitutional interpretation (99:1500)." "The Court cooked up some pretty funny menus. Now we have double implied rights and that's horrible (2:2630)." They were "silly cases, silly decisions (5)," "results-oriented (10)," "sneaky (52)," "the worst single feature of Australian constitutional law in the last twenty years (3:240)," "madness let loose (3:1750)" that created a "loose leaf constitution (128)" through "Rorschach inkblot reasoning (89:4630)." One judge resented having "this forced upon us by the left-wing. Now we suffer the consequences.... We've said bugger the constitution. We'll tell you what should be there. It's very distressing (3:1730)."

Critics voiced several concerns about the cases' consequences for law and the judiciary. "There are great difficulties, I find, personally with that sort of approach," said one judge, "because it leads to a degree of uncertainty in the law. An injustice occurs when people go about their business on a set of assumptions and all of a sudden find out they're wrong because a court implied this right (60:4545)." Another expressed institutional reservations: "The judiciary must be conscious that while it can advance the law...if it pushes too far ahead of majoritarian sentiment or...state and federal governments, you'll get a backlash and you'll end up with a permanent undermining of the judiciary (89:4630)." Still another feared that the Court's unconventional reasoning could rub off on lower court judges.

> The difficulty I have with it is that it gives license to judicial creativity at the lower end of the spectrum, which I think may not be tight enough to justify its existence. If you look at judges in the district court you wouldn't necessarily expect them to have the same analytical approach to legal doctrine and principle as you would get in [the Court of Appeal] and the High Court. For the most part, it's not their task to have it. It's more their task to have a grasp of fundamental legal principles to apply to the numerous fact situations which they deal with.... Once you start opening up these concepts—many of these people are my friends—lower court judges grabbed on to this concept and thought, "Terrific, this is something we can apply." I just felt that it was starting to create something that shouldn't be there but was.... When you have a principle like that you'll get people in the lower order of judicial office who will snatch at that and say, "Look

the High Court has said we can do this," and start applying it in a whole range of circumstances where it just doesn't apply (58:10100).

Detractors regretted the *Nationwide News* and *ACTV* cases and welcomed its pullback in *Lange*. "The tide has turned with the implied rights cases and this is just as well. There are great difficulties about implying rights of that kind absent a bill of rights (100:700)." Another judge remarked, "I thought the method was wrong.... [The approach] won't survive. The implied rights cases were a flower that popped up its head but never bloomed—and that's where it should be (79:3000)."

How did defenders of the implied rights decisions justify them and the methodology? One group of informants justified the decisions based on the fact that the Court regularly draws text-based implications in other areas of law. A judge said, "I have no difficulty with it. As a commercial lawyer the idea of implied rights I grew up with. Every time you enter into a contract...you'll find some things that are said, but no contract has ever been written that would cover every possible occurrence that could be foreseen. If something occurs that's not foreseen you look to see how the contract applies to what has occurred—you imply terms. That's been done since time immemorial." Turning his attention to constitutional interpretation, the judge continued, "The argument is that with constitutional rights, they're so important that you wouldn't think parliament intended there to be any implied right—only expressed rights. If you want laws written in stone and never changed even though society changes then that's what you do. I don't want that. Would anyone want to be governed by the Ten Commandments alone? (105:5330)" This sentiment was echoed by another judge:

> It's a question of what your attitude is toward what the law is.... [T]he purposive construction is based upon developments in the law, within which the [constitution] has to be construed. If you're doing that then I don't see that there's a real problem about implications. It's been part and parcel of the law for so long. Relying upon implications is an integral part of the judicial process. There is no reason to take it away with respect to the constitution (118:3745).

Another said, "I don't think that [implying rights] is inappropriate and it has precedents in other fields of the law. It's a common judicial technique full stop, whatever the topic is (25:3400)."

A second group of defenders justified the decisions on grounds that Australia's constitution was antiquated and required a judge-sponsored tune-up. Many in this second group considered it shortsighted for the Court to employ strict textualism or originalism. "In a sense, the constitution and method of altering it invite this sort of development because it's extremely hard to alter," said one judge. "There's a sense that if you don't let it grow it will ossify and become an obstacle to good government (60:4545)." Another judge asked rhetorically, "How do you interpret a constitution that came into operation a hundred years ago in contemporary society?...It would be easy to say you interpret it by reference to what they had in mind at the time. But we don't even do that with the interpretation of contracts. In contracts between individuals we ask the question, 'What would they have had in mind if this occurred at that time?' (74:4415)" Another judge put it this way:

> Judge: We've got this horse and buggy constitution written in the late 1890s for the day, in a very different social context from today. A hundred years later it's a completely new ball game, so the High Court over a long period of time had to read things into the constitution that hadn't been invented or existed in 1900. In the absence of a bill of rights, I don't see any problem with the High Court reading by implication some implied rights into the constitution. I'd do it myself if I had the chance.
>
> Q: Do you fear that this methodology could open Pandora's box?
>
> Judge: The Pandora's box argument is a bit like the floodgates argument, which is used in several respects, particularly in relation to liberalizing standing. I've experienced twenty years of open-standing provisions and I'm fond of saying I've never got my willies wet because the floodgates never opened....I'd say the same thing in relation to implied interpretations (36:2645)."

A third group justified the implied rights decisions as instances where the Court simply fulfilled its constitutional duties. Some informants characterized the decisions in rather benign language, as if the Court had no alternative but to reach the decisions it did. Another concluded, "I would not call them overtly political decisions. They follow traditional legal methods....Don't forget these were arguments addressed by counsel that have to be approached by the Court....Forced into looking at it, if you really think about it, it's not an unfair inference (11:10130)." One judge concluded that the method could not be faulted. "It's a legitimate development in jurisprudential analysis. It puts flesh on the bones of the constitution, which is not a steely framework that doesn't have any give in it. We're beginning to realize that it's a much more pliable document than we thought ten or twenty years ago (18:530)."

Other proponents described the implied rights decisions as byproducts of parliaments failing to protect human rights adequately. A Federal Court judge pointed out, "With two houses of Parliament and the difficulties of Governments securing majorities in both, it's a very clever system because it really does give courts the ability to move where the legislature can't. Isn't that what you saw with the implied rights cases? It's an invidious position to put the judges in when parliaments get jammed up (12:1130)." Another explained:

> In the absence of a bill of rights, there is a void there that from time to time has to be filled. I don't think there is anything terribly sophisticated about it. They've stepped in and found an excuse....This implied approach came out of left field only a few years ago. No one ever heard of it until then. They've done it because there is a need to address certain problems with no bill of rights....Don't be too sophisticated about this. It's the doctrine of necessity in another form (14:4715).

Whatever justifications were offered, defenders readily admitted to the limitations inherent in a doctrine that lacks a firm constitutional or statutory grounding and one that is contingent on judges' individual predilections. Even among its most strident supporters, the implied rights jurisprudence was not seen as a sufficient elixir for rights protection. A High Court judge offered, "The best argument for a bill of rights in Australia is that if Australia doesn't get one, you'll get seven different ones from the High Court (92:2745)." A Queensland judge said, "[The implied rights cases] require a degree of legal artificiality, which is limiting and coercive for the future because it's easy to overthrow." He continued,

> The free speech, which was moving forward so effectively, has been taken back by the post-Mason court. It had no solid foundation except in some notion of implications in the constitution....It had no formal basis there where you could actually look and see it. So the critics who want to move back to majority will are able to say the Court's acting illegitimately and not acting within their proper role....We don't have the formal structure that lets the Court play this balancing role (87:2600).

A High Court judge admitted, "As far as the outcomes are concerned, I was rather pleased....As far as the legitimacy of what was done by the Court, I had some doubts....Some of those decisions tended to go rather far toward imaginative interpretation, but I think the outcome was a good one....*Perhaps it's illegitimate to pull the rabbit out of the hat, but it's nice to see the rabbit emerging* (37:5045) (emphasis added)." Another judge said

> I do support it, but it was a little stretched to get it. It's not easy to get it out of the words of the constitution. But I'm happy enough that

they got it....I think it would be better to have a bill of rights...because it is a little stretched and it will change with the make-up of the Court. There is that inevitable degree of uncertainty; whereas a bill of rights will give more certainty (1:3400).

The Chief Justice of a state supreme court admitted

I have reservations about the method...although I agree with the results. I think it is the function of Parliament to identify the fundamental rights for society...because it is so much a value-laden function. I hesitate about courts getting into this area because if you can distill things you like, others can also distill things you don't like....I think there are basic principles in the constitution and identifying them is difficult. But the answer is not to retreat to Dixonian legalism (82:1130).

Sources for Constitutional Interpretation

The Mason Court's second notable development in constitutional interpretation concerns the sources upon which the Court draws. The Mason Court explicitly expanded the corpus of legitimate sources for constitutional interpretation. The Court departed from the orthodoxy's preference for Australian and British precedent (or as Australians say, "authorities") and willingly considered relevant precedent from other Anglo-American and European systems. A state appellate judge said, "The mindset of Mason was to no longer give priority to English decisions....The Australian High Court looks now at a wide range of comparative law for solutions (123)." A former Commonwealth Solicitor-General concurred:

[T]here has been a great opening up of Australian jurisprudence, particularly constitutional jurisprudence, to international elements.... [G]enerations ago we would look no further than the U.K., which would not be of much assistance—not having a written constitution. Now it's the case that we would rarely cite U.K. authority, but I certainly do it, but very irregularly and with reluctance. We draw in constitutional litigation such analogs and authority we can from the United States, Canada, Europe...and we do it with an openness that basically still doesn't exist in the U.S. (127).

The move away from considering only British judgments was confirmed in several interviews with Mason Court judges. In response to a question about whether they were cognizant of their novel approaches, one Mason Court judge answered: "They weren't waters that were uncharted by reference to experience elsewhere. The approaches adopted by the Court were clearly approaches which had been explored elsewhere and by writers elsewhere.... *The Canadian experience I thought was particularly illuminating...the change from a court that was not progressive but became a very progressive court* (122:1000) (emphasis added)." This judge downplayed the profundity of change during the Mason era by suggesting the Court was simply following reforms underway elsewhere. Within the expanded pantheon of foreign authorities, many informants affirmed the importance of the Canadian experience. A Federal Court judge said:

> Another thing the High Court did—a real storm center because of all the fuss it creates among all the other judges in the system who still love England and vote against republics—they started to look away from England, as the quality of the English judiciary deteriorated, and looked more to North America. [The Court was] a bit more comfortable with Canada because the common law in Canada is seen a bit like we see it and you don't have the problem that you have in America...with due process....It's very hard [in the U.S.] to discern when a judge is talking about a common law principle or how much of it is infected by constitutional principle. So there's a danger in following too closely U.S. jurisprudence....We do business with Americans and Canadians every day. Can we have a system that says if you fight your case in Australia the plaintiff will win, but if you fight the case in America the defendant will win? Same facts? [The High Court] started to shed the insular approach, which they've always had. [It said that] if you want to know the answer you look to the English House of Lords or the Court of Appeal and that's your search (85:1430).

The heightened attention directed toward Canadian decisions explains, in one judge's mind, the contours of the Mason Court's native title cases.

> I've got to point a finger to North America—more Canada than the U.S.—for the *Wik* decision. There were developing pressures around the world about the rights of indigenous people....We were feeling those forces.... [A]s those cases were decided, the jurisprudence started to mount about it. Legal and social agitation in Australia reflects a lot of that as well. The High Court came to the point where cases were put that needed to be decided and you had a court with the instincts...coming to struggle with these decisions very much as Canada had gone (17:1930).

Another High Court judge remarked, "We still looked at the precedents in U.K. courts—not only U.K. courts but also quite extensively at the U.S. and Canadian cases....It varied from judge to judge. Some judges extensively look at overseas precedents in the common law world—a lot really of the U.S. Supreme Court for the very reason that our constitution finds much of its origin in the U.S. (37:1415)." High Court Justice Kirby was seen as the strongest proponent of incorporating foreign authorities. "Justice Kirby was particularly a man of the world and would insist on counsel citing decisions from other jurisdictions....So people suddenly had to prepare to take to the Court these things....When it started fifteen years ago it was heresy but even Brennan adopted it in *Mabo* (123)."

Empirical research largely affirms these qualitative assessments. Grouping High Court decisions by decade, Bruce Topperwien, for example, finds that British cases have long and consistently appeared in High Court judgments. Since 1903 no less than 70 percent of cases decided in a given decade cite British cases. For the years 1991 to 1999, British citations appeared in 88 percent of cases. Beginning in the 1980s, however, the frequency of American, Canadian, and New Zealand citations precipitously increased. The Court cited American cases in 13 percent of its decisions from 1971 to 1980. This increased to 25 percent and 41 percent during the 1980s and 1990s, respectively. Canadian citations went from 10 percent in the 1970s to 21 percent in the 1980s and then 37 percent in the 1990s. New Zealand cases enjoyed a similar presence (Topperwien 2001).[21]

The Mason Court also expanded the corpus of legitimate foreign sources by relying increasingly on international law and appealing to international legal norms. "The impact of international law is an ongoing and powerful influence, certainly in the High Court. [It's] something that you wouldn't have found previously...because the limited volume of international law in comparison with the flood of it that's coming out now (83:930)," said one judge. A Federal Court judge assessed:

> There's another radical move...where the view took hold that you should also look to international law. I'm not sure how it works in the U.S., but international law is not part of domestic law in this country unless it's enacted....By and large, we could sign a treaty, but unless we enact the treaty, the treaty is just a piece of paper. We can sign nice pieces of paper but it doesn't affect the citizens. More and more, the High Court was construing statutes by reference to international standards, developing the common law by reference to international standards, and

---

21. See also Allen & Anderson (1994).

so on. In as many areas as you want to look—basic, bread and butter areas of law like torts and contracts—we were looking around the world. When you start to look at the international community and Europe you start to pick up things we never thought of twenty-five years ago [such as] how should human rights be protected (85:1700)?"

As intimated in this remark, international standards and international law was brought to bear particularly on the rights front. A Queensland appellate judge said, "Identification of [human rights] is extremely difficult, but there has been a great deal of work done on it in the fifty years since the Second World War. There is now an emerging human rights consensus.... What I think we saw in Australia was an attempt to give effect to those international norms without a constitutional framework for doing so. It was done by reading implications into the constitution (87:4345)." Another judge offered an example of how the heightened interest in international obligations impacted his litigation as a barrister before his appointment to the bench.

When I got more senior and richer, I started the American practice of running some of these mad cases for nothing if they took my fancy. There was some fellow who was Victoria's worst prisoner. They kept him in a maximum security prison, kept in his cell twenty-three out of twenty-four hours shackled. I said no power to do that, cruel and unusual punishment. That's the sort of argument you would not have even thought about running twenty-five years ago.... Twenty-five years ago you could not have even walked into court with that. They would have said, "Get out, we've got serious cases on next week, we can't waste our time on this." The whole mood changed (85:1700).

Two cases well illustrate how the Court in the last twenty years has relied increasingly on international law and international legal norms to interpret the constitution. The first case, *Commonwealth v. Tasmania* (known more commonly as the Tasmanian Dam case) was decided in 1983.[22] The case arose after the newly elected Hawke Labor Government took action under the *World Heritage Properties Conservation Act* to prohibit the damming of the Franklin River system in Tasmania. The Government justified this as a valid exercise of its external affairs power (Section 51(xxix)). This power is thought to enable

---

22. (1983) 158 CLR 1. This case was decided two years before Anthony Mason was promoted to Chief Justice. I group it with other Mason Court decisions because most of the key players in the role transformation were in place by May 1983 and the case is emblematic of my thesis.

Parliament to pass legislation giving effect to international obligations made under various conventions and treaties. Australia became a signatory in 1975 to the Convention Concerning the Protection of the World Cultural and National Heritage, so the question facing the Court was whether Parliament could give effect to this international convention through the external affairs power. Parts of Tasmania had been listed on the World Heritage List and were to be deleteriously impacted by the dam. The Tasmanian government supported the dam's construction for the purpose of generating electricity at low cost and in hopes of stimulating economic development and employment. It found itself at loggerheads with the Commonwealth.

A majority of the Court held that the Commonwealth was under international obligation to protect Australia's sites included on the World Heritage List and that it could legislate under its external affairs power to prohibit the dam's construction. Then Justice Mason wrote in the majority:

> [E]ntry into...and ratification of...an international convention evidences the judgment of the executive and of Parliament that the subject-matter of the convention is of international character and concern and that its implementation will be a benefit to Australia. Whether the subject-matter...is of international concern [and] whether it will yield...a benefit to Australia...are not questions on which the Court can readily arrive at an informed opinion. Essentially they are issues involving nice questions of sensitive judgment which should be left to the executive government for determination. The Court should accept and act upon the decision of the executive government and upon the expression of the will of Parliament in giving legislative ratification to the treaty or convention.[23]

The High Court's appeal to international obligations in this case caught the ire of at least one informant. A Queensland appellate judge remarked:

> The Tasmanian Dam decision is one of the worst decisions because the High Court said that whatever you get under the head of external affairs by treaty you can fix up here. That put an enormous number of people out of work in Tasmania....You can't afford to have...the constitution interpreted that way. That decision turned many against the judiciary because it seemed absurd. I mean if we enter into a treaty with Sierra Leone about something and it gives the central government the right to take those powers from the state, that can't be right (2:2630).

---

23. Ibid., 125.

A second case illustrating this trend was decided at the end of Mason's tenure as chief justice. Decided in 1995, the *Teoh*[24] case addressed to what extent domestic lawmakers must consider international treaties that Australia has ratified as they enact legislation or make administrative decisions. The question before the Court was whether a person has a legitimate expectation that domestic laws comport with relevant international treaties. Teoh, a Malaysian, was denied permanent residence in Australia despite his marriage to an Australian and having several children born in Australia. The immigration authorities denied his application primarily because he had been convicted of six counts of drug possession—crimes he apparently committed to feed his wife's drug addiction. The Mason Court concluded that because Australia had ratified the United Nation's Convention on the Rights of the Child in 1990, immigration authorities should have given greater consideration to the impact that Teoh's deportation would have on his children. Chief Justice Mason led a majority in concluding

> [I]t does not seem to us that the [Immigration Review Panel] or the [Immigration Minister's delegate] regarded the best interests of the children as a primary consideration. A decision-maker with an eye to the principle enshrined in the Convention would be looking to the best interests of the children as a primary consideration, asking whether the force of any other consideration outweighed it. The decision necessarily reflected the difference between the principle and the instruction.[25]

The Tasmanian Dam and *Teoh* cases are but two of several contemporary decisions that drew upon international conventions or treaties and international legal norms. Others include *Polyukhovich v. Commonwealth*[26] where the external affairs power was extended to include a federal law that identified as "war crimes" certain crimes committed in Europe during the Second World War and enabled prosecution; and *Kruger v. Commonwealth*[27] where the Court confronted and ultimately answered in the negative whether a federal policy of forcibly removing Aboriginal children from their homes and culture constituted genocide under the Convention on the Prevention and Punishment of the Crime of Genocide.

---

24. *Minister for Immigration and Ethnic Affairs v. Teoh* (1995) 183 CLR 273.
25. Ibid., 292.
26. (1991) 172 CLR 501.
27. (1997) 146 ALR 126.

Consulting the Conventions

The third change that the Mason Court brought to constitutional interpretation concerned its outlook on the history surrounding the constitution's
framing, specifically the conventions held in the 1890s. Whereas the U.S.
Supreme Court can point to no authoritative recording of the proceedings and
debates that occurred in Philadelphia in the summer of 1787 (secondary
sources certainly are available), the High Court can. An official transcript of
all plenary speeches, debates and public deliberations was kept for each convention. The proceedings were published in six volumes covering the 1891,
1897, and 1898 sessions (Craven 1986). For eighty-plus years the High Court
did not rely upon or entertain arguments based on the conventions' official
records, even when questions about the framers' intent arose. The Mason
Court turned this practice on its head. In what may seem paradoxical to U.S.
court scholars, given the political aim of those who advance an originalist
mode of constitutional interpretation, the Mason Court entertained arguments on the framers' intent for what were progressive legal reforms. Rather
that kicking back constitutional interpretation to 1901, the convention proceedings were utilized to foment legal change. The Mason Court did not simply want to ascribe meaning to the constitution's clauses based on what the
words meant in 1901. The convention debates did not define the words necessarily, but provided perspective on what the framers intended by certain
clauses. A NSW appellate judge explained: "In constitutional reasoning, a significant change occurred because people started looking at the convention debates, which Dixon and his courts professed not to look at and didn't allow to
be cited. The person, Greg Craven, who is an academic, claims that it was because he published a new edition of [the convention debates] that it all happened. Suddenly they became accessible, just physically (123)."[28]

Craven's publication at least coincides with Mason Court decisions that
drew upon the conventions. This interpretive transition is marked, for example, by the 1988 *Cole v. Whitfield* case.[29] As discussed earlier, this case brought
significant clarity to the hitherto muddied meaning of the interstate commerce
clause, Section 92. The Court accomplished this, in part, by reference to the
convention debates. Its motivations were not to substitute the scope and effect of the actual words with a meaning "the founding fathers subjectively in-

---

28. Professor Craven published in 1986 a fully edited and indexed version of the convention debates, which some suggest made judicial reference to the debates all the more
accessible. See Craven (1986).

29. 165 CLR 360.

tended the section to have." Rather, studying the debate proceedings enabled the Court to assess "the contemporary meaning of language used, the subject to which that language was directed and the nature and objectives of the movement towards federation from which the compact of the Constitution finally emerged."[30] With this in mind, the Court traced the changes in Section 92's phrasing from convention to convention and made frequent references to the debates surrounding the requirement that trade remain "absolutely free."[31] "Until recently," confirmed a Federal Court judge, "the High Court ignored the historic context of federation. The Australian tradition has been textual and not historical. *Cole* changed all of that (102:5238)."

Members of the Mason Court generally agreed with this account. One judge who participated in *Cole* explained: "Yes, [the Mason Court] marked a difference in approach....In *Cole*, the Court did some things that wouldn't be regarded as remarkable by a United States lawyer, but would be regarded as very significant...in Australian constitutional law; that is, interpreting the constitution by reference to convention debates and antecedent history [was unique] (122:10400)." But at least one High Court justice expressed some reservations about looking at these materials. "We're not going to psychoanalyze the authors of the constitution. We're very interested in the received understanding of the constitution for two reasons. First, it's evidence of a possible meaning of the constitution. Second, as a matter of principle, whilst we're free to depart from decisions of earlier courts, we're slow to do so." The judge continued, "Instead of looking at speeches made for the purpose of divining the subjective intention of the framers, look at the drafting history— the *travaux préparatoires* [preparatory work] in international law. The drafting history will often throw some light on the meaning of the words. But I don't think you get a great deal of comfort from having an assertion by an individual at a convention that he thinks the words mean something, except it tells you a possible meaning (96:2400)."

By way of summary then, the Mason Court ushered in several changes to constitutional interpretation. It conceived the document as much more than simply a power-distribution document. It contained express and implied rights that the Court was obligated to identify and protect. The implied rights jurisprudence generated intense reaction. Supporters saw it as a necessary step given the constitution's nature. Opponents thought it dangerously unhinged the Court from the constitution's text and structure. The Mason Court also

---

30. *Cole*, 385.
31. *Cole*, 385–91.

departed from a strict reliance on Australian and British sources and cast its eye to North America and Europe for relevant precedent. In a related development, international law, legal norms and treaty obligations were relied upon increasingly to guide constitutional interpretation, as were the convention debates.

DIMENSION #5: STARE DECISIS AND THE NATURE OF LEGAL TESTS

The orthodoxy exhibited a robust practice of stare decisis, so much so that several informants suggested that in yesteryears High Court judges followed precedent even if they thought it was wrongly decided. Such a characterization probably overstates the case, but it became clear from the interviews that today's appellate judges perceive the Court following a weaker tradition of stare decisis, a trend that began during the Mason era. One judge claimed, in fact, that the judicial system experienced in the 1990s a "breakdown of stare decisis." "The impression that I get," the judge continued, "is that within the High Court itself, it's a little bit like what happened with the English House of Lords. There is a clear acknowledgment that the Court can depart from earlier precedent. Now that was always the case in the High Court, but there is much more discussion and willingness to entertain the argument, 'Yes they said that but that was twenty years ago (103:2430).'" Another judge said, "Traditionally this country has had a very structured approach to judicial decision-making. The High Court would depart from precedent only where it considered it proper to do so and in those instances it was very careful (81:430)." The Mason Court, on the other hand, "saw itself in a different role from what it previously had," according to one informant. "The function of the High Court has changed. It's increasingly willing to restate the law as they see it. They're less constrained by precedent (67)." As one Federal Court judge put it, precedent is now "just something to toy with (87:5000)."

That the politicized role incorporates a weaker tradition of stare decisis means that the Court may be more skeptical about a precedent the longer it is on the books. A South Australia judge remarked, "Previously the High Court would have accepted that if there was a lot of established precedent the precedent would stand. Whereas now, the question is if there is a long established precedent, perhaps it's time to look at it again." The judge offered this example:

I had a case that I decided in this court on the construction of an insurance policy's term that had been used in commerce certainly for

150 years—established in the 1860s or 1870s. It had been construed and given a particular definition. The full court upheld my decision.... When [the case went before the High Court] the respondent said, "I'll draw the Court's attention to the fact that this is a well established principle." One of the judges on the High Court said, "Well that's good enough. It's about time we had another look at it!" It was obviously said partly tongue-in-cheek but this is the attitude of the Court—to look at everything and test it in light of social conditions (48:2215).

A colleague remarked, "Earlier courts [here] were less likely to change precedent. They conceived themselves more enthralled with the past (65:1300)." Another judge quipped, "Now everybody is saying that we can change the law (123)." The Mason Court, according to one High Court judge, "showed they were willing to disregard precedent" even if the law in a particular area was accepted (94:900). As one informant said, "There is no reason why the High Court can't change it (104:345)."

Mabo is the classic example of the Mason Court's willingness to overturn long-established precedent, in this case the 200-year-old application of *terra nullius* in Australia. Brennan confronted squarely the orthodoxy's contention that a precedent's persuasiveness rests, in part, on the fact it was decided long ago. He stated in *Mabo*, "Although our law is the prisoner of its history, it is not now bound by decisions of courts in the hierarchy of an Empire then concerned with the development of its colonies.... The law which governs Australia is Australian law."[32] He then explained why the *terra nullius* doctrine and its supportive precedents were no longer relevant: "[N]o case can command unquestioning adherence if the rule it expresses seriously offends the values of justice and human rights (especially equality before the law) *which are aspirations of the contemporary Australian legal system* (emphasis added)."[33] The case he had in mind was none other than *Cooper v. Stuart* (1889), where the Privy Council affirmed the application of *terra nullius* to Australia.[34] Long established precedent is prone to review according to Brennan when its principles offend contemporary values or aspirations of Australian society. He concluded, "[A]n unjust and discriminatory doctrine of that kind [*terra nullius*] can no longer be accepted. The expectations of the international community accord in this respect with the contemporary values of the Australian people."[35]

32. *Mabo*, 29.
33. Ibid.
34. 14 AC 286.
35. *Mabo*, 42.

This weakened tradition of stare decisis also meant that the Mason Court was increasingly willing to overturn recently established precedent. The long entrenched and the newly established precedents seem equally vulnerable. The latter is remarkable because under the orthodoxy it is unacceptable to reconsider recently decided cases simply because the vehicles present themselves and change to the Court's composition may produce different results. Nonetheless, this was observed in a case concerning professional privilege, *Esso v. Commissioner of Taxation*.[36] This 1999 case considered when communications between an attorney and client fall under the attorney-client privilege. The High Court had answered that question in its 1976 *Grant v. Downs* decision,[37] where it propounded a "sole purpose test." The attorney-client privilege would extend under this test to communication only if its sole purpose was to offer and receive legal advice. In *Esso*, the Court reargued and ultimately overturned *Grant v. Downs* (itself decided by a 6-1 majority) on a 5-2 vote. It concluded that while the "sole purpose test" appeared as an easily understood and applicable test, they lamented that a single purpose to a communication in addition to legal purpose would defeat the privilege if applied literally. A fairer test in their minds, the "dominant purpose test" would apply the privilege when the cause of communication is the solicitation or provision of legal advice (Palmer 2000).

As one judge put it, "That is something that just wouldn't have happened, until the last fifteen years (103:730)." Indeed, the dilemma of when an established precedent can be reviewed was addressed during oral argument in *Esso*. Justice McHugh asked counsel, "But is not the problem in this case [that *Grant v. Downs*] has now stood for 23 years [and] it has been applied in this Court on a number of occasions. Why should it now be overturned?...Would you not have to show that it has become really unworkable in practice?"[38] *Esso's* majority was sensitive to this concern:

> *Grant v. Downs* has, for more than 20 years, been accepted in Australia as authority for the sole purpose test of legal professional privilege, and it has been consistently followed in later decisions and has been applied in this Court.... The power to disturb settled authority is, as Gibbs CJ said, one to be exercised with restraint, and only after careful scrutiny of the earlier course of decisions and full consideration of the consequences.[39]

---

36. (1999) 201 CLR 49.
37. (1976) 135 CLR 674.
38. *Esso*, transcript of proceedings, 28 September 1999, Canberra, 10:19 a.m.
39. *Esso*, 71.

Justice Kirby objected to overturning *Grant v. Downs* and its sole purpose test, saying, "It has been accepted and applied...in the numerous cases...in countless appeals and trials and even more numerous pre-trial and pre-litigation decisions made in every jurisdiction of Australia since 1976. This is not an obscure rule of the substantive law visited only occasionally by the courts. It is part of the woven texture of the law."[40] The decision in *Esso* to overturn *Grant v. Downs* illustrates how the Mason Court was willing to overturn recently established authorities.

My informants reported that the politicized role justifies this weaker tradition of stare decisis on two grounds. First, the politicized role leaves room for the possibility that extant precedent may not necessarily exhaust a legal concept. As one High Court justice put it, "The emphasis [under the politicized role] has been on identifying the basic principle, however expressed. Earlier decisions had been followed as though that articulation exhausted the whole concept. This means there is a more realistic approach toward precedent (63:1230)." Second, the politicized role reconceives the bases on which precedent is considered persuasive. Informants thought the orthodoxy values precedent simply because it was decided by an earlier court. The politicized role values precedent because of its persuasiveness today. "From time to time, the High Court is accused of judicial activism," said one judge. "But in reality the Court seems more concerned with saying to people why is that principle correct, rather than why did our predecessors think it was correct thirty years ago (74:1530)." Another judge remarked that since the role transformation, "[I]t's the persuasiveness of the argument [that matters] rather than its precedential effects. So we were suddenly...required to look in appellate advocacy to U.S. cases, English cases, New Zealand, and increasingly to European patterns of legal thought. The library was opened (123)."

Several informants noted that barristers appearing before the High Court during the last fifteen years were more likely than earlier generations to ask the Court to revisit precedent. One judge concluded:

> Counsel are encouraged to be more adventurous than they used to be, although that's not entirely true. Sir Robert Menzies argued a case in the High Court...in the late [19]20s probably where he said, "Look, I have an argument but it's completely at variance with this Court's recent authority, but with the Court's permission I'd like to raise it."...The Court heard the point and overruled the previous authority. So, the High Court overruling previous authority and being

---

40. Ibid., 87.

invited by counsel to do so is not recent, but it may have been...a little more frequent...since 1980 (104:1745).

Another judge thought that since the 1980s, the Court has not "felt the same
obligation to precedent" as its predecessors. The informant continued, "Now
it says they'll look at any common law jurisdiction and it's not bound by any
of them (24:1930)."

This breakdown in stare decisis appears to have trickled down from the
High Court. Some informants reported that intermediate and trial court
judges are feeling less bound by precedent since the Mason Court introduced
the politicized role. Their rationale is that if the High Court entertains arguments for overturning established precedent, then perhaps so too should they.
A state supreme court chief justice conceded this trend, but cautioned against
thinking it is simply a lower court power grab.

> In the state courts, there has been more readiness to reconsider ear-
> lier decisions. That's been forced because you find out that there are
> conflicting decisions in other states and you're then presented with
> whether you just allow the High Court to sort it out. As the High
> Court has gotten busier and busier and as appeals to [it] are now all
> by special leave, that's put greater pressure on the state courts to keep
> the law up to date themselves. The High Court has actually said to
> the states, "We can't sort out all the problems. If you have split deci-
> sions or conflicting precedents within your hierarchy, sort them out
> (123)."

A Victoria appellate judge affirmed, "All this trickles down to other judges and
I'm no exception myself. Appellate courts have more power to restate the law
as they see it. That's good because reasoning should be from the principles to
the cases....But with everyone less constrained, we all live out this fairy tail
that the great judges develop the law (67)." One judge illustrated how his own
legal reasoning changed since the High Court's transformation.

> I decided a case...in which an Aborigine was arrested outside the
> workers' club at 11 p.m. on a Friday night. He [verbally insulted] the
> police officer....The officer arrested him for behaving in an offensive
> manner. The guy...was taken to jail....When three [officers] entered
> his cell, he panicked and pushed one of them. So he was then charged
> with assault. I decided that it wasn't offensive to say [that insult] to a
> police officer at 11 o'clock at night outside the workers' club. There
> being an absence of shoals of school children or passing members of
> religious orders, telling the police officer [that] was hardly likely to

be offensive to anyone there....Second, that it was not unreasonable for an Aborigine who had conceptions about police conduct toward Aborigines to believe that when those officers entered his cell they had some hostile intent....That sort of decision...fifteen years before would not have been reached...but that's common among the modern judiciary (104:1230).

A corollary development to weakened stare decisis is the increasing use under the politicized role of indeterminate legal tests. Legal tests are constructs that courts develop when deciding cases that are of a generalizable nature and explain their rationale and guide future courts in analogous cases. For example, the High Court's "dominant purpose" test proffered in its 1999 *Esso* decision is an example. This construct holds that if communication was conducted for the *dominant purpose*, not sole purpose, of obtaining or giving legal advice then the common law standard for professional privilege is met. Legal tests are designed to provide guidance on legal questions and to elevate the judge's reasoning in a particular case beyond the specific circumstances of that case.

Many informants thought that the legal tests generally propounded during the Mason era were less determinate in language, giving judges greater flexibility in decision-making, more discretion, and therefore more power. "There has been a move to making legal tests more indeterminate," said one judge, "with a view to fit justice to the individual case." He continued:

> That creates its own tension because that means there is greater uncertainty. The rigor of the legal reasoning of the past has been cut down by that trend. That's why you get in a number of High Court cases now a lot of words written in an endeavor to state or apply these indeterminate tests in an intellectually satisfying way, which is difficult....That is a change from years ago where there was a greater emphasis on strict rules (95:2500).

One area where several informants noted the Court's tendency toward indeterminacy was the law of negligence. Negligence is but one of several private law claims that falls under the general law of torts. The overarching concern in a tort claim is whether compensation for a civil wrong—that is, something not criminally punishable—should be awarded for damage suffered as a result of another's acts or omissions.

Dating back to eighteenth-century English common law, the law of negligence concerns whether a person (or "tortfeasor") has a "duty of care" in a particular situation not to harm others. Common law legal systems the world over failed to develop generalized principles for determining duty of care standards until the House of Lords handed down *Donoghue v. Stevenson* in 1932.[41] *Donoghue*, which dealt with whether a soft drink manufacturer had a duty of care to those who consumed the beverage, laid down the following standard: "You must take reasonable care to avoid acts or omissions which you can reasonably foresee would be likely to injure your neighbor."[42] Despite *Donoghue's* apparent parsimony, courts have stumbled and fumbled over how to apply the reasonable care standard. Just how does one systematically evaluate whether reasonable care was given? For the first fifty years after *Donoghue*, British, Australian, and New Zealand courts approached this question by categorizing the type of alleged harm. Was it physical harm or harm to property? Was it purely economic harm? Courts in these countries developed different tests for duty of care depending upon the nature of the harm. Physical or property harm had one standard and purely economic harm had another. This was known as the "categorical approach."[43]

In the 1980s and early 1990s the High Court abandoned the categorical approach and tried to elevate a single, overarching principle to guide duty of care cases. "Proximity" became the determinative factor.[44] Proximity involves "the notion of nearness or closeness and embraces physical proximity, circumstantial proximity [such as the relationship between employer and employee]...and causal proximity, in the sense of closeness between a particular act and the injury sustained."[45] Elsewhere the Court said that proximity "reflects an assumption by one party of a responsibility to take care to avoid or prevent injury, loss, or damage to the person or property of another" due to the relative closeness or nearness of the parties.[46] Proponents of the proximity standard saw it getting at the core question in negligence cases: Was there enough of a relationship between the parties to obligate a duty of care?

---

41. [1932] AC 562.

42. Ibid., 580.

43. See *Bourhill v. Young* [1943] AC 92; *Glasgow Corporation Muir* [1943] AC 448; *National Coal Board v. England* [1954] AC 403; *Carmarthenshire County Council v. Lewis* [1955] AC 549; *Chester v. Waverley Municipality* (1939) 62 CLR 1; *Green v. Perry* (1955) 94 CLR 606; *Caledonian Collieries Ltd v. Speirs* (1957) 97 CLR 202; *Everitt v. Martin* 1953 NZLR 298; *Furniss v. Fitchett* 1958 NZLR 396; *MacKenzie v. Sloss* 1959 NZLR 533.

44. See *Jaensch v. Coffey* (1984) 155 C.L.R. 549; *Sutherland Shire Council v. Heyman* (1985) 157 CLR 424; *San Sebastian Pty Ltd. v. Minister Administering the Environmental Planning Act 1979* (1986) 162 CLR 340.

45. *Jaensch v. Coffey* (1984) 155 CLR 549, 584–85.

46. *Sutherland Shire Council v. Heyman* (1985) 157 CLR 424, 497–98.

The Mason Court saw proximity as a valuable legal test for determining duty of care. It enabled judges to consider a host of administrative, moral, ethical, political, and economic factors given the variegated notions of "nearness." Several appellate judges saw the proximity test as a prime example of the Mason Court's preference for indeterminate legal tests. Said one judge:

> Just what proximity was and how you decided there was proximity was something that caused an awful lot of trouble. Nonetheless, the Court mouthed these words about "proximity." Undoubtedly there was, from a political science view, power because of the indeterminacy of what this notion of proximity meant. In the last couple years the High Court has abandoned this proximity standard and said that it's not really a helpful way of looking at things. It's a statement of the result, rather than helpful to state how one gets a result (95:2700).

The post-Mason Court abandoned proximity as the lodestar for duty of care beginning in the late 1990s, but it has shown little capacity to develop consensus around alternative conceptual approaches.[47] The contemporary Court has backed away from proximity in part because of the substantial amount of intellectual wiggle room that it afforded the judges. The Mason Court thought that this wiggle room enabled judges to ensure just and fair decisions by being fact responsive and not rule bound.

DIMENSION #6: DEVELOPMENT OF THE LAW

The orthodox role recognizes that law develops interstitially and that litigants and their attorneys are the primary engines for this development. In other words, judges play a passive role in legal change, depending on litigants to bring cases that raise the opportunities for change. Moreover, when law develops under the orthodoxy, it does so in small steps. The politicized role, on the other hand, foresees occasions and justifications for larger legal leaps. Mason Court proponents supported the idea that there are occasions when interstitial development is inadequate and more profound change is warranted. Illustrative is this exchange with a Federal Court judge.

> Q: There is the possibility of backlash when the Court introduces profound change. Do you see a possibility for a snap forward? In theory, is it possible for the judiciary to be at the vanguard of an issue and

---

47. See *Hill v. Van Erp* (1997) 188 CLR 159; *Perre v. Apand* (1999) 198 CLR 180.

jump start the political system on a topic, moving the political system to where the Court is?

> Judge: Yes, I think that's possible. It's a question of how often you can do it and how radical you can do it. *Mabo* is the most radical example I think of that. Ultimately the sentiment has moved to accommodate *Mabo*. There has been an acceptance of the reality of native title. There had been a lot of mucking around the edges [on native title]. I don't think the basic principle has been diminished.... Even Prime Minister Howard has gone on record saying it was a sensible decision....Plainly if it happens too often or you leap too far forward you'll get a snap back....Maybe the Court has to put aside those considerations and say what they think the constitution says (89:4830).

Or consider this exchange with a Victoria appellate judge:

> Decisions from the High Court can make an impact in our society.... What you need is an accumulation of members of the High Court who are adventurous. If you get a majority who are, then the High Court has a real role to play. But if it goes back to its box, then it doesn't do much more than an intermediate appellate court....Our society is so conservative, it needs a prod occasionally.
>
> Q: Critics in the U.S. would say that the U.S. Supreme Court hasn't stopped prodding.
>
> Judge: That's what [Chief Justice] Gerry Brennan was afraid of.... I've always thought many Supreme Court decisions were good because they stimulate public debate. We haven't seen a civil war in America yet.

Accepting that it could bring more significant and rapid change to law, the Mason Court also altered how it justified that change, particularly in regards to constitutional doctrine. Orthodox judges justified constitutional development based on an antecedent admission that the common law develops interstitially. The Court was authorized to change the meaning of the constitution because it exercised an analogous power with the common law. The prominence that the orthodoxy gave to the common law justification is well illustrated in a speech that the current chief justice gave, where he said: "There is but one common law in Australia which is declared by the High Court as the final court of appeal. This is the principal unifying force in our legal system."[48] Rather than viewing the constitution as the unifying legal force and justification for change, the orthodoxy sees the common law playing that part. What was lacking under the orthodoxy was a justification for constitutional change based on the Court as final arbiter of constitutional disputes, something like the U.S. Supreme Court's claim in *Cooper v. Aaron* (1958). There the Court asserted that it alone was charged with this duty and was uniquely skilled to carry it out.[49]

The Mason Court supplemented the orthodoxy's common law justification with an institutional one. As one Mason Court judge remarked, "*Yes the High Court can place limits on Parliament because the judiciary is the ultimate interpreter of the constitution* (122:3703) (emphasis added)." Another remarked, "The High Court is the court which interprets the constitution. There is no other court in this country. Therefore, to the extent that it does that, it has enormous power (70:2100)." The admission that the High Court is the final interpreter of the constitution may seen inconsequential and, on one level, stating the obvious. It stands, however, in sharp contrast to the orthodoxy's common law justification for constitutional change.

A final way in which the Mason Court altered conceptions of legal development concerns who are seen as legitimate agents for that change. Under the orthodoxy, litigants and their attorneys were thought responsible for generating cases and arguments that precipitated legal change. Judges took a more passive approach, filling in the gaps as cases arose. The politicized role, on the other hand, envisions judges playing a larger role, moving from passive responders to active agents for legal change. This chapter and earlier chapters have mentioned several dimensions to the politicized role that facilitate judges functioning as

---

48. Chief Justice Murray Gleeson. October 10, 1999. "State of the Judicature." Australian Legal Convention, Canberra. See http://www.hcourt.gov.au/speeches/cj/cj_sta10oct.htm.

49. In *Cooper v. Aaron*, 358 U.S. 1 (1958), the Court wrote, "Article VI of the Constitution makes the Constitution the 'supreme Law of the Land.' In 1803, Chief Justice Marshall, speaking for a unanimous Court, referring to the U.S. Constitution as 'the fundamental and paramount law of the nation,' declared in the notable case of *Marbury v. Madison*, 1 Cranch 137, 177, that 'It is emphatically the province and duty of the judicial department to say what the law is.' This decision declared the basic principle that the federal judiciary is supreme in the exposition of the law of the constitution, and that principle has ever since been respected by this Court and the Country as a permanent and indispensable feature of our constitutional system. It follows that the interpretation of the Fourteenth Amendment enunciated by this Court in the *Brown* case is the supreme law of the land, and Art. VI of the Constitution makes it of binding effect on the States 'any Thing in the Constitution or Laws of any State to the Contrary notwithstanding.'"

agents for legal change. This difference in perspective can be seen in several remarks from informants. One judge concluded that the implied rights jurisprudence did not occur solely because of litigants advancing the argument, but also was "an act of frustration by the High Court faced with parliaments who won't work and who won't address big issues (126:4245)." The Court, in other words, was called to act. Another judge described the Mason Court judges not as passive dispute resolvers, but as a "breed of lawyers who saw law as a means of shaping and changing society....They didn't get there with political motives but their instinct was to see social problems and question why the law didn't deal with this. If the problem was that politics failed then law was the only other way.... They're all my friends....They saw law as a mechanism to help society cure its difficulties rather than law as an intellectual dispute (17:11220)." Finally, a Mason Court judge spoke about the institution's capacity to educate the community using language that envisaged more active roles for judges. The judge said:

> The legacy of the Warren Court is that people of the United States understand the constitution much better than they ever did. They have a better understanding of the judicial role. The Court can actually educate the legal community and the people; in fact, it's harder to educate the legal community than it is to educate the people....A lot of the criticism of the Warren Court and *Mabo* and *Wik* comes from those elements in the community that have no sympathy for liberalism. A lot of these people are vociferous red-neck people (122:5600).

The pertinent language here is the judge's conviction that the Court can impact public opinion and even promote liberalism, notwithstanding those unsympathetic to the cause. Underpinning this response is a conception of the High Court as a legitimate agent of change within the broader political system.

SUMMARY AND CONCLUSIONS

This is the second empirical chapter to explore the contours of the politicized judicial role. The chapter's main thesis is that the Mason Court ushered legal realism into a judicial culture long steeped in formalism. Most informants clearly saw the general shift in legal reasoning, but while the changes were palpable to them, many struggled to find an adequate label for the changes. Typifying many of his colleagues, a state Supreme Court Chief Justice said, "Yes a shift has occurred in legal reasoning, undoubtedly. A shift toward what I don't know (6:15115)."

This shift toward realism was evident in several general changes that the Mason Court brought to legal reasoning, most notably an admission that choice and discretion are unavoidable and that judges should be forthright in acknowledging actual influences on their legal reasoning, including community values. Constitutional interpretation underwent profound, even explosive, changes. The Mason Court developed an implied rights jurisprudence that admittedly waxed and then waned in scope. Appeals to international law, foreign precedent, and constitutional convention debates opened the library on constitutional interpretation. This chapter has also described how precedent became less stringent and legal tests more flexible during Mason's watch. The collective result was that the Mason Court became more comfortable than its predecessors as an agent of legal (and political) change.

6

The Causes and Timing of the Transformation

Having presented evidence that the Mason Court transformed its institution's role, this chapter tackles the question why the transformation occurred at all and why between the mid-1980s and mid-1990s. Explaining the causation, much less the timing, of Australia's judicial role transformation is no simple matter. The cast of players was large. High Court judges and other judicial officers played central roles. The political dynamics that brought many of the controversial disputes to the High Court, such that it could reach the decisions it did, involved myriad federal and state politicians, not to mention the litigants and their attorneys. The High Court judges at the transformation's core acted with an important degree of common purpose, yet possessed personal and idiosyncratic motivations, norms, and preferences that influenced why they reached their decisions. It is important to recognize that the transformation occurred within an institution that has its own history, rules, norms, and patterns of behavior separate and apart from the judges who fill its ranks. One must also recognize that it took place within a broader political system that frequently pressed upon and reacted to what was occurring in the Court. To make matters still more complex, the role transformation did not occur simply by judicial fiat. The Mason Court judges advanced their reforms, some with more forethought than others, within the parameters of actual cases where litigants sought resolution to particular problems. In the end, causation and timing were highly contextual and involved an array of actors and institutions. Given the complexity of the phenomenon described, the more accurate task for this chapter is to present the judges' perceptions of why the transformation occurred when it did. Their collective accounts suggest that an interplay of individual, political, and institutional factors coalesced to bring about the transformation. No single variable can explain it. Indeed, my informants were adamant that selecting one causal variable to the exclusion of others yields an incomplete and misleading picture. My data also demonstrate that the judges themselves did not hold to single causal explanations, but instead recognized multiple causes. Those who observed Australia's transformation firsthand identified the importance of individuals, institutions, and politics not out of intellectual confusion but in recognition of the complexity involved.

THE IMPORTANCE OF INDIVIDUALS

When exploring the causes and timing of the High Court's role transformation, a rather obvious yet critical factor is the Court's composition. Individuals matter. To say a court's decisions reflect who sits on the bench is prosaic to all but the most quixotic defenders of a mechanical jurisprudence. For them, law's clarity and comprehensiveness remove judicial discretion and enable different judges confronting the same case to reach the same conclusion. They would reject the notion that who sits on a court impacts the court's outputs. However, one need only look at how closely nominees to U.S. federal courts are vetted to see the intellectual vulnerabilities of this notion. Australia's High Court judges do not undergo formal confirmation hearings, but the media and legal community certainly pay attention when Prime Ministers announce new High Court appointees. As with a U.S. Supreme Court vacancy, speculation immediately surfaces over who is on a short list and what sort of impact an appointee may have on High Court decisions. Barristers who appear before the Court, academics who study it, and even lower court judges who read High Court decisions would all agree that the Court's composition influences its decisions, the rationales for those decisions, and the Court's broader institutional role. Individual judges can clearly shape a court's trajectory. It is necessary to begin then by assessing how changes in the High Court's membership contributed to the transformation's occurrence and timing.

Because Australia's appointment system enables the Prime Minister to fill vacancies on the High Court with little review, changes to the Court's composition must be contextualized with party politics at the federal level. Table 6.1 charts the tenures of recent Prime Ministers and the timing of their High Court appointments. It also records the chief justices' tenures. The last thirty years can be divided into three periods: 1972–1982, 1983–1995, and 1996–2005.

The first period begins with Gough Whitlam's Labor Party coming to power in 1972, the first Labor Government in twenty-three years. Whitlam's tenure was cut short by the infamous 1975 constitutional crisis. In October of that year the Senate, controlled by the opposition, refused to pass several of Whitlam's budget bills. Their refusal was in objection to a loan controversy that

Table 6.1 Tenures of Recent Prime Ministers and Chief Justices, 1972–2005

	1972	1973	1974	1975	1976	1977	1978	1979	1980	1981	1982
Prime Minister	Whitlam (ALP) 12/72–11/75				Fraser (Liberal) 11/75–3/83						
High Court Appointment	Stephen (Lib) Mason (Lib)		Jacobs	Murphy	Aickin			Wilson		Brennan	Deane Dawson
Chief Justice	Barwick								Barwick/ Gibbs	Gibbs	

	1983	1984	1985	1986	1987	1988	1989	1990	1991	1992	1993
Prime Minister	Hawke (ALP) 3/83 – 12/91									Keating (ALP) 12/91–3/96	
High Court Appointment					Toohey		McHugh				
Chief Justice	Gibbs				Gibbs / Mason	Mason					

	1994	1995	1996	1997	1998	1999	2000	2001	2002	2003	2004-05
Prime Minister	Keating (ALP) 12/91–3/96		Howard (Liberal-Coalition) 3/96–Present								
High Court Appointment		Gummow	Kirby (ALP)	Hayne	Callinan Gleeson					Heydon	Crennan
Chief Justice	Mason	Mason/ Brennan			Brennan/ Gleeson	Gleeson					

Note: Judicial appointments are listed by year. If in a given year a Government made an appointment only to lose later that year in the federal election, the appointing Government is listed in parentheses.

had enveloped Whitlam's Minerals and Energy Minister. A standoff ensued between the Government and the Senate. Australia's Constitution gives the Governor-General, the Queen's representative, the power to call for new elections when the Government is unable to pass its budget. Prime Minister Whitlam threatened to dismiss Governor-General Sir John Kerr if Kerr acted. With public pressure mounting on Whitlam and to the surprise of many, Kerr acted first. On November 11, 1975, he dismissed without consultation or warning the Whitlam Government and installed the Liberal Party leader, Malcolm Fraser, whose party was not in the majority, as a caretaker prime minister. A double dissolution election (where all House and Senate seats are put up for election) was held in December 1975, resulting in a sound Whitlam defeat. Prime Minister Fraser led the Liberal Government from 1976 to 1983.

The second period begins with the Labor Party wrestling control from the Fraser Government in the 1983 federal election. This victory ushered in an unprecedented thirteen years of Labor Government. Robert Hawke, Prime Minister from 1983 to 1991, successfully passed the baton to his Labor colleague Paul Keating, whose Government lasted an additional five years. The Liberal Party returned to power (in coalition with the National Party) under the leadership of John Howard in 1996, marking the start of the third period. Howard remains Prime Minister, successfully navigating three additional elections since 1996.

Keeping these three eras of federal politics in mind is important to understanding the High Court's transformation. Each of the five prime ministers made critical appointments. Prime Ministers Whitlam made two appointments (Jacobs, Murphy), Fraser racked up five (Aickin, Wilson, Brennan, Deane, Dawson), Hawke made two (Toohey, McHugh), Keating accounted for two (Gummow, Kirby), and Howard has made five (Hayne, Callinan, Gleeson, Heydon, and Crennan). In all, Labor Governments made six appointments and Liberal Governments accounted for ten. If popular convention holds true about the type of judges Labor and Liberal Governments appoint—the former more liberal and the latter more conservative—the High Court has been predominantly filled by conservative judges over the last thirty years. How then could it be said that federal politics during this time contributed to a more liberal Court? As with appointments to the U.S. Supreme Court, High Court justices do not always live up to the expectations of the Prime Ministers who appointed them. For example, the conservative Fraser Government (1975–1983) thought it was appointing conservative judges, but several embraced the politicized role more than Fraser would have anticipated. Similarly, the Hawke and Keating Labor Governments (1983–1996) appointed justices who, somewhat surprisingly, revealed more conservative judicial attitudes than expected. Who made the appointments mattered, but the story about the Court's transformation is more nuanced than this single factor. Once on the Court, several appointees exhibited role conceptions that were at odds with how the appointing Government envisioned the Court's role.

My informants emphasized that the Court's composition contributed to the transformation in the 1980s, but also to the orthodoxy's longevity and vitality earlier in the century. Since 1949, the Liberal Party (usually in coalition) has been in power 40 of 55 years, and enjoyed uninterrupted power between 1949 and 1972. Its dominance in federal politics over the last half century contributed to a conservative High Court that upheld the orthodoxy. Twenty-seven appointments to the High Court occurred from 1950 to 2005, with Liberal-National (Country) Governments making twenty-one of them, and Labor Governments making only six. The timing of these appointments partially explains why the transformation occurred when it did. Between 1950 and 1987 Liberal-led coalition Governments made sixteen appointments, while Labor Governments made but two.[1] Table 6.2 charts the partisan composition of the High Court in each of the thirty-eight natural courts that formed from 1903–2004. This term—a natural court—is used to demarcate the compositional change that comes with each new appointment.

The shading demonstrates vividly how dominant Liberal Government appointees have been. They enjoyed majority status on nineteen of thirty-eight natural courts, compared to nine natural courts for Labor Government appointees. Most significant, the Court had an uninterrupted Liberal majority from 1952 to 1989—a staggering 37 years. Indeed, it was not uncommon for Liberal appointed judges to occupy six of the seven positions, as it did from 1964 to 1974 and 1979 to 1987. This lopsidedness made for a more conservative Court during these decades, one more faithful to the orthodoxy. High Court judges bespeak often (and accurately) of their neutrality and independence. The aggregate picture from Table 6.2 suggests that more times than not during the institution's history, this message was offered with a Liberal accent.

It is not simply bad timing that explains Labor's historically spartan influence. Labor could not win an election, period, from 1949 to 1972, and its victory in 1972 was cut short by the 1975 constitutional crisis. That put Labor out of power for nearly another decade. The tides turned in 1983 with Bob

---

1. Liberal Government appointees in order of appointment: Justices Kitto (1950), Fullagar (1950), Taylor (1952), Menzies (1958), Windeyer (1958), Owen (1961), Chief Justice Barwick (1965), Justices Walsh (1969), Gibbs (1970), Stephen (1972), Mason (1972), Aickin (1976), Wilson (1979), Brennan (1981), Deane (1982), and Dawson (1982). The two Labor appointees were Justice Jacobs (1974) and Justice Murphy (1975).

Table 6.2 Natural Courts in High Court History, 1903–2004
(*Chief Justice Italicized, New Appointee in Bold)

Natural Court	Party Making Majority of Appointments**	\: Justice Positions							Date of Change	Length of Natural Court
		1	2	3	4	5	6	7		
1	Protectionist	*Griffith*	Barton	O'Connor					05.10.03	1903–1906
2	Protectionist	*Griffith*	Barton	O'Connor	**Isaacs**	**Higgins**			12.10.06	1906–1913
3	Protectionist	*Griffith*	Barton	**Duffy**	Isaacs	Higgins			11.02.13	1913–1913
4	Protectionist	*Griffith*	Barton	Duffy	Isaacs	Higgins	**Powers**	**Rich**	05.03.13	1913–1919
5	—	***Knox***	Barton	Duffy	Isaacs	Higgins	Powers	Rich	18.10.19	1919–1920
6	Labor	*Knox*	**Starke**	Duffy	Isaacs	Higgins	Powers	Rich	05.02.20	1920–1929
7	Nationalist	*Knox*	Starke	Duffy	Isaacs	**Dixon**		Rich	04.02.29	1929–1930
8	Labor	**McTiernan**	Starke	Duffy	*Isaacs*	Dixon	**Evatt**	Rich	20.12.30	1930–1931
9	Labor	McTiernan	Starke	*Duffy*		Dixon	Evatt	Rich	21.01.31	1931–1935
10	—	McTiernan	Starke	***Latham***		Dixon	Evatt	Rich	11.10.35	1935–1940
11	Nationalist	McTiernan	Starke	*Latham*		Dixon	**Williams**	Rich	15.10.40	1940–1946
12	Nationalist	McTiernan	Starke	*Latham*	**Webb**	Dixon	Williams	Rich	16.05.46	1946–1950
13	—	McTiernan	**Fullagar**	*Latham*	Webb	Dixon	Williams	Rich	08.02.50	1950–1950
14	Nationalist	McTiernan	Fullagar	*Latham*	Webb	Dixon	Williams	**Kitto**	10.05.50	1950–1952
15	Liberal	McTiernan	Fullagar	**Taylor**	Webb	*Dixon*	Williams	Kitto	03.09.52	1952–1958
16	Liberal	McTiernan	Fullagar	Taylor	**Menzies**	*Dixon*	Williams	Kitto	12.06.58	1958–1958
17	Liberal	McTiernan	Fullagar	Taylor	Menzies	*Dixon*	**Windeyer**	Kitto	08.09.58	1958–1961
18	Liberal	McTiernan	**Owen**	Taylor	Menzies	*Dixon*	Windeyer	Kitto	22.09.61	1961–1964
19	Liberal	McTiernan	Owen	Taylor	Menzies	***Barwick***	Windeyer	Kitto	27.04.64	1964–1969
20	Liberal	McTiernan	Owen	**Walsh**	Menzies	*Barwick*	Windeyer	Kitto	03.10.69	1969–1970
21	Liberal	McTiernan	Owen	Walsh	Menzies	*Barwick*	Windeyer	**Gibbs**	04.08.70	1970–1972
22	Liberal	McTiernan	Owen	Walsh	Menzies	*Barwick*	**Stephen**	Gibbs	11.03.72	1972–1972
23	Liberal	McTiernan	**Mason**	Walsh	Menzies	*Barwick*	Stephen	Gibbs	07.08.72	1972–1974

Table 6.2 Natural Courts in High Court History, 1903–2004, *continued*

Natural Court	Party Making Majority of Appointments**	Justice Positions 1	2	3	4	5	6	7	Date of Change	Length of Natural Court
24	Liberal	McTiernan	Mason	Jacobs	Menzies	Barwick	Stephen	Gibbs	08.02.74	1974–1975
25	Liberal	McTiernan	Mason	Jacobs	Murphy	Barwick	Stephen	Gibbs	10.02.75	1975–1976
26	Liberal	Aickin	Mason	Jacobs	Murphy	Barwick	Stephen	Gibbs	20.09.76	1976–1979
27	Liberal	Aickin	Mason	Wilson	Murphy	Barwick	Stephen	Gibbs	21.05.79	1979–1981
28	Liberal	Aickin	Mason	Wilson	Murphy	Brennan	Stephen	Gibbs	12.02.81	1981–1982
29	Liberal	Aickin	Mason	Wilson	Murphy	Brennan	Deane	Gibbs	25.06.82	1982–1982
30	Liberal	Dawson	Mason	Wilson	Murphy	Brennan	Deane	Gibbs	30.07.82	1982–1987
31	Liberal	Dawson	Mason	Wilson	Toohey	Brennan	Deane	Gaudron	06.02.87	1987–1989
32	Labor	Dawson	Mason	McHugh	Toohey	Brennan	Deane	Gaudron	14.02.89	1989–1995
33	Labor	Dawson	Gummow	McHugh	Toohey	Brennan	Deane	Gaudron	21.04.95	1995–1996
34	Labor	Dawson	Gummow	McHugh	Toohey	Brennan	Kirby	Gaudron	06.02.96	1996–1997
35	Labor	Hayne	Gummow	McHugh	Toohey	Brennan	Kirby	Gaudron	22.09.97	1997–1998
36	Labor	Hayne	Gummow	McHugh	Callinan	Brennan	Kirby	Gaudron	03.02.98	1998–1998
37	Labor	Hayne	Gummow	McHugh	Callinan	Gleeson	Kirby	Gaudron	22.05.98	1998–2003
38	Liberal	Hayne	Gummow	McHugh	Callinan	Gleeson	Kirby	Heydon	11.02.03	2003–2004

Key:

Protectionist

Nationalist, Nationalist-CP Coalition, or UAP-CP Coalition

Liberal-CP, Liberal NCP, or Liberal-NPA Coalitions

ALP

Shading indicates the appointing Prime Minister's party. If a sitting justice was later appointed chief justice by a party other than the original appointing party, that is reflected.

**For parsimony, I ignore coalition components and use the most recent name for the parties.

Hawke, who brought Labor four election victories (1983, 1984, 1987, and 1990). Paul Keating's successful reelection bid in 1993 meant that Labor stayed in power for an unprecedented and uninterrupted thirteen years. The 1980s and early 1990s represented, then, the first real occasion for sustained Labor influence on the Court's composition. Five Labor appointments were made between 1983 and 1996: Justices Toohey (1987), Gaudron (1987), McHugh (1989), Gummow (1995), and Kirby (1996). This run meant that from 1989 to 2003 (natural courts #32-37) Labor appointed judges were in the majority. There was only one other occasion in High Court history when Labor appointed judges sustained majority status across two or more consecutive natural courts. In December 1930, Justice Herbert Evatt's appointment created a Court where five of the seven judges were Labor appointees. One month later, January 1931, Justice Isaacs left the Court, leaving four of six Labor appointees. The Court operated at this reduced size as a cost saving measure through the Second World War, but Labor appointees lost their majority status in October 1935 with Chief Justice John Latham's appointment. After this near five year run, Labor appointed judges would not constitute a majority— much less sustain majority status across two or more natural courts—until 1989, some sixty-four years later. These statistics underscore the historical significance of the Hawke and Keating Governments' influence on the Court.

Some readers may object, particularly Australian court observers, to my use of the term "majority status," suggesting that it inappropriately implies that judges appointed by the same party behave in coalition. That is not what I intend. Rather, Table 6.2 shows the relative and evolving influence that the major political parties have had on the Court's composition. Furthermore, while it is unfair to lump together automatically judges appointed by the same party and assume their decisions comport with others in the majority, one cannot ignore the reality that the major parties favor judges with different judicial philosophies. The table provides in very broad brushstrokes, then, a sense of the intellectual ebbs and flows over time.

Can a causal argument be made that the transformation was simply a byproduct of the Labor Party coming to power in 1983? If political events had panned out differently—if, say, the Labor Party controlled Government from 1950 to 1983 instead of the Liberal-Country coalition—would the transformation have occurred much earlier, coinciding perhaps with the U.S. Warren Court revolution? In a famous 1957 article, American political scientist Robert Dahl observed that, "The policy views dominant on the Court are never for long out of line with the policy views dominant among the lawmaking majorities of the United States (1957, 285)." U.S. Supreme Court scholars have noted how the Court's role has tended to follow major party realignments and shifts in governing majorities. The Court may lag behind the governing majority at times. With lifetime tenure, it is possible for judges to remain on the Court long after the appointing president (and governing majority he represented) leaves office and the current majority moves in a different direction. As vacancies occur, the lag diminishes. The larger point of Dahl's research is that a court's outlook mirrors broader political shifts in the governing majority. The same appears to be true in Australia. The judicial orthodoxy's hold in Australia was so great, in part, because conservative governments remained in power so long. The change in judicial outlook and temperament occurred exactly when Dahl would predict: after the Labor Party came to power in 1983 and made several High Court appointments that shifted the balance of power on the Court.

There is a case to be made that changes in party control of government contributed to the Court's transformation. My informants tended to think that to properly understand the transformation, one must begin with the two chief justices who led the Court from the 1960s to the 1980s. Chief Justices Barwick (1964–1981) and Gibbs (1981–1987) were both Liberal Party appointees. Barwick came to the bench from political circles, having served as Commonwealth Attorney-General from 1958 to 1963. Prime Minister Menzies appointed Barwick straight to the chief justiceship in 1964 when Chief Justice Dixon retired due to health concerns. My informants placed Barwick and the Barwick Court in the orthodox camp, although they regarded it as less orthodox than the Dixon Court (1952–1964).[2] The difference was one of degree, not kind.

According to my informants, Barwick earned his orthodox stripes for the consistent leadership he brought to the Court's tax decisions. The Barwick Court dedicated a disproportionate amount of its docket space to tax cases; indeed, it was not uncommon for a half-dozen tax cases to appear in a single volume of the *Commonwealth Law Reports* during Barwick's tenure. Foremost in this jurisprudence were cases concerning section 260 of the *Income Tax Assessment Act*, a provision designed to close off tax loopholes. In a series of cases, the Barwick Court diluted the potency of this section, concluding that the section's language was too vague and absent more specific prohibitions individuals could creatively (and legally) avoid tax obligations.[3] Reading down

---

2. The following biographies provide extensive analyses of Chief Justices Barwick's and Gibbs' judicial philosophies: Barwick's *A Radical Tory: Garfield Barwick's Reflections and Recollections* (1995); also Joan Priest's *Sir Harry Gibbs: Without Fear or Favour* (1995).

3. See *Mullens v. Federal Commissioner of Taxation* (1976) 135 CLR 290; *Slutzkin v. Federal Commissioner of Taxation* (1977) 140 CLR 314; and *Cridland v. Federal Commissioner of Taxation* (1977) 140 CLR 330.

section 260 in this way required a narrow, literalist approach to statutory interpretation. Barwick would later justify these decisions in his autobiography:

> The obligation to pay [taxes] is a legal one. Some politicians try to treat it as a moral obligation. But it is not. The citizen is bound to pay no more tax than the statute requires him to pay according to the relevant state of his affairs.... In the language of the layman, the citizen is entitled to minimise his liability to pay tax.... On this principle, I regularly acted. Provided the citizen's transactions were not shams, pretences, the form of his transactions and their legal consequences would affect his liability to tax, even though that form might be unusual and adopted for the express purpose of limiting the liability to pay tax (Barwick 1995, 229).

A judge who served on the Court with Barwick offered the following assessment:

> In my early days on the Court, I saw a strong feeling of animosity directed towards taxation generally. This was led by Barwick. That was fairly dominant in the Court—a feeling that it was legitimate for taxpayers to have recourse to any steps...within the law to reduce the incidence of taxes, and that it was for the Court to give a strict interpretation that would allow them to do it. It was up to the legislature to block those efforts...rather than for the judges to strain an interpretation to achieve what they might regard as a good policy outcome (37:5300).

Barwick's influence went beyond tax law. He also exerted significant control over the Court's broader agenda, displaying a penchant for Section 92 cases. A Federal Court judge, who clerked at the High Court during Barwick's tenure as chief justice, remarked:

> To an associate it appeared that Barwick controlled the Court, not only in administrative terms, but very much in where the Court was prepared to go in developing constitutional theory. The best example I can think of were the Section 92 cases...where you saw judges trying to tease out one workable standard.... The effort failed. Within the Court at that time, the sense was that the judges were really fighting against Barwick's desire to hold the Section 92 line back to its original form, which was very much to give Section 92 very little bite at all. I remember asking [a High Court Justice] why the members of the Court were so careful to negotiate with the Chief.... His answer was because they had enormous respect for

him. So there was a generational respect for Barwick as Chief Justice which my generation didn't share. We saw him as an old man (113:1350).

These cases earned Barwick a conservative reputation. According to a Western Australia judge, "Barwick was a brilliant lawyer, but he was always English. He was back in England. He grew up on English law (43:1200)." Another judge remarked, "I knew Barwick well and personally. He and I were yachtsmen. Barwick was a black letter lawyer." Asked to define this term, he continued:

Black letter lawyers are civil lawyers who think they know everything about law. They regard it as a science and up themselves. They're usually highly qualified judges who think they know the law. An elitist is a good way to describe a black letter lawyer. They're more interested in the science, the letter and theory of the law than how it affects the person standing over there (43:1815).

Still another judge described him as "a lawyer in the conventional mold (48:2600)."

I noted above that Barwick was not as strongly associated with the orthodoxy as Dixon. One way in which this came to light was how my informants thought about Barwick's black-letter lawyering. According to my informants, his commitment to literalism, at least in the tax cases, was not to its method per se but to the economic results the method produced. It was not literalism for literalism's sake. "The High Court has done things in the past that was social engineering in a secretive way," said one judge. "Barwick's interpretation of income tax legislation, for example, was social engineering. Now that's acknowledged (65:1100)." Another put it this way: "In Barwick's time, the Court looked at tax cases and took a parsing approach rather than a purposive approach. Deconstructionists would say that that was just a cloak for outcomes that Barwick wanted (89:1800)."

Barwick's retirement in 1981 led to the promotion of Sir Harry Gibbs as Chief Justice. Gibbs was not thought to exercise the same degree of control as Barwick, but he was seen by many informants as an orthodox judge. A Queensland judge claimed, "Gibbs was a conservative—a black letter lawyer. He treated law in a blinkered way (1:1700)." While Gibbs himself promoted the orthodoxy, rumblings of discontent were heard among other justices during his chief justiceship. "When Chief Justice Barwick retired, it was the start of a new era," said a Western Australia judge. "It was followed by the Gibbs Court. The [Barwick] Court was a good degree more conservative than [the Gibbs Court]. Judges were less restrained under Gibbs…and under Justice Mason they came out of their shell. Under Mason there was unparalleled judicial activism. But there were…signs in the early 1980s (126:130)." This judge's description of two progressive steps from Barwick's orthodoxy to Mason's transformative court was generally agreed to among informants. The Gibbs Court was the stepping stone. As a Federal Court judge said, the Gibbs era was "an interlude," "a time of peace for the Court," and "marking time (114:1630)."

I found strong consensus that the retirements of Chief Justices Barwick in 1981 and Gibbs in 1987 were critical to the transformation. When Barwick retired, Prime Minister Fraser's Liberal Government promoted Justice Gibbs to the top position, who had been on the High Court since 1970. Sir Gerard Brennan, previously on the Federal Court and the ACT Supreme Court, filled Gibbs' vacancy. When Gibbs retired as Chief Justice in 1987, Anthony Mason was promoted from within to lead the Court. The year before Mason became Chief Justice, Justice Lionel Murphy died, creating, with Gibbs' departure, two vacancies for the Hawke Labor Government to fill in 1987. John Toohey from the Supreme Court of Western Australia and Mary Gaudron from the NSW Court of Appeal were appointed. Two years later the Hawke Government made a third appointment—Michael McHugh from the NSW Court of Appeal—upon the retirement of Justice Ronald Wilson, a Fraser Liberal Government appointee. In three short years, 1987 to 1989, the Court's composition changed dramatically with three Labor appointments.

The correlation between the party in power and the appointees' proclivities for the orthodox or politicized High Court roles appears all the stronger when one looks at the composition of Labor and Liberal Government justices on the Court from year to year. It was not until Labor appointees found themselves in the majority that the Court issued the controversial decisions that confirm the politicized role's emergence. Dahl's thesis appears to be correct: the transformation occurred when it did because the Court was reflecting the new governing majority. As one judge put it, "What the public doesn't realize is that the judiciary is the product of who the executive government appoints. If they appoint liberal thinkers and you get a court full of them, you'll get changes. If you appoint liberal thinkers—Kirby is a good example—you get judgments of a different type that Barwick (53:1645)."

The idea that the transformation was a natural consequence of Labor Party appointees breaks down upon closer scrutiny, however. First and foremost, the strongest protagonists in the transformation—those who provided its intellectual leadership—ironically were Liberal-Country coalition government appointees. If the liberalism of U.S. Chief Justice Earl Warren and Justice William Brennan surprised and disappointed President Eisenhower, Liberal Prime Ministers McMahon and Fraser were probably just as surprised that their appointees—Justices Anthony Mason and William Deane—would some-day spearhead such radical reform, much of it at odds with Liberal Party ideology.

A second reason why Dahl's thesis breaks down in the Australian context has something to do with lag time. His primary thesis is that U.S. Supreme Court decisions will rarely be long out of line with governing majorities because of the regularity with which presidents make appointments. When lags occur between the Court's and the governing majority's ideologies, the Court usually finds itself reaching decisions that an erstwhile governing majority would favor but are at odds with the present governing majority. Australia's judicial role transformation presents something of an anomaly in this respect. The transformation occurred largely during two Labor Governments, led by Prime Ministers Hawke (1983–1991) and Keating (1991–1996), that were more receptive to at least some of the reforms than the Liberal Party. Dahl's thesis seems vindicated. Yet the intellectual leadership for the transformation came from Liberal Government appointees put on the bench during the 1970s and 1980s, namely Anthony Mason and William Deane.

The critical change was Anthony Mason's promotion to Chief Justice in 1988. With near unanimity, my informants thought that Chief Justice Mason provided the intellectual leadership for the transformation. To say merely that the change occurred "during" his tenure belies his critical role. A Federal Court judge offered the following regarding Mason:

> By the time you get to the Mason Court there was a greater willingness to experiment with developing different theories and not feeling constrained by the Chief Justice into going one way. It may sound odd then to call it "The Mason Court." But the strength of Mason was he could lead from the front. He was fast with writing judgments. He picked up the tenor of his brother judges and provided something that they were prepared to follow or develop. That was not through generational respect, but more sympathetic assessment of where Australian law was going and where his Court wanted to take it. If you appeared in the Mason Court, you could never avoid being aware of the Chief, even if he said nothing and looked as if he was writing another judgment [during oral argument]. I don't know if he was or wasn't. Even if he was, he dominated. He didn't dominate the Court in the Barwick sense by controlling the dialogue, but he brought it all towards himself. He had that ability to channel what was going on (113:1630).

"We had a very radical High Court for a while, when you had Mason, Deane, Toohey, and Gaudron forming a majority group who were prepared to make changes, (77:1200)" said one judge. A Victoria appellate judge claimed, "Circumstances arose in the 1980s which gave the opportunity for the Court to decide some landmark cases. Because of the members of the Court—Mason and Deane in particular—there was more liberal, lawmaking activity by the Court (70:600)." The advocates for reform were, according to a Federal Court judge, "Mason, Brennan, Deane, Gaudron, and Kirby—Mason and his mates—and to a lesser extent members of the Brennan Court (85:1000)." The reform, according to another judge, "[C]ame with Sir Anthony Mason. It was not just his doing....The Court then was composed of a group of judges who felt free to break out....People like Deane and Mason were prepared to look beyond the black letter law (113:1025)."

Mason's leadership in the transformation is all the more fascinating because few foresaw it when he was appointed as a puisne High Court judge in 1972. His practice as a barrister had primarily been in equity and commercial law, hardly areas where budding reformers cut their teeth. He was appointed Solicitor-General for the Commonwealth in 1964, which afforded regular appearances before the High Court, particularly in constitutional matters. He served on the NSW Court of Appeal from 1969 to 1972 before his appointment to the High Court. Signs of Mason's reformist spirit did not appear in his early years on the Court. In fact, he wrote in a 1979 decision regarding his institution's lawmaking capacity that, "[T]here are very powerful reasons why the court should be reluctant to engage in such an exercise. The court is neither a legislature nor a law reform agency. Its responsibility is to decide cases by applying the law to the facts as found. The court's facilities, techniques, and procedures are adapted to that responsibility; they are not adapted to legislative functions or to law reform activities."[4]

Much has been said about the Mason Court endorsing a mode of constitutional interpretation that enabled it to imply certain rights from the document. Mason did a substantial amount of intellectual lifting in these cases. For instance, in *Australian Capital Television*, Mason advanced the argument that the Court has a long tradition of drawing implications from the constitution, reminding his readers that none other than Sir Owen Dixon admonished his colleagues to "avoid pedantic and narrow constructions."[5] Mason wrote:

> [T]he court has drawn implications from the federal structure prohibiting the Commonwealth from exercising its legislative and exec-

4. *State Government Insurance Commission v. Trigwell* (1979) 142 CLR 617, 633.
5. *Australian National Airways Pty Ltd. v. Commonwealth* (1945) 71 CLR 29, 85.

utive powers in such a way as to impose upon a State some special disability or burden unless the relevant power authorized that imposition or in such a way as to threaten the continued existence of a State....*But there is no reason to limit the process of constitutional implication to that particular source* (emphasis added).[6]

Only six years before Mason endorsed this constitutional methodology, he participated in *Miller v. TCN Channel Nine Pty.* (1986). Having been prosecuted for erecting a wireless telegraphy station without the required license, Miller alleged, *inter alia*, that the state law requiring this license violated an implied right to a freedom of communication contained in the constitution. After addressing Miller's other arguments, Mason turned in his last paragraph to the implied rights issue. He pithily dismissed it with the following:

There was an alternative argument put by the defendant, based on the judgment of Murphy J. in *Buck v. Bavone* (1976) 135 CLR 110 at 137, that there is to be implied in the Constitution a new set of freedoms which include a guarantee of freedom of communication. It is sufficient to say that I cannot find any basis for implying a new s.92A into the Constitution.[7]

It is true that *Miller* and *Australian Capital Television* dealt with different sections of the constitution. It is also true that Miller's "speech" was certainly different from banning political advertisements leading up to an election. Miller's station was erected to serve exclusively as a linking station to transmit signals from Sydney to Brisbane. Nonetheless, it is striking that Mason made such quick work dismissing the implied rights argument in *Miller* only to change his mind six years later.

With these examples in mind, it is hardly surprising that Mason's reforming spirit went undetected in the legal and popular media at the time of his promotion to chief justice. Perhaps his reforming spirit remained latent. Perhaps it had not yet formed. The popular media focused, if the promotion was covered at all, on administrative and stylistic changes that Mason may bring to the Court. There was little or no speculation that any substantive changes in law or legal reasoning would come. A typical prognostication was, as one reporter wrote, that Mason's promotion would "result in a streamlining of court procedures," "more joint judgments," and "greater consultation among the members of the court." Stressing the stylistic changes that Mason would

---

6. *Australian Capital Television*, 134.
7. 161 CLR 556, 579.

bring, another wrote that Mason is "firm like Barwick," but "lacks the open aggression Barwick displayed." He is a "stickler for the rules," and someone with "an acute memory of the case law" who will "keep cases moving fast."[8]

How does one reconcile Mason's 1979 obiter dictum with the Mason described in the previous two chapters? Some informants spoke in religious terms about Mason undergoing some kind of conversion from "a black letter lawyer" to an institutional reformer. A Victoria judge claimed, "We saw two phases of Mason. The first was as a conservative judge in the 1980s and then the second— more innovative—later on (67)." A Federal Court judge concurred: "Mason himself went through an evolution I think which made him much more of an activist than he was in his early years (89:1400)." A Queensland judge offered: "Sir Anthony Mason himself moved from…a very traditional, conservative, black letter legal position to a much more radical position. The position was then reached that the Court's Chief Justice and its resident intellectual—Justice Deane—were both willing to adopt a wider, more progressive attitude toward the development of the law (87:1245)." Others thought Mason just expanded to fit the office. A Commonwealth attorney said simply: "Mason grew into the role of chief justice. He grew into the big picture idea—that it was the High Court's responsibility to lead in the development or creation of law (66)."

Still others were less charitable. "The Jacobins at the High Court" should have returned "to the way it was between 1960 and say 1985," said one judge. He continued:

> The basic approach was sounder before 1985. Mason-I was sounder than Mason-II…meaning from 1982 onwards. Mason-I was an equity lawyer. The most striking feature of his judgments from 1971 to 1981 are the very useful analysis of the law on any particular subject by reference to everything that had gone before, and there's not too much novelty. Mason-II you don't bother with what everyone said before. You just work it out from first principles (103:5200).

Another critic regretted, "Sir Anthony Mason was a first-class lawyers' lawyer and he suddenly felt sick of lawyers' law. He had been there, done that. He didn't find it exciting any longer. He would find it very exciting if he started interpreting things the way Marx, Freud, or someone would have done. [Mason succumbed to] the siren song of the left-wing intellectuals (3:1730)." The *Sydney Morning Herald* was excruciatingly mistaken when it ran an article in 1986 about the

---

8. See, e.g., Verge Blunden, Dec. 9, 1986, "After Troubled Years, High Court Enters Calmer Waters," *Sydney Morning Herald*, p. 4.

Court under Mason titled "After Troubled Years, High Court Enters Calmer Waters." The article included the following: "A new Chief Justice and the first woman judge [Gaudron] should provide an interesting phase in the history of the High Court. *But at least it should be sailing into calmer waters* (emphasis added)."[9]

Mason assumed the helm in February 1987. There were no explicit harbingers in his public remarks for what was to come, although hindsight allows one to find some subtle hints. In the annual State of the Australian Judicature speech in September 1987 Mason described the mid-1980s as "quite eventful for the Australian judiciary." Topping the list of memorable developments was the elimination of appeals to the Privy Council from state supreme courts and the implementation of the special leave procedure. Mason tersely said that the former "has finally cemented the position of the High Court as the ultimate court of appeal for Australia." He spent the bulk of his speech affirming the merits of the latter. He remarked, "From the Court's point of view the new system has achieved the benefits expected of it. It has placed a limit on our increasing burden of work by winnowing out those cases that have no general or public importance. Consequently the work is generally more difficult. The questions of law are invariably significant so that the average case now requires greater consideration." Critics of the special leave process argued that it denied litigants a right to a second appeal. The language that Mason used—distinguishing between private and the public's interests—elliptically hints at his desire for a more powerful court:

> But in common law systems elsewhere it is generally recognized that one appeal is a sufficient satisfaction of the private interests of the litigants. It is legitimate to expect the state to provide one appeal to an intermediate court to guard against the possibility of error at the trial. But it is going a long way to ask the state to provide a second appeal.... The justification for a second appeal, an appeal to the ultimate national court of appeal, is that it serves the public interest (Mason 1987, 1122).

Mason also called for a close examination of Australia's intermediate appellate courts. Intermediate courts are the final courts to review most cases so they must be staffed with judges who can promote uniformity in the law and still satisfactorily resolve the immediate cases before them. Not every judge, according to Mason, is up to the task. He did not go as far to say what type of judge makes a good appellate judge, but he noted, "Appellate and trial work call for different judicial qualities," and that politicians should look for those "best fitted to undertake appellate work (Ibid.)." Here we see Mason trying

---

9. Ibid.

from the very start to distinguish the High Court's work from other courts. The Canberra Court has a special charge. Acknowledging these differences is key to the transformation's genesis.

The first indication that the new Chief Justice was likely to promote more than stylistic reform came on May 5, 1988 with the *Cole v. Whitfield* decision about interstate trade. Back peddling from its earlier prognostication for calmer waters under Mason's leadership, the *Sydney Morning Herald* ran a lengthy article about the Chief Justice where, after detailing Mason's archetypal conservative background and legal experience, it concluded that, "Such impeccably conservative credentials make him an unlikely candidate to be 'the most radical Chief Justice we have ever seen,' which is how one of Australia's leading constitutional lawyers describes him."[10]

Just as the popular press failed to foresee the radical change that would come under Mason's leadership, so too did the legal press and law journals. The announcement of his promotion caused nary a stir and certainly not articles alerting the legal profession to the revolution just around the corner. None of Australia's major law reviews or any of the legal journals made such a claim. They should not be faulted for shortsightedness. The nonplus reaction was not from missed signals. There was something quite unexpected about Mason's conversion. It caught court observers and many of my informants by surprise.

I should mention that Sir Anthony Mason participated in my research and he is quoted regularly within these pages. He sat for a lengthy, forthright interview. Like all other informants, Sir Anthony spoke on condition of anonymity, so I am unable to utilize his comments to speak one way or another about any conversion that he underwent. To mention even elliptically any such discussion would violate the conditions for the interview. However, I can say that my interviews with him and with his colleagues who constituted the Mason Court confirm the importance of appointments. Who serves on the bench obviously matters. Appointments (and retirements) were critical to the timing of the role transformation.

The sheer force of Chief Justice Mason's intellect and leadership would prove inadequate to realizing change if at least a majority of the bench did not share, in some measure, Mason's vision. By the late 1980s a coterie of like-minded, reform-oriented judges was assembled, skeptical about the orthodoxy and intent on advancing a new institutional vision. My informants tended to identify

---

10. Milton Cockburn, June 30, 1988, "Mason Sets the Benchmark," *Sydney Morning Herald*, p. 7.

three associate justices as key collaborators in the transformation: Justices William Deane, John Toohey, and Mary Gaudron. Each provided intellectual leadership at different times in the transformation and in different areas of law. With Chief Justice Mason, they forged a consistent majority in several signature cases. Their success promoting the politicized role was possible, in part, to the eight years that all four shared the bench (1987–1995, natural courts #31 and #32).

As a barrister, William Deane had an extensive practice in equity, trade practices, and commercial law. He was appointed to the Federal Court in 1977 as President of the Australian Trade Practices Tribunal, before accepting an appointment by the Fraser Government to the High Court in 1982. After thirteen years on the Court, Deane served as Governor-General from 1995 to 2001. His influence on the Mason Court can be seen in several decisions. It was he who advocated for an alternative to reasonable foreseeability as the standard for determining when to impose a duty of care in negligence claims. In *Jaensch v. Coffey* (1984), Deane was the only judge who argued that the concept of proximity should guide duty of care questions. As discussed earlier, this standard gained wider acceptance by Mason Court judges in the late 1980s and early 1990s.

Deane also contributed to the Mason Court's expansion of constitutional freedoms. In language akin to the U.S. Constitution, Chapter III of Australia's Constitution vests "the judicial power" in the High Court and other federal courts that Parliament may create. Deane defined "judicial power" in a manner that served as a source of liberty. In his mind, the exercise of judicial power obligated the courts to recognize certain due process rights and procedural protections. For instance, he concluded in *Polyukhovich v. Commonwealth* (1991) that the concept of the "judicial power" prohibited an ex post facto law that designated certain acts committed during the Second World War as "war crimes." Such a law violated a foundational juridical tenet that criminal convictions must be based upon acts deemed illegal at the time they were committed. Deane also supported the Mason Court's implied free speech cases and pushed the implication envelope further than some of his colleagues. For example, *Leeth v. Commonwealth* (1992) concerned the legality of the procedures for sentencing federal criminals, who typically serve their time in state prisons. The sentencing procedures required judges to follow relevant state criteria in setting a minimum non-parole period. These criteria varied from state to state, thus resulting in widely varying sentences for federal offenders who committed the same crime. Justices Deane and Toohey concluded that this practice violated a right to substantive equality implicit in the free agreement of "the people" to unite in a federation and "in the Constitution's separation of judicial power from legislative and executive powers."[11]

If one found any press speculation in the 1980s about forthcoming judicial activism, it was not about Mason's or Deane's potentiality. Much more speculation swirled around John Toohey and Mary Gaudron, both appointed in 1987. Regarding these two, the *Australian Financial Review* wrote, "The Federal Government has produced the unlikely result of an ecstatic Labor Party.... The Gaudron-Toohey team also delivers the type of liberalization of the court which will appeal to Labor supporters."[12]

Toohey came from the Western Australia bar and had served concurrently on the Federal Court and the Supreme Court of the Northern Territory, which afforded him significant adjudicative experience with property disputes and Aboriginal people. This experience no doubt informed his *Mabo* and *Wik* judgments in which he sided with the Aboriginal claimants. Toohey's judgments in these cases garnered much attention and have gained particular recognition in ensuing years for their clarion call against reaching adverse legal conclusions based upon cultural differences, his assertion of a fiduciary duty to protect indigenous Australians' land rights, and his recognition that native title to particular lands may coexist with other titles. In a later indigenous case, *Kruger v. Commonwealth* (1997), Toohey would be one of two justices to conclude that the legal claims of the "stolen generation" were satisfied based on a constitutionally implied right to freedom of movement and association. He also reached the controversial conclusion in *Leeth* (1992) that the constitution implied a substantive right to equality. Toohey joined the majority in a number of other cases that signaled the role transformation: *Cole v. Whitfield* (1988) which brought much clarity to Section 92 interstate trade jurisprudence; *Dietrich v. Queen* (1992) concerning a common law right to a fair trial; and *Cheatle v. Queen* (1993) affirming that the constitutional right to a jury trial includes a unanimity standard for convictions.

Appointed in 1987, Mary Gaudron was the first woman to serve on the High Court. She came to the Court having had an active practice at the bar working for six years as NSW Solicitor General, which had her appearing regularly before the High Court. Justice Gaudron consistently supported the most controversial Mason-era decisions, including *Cole v. Whitfield*, *Mabo*, *Wik*, *Australian Capital Television* and *Nationwide News*, *Dietrich* and *Kruger*, and occasionally would have pushed the Court even further, such as in *Leeth*. Her joint judgment with Deane in *Mabo* caught much controversy because of its

---

11. *Leeth v. Commonwealth* (1992) 174 CLR 455, 486.

12. David Solomon and Greg Earl, December 9, 1986, "Gaudron, Toohey Get Nod as New High Court Judges, *Australian Financial Review*, p. 1.

direct, emphatic tone: "The acts and events by which that dispossession in legal theory was carried into practical effect constitute the darkest aspect of the history of this nation. The nation as a whole must remain diminished unless and until there is an acknowledgment of, and retreat from, those past injustices."[13] Many politicians saw this as over the top. It was one thing for the Court to overturn *terra nullius* but quite another to do so with such moralizing tones.

As these brief paragraphs demonstrate, the role transformation depended heavily upon the right collection of judges assembling at the Court. Chief Justice Mason was central to the transformation, but he needed willing collaborators—judges who shared in a larger, more politicized vision for the Court. He got just that with the appointment of Deane, Toohey, and Gaudron. Other judges contributed as well, but not as consistently as these three. From 1987 to 1995 the Court had a majority of judges whose proclivities favored the politicized over the orthodox role. Getting the right mix of justices was important, but not singularly important to the role transformation.

THE IMPORTANCE OF INSTITUTIONS

Australia's judicial role transformation cannot be explained exclusively through appointments. It stems from an interplay of individual, institutional, and political variables. This section identifies a number of institutional precipitants critical to the role transformation. I use the term "institutional" in the broad sense of formal structures and rules, as well as informal norms and practices that set the parameters and context within which political power is exercised, in this case High Court decision-making. Three institutional precipitants fostered favorable conditions for the Mason Court to advance the politicized judicial role. These precipitants were the introduction of mandatory retirement reforms for High Court judges, the creation of a mechanism for the High Court to decide only those cases it wants to hear, and the abolition of appeals from Australian courts to the Privy Council. They all were necessary conditions, though non sufficient for the transformation. Each institutional precipitant had its own unique effect on how the Court exercised its power.

Institutional Precipitant #1: Mandatory Retirement

Section 72(ii) of the Commonwealth Constitution originally provided that justices of the High Court and of other courts created by Parliament "shall not

---

13. *Mabo*, 109.

be removed except by the Governor-General, on an address from both Houses of Parliament in the same session, praying for such removal on the ground of proved misbehavior or incapacity." The Court interpreted this in *New South Wales v. Commonwealth* (Wheat case) to mean that federal judges enjoy lifetime appointments.[14] Many justices fully lived out this charge. The ranks of High Court justices are peppered with several judges who had remarkable staying power. For example, Australia holds the record for the longest serving final appellate court judge in the common law world: Justice Edward McTiernan served for forty-six years from 1930 to 1976. He was appointed at the spry age of thirty-eight and retired at age eighty-four. Sir Owen Dixon was a close second, serving as a puisne judge or chief justice for thirty-five years (1929–1964). Since federation in 1901, only thirty-eight individuals have served on the Court, excluding its seven current members. Twelve died while on the bench or within a year of leaving it. Justice McTiernan will likely retain his marathon record because in 1977 Australian voters passed a constitutional amendment fixing a mandatory retirement age of 70 for High Court judges. Parliament cannot change this age. The amendment also set the maximum age for all other federal judges at 70, but Parliament retains the right to alter this, should it so desire. For a contemporary aspirant to exceed Justice McTiernan's forty-six years on the Court, the prodigy would have to be appointed at the age of twenty-four. The high threshold of popular support required for constitutional amendments to be passed usually means that successful amendments must enjoy bipartisan support. The 1977 reform secured the support of all major parties on the basis that it would promote a more dynamic Court by fostering more turnover and appointment of younger, qualified barristers who, under the old regime that produced fewer vacancies, might not be appointed at their professional peak. All High Court appointments made after 1977—puisne and chief justice positions alike—were affected.

Had the 1977 mandatory retirement provision been in effect since federation, fourteen of the thirty-one judges who served before 1976 would have been forced to retire. Only four of the thirty-one judges retired before reaching age seventy. Nearing its thirtieth anniversary, the mandatory retirement provision has increased turnover and produced a younger bench. Thirty-one appointments were made during the High Court's first 75 years (1903–1977). The average lapse in time between these appointments was 2.87 years. From 1978 to 2004, nineteen judges were appointed. The average time lapse between

---

14. (1915) 20 CLR 54.

these appointments was 2.18 years. Moreover, the average tenure for a High Court judge has decreased since the reforms. From 1903 to 1977 the average judge spent 17.16 years at the High Court. Since the reform, it has dropped to 13.2 years.[15] The larger point to these statistics is that the 1977 reforms fostered greater turnover in the High Court's composition and quickened the assemblage of a cohort of judges favorably disposed to the politicized role.

Its impact was observable as early as 1981 when Chief Justice Garfield Barwick retired from the Court at age eighty-eight. Appointed to the chief justiceship in 1964 by a Liberal Coalition Government, Barwick was exempt from the retirement provision. Scholars tend to agree that Barwick carried the orthodoxy's banner during his seventeen year tenure. Prime Minister Fraser elevated a puisne judge, Harry Gibbs, to the top job that year. He too supported an orthodox judicial role. Gibbs' promotion came four years after the retirement reforms, which meant that although he had served as a puisne High Court judge since 1970, he came under the mandatory retirement rule with his promotion. Gibbs was 64 years old at the time of his promotion. Treating Gibbs' promotion as a "new appointment," susceptible to the 1977 reforms, proved critical to the transformation's genesis. Gibbs would only serve six years as chief. Had the amendment applied only to new appointments and not promotions within the Court, the transformation very well may have never occurred or it certainly would have been delayed.

Gibbs served as Chief Justice only six years before he was forced to retire in 1987. By then, the Liberal Coalition Government had lost power to the Hawke Labor Government. On the occasion of Gibbs' retirement in 1987, Hawke promoted Anthony Mason, leaving Gibbs with the ironic legacy of ushering in the transformation by simply entering into his septuagenarian years. Gibbs' mandatory retirement was also critical because it enabled the Hawke Labor Government to appoint Mary Gaudron to fill the vacancy created with Mason's promotion. Justice Gaudron frequently lined up as a Mason reformer and promoted the politicized role. Sometimes she provided just her vote. Other times she pushed reforms even further than her reform-minded colleagues.

To complete the Court's picture in 1987, one must note the death of High Court judge Lionel Murphy one year earlier. A colorful and controversial High Court judge from 1975 to 1986, Murphy had served as Commonwealth Attorney-General from 1972 to 1975 under the Whitlam Labor Government.

---

15. These figures ignore Albert Piddington's appointment in 1913, who resigned before taking up his appointment, and reflect the Court at the end of 2004.

Murphy himself has an important part to play laying the groundwork for the Mason Court revolution, but here I will only note that his death in 1986 enabled the Hawke Labor Government to appoint John Toohey to the Court in 1987. With this appointment, the key proponents for the transformation were in place: Chief Justice Mason, Justices Deane, Brennan, Toohey, and Gaudron. The mandatory retirement provision precipitated these changes in the Court's composition.

Institutional Precipitant #2: The Special Leave Requirement

The second institutional precipitant emerged from reforms during the mid-1980s to the mechanism by which the Court controls its workload. The constitution specifies some matters included under the Court's original jurisdiction, including cases where the Commonwealth is party to a suit (Section 75(iii)), cases involving Commonwealth officers (Section 75(v)), and suits between residents of different states (Section 75(iv)). Parliament has assigned other matters to the Court's original jurisdiction, notably cases concerning the constitution and its interpretation. The Court's appellate jurisdiction, promulgated in Section 73, extends judicial review to decisions from single High Court judges, all federal courts, and state supreme courts. Unlike its original jurisdiction, the Court's appellate jurisdiction is general in nature, meaning that it may review any public or private law as a general court of review.

Until 1984 the High Court lacked any filtering mechanism for cases filed under its appellate jurisdiction. This meant that if a case was properly appealed, the Court had to hear it. The U.S. Supreme Court found itself in a similar position, having little control over which cases made it to its appellate docket, until the Judges' Bill of 1925. That year, some sixty years before comparable reforms in Australia, amendments to the *Judiciary Act* provided the Supreme Court with a filtering mechanism to review only those appeals that it agreed to consider. In 1984, reforms to Australia's *Judiciary Act* required litigants to secure henceforth the High Court's permission to proceed with an appeal. Litigants appealing decisions of single High Court judges were required to secure "leave to appeal" and those appealing from the Federal Court or state supreme courts needed "special leave to appeal."[16] The difference between the two obviously stems from the origin of the dispute. Judges tend to use the moniker "special leave" for both types. The procedures for evaluating

---

16. Individual High Court judges frequently handle interlocutory matters, constitutional writs, and election contestations.

them are the same. To secure either, appellants must first make written submissions. The High Court reviews these applications using two judge panels. If before oral arguments on a special leave application it appears that the two assigned judges disagree on whether to grant leave, a third judge participates in oral arguments to break the tie. The special leave requirements were designed to alleviate workload pressure generated from appeals by right. Previous chapters detailed the criteria used to evaluate petitions for leave.

Scholarship regarding the U.S. certiorari process concludes that it effectively enables the Supreme Court to construct agendas (Perry 1991; Pacelle 1991). Indeed, given the Court's ability to grant a fraction of the thousands of petitions, it exercises extensive agenda building capacity. Attitudinal public law scholars contend that because policy preferences animate Supreme Court judges, it follows that they grant review to cases that best enable them to advance these preferences. Finite resources and time also mean they are unlikely to review cases where they agree with the lower court's decision and reasoning. The judges instead concentrate on reviewing those cases which, if overturned, would promote their policy preferences (Tanenhaus et al. 1963; Provine 1980; Caldeira and Wright 1988).

H.W. Perry's *Deciding to Decide* offers a more nuanced explanation for certiorari decisions. Drawing from interviews with Supreme Court judges and clerks, Perry concludes that individual judges cast their certiorari votes based on a number of sequential decision gates. Answering "yes" or "no" to each question leads the judge closer to a decision. In short, judges can follow an outcome mode or a jurisprudential mode. Judges follow the former if they care about the case outcome. If not, they follow the latter. The outcome mode presents fewer decision gates that must be passed to grant certiorari: Does the judge think she will win on the merits? Would it be institutionally irresponsible to not take the case? Is this a good vehicle or is a better case coming down the pipeline? The jurisprudential mode is followed if the judge does not care about the case outcome. In this mode, a judge would vote to grant certiorari if there is inter-circuit conflict, if the case raises an important issue, if the issue has sufficiently percolated in lower courts, and if a better vehicle is unlikely to come. As a hierarchical process involving several decisional steps, judges have any number of devices at their disposal to handle extant petitions and even cue future petitions (271–84).

Implicit in Perry's decision-gate schematic is the notion that the Supreme Court crafts its workload agenda using the certiorari process. The discretion it affords the justices enables them to review only those cases they deem worthy. The aggregate effect of these individual certiorari decisions is that the Court constructs an agenda—a vision of its institutional responsibilities and priorities. That the Supreme Court uses the certiorari pool to construct an agenda is accepted by most Supreme Court scholars. The same cannot be said about the High Court and its special leave requirement. Indeed, the idea that the High Court has "an agenda" was altogether an anathema for my informants.

Perspectives on the High Court's special leave process tended to divide into two distinct camps: the judges, on the one hand, and the barristers who appear before the judges on the other. Those who filed special leave applications said one thing about the process, while those who decided them said another. I confronted near universal aversion among judges at all levels to the suggestion that special leave enables High Court judges to accept cases they prefer to review and reject those they do not. None would consider that special leave decisions enable the justices to promote their policy preferences. Special leave was seen to filter out unwarranted cases, but not filter in wanted cases. Moreover, it was a benign filtering process, disconnected from judges' normative role conceptions or legal and policy preferences. Consider these two responses from High Court judges when asked about the special leave process.

> [The Court's] control over major constitutional cases is extremely limited. That is because first it is open usually to any party who wishes to agitate a constitutional question.... Sometimes it is possible for the Court to remit proceedings to a lower court for trial, but then there will always be the possibility of the matter coming back to the High Court on appeal. In the case of litigation in other courts, not only is there a prospect of special leave to appeal, but there is also a procedure by which an attorney general of the Commonwealth, states, or territories can require a court to remove a matter into the High Court in order to have it determined. When there is a live question of some substance relating to the constitution, the High Court's practice universally has been to adopt a procedure which will result in the Court giving a ruling on a point. The High Court does not in fact abjure any opportunity to determine an important constitutional question (63:2630).

A second High Court judge offered this description:

> Under Section 75, parties have the power to approach the High Court directly with constitutional writs. No special leave is required. Now under the *Judiciary Act*, the High Court has the power to remit such cases, and it usually does. It's possible to by-pass the special leave application, given that important constitutional cases come straight to the Court.... Special leave in state courts is different from special leave at the High Court. Here special leave focuses on the merits of the

cases, but also about the national importance of the point being discussed. If the issue concerns one state's statute, it's unlikely that the
Court will grant special leave. If it's a federal statute, the matter is
usually left at the Full Federal Court because the High Court doesn't
have the time.... As an appellate judge, I looked also to ensure justice
in individual cases, so it was hard for me to make the transition to
the High Court.... Now High Court cases must have national importance or a sufficient injustice to require the Court's attention and send
a message to lower courts (116:1300).

The two excerpts illustrate the benign role the High Court judges ascribe to
themselves in the special leave process. No comments were made about agenda
setting or policy preferences, aside from amorphous references to what might
be in the country's best interest. Indeed, High Court judges saw themselves as
passive observers to the assemblage of cases. Judges don't craft agendas. The
litigants who bring cases exercise the agenda setting power. Consider a High
Court judge's supine description of his institution:

The question you ask is wrong. There is no agenda. We do not construct
an agenda....Our options are limited. We have original jurisdiction. Unless it can be remitted, it has to be determined. By and large there is no
point in remitting something if you know it's going to bounce back up
as an appeal. In those areas there isn't a big choice. You have got a choice
in your civil and criminal appeals....People will never believe it, but
those cases chose themselves. Things go on out there that conspire us
to take the cases....In general, the cases choose themselves (92:5500).

Another High Court judge suggested the same:

The question so phrased seems to suggest that the Court itself has some
initiative to undertake. I don't think there is any....The Court's function is to simply resolve the question that arises from the litigation that
is put before it. The Court has no agenda of its own....I think it's not
a question of whether the Court wishes to intervene....The question
is whether the instruments of the democracy have purported to act
within the powers which the constitution confides on them (63:2500).

Several intermediate appellate judges held equally skeptical views about the
High Court's agenda setting capacity. By way of illustration, a NSW appellate
judge suggested, "I don't think judges, when they consider cases brought to
the Court, think to themselves, 'Well, we should jump start something.'" He
continued:

Judicial thinking is different from that. In the first place, the cases that the High Court deals with are the cases that the parties bring before them. True we have a system now where you can't get to the High Court without special leave, but broadly speaking the High Court can't set an agenda and say, "This year we're going to fix up this and next year we'll get around to fixing something else." Judges are faced with cases that are presented by particular parties in a particular way (34:1215).

If the High Court judges and many of their lower court colleagues resolved to see no discretion entering the special leave process, the barristers who appear before the Court and navigate this process for clients saw little besides discretion. To deny the agenda building capacity is to ignore their firsthand experiences. Nearly all of the lawyers I interviewed found it next to impossible, drawing from their own experiences, to determine when and why the Court grants or denies requests for leave. Several thought that the judges' personal proclivities inevitably come into play. Reflecting on his appearances before the Court, one informant remarked, "I don't think anyone is yet able to say, possibly not even the High Court judges themselves, on what basis the judges decide really whether to give special leave or not. It was my experience and from talking to others...you just could not predict whether special leave would be granted (95:2130)." A Federal Court judge with substantial High Court experience offered his view on the special leave's logic.

The Court handles only a tiny, minute fraction of the matters that are put up to it...through the filtration process—the grant of special leave. It's still very difficult to get a case before the Court through a grant of special leave. It's a pure lottery. It depends very much on what appeals to the judges on the day when special leave is sought from the Court. I can't for the life of me, having done dozens of cases before the High Court, predict with confidence whether the Court will be prepared to take a case....Sometimes they grant special leave in a case that I would have confidently said there is no special leave point here. Sometimes they might reject a case and wouldn't consider it while I think the case is an absolutely clear-cut suitable vehicle for the grant of special leave. *So what the Court does is the product of a fairly indiscriminate scratch-off lottery* (44:1330) (emphasis added).

Other informants emphasized that while special leave decisions are unpredictable, the process provides the Court with greater control over its workload.[17] A Commonwealth attorney confessed, "Yes of course the High Court has the power to control its agenda because of the special leave process (66)." A High Court barrister offered such an assessment.

> They would say, "We have no agenda," but I would regard that as simplistic because whether you have one or not, or whether you recognize you have one or not, the approach taken over time in dealing with granting leave to appeal to the High Court is itself a manifestation of some view about what types of cases should be reviewed. I think it's simplistic to say that a case gets to the High Court by reason of the activity of those involved in bringing them—that the activities of the High Court play no part in them getting there. The reality is that if, in effect, decisions in cases A and B indicate the possibility of there being a change of view on the part of the Court, then the likelihood is that a case which raises that issue will be there pretty shortly. That's what can happen of course (106:3500).

Those last two sentences are crucial. They indicate that the bar responds to the Court's cues on what issues or precedents it is keen to review. Agenda setting then goes beyond choosing among extant special leave applications. Through formal judgments, speeches or other informal means, the Court also can influence what special leave applications are filed in the first place. Supreme Court scholarship finds similar effects (Tanenhaus et al. 1963; Ulmer et al. 1972). A Western Australia judge thought special leave focuses the Court on the most important (controversial) issues:

> Not having appeals of right—not having their time taken up with boring property cases—means that they will end up with more hard questions. So, they end up with more things where it can look simply wrong. One of the criteria for granting special leave is that the question

---

17. There are some admitted dilemmas in conceptualizing the special leave process as the Court's agenda-setting mechanism. First, the Court cannot survey at a single point in time all of the special leave applications that will come before it that year. It operates with imperfect information, obviously surrendering much control over the timing of applications. In other words, if the Court decided to dedicate attention to a cluster of issues, it could proceed only on the knowledge of those special leave applications before it. Its agenda-realizing capacity is limited by this. Second, not all judges hear every special leave application. Panels of two (sometimes three) judges review the written submissions, conduct the hearings, and make determinations on the applications. This means that any discussion of the Court acting on special leave applications as an institution must recognize this qualification.

has a broad importance across Australia, so you're going to annoy more people....What the High Court [does now] has more effect on the Australian political system and is the focus of more discontent (45:5500).

An ACT judge made a similar connection:

> The High Court in the 1980s took the view that it was no longer feasible to hear every appeal that came before it. By virtue of a consultation between the Government of the day and the Court, it was decided that the High Court would hear appeals only by leave. That naturally meant that the High Court would choose cases that it wished to hear. There would be more that raise questions of constitutional importance or general legal significance, so I guess it's understandable there would be a greater number of significant cases then being decided in the Court (104:1800).

The real rub is whether special leave enables the judges to review those cases that promote their judicial role conceptions. American public law scholars viewing the Australian scene would conclude that the judges possess that capacity and exercises it, even if they do not admit to it. Most remarkable was the failure (or unwillingness) of High Court justices to see that their special leave decisions say volumes about their judicial role conceptions.

The question then becomes whether the barristers or High Court judges more accurately describe the special leave process. My sense from the interviews was that this was one area where Australia's judicial culture has yet to pierce the pre-legal realist orthodoxy. High Court judges were not prepared to say they have control over their institution's agenda. Even the strongest proponents of the transformation abided by this passive vision of the Court and its agenda. One might anticipate this hesitancy. For them to admit to realist explanations for special leave decisions risks much criticism and potential loss of legitimacy.

Empirical data lend some credence to the barristers' viewpoint. The data suggest that the special leave reforms not only heightened the Court's control over its workload, but since the reforms, the judges are inevitably advancing, consciously or otherwise, their normative role conceptions through special leave decisions. Figure 6.3 charts the annual number of special leave applications filed at the High Court and certiorari petitions filed at the U.S. Supreme Court from 1977 to 2000. It also charts the number of cases decided by each court.[18]

---

18. The High Court data came from the *High Court of Australia Annual Report* for the years 1980 to 2000 and the Australian Law Reform Commission's 2001 report, *The Judicial Power of the Commonwealth, Report: A Review of the Judiciary Act 1903 and Related Legis-*

Figure 6.3 High Court Special Leave and U.S. Supreme Court
Cert. Petitions Filed versus Cases Decided, 1977–2000

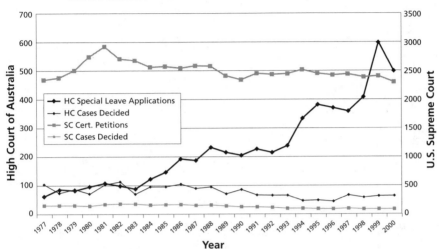

Many more petitions for review are filed in the Supreme Court than the High Court. One could hypothesize that this difference is due to Americans being more litigious or rights-conscious than Australians (Glendon 1993). Relative population may also account for the difference. Australia's population is nearly fourteen times smaller than the U.S. population. Consider the number of petitions filed in each court in 2000: 2,305 (U.S.) and 370 (Australia). If the relative population explains the difference, then only 164 applications should have been filed in Australia to the 2,305 filed in the U.S. In fact, nearly double the predicted number were filed that year. Population alone cannot explain the difference. It is noteworthy that in the mid-1980s the number of special leave applications filed in the High Court grew precipitously in response to the reforms under discussion. Given these statistics, the High Court has found itself increasingly in a position not unlike the U.S. Supreme Court, whereby it exercises growing discretion over which cases to review. The gap between the number of cases actually decided and the pool of petitions for special leave provides a measure for its agenda-setting capabilities. The smaller the number of petitions, the fewer choices the Court faces. The larger the pool, the more choice the Court faces. If, for example, the judges identify an

lation. The U.S. Supreme Court data came from Epstein et al.'s *The Supreme Court Compendium: Data, Decisions, and Developments.*

Figure 6.4 Annual Number of Special Leave and Certiorari Petitions Filed Per Decided Case in the High Court and Supreme Court, 1977–2000

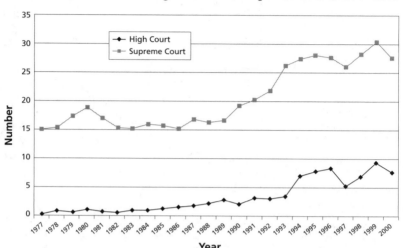

area of law requiring development or clarification, a larger special leave pool would provide more and perhaps better suited cases to pursue this clarification than a smaller pool.

One measure of the High Court's agenda setting capability is how much of a filtering effect the special leave process provides. Figure 6.4 charts the annual number of special leave and certiorari petitions filed per decided case in the High Court and Supreme Court from 1977 to 2000. It shows that the Supreme Court's certiorari process provides a much greater filtering effect than the High Court's special leave process. Perhaps one factor contributing to this difference is the relative adolescence of Australia's requirement. Australia's special leave requirement is less than twenty years old, whereas the certiorari requirement is eighty. A more suitable comparison to the contemporary High Court might be the U.S. Supreme Court from 1925 to 1941. This sixteen year block represents the same number of years out from the point at which reforms were undertaken in Australia. Figure 6.5 compares the filtering effect of Australia's special leave process (1985–2000) to the Supreme Court's certiorari requirement (1925–1941). The data show fairly comparable filtering effects in both courts during these initial years. The courts diverge initially in the ninth year (1934 and 1993, respectively) and in earnest starting in the fourteenth year, where the High Court (1998) significantly outpaced the Supreme Court (1939).

Figure 6.5 Annual Number of Special Leave and Certiorari Petitions Filed
Per Decided Case for First Sixteen Years After Reforms
(U.S. Supreme Court 1926–1941, Australian High Court 1985–2000)

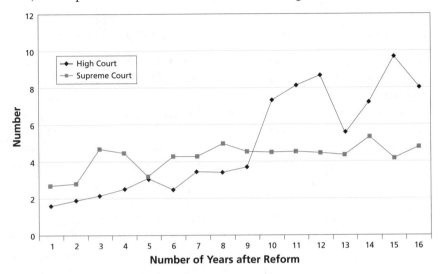

This raises an important empirical question, that I can only pose at this point and leave for future research: Was there a common development pattern as these institutional reforms became routinized in both countries? It is unlikely, of course, that Australia's special leave process will ever have the filtering effect that the certiorari process has, given differences in population and litigation rates. The data confirm, however, that the High Court's agenda-setting capacity increased consistently since the reforms were initiated. Indeed, its filtering effect outpaced the U.S. court in its early years.

This reform was necessary but insufficient for the judicial role transformation. It was necessary because without this the Mason Court would have had less control over its docket because the right of appeal would have remained. It shifted the locus of power from litigants to the judges. Rather than litigants shaping the agenda, the judges were. With the number of special leave applications increasing by nearly 800 percent from 1983 to 2000 and with a special leave success rate hovering between 18 and 31 percent for those years, the reform also gave the judges permission to focus their limited time and resources on issues they considered most important.

This was just one piece of the puzzle. Controlling the docket only makes a change in the Court's mission more possible. Its efficacy depends completely on what cases the judges deem most important. In truth, the special leave reform coincided with another institutional precipitant that heightened the Court's control over its work.

Institutional Precipitant #3: Abolition of Privy Council Appeals

Judge Learned Hard wrote, "For myself it would be most irksome to be ruled by a bevy of Platonic Guardians, even if I knew how to choose them, which I assuredly do not. If they were in charge, I should miss the stimulus of living in a society where I have, at least theoretically, some part in the direction of public affairs (1958, 73–74)." Australia's High Court operated for over eighty years under such a bevy. Chapter 2 described the historic concession that Australia's constitutional framers made with Colonial Secretary Chamberlain to secure enactment of the constitution in the Imperial Parliament. To placate British investors and promote legal uniformity throughout the Empire, Chamberlain insisted that the constitution provide litigants the option to appeal decisions from Australian courts to the Empire's appellate court in London, the Judicial Committee of the Privy Council (henceforth "Privy Council"). The Australian delegates conceded to this demand, provided that the High Court would be the final arbiter in all constitutional matters. Thus, when the constitution was ratified in 1901, litigants could appeal decisions from state courts and from the High Court in non-constitutional matters. This section makes the argument that the gradual abolition of the appellate route to the Privy Council provided a final institutional precipitant for the transformation. To appreciate the significance of this reform, it is necessary to provide some historical detail on the Privy Council's jurisdiction and then explore its practical impact on Australian judges.

At its apex, the Privy Council, sitting in London and composed primarily of members from the House of Lords, functioned as the final appellate court for nearly 100 countries, dominions, and territories throughout the British Empire. Today's Privy Council is a nineteenth century statutory creation, but its jurisdiction can be traced back to the Curia Regis, when the King was the ultimate dispenser of justice. Australia's constitutional delegates were not the only ones debating the relevance and jurisdiction of the Privy Council in the nineteenth century. Debate extended to Whitehall as well. Although many heralded the Privy Council as the most august judicial body the world over, a sustained effort to consolidate the Privy Council and House of Lords into a single appellate court occurred in the nineteenth century. With these two institutions exercising overlapping jurisdictions, the possibility of conflicting decisions on legal questions was well appreciated and a point of concern. Advocates for each institution pushed various legislative efforts in the 1830s and 1840s to transfer the appellate jurisdiction of one court to the other and vice versa.[19] In 1872 Lord Hatherley successfully passed an act that would have created a new Imperial Supreme Court of Appeal, but it was never realized.[20]

The Imperial Conferences from 1911 to 1918, attended by delegates from each British colony and territory, grappled with what appellate structures should exist in Great Britain and its dominions. Australia took the lead in championing reform, calling for the creation of a truly imperial appellate court—one whose members represented all dominions and whose decisions spoke for the entire Empire, including Great Britain. The Privy Council at that time did not hear domestic cases and its decisions were not binding on other British courts. In fact, its decisions applied only to the dominions involved in the disputes. Although one of its chief duties theoretically was to promote legal uniformity across the Empire, this setup made it possible for the Council to undermine uniformity in fact. Although the idea of an Imperial Court of Appeal was bantered around for nearly twenty years, the exigencies of World War I interceded and the idea lost steam until Britain revived it in the 1960s (Swinfen 1987).

The inter-war period represented a time in which debate over dominion status unfolded. Reforming the constitutional relationship between Great Britain and her dominions percolated throughout the Imperial Conferences in the 1910s and 1920s. What role the Privy Council should play in the evolving relationship between dominions and London was central to the debate. Should there be an Imperial Court of Appeal? Should the Privy Council play any role in the dominions' legal affairs? These questions were formally addressed when the 1926 Imperial Conference adopted what came to be known as "the Balfour Declaration," named after Lord Balfour who chaired the Committee of Prime Ministers that drafted it. The non-binding declaration called for a new constitutional relationship: "[Great Britain and the dominions] are autonomous communities within the British Empire, equal in status, in no way subordinate one to another in any aspect of their domestic or external affairs."[21] This was a significant first step because it questioned the future applicability of the *Colonial Laws Validity Act*. Passed in 1865, this Act forbade dominions from passing laws that contravened or were repugnant to imperial law, and it lim-

---

19. Lord Brougham led an effort to transfer the House of Lords' appellate jurisdiction to the Privy Council. See Swinfen (1975). Lord Campbell pushed for legislation that would have done the opposite. See (1842) "Debates 3rd Series," Hansard LXII, columns 175, 179.

20. 36 & 37 Vic., c 66. See Childers (1901).

21. Imperial Conference. *Command Paper 2768—Summary of Proceedings*. Imperial Conference of 1926. London: H.M.S.O.

ited the extent to which colonial legislatures could have effect outside their im-mediate borders. These were known as the repugnancy and extraterritoriality doctrines. The Privy Council was responsible under the Act for policing do-minion statutes to determine if they violated these doctrines. The principle of equal status declared in the Balfour Declaration secured legislative footing in 1931 with the *Statute of Westminster*.[22] The statute freed the dominions (then Canada, Australia, New Zealand, the Union of South Africa, the Irish Free State, and Newfoundland) from the repugnancy and extraterritoriality doc-trines. No longer were dominion laws invalid because they were repugnant to the laws of England; moreover, dominion legislation could have extra-territo-rial effect.

Under the Statute, the British Parliament could still legislate for Australia, but it required the "request and consent" of the Commonwealth Parliament. While it freed Australia's Commonwealth Parliament, it left the state parlia-ments still bound by the *Colonial Laws Validity Act* and the doctrines of ex-traterritoriality and repugnancy. Section 2 authorized dominion legislatures to amend or repeal acts of the United Kingdom Parliament applying to the dominions. The statute broadened dominions' legislative powers, including the power to restrict Privy Council appeals. Retention of the appellate route was a matter of discretion. Some dominions responded sooner than others to the green light that the statute gave in curbing Privy Council appeals. Canada abolished criminal appeals in 1933 and civil appeals in 1949. South Africa followed suit in 1950. Australia's verve did not match that of her Commonwealth cousins. Its path toward abolition was long and marked by fits and starts.

Australia's first step to limit Privy Council appeals occurred shortly after federation, but was rather narrow in scope. The *Judiciary Act 1907* prevented direct appeals from state supreme court in cases that raised *inter se* questions. An *inter se* question is a narrow constitutional question involving the limits of government power *inter se* (that is, between) the Commonwealth and the states. With it the High Court became the final arbiter of *inter se* questions. All other state matters could still go to the Privy Council after 1907.

The real push to abolish Privy Council appeals began in the late 1960s and concluded in the mid-1980s. The first step occurred in 1968, when the Gorton Government passed legislation that limited the matters for which leave to the Privy Council could be sought. The *Privy Council (Limitation of Appeals) Act 1968* allowed appeals from the High Court to the Privy Council only in non-

---

22. 1931. 22 & 23 Geo. 5, c4.

federal matters. In other words, all constitutional and federal jurisdictions came exclusively under the High Court's authority. It was still possible, however, to appeal High Court or state supreme court decisions concerning purely state questions. The Whitlam Government took the next step in 1975 when it enacted legislation that ended all appeals from the High Court, regardless of whether federal or state jurisdiction was involved.[23] Appeals from state supreme courts were still possible after 1975 in purely state matters. This produced a schizophrenic judicial hierarchy, where it was possible to appeal a state supreme court decision either to the Privy Council or the High Court. Former Chief Justice Mason concluded that this duality produced much confusion, unnecessary complexity, and delay (2000). This strange duality ended in 1986 with passage of the *Australia Act* (Cth). This act marked Australia's full and complete legal independence from Britain and ended, *inter alia*, all appeals from state supreme courts to the Privy Council. Lest the significance of these statutory developments be lost, it deserves reiteration that the High Court of Australia was not considered the final, ultimate authority over all Australian legal matters (federal and state) until 1986. In other words, Australia's High Court achieved a mere twenty years ago what the U.S. Supreme Court secured in 1793!

It became patently clear from my interviews that the Privy Council profoundly shaped how High Court justices viewed their institution's role within the legal system and prolonged the orthodoxy's dominance. My informants had strong convictions that closing this appellate route opened the High Court to profound change. I contend that this institutional reform served as another institutional precipitant to the transformation.

Australia's appellate judges perceive that retention of Privy Council appeals had a constraining force on the High Court. At a technical level, the High Court was bound to accept and follow Privy Council decisions. As a High Court judge explained, "Of course we were bound by decisions of the Privy Council directly on point. It had to follow them as matter of precedent. It gave very great weight to decisions of the House of Lords, although it was not technically bound because the Privy Council is often constituted by members of the House of Lords. They're likely to come to the same conclusion (94:1500)." Another High Court judge confirmed that before the reforms, Privy Council decisions had a "binding nature" on the High Court. This should surprise few because the Privy Council was legally the High Court's court of review. Several informants noted de rigueur deference to other English courts as well.

---

23. *Privy Council (Appeals from the High Court) Act 1975.*

[T]here was an attitude of mind on the part of Australian judges that although they weren't strictly bound by…decisions of English courts…because the Privy Council was constituted by judges who sat in the House of Lords there was a natural tendency…to follow a House of Lord's decision. That was carried to the extent that [a former Chief Justice] wrote a judgment in which he said Australian judges were bound to follow the decision of the English Court of Appeal, a view which I think is clearly unsupportable. But I only mention it to indicate the attitude taken by the bulk of Australian judges [before the 1980s] (122:630).

The obeisance to the Privy Council and other English courts was done, however, for more than mere legal obligation. Earlier generations of judges, many good Anglophiles, held the Council in high esteem and relished opportunities to participate in its proceedings. Australian barristers took appeals to London. Certain Australian judges even sat on the Privy Council, following early twentieth century reforms that enabled the Crown to appoint judges from colonial and dominion supreme courts. This reform was designed to ameliorate the workloads placed on English judges and provide dominion courts a greater sense of inclusion in imperial legal development (Beth 1975, 235).[24] "Going to London had its attractions," said one High Court judge. "That's one reason why some people took cases there (95:1700)." Another High Court judge made the following assessment of ending Australian appeals: "There was regret on the part of some members of the Court, I'm sure, partly because they very much enjoyed going over—this is a purely selfish view I suppose—as members of the Privy Council and sitting on very interesting cases coming from all over the Commonwealth of Nations (37:1145)."

The Privy Council did more than simply engender nostalgia for the motherland. Several judges asserted that the mere existence of an appellate route impinged the High Court's ability to shape Australian law as it saw fit. A High Court barrister said, "The fact that you could have another court as the ultimate appellate court in relation to Australian law I think did have an inhibiting effect in a couple of ways. One way was that with the possibility of appeal…the

---

24. *Judicial Committee Amendment Act 1895* (58 & 59 Vict. c. 44) and the *Appellate Jurisdiction Act 1908* (8 Edw. 7, c. 51). Such opportunities depended, of course, on judges having reasons and resources for travel to England. Some were more apt than others to accept the invitation. Indian jurist Syed Ameer Ali, for example, sat on over 400 cases from India, Burma and Ceylon.

state of the High Court was diminished. [Second,] the ultimate determinant of what would be the proper model of legal reasoning was to be found in what the Privy Council said (106)." An ACT judge concluded that before appeals ended,

> The High Court always felt—Sir Owen Dixon felt—that they really did not want to get out of kilter with what was happening in the U.K. That was the source of the common law. The common law was developed in the U.K., with the Privy Council at the apex. The Privy Council could always overrule the High Court on matters other than Australian constitutional things. So they really didn't want to go too far in developing the common law in any way inconsistent with what they'd expect the Privy Council to do (6:1515).

These quotes suggest that the High Court limited itself by following Privy Council precedent and legal reasoning. The development of Australian law was also limited by the fact that the Privy Council often proved ill-prepared and unfamiliar with the disputes arising from a federal system of government established in a written constitution. A High Court judge offered:

> What was significant was getting rid of the Privy Council....There were three factors making the Privy Council less relevant to Australia. [First,] the Brits never understood federation—just didn't understand what was involved in it. They simply had no conception of the quite different role of the judiciary in a federation. The second thing was their absolute inability to understand that the common law might develop differently in one place from another....Third, their entry into the European Union frustrated the development of the common law in Australia because the British courts were not addressing them (92:245).

A High Court barrister elaborated on the challenge of the Privy Council interpreting Australia's written constitution when its own government lacked one. "The Privy Council had no experience in constitutional law in any sense comparable to the way you have it in the U.S. or Australia. That I think does have an effect on the modes of reasoning because if you have to decide constitutional cases, there are so many factors you take into account. Sometimes very few of them have much to do with legal reasoning in any traditional sense (106)." A High Court judge concurred: "I know in early years it never came easy to members of the Privy Council—English and Scottish judges—to treat a legislature as subject to limits in a written constitution. They had to adjust their thinking.

That's probably changed now with the European context in which they have to operate (37:2300)." Finally, another High Court judge confessed, "The point had come where the [Privy Council] was perceived as no longer relevant.... What the Privy Council might say today on a legal issue is likely to be entirely irrelevant to us. If you think about significant developments in the law, the last time the Privy Council made a significant development in Australian law was in the *James* case. They really haven't made any significant contributions [since] (92:1330)." For clarification, the Privy Council decided *James v. Cowan* in 1932.[25]

Even judges who found value and benefit in having Privy Council review recognized the limitations and challenges in having a foreign court decide domestic cases. One Queensland judge asserted, "The Privy Council at least had this advantage to it: It knew nothing about local politics anywhere. So, it just sort of decided it according to the law or perhaps whether they wanted to get away for the weekend. They did a good job sometimes." The judge continued, "I'm quite conscious of the disadvantage of having foreigners sitting in cases....Mistakes can be made if we think other political systems are the same as ours. The advantage you get is independence and impartiality. The disadvantage is they know nothing about what's happened (2:11415)."

Whatever the relative merits or demerits in having Privy Council appeals, I confronted strong sentiment that closing this appellate route encouraged the transformation. Abolition was the "trigger," "a watershed event (126:130)," that enabled the Court to take "a completely different approach as a court at the apex (48:1215)." It "opening the library" and "released a creative impulse (24:1930)" through the Court. A High Court justice admitted, "Abolition of appeals...had something to do with the activism that developed in the 1990s. The High Court would not have been so prone to depart from established principles had there been appeals to the Privy Council (94:1615)." Another High Court judge suggested, "Undoubtedly there was a feeling of liberation, if you like. One hopes that didn't extend to irresponsibility. There certainly was a feeling that no longer was the Privy Council breathing down our necks once the appeals ended (37:1100)." Yet this same judge then confessed, "I'm sure that parties involved are better off [after appeals ended].... The time this took and the cost involved were well rid of.... I suppose as an Australian I should feel rather pleased that now the High Court is the ultimate court of appeal, but I don't have any strong feelings in that respect (37:1415)." This is a remarkable statement coming from a judge whose decisions came under Privy Council review.

---

25. *James v. Cowan* [1932] AC 542.

A Queensland judge offered a strong case for the liberating impact that abolition had. "After Privy Council appeals were abolished, it let the High Court go free. They went freer than I thought they would....There was a huge change with abolition of appeals...and people don't realize the social impact. Until appeals were abolished, the High Court was reined in by the fact that they might be inconsistent with the Privy Council. That's been the trigger for the High Court to take a completely different approach as the court at the apex (2:11800)." And with great parsimony, another judge concluded, "Since the *Australia Act* there has been greater activism. The High Court has had a tendency to go its own way and be unbound by English authority (126:130)." Not all judges embraced the Court's politicized role, but even the harshest critics acknowledged the significance of closing the appellate route. A NSW appellate judge claimed, "Delusions of grandeur have precipitated the notion that judges can move the goal posts. Power has gone to [the High Court's] head. *We abolish the Privy Council appeals and they think they ought to do something (99:700) (emphasis added)*."

The Privy Council: A Bedeviling Institution?

My interview data present a clear case that Australia's appellate judges perceived the Privy Council as a constraining force. It thwarted and stymied developments that otherwise may have occurred. Are these perceptions supported empirically? Is there evidence that the Privy Council discouraged High Court attempts to venture out on its own? One way to answer this is to explore whether the Court fared any better or worse than other countries' courts in the rate at which decisions were reversed. I assembled a data set of every Privy Council decision handed down last century to compare the frequency with which the Privy Council reversed Australian courts vis-à-vis other countries' courts. Every appeal to the Privy Council can be seen as an occasion where an overseas decision came under review. To compare Australia's experience with that of other countries, I ignore the fate of the overseas courts' legal reasoning and focus exclusively on the end result: Did the Privy Council affirm, vary, or reverse the overseas court? Assembling these data would be no Lilliputian effort, save for the Lord Chancellor's detailed annual reports to Parliament,[26] which include the annual number of cases the Privy Council af-

---

26. A note on my data source: the Lord Chancellor's Department submitted since 1857 an annual command paper to Parliament summarizing the judiciary's activity for the preceding year, including the Judicial Committee of the Privy Council. These reports, currently titled *Civil Judicial Statistics*, provide the most reliable and accessible source for aggregate data on the Privy Council. Lord Brougham introduced legislation in 1856 that

Figure 6.6 Annual Number of Australian Cases Decided by Privy Council, 1900–1999, with 5-Year Moving Average

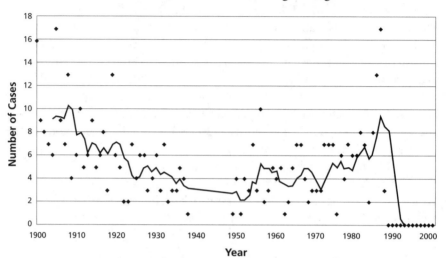

firmed, varied, reversed, and resolved without a hearing from each overseas court.[27]

The Privy Council handed down 6,157 decisions from 1900 to 1999. Australian cases accounted for 444 of these decisions, the third highest number from any single country next to India (2,390) and Canada (713).[28] Figure 6.6 charts the annual number of Australian cases that the Privy Council decided,

---

would have established a system for reporting judicial statistics for all courts in England and Wales. The bill failed but a few years later an agreement was reached requiring all courts to report statistics. Judicial statistics were first reported in 1859. Typically, the Lord Chancellor's Report for a given year is published one or two years later as a Command Paper in the *Parliamentary Papers* series. I rely upon these command papers for my analyses. The Second World War marked the only hick-up in this annual reporting scheme. Judicial statistics were not assembled (according to the Privy Council's Chief Clerk) for the years 1939–1948 due to the war effort.

27. For clarification, a case is "varied" when the Council tweaks the lower court's decision without changing the winner or loser. Cases that are settled, abandoned, or dismissed for non-prosecution are reported as "resolved without a hearing."

28. Only twelve of the nearly 100 different jurisdictions had a hundred or more appeals decided last century. In rank order, those jurisdictions and the number of cases are as follows: India (2390), Canada (713), Australia (444), Ceylon (257), Hong Kong (222), New Zealand (216), Jamaica (186), Malaysia (148), Trinidad & Tobago (145), and Singapore (104). Collectively, these twelve countries account for 4,869 decisions—79 percent of all decisions last century and 85 percent of all overseas decisions.

while Figure 6.7 disaggregates these data to indicate the annual proportion of cases from state courts versus the High Court. Finally, Figure 6.8 shows the annual proportion of the Privy Council's agenda dedicated to Australian cases.

Australia's appearance before the Privy Council last century exhibited a bi-modal distribution. The most cases were handled in the first several decades after federation and in the 1970s and 1980s, with a slump from the 1940s to the 1960s. It was during mid-century that High Court cases—not state supreme court cases—accounted for most Australian appeals. In fact, the 1950s brought five years in which all of Australia's appeals originated in the High Court. When looking at the entire century, however, New South Wales out-paced all other states and the High Court in terms of the raw number of Privy Council cases. New South Wales provided the lion-share (191 cases or 43 per-cent), with Queensland (38 cases) and Victoria (37 cases) nudging out West-ern Australia (33 cases), South Australia (18 cases), and Tasmania (3 cases).

How did Australian cases fare before the Privy Council? Were Australian cases more or less likely to get overturned than cases originating in other countries? Within the universe of all Privy Council decisions last century (6,157 cases), the Council affirmed 59.4 percent (3,660 cases), reversed 35.6 percent (2,194 cases), and varied 5 percent (304 cases) of the lower court decisions. Thus, in about four out of ten cases, the Council altered the lower court decision to some degree. Out of the 444 Australian cases the Council decided, it affirmed 58.7 percent (261 cases), reversed 37.3 percent (166 cases) and varied 3.8 percent (17 cases). Thus, in 41.2 percent of Australia's cases, the Council amended the courts' decisions in some fashion. By way of comparison, Table 6.9 presents the reversal rates for the twelve countries that had more than 100 cases decided by the Privy Council last century, as well as the reversal rates for Australian courts.

Variance exists in the reversal rates for each country and also between Aus-tralian courts. Is this variance statistically significant? In other words, were cases from the Queensland Supreme Court less likely to get reversed than cases from the NSW Court of Appeal? Similarly, were Canadian cases less likely to get reversed than Malaysian cases? To answer these questions, two statistics were calculated using country-year as the unit of analysis. First, I calculated a "NegTotal" statistic by adding the annual number of varied and reversed cases from each country. This statistic reflects the sum number of "negative" decisions handed down for each country-year. My assumption is that lower courts perceive varied and reversed decisions in similar light—in both cases their decisions are impugned and altered. Second, I calculated a reversal rate statistic ("RR") for each country-year. This statistic indicates the percentage of decisions that were reversed or varied for each country-year. Thus, if the Privy Council hypothetically affirmed one decision, reversed two

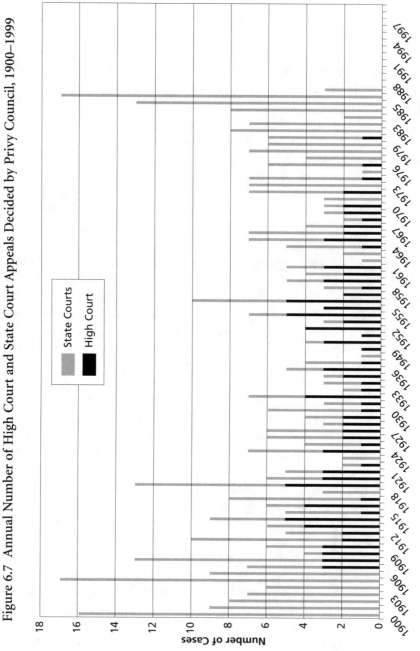

Figure 6.7 Annual Number of High Court and State Court Appeals Decided by Privy Council, 1900–1999

**Table 6.8 Annual Percentage of Privy Council Agenda
Dedicated to Australian Cases, 1900–1999**

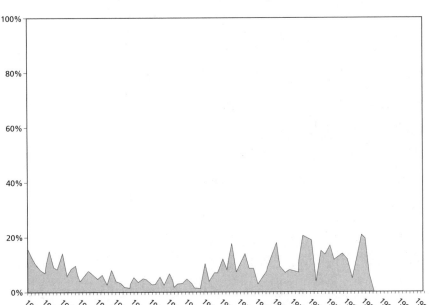

decisions, and varied one decision in 1950 from Country X, the reversal rate
for that country-year would be 75 percent. Calculating a percentage reversal
rate for each country-year enables comparisons between countries and years
despite variation in the number of decisions for each country-year.

Did the Privy Council's tendency to affirm or reverse decisions vary from
country to country and between Australian courts? To answer this question,
I conducted W.L.S. regression analysis on dummy variables for each country.[29] Each Privy Council decision was coded according to the originating
court. I then regressed the reversal rates percentage (Y) on C-1 of the country dummy variables, controlling for time. The null hypothesis for this regression holds that the reversal rates do not vary from country to country:
Ho: $\beta_1 C_1 = \beta_2 C_2 = \beta_3 C_3 \ldots \beta_n C_n$, where C is the country. Any regression on a
country dummy variable that produced a significant coefficient indicates that

---

29. Regressing the reversal rates on country dummy variables is equivalent to conducting difference of means tests between the years. Because of heteroscedasticity problems, however, I used W.L.S. regression, weighted by the number of cases actually decided
for each country-year.

Table 6.9 Mean Reversal Rates for Australian Courts and
Eleven Other Countries, 1900–1999

Court	Mean Reversal Rate (%)	Number of Cases Decided
Australia	41.2	444
High Court	44.4	124
New South Wales	42.4	191
Queensland	18.4	38
South Australia	50	18
Tasmania	100	3
Victoria	37.8	37
Western Australia	42.4	33
India	41	2390
Canada	43.1	713
Ceylon	41.6	257
Hong Kong	41.4	222
New Zealand	38	216
Jamaica	43.5	186
Malaysia	42.6	148
Trinidad & Tobago	46.2	145
Singapore	41.4	104

the reversal rate for that country is statistically different from the constant. A statistically insignificant coefficient on the country dummy variable indicates no statistically significant difference between that country's reversal rate and the constant.

Table 6.10 reports the regression coefficients and levels of significance for Australian courts and the eleven other countries with the most frequent Privy Council appearances.

There are several conclusions to draw from this table. Recall that the Privy Council reached decisions from over one hundred countries, territories, and dominions last century. Given the myriad disputes that came from this expansive jurisdiction, one would anticipate that statistically significant differences of means would emerge for many of these jurisdictions. One might expect cases from certain countries to be more likely overturned than cases from others. However, the W.L.S. regressions indicate a remarkable consistency in the Privy Council's decision-making. Only three of the overseas jurisdictions had mean reversal rates that were statistically significant (Botswana, West Africa, and Queensland). The reversal rates for the remaining ninety-plus jurisdictions were statistically insignificant, meaning that whatever variance might exist was due as much to chance. In other words, the Privy Council was remarkably consistent in its tendency to reverse overseas courts, despite changes in the Council's composition and jurisdiction.

Table 6.10 W.L.S. Regression Results for Australian Courts and Other Countries, 1900–1999

Court	Unstandardized Coefficients (β)	Std. Error	t	Sig.
Australia (High Court)	−.0245	0.056	0.436	0.663
New South Wales	−.0439	0.049	0.894	0.371
Queensland	−0.284	0.089	−3.19	0.001
South Australia	.032	0.125	0.257	0.798
Tasmania	0.532	0.297	1.792	0.073
Victoria	−.0896	0.09	−0.996	0.32
Western Australia	−.0438	0.095	−0.462	0.644
Indian Courts	−.0592	0.034	−1.743	0.082
Ceylon	−.0517	0.045	−1.138	0.255
Hong Kong	−.0536	0.047	−1.137	0.256
New Zealand	−.0292	0.036	−0.803	0.422
Jamaica	−.0325	0.049	−0.657	0.511
Malaysia	−.0423	0.053	−0.799	0.425
Trinidad & Tobago	−.0059	0.053	−0.111	0.911
Singapore	−.0545	0.06	−0.915	0.361

Second, the High Court was not reversed at any higher rate than other courts. The Queensland Supreme Court was the only Australian court that differed statistically from its cohort. These analyses indicate that Queensland's cases were less likely to get overturned—only 18.4 percent when controlling for time. Why this was the case demands further investigation, but that falls beyond the scope of this chapter. The third, and most significant, conclusion is that while the High Court's experience before the Privy Council was statistically no different from other countries' supreme courts, the mere presence of the appellate route had a profound psychological impact on the judges. The Council did not treat High Court cases any differently, but the judges attest to the soft influence it had on the Australian judicial mind. It shaped and shepherded Australian law merely by its formal hierarchical authority and the reverence the judges afforded it. Lifting this barrier had a significant psychological impact.

THE POLITICAL PRECIPITANT

A final precipitant to the transformation was political in nature. This section will demonstrate that the state and national governments encouraged, or were at least complicit with, components of the transformation. By no means did the elected branches endorse the politicized High Court in toto, but they welcomed some of the Mason Court's reforms. Mark Graber (1993) wrote about occasions in U.S. Supreme Court history when it tackled issues that were too controversial or too divisive for popularly elected bodies to handle. He demonstrated that on occasion the elected branches abdicate purposively their decision-making authority to the Court on issues that are too politically controversial for democratic political processes.

Graber's "hot potato thesis" explains some of the Mason Court's success in introducing and advancing the politicized judicial role. One reason for the transformation's timing was that the Mason Court acted on a powder keg issue that the elected branches were unwilling to tackle: native title land rights. This was clearly a "hot potato" in Australian politics. *Mabo* was the High Court's first native title decision, handed down halfway through Prime Minister Keating's term (1991–1996). Keating came into office after his Labor colleague, Bob Hawke, completed four consecutive terms as prime minister (1983–1991). Over these thirteen years of ALP Government, Hawke and Keating strived to revamp their party, moving it away from the protectionism, paternalism, and trade union base that historically defined it. Reaching out to suburbia, Labor's watchwords became multiculturalism, trade liberalization, deregulation, and globalization. When the High Court handed down *Mabo*, Keating had to decide what, if any, the Government's response would be. The Court had secured native title—something Keating supported—and provided a common law mechanism for indigenous people to secure native title rights. They could litigate their claim in court. But *Mabo*'s political implications were complex and far reaching. Early government reports estimated that as much as ten percent of the continent (mostly in Western Australia) might be affected by new native title claims.[30] *Mabo* left unanswered a host of questions about native title rights, most notably how it was to be balanced against other property rights. It also raised fears about the eventual creation of "black states" and politically disastrous native title claims in major metropolitan areas. While Keating supported *Mabo*, the decision met vitriol from many corners. The High Court's ruling was described as "naive adventurism," exhibiting "a perverse and politically driven logic," and utilizing the language of "the guilt industry."[31]

The election of Pauline Hanson and her One Nation Party to the Commonwealth Parliament in September 1996 crystallized the political upheaval caused by *Mabo*. As a Liberal parliamentarian from Queensland, Hanson soon

---

30. Heather McRae et al. 1997. *Indigenous Legal Issues*. North Ryde, Australia: LBC Information Services, p. 16.

31. G. Hughes. July 1, 1993. "High Court Failed Nation with Mabo, Says Mining Chief," *The Australian*, pp. 1, 2.

tapped into the fears of rural farmers and miners that do-gooder elites were handing Australia over to its indigenous people. Thus, in her famous maiden speech in the House of Representatives in 1996, she said:

> We now have a situation where a type of reverse racism is applied to mainstream Australians by those who promote political correctness and those...that flourish in our society servicing Aboriginals, multi-culturalists and a host of other minority groups....I am fed up to the back teeth with the inequalities that are being promoted by the Government....This nation is being divided into black and white, and the present system encourages this. I am fed up with being told, "This is our land." Well, where the hell do I go? I was born here....Like most Australians, I worked for my land; no one gave it to me.[32]

Recognizing that uncertainty, expense, and delay were the likely consequences of a purely judicial (common law) mechanism for handling native title claims, Keating concluded that some statutory response was necessary. He could not afford to do nothing. Two months before the 1993 election, he announced that the Government would draft legislation to give statutory force to *Mabo* and provide institutional processes for native title claims. After year-long consultations with a myriad of interests, his Government enacted the *Native Title Act of 1993*. This established a national Native Title Tribunal to receive and consider native title claims. After a prima facie case is made out that native title to land may exist, the Tribunal was meant to assist the parties involved in negotiating a settlement. Appeals from the Tribunal go to the Federal Court. The *Native Title Act* also required that extinguishment of native title rights could occur only with just compensation and assurances that native title holders would be treated no differently than other land holders.

The *Native Title Act* was enacted in response to *Mabo;* Keating was not leading the country in reform but responding to the High Court's prompting. Providing statutory protection for native title was something that the Commonwealth Parliament could have done at any point. Indeed, the Hawke Government flirted with the idea in the 1980s, but backed down. According to my informants, the *Native Title Act* would not have materialized without *Mabo.* As one informant said, "The High Court was prepared to make changes and assume a role the elected government wasn't assumed to make. The fed-

---

32. Inaugural speeches before Parliament for new members are given a significance absent in the U.S. Congress. First speeches, for instance, are commonly posted on members' web pages along with other information. For Hanson's speech see L. Tingle, November 15, 1996, "Behind the Lines: The Speech that Split a Nation," *The Age*, p. 15.

eral Labor Government was happy to run with *Mabo*—'You forced us, so we'll legislate!'—but even the Labor Government would not have legislated without *Mabo* because of electoral backlash (77:2200)."

Keating's Labor Government lost the March 1996 federal election to John Howard's Liberal-National Party coalition. In December 1996 the High Court extended and affirmed *Mabo* in its *Wik*[33] decision. Disputed in *Wik* case was whether native title claims to government land could coexist with pastoral leases that a government had granted to the same land. The Court's decision that native title and pastoral leases indeed could coexist further enraged Australian farmers and miners, who feared that their livelihoods were in still greater jeopardy. Responding to the *Wik* turmoil, the Howard Government proposed a piece of legislation known as The Ten-Point Plan. It supposedly implemented *Wik* by specifying procedures and rules for reconciling native title land claims with competing leasehold claims. This legislation was twice rejected in the Senate, and it brought Australia to the brink of only the seventh double-dissolution federal election since federation. After much wrangling and the longest debate in Parliament's history, the *Native Title Amendment Act 1998* was passed, specifying in statute the procedures and rules for settling native title claims.

The 1998 Act modifies the original legislation in several ways. First, it limits instances where Aborigines retain a right to negotiate native title claims. This right is no longer available for cases involving certain mineral explorations and the compulsory acquisition of land by governments. Second, the Act provides that native title is extinguished by a variety of other land rights, including private freehold grants, residential and commercial leases, exclusive possession leases, community purpose leases, and public works. Third, it requires all applications for native title to be submitted first to the Federal Courts. Only those applications potentially settled through mediation are forwarded to the Native Title Tribunal. Finally, it adopts a more stringent registration test for potential native title claims. Applicants must represent a clearly defined group, the application must be lodged with that group's consent, and applicants must demonstrate continuous association with the land. The Native Title Tribunal reports that since these amendments, the number of applications lodged and determinations of native title have increased.[34] Formulation and passage of this thorny legislation consumed the Howard Government and the country like no other policy undertaking.

---

33. *The Wik Peoples v. The State of Queensland* (1996) 141 ALR 129.
34. Native Title Tribunal. *Annual Report 2003–2004.* See http://www.nntt.gov.au/publications/data/files/Annual%20Report%202003-2004.pdf. Last accessed May 30, 2005.

Since the 1998 amendments, the High Court has issued several important decisions clarifying native title rights. These decisions have generally narrowed the scope of native title rights and decreased the range of people who might successfully claim such rights to land. In its 1998 decision, *Fejo v. Northern Territory of Australia*, the Court considered two critical questions: 1) whether a grant of freehold title extinguishes any native title rights, preventing the two from coexisting; and 2) whether extinguishment of native title is permanent or can be re-recognized if the land in question reverts to the Crown. Here the Court concluded that freehold grants extinguish any underlying native title claims to the land and prevent co-existence. It also decided that a grant of freehold permanently extinguishes any native title claims to the land, even if the land reverts to the Crown.[35] In *Western Australia v. Ward* (2002),[36] the Court considered whether partial extinguishment of native title is possible under the amended *Native Title Act* and what criteria must be met for extinguishment to occur. This case concerned a native title claim in the Kimberley area of Western Australia. The Court concluded that when governments grant exclusive possession to non-indigenous interests, all native title claims are exhausted. On the other hand, when non-exclusive grants have been issued, native title can be extinguished only to the extent that the indigenous and non-indigenous interests conflict or are "inconsistent" with each other. Handed down the same day as *Ward*, *Wilson v. Anderson*[37] considered how *Wik*'s coexistence principle was to operate after the 1998 amendments to the *Native Title Act*. This case concerned whether a perpetual grazing lease in New South Wales extinguished native title claims. The Court ended up distinguishing *Wik* as precedent and concluded that the perpetual grazing lease amounted to an exclusive possession and denied native title. This decision's net effect was to insulate roughly forty percent of New South Wales from native title claims. The final case, *Yorta Yorta v. Victoria* (2002)[38] concerned a native title claim to lands bordering Victoria and New South Wales, made on behalf of the Yorta Yorta indigenous community. This indigenous community lodged its native title claim acknowledging that European settlement and the numerous Aboriginal policies initiated by the states and Commonwealth had fractured their once strong connection to the land. The Yorta Yorta community argued that despite these lapses native title rights should be extended. In the end, they lost their case because they could not demonstrate an uninterrupted connection to the land.

---

35. 195 CLR 96.
36. 1991 ALR 1.
37. (2002) 190 ALR 313.
38. 194 ALR 538.

The Court interpreted the *Native Title Act* to mean that native title would be granted if a community demonstrated "a continuity of acknowledgment and observance" of traditional laws and customs pertaining to the land.

Most indigenous advocates see these post-*Wik* cases illustrating the gradual erosion of native title rights secured in the early 1990s. Articles appeared in the popular and legal presses foretelling native title's death. *The Australian's* headline for its article on the *Yorta Yorta* decision asked, "Is this the end of native title?"[39] Similarly, a recent *Melbourne University Law Review* article led with the title, "A Hope Disillusioned, an Opportunity Lost?" These headlines capture a growing sentiment that an expansive and robust form of native title thought possible after *Mabo* and *Wik* will not be realized. There is a certain irony in how native title litigation has progressed since the 1990s and the evolving relationship it has brought between parliaments and the High Court. It began out of legislative inaction. Native title was too controversial for the parliaments to tackle it without prompting. Legislators needed the Court to provide cover. Now it is the Court seeking cover under the legislation. Having made the tough calls and jumpstarted the legislative process, the Court has pulled back in deference to the statutory guidelines.

Before continuing, let me restate this section's argument: that the role transformation occurred partly in response to inaction in the other branches of government. Inaction was a precipitant. Politicians were unwilling or unable for electoral reasons to tackle the native title question through legislation without the cover of saying that the Court made them do it. Many of my informants saw *Mabo* and *Wik* not as judicial power grabs, but instances where the Court was compelled to address an unresolved issue.

As one Queensland judge remarked, "The political process was unable to deal with that social issue, native title. The politicians were grateful the High Court was taking the flack (87:1400)." A barrister who was intimately involved in native title litigation offered the following: "Yes there was [parliamentary deference]. *Wik* is an example of that. It suited Keating politically to not resolve native title, so he left it with the Court....Everyone knew that *Wik* was not resolved by the *Native Title Act* in 1993, that it had to be resolved by the High Court. Everyone knew it, but no one admitted it (68)."

To summarize, securing and protecting native title rights was a hot potato issue in Australia for several decades. My informants indicated that Governments from both major parties faced electoral disincentives for providing

---

39. Stuart Rintoul, "Is this the end of native title?" *The Australian*, December 13, 2002, p. 1.

statutory native title protection. The elected branches needed the Court to provide an institutional trigger for enacting the original *Native Title Act*, as well as later amendments to it. The political system's inability to grapple with Aboriginal land rights through democratic channels invited at least part of the Mason Court transformation, in so far as *Mabo* and the other native title cases constitute cornerstones of it. Although *Mabo* was not the genesis of the transformation, it was clearly the transformation's most dramatic manifestation.

This chapter has presented three types of precipitants to the transformation: individual, institutional, and political. It should be clear from the interview data presented that the transformation had no single cause. Some of my informants stressed the individual over the institutional. Others stressed the institutional over the political. The collective portrait that emerges is that the interplay of these precipitants caused the transformation.

The reader may have noticed that I speak about the transformation using past-tense verbs. This is not a grammatical mistake. Just as an interplay of factors caused the transformation, a set of judicial appointments, institutional constraints, and political precipitants consolidated the transformation's gains in the late 1990s and brought an end to the politicized role's ascendancy.

7

Recent Retreats from the Politicized Role

[The Mason Court] wanted to obtain immortal glory by this kind of continuing revolution. But all that happens with continuing revolutions is that the Girondins come in and they get executed by the Jacobins, Danton gets executed by Robespierre, who in turn gets executed by the Thermidorians, and then you end up with a military dictatorship!" (103:10619)

Previous chapters described the onset of Australia's judicial role transformation as a two-step process, whereby the Gibbs Court (1964–1981) marked a transition from the Barwick Court's orthodoxy to the Mason Court's politicized role. This transformation had no single cause, but resulted from the interplay of individual, institutional, and political precipitants. When Chief Justice Mason retired in 1995, the Keating Labor Government promoted Justice Gerard Brennan to the top job. Brennan's tenure was relatively brief, 1995–1998. Originally appointed as a puisne justice in 1981, he had experienced two worlds: the inconspicuous and politically tranquil years that marked the Gibbs Court and the tempest that was the Mason Court. The mandatory retirement law forced Brennan's departure in 1998, but a part of him may have appreciated the exit opportunity. He inherited an institution battered and bruised a bit from the hits it sustained under Mason. Cognizant of this, Brennan's speech at his swearing in ceremony carried an educative tone, as if Brennan was attempting to make sense of the Mason Court's revolution and how it could have occurred given the Court's historically orthodox role. He begins by noting that the 1980s and 1990s were decades of profound legal development, but that this should not be surprising.

If right is to be done according to law, right will be done only if the law be just. Such tension as there is between justice and the rules of law surfaces most acutely in litigation before the High Court, partly because of history, partly because of procedure. With the abolition of the last appeals from Australian Courts to the Privy Council, this Court was charged with the ultimate responsibility of declaring the law for this country. This did not mean that we were free to cast aside the priceless heritage of the common law of England, but it did mean that this Court had to examine critically those rules of the common law including the rules of statutory interpretation in the light of our own history, culture and social conditions. Long-standing rules of tort and contract, of land law, equity and administrative law have been revisited in recent years. The same factors and the ever-changing problems of government have evoked renewed examination of the spare text of our Constitution (Brennan 1995).

After attempting an explanation for why so much change occurred during the Mason Court, Brennan turned to the public's reaction to it. He tried to walk a narrow path, acknowledging that public attention on the courts is normal in a democracy, but that this attention was ill-informed at times due to an ineptly trained media.

The work of this Court is rightly a subject of considerable public interest. Though the arguments heard here are often at a high level of abstraction, the emerging principles have a concrete effect on the liberties, relationships and property of individual persons, both natural and artificial. Therefore the work of this Court should be subject to informed public scrutiny. But how is it possible for the public to be informed? It is unrealistic to expect the arid fields of law to be tilled in the popular press, much less in the brief and adversarial encounters of the television screen. Of course, there are some few highly competent legal journalists but an adequate analysis of legal principle and its significance may be precluded by limited space or may give way to a story of more gripping, if ephemeral, interest. The problem of fostering informed public appreciation of the laws by which we are governed and protected is, I venture to suggest, a problem far from satisfactory solution. It will not be resolved by superficial comment or by an expression of pleasure or disappointment in advancing policy or interest (Brennan 1995).

He concluded by trying to deflect attention away from the High Court, noting, "[T]he public interest in the judgments of this and other Courts is a clear and gratifying indication that, in this country, we are governed by the rule of law.... Today's focus is on the work of the High Court, but it must be remembered that the face of justice is more often the face of the magistrate and the judge at trial (Ibid.)." Brennan's own evaluation of the Mason Court and his desire to reflect attention elsewhere proved a harbinger for his tenure.

If the Gibbs Court experienced judicial rumblings about the orthodoxy, justices on the Brennan Court aired their misgivings and uncertainties about many of the revolutionary changes wrought under Mason. The year 1995 marked the beginning of a gradual rollback in the politicized role's popularity among the justices, a pullback quickened when NSW Supreme Court Justice Murray Gleeson replaced Brennan as High Court Chief Justice in 1998.

This chapter focuses on what happened to the politicized role after the Mason Court. The question of how to characterize accurately the post-Mason High Court has attracted significant attention in recent years. By post-Mason Courts I mean the High Court under Chief Justices Brennan (1995–1998) and Gleeson (1998 – present). It is a complex picture that requires an increasingly nuanced eye as the Gleeson Court's years unfold. Scholars tend to divide into two camps: those who perceive the Gleeson Court significantly retreating from the Mason Court reforms and those who do not (See Patapan 2002 and Selway 2003 contra Zines 2002). My informants consistently sided with the former group of scholars, concluding from their firsthand observations that the transformation stalled in the late 1990s. High Court judges abandoned several components of the politicized role and new appointments brought judges to the Court who fundamentally opposed it.

The chapter begins by advancing the argument that the contemporary Court has retreated from some of the more controversial and consequential Mason Court doctrines. This section does not exhaustively chronicle these retreats; indeed, to map systematically the ebbs and flows of legal doctrine from the Mason Court to the Brennan and Gleeson Courts is beyond this book's scope. Instead, it delves deeply into a single pullback in substantive law that was of central import to the Mason Court and that my informants deemed salient at the time of the interviews. The chapter then moves to ways in which the post-Mason Courts have trended toward the orthodox role conception. It concludes by identifying reasons why the politicized role failed to outlive, in any consequential or thoroughgoing manner, the Mason Court. Why did the transformation stall? The answer again involves the interplay of individual, institutional, and political variables. Central to the rollback were the following facts: a High Court exposed to unprecedented levels of public criticism, a judicial community profoundly divided over the politicized role's merits, a constitutional infrastructure inadequate to support many of the Mason Court reforms, and the failure to secure transformation-sustaining High Court appointments.

Consolidating the Implied
Rights Jurisprudence

Appellate judges I interviewed perceived with near unanimity that the High Court since Chief Justice Mason's retirement has undergone a retrenchment. By that they meant that many legal reforms instigated during the Mason era have progressed no further, or more common, undergone consolidation. My informants marked the beginning of this retreat with the Brennan Court and see that it has continued apace under the Gleeson Court. By way of example, an ACT judge thought, "The Brennan Court was different from the Mason Court.... When Brennan became Chief Justice, the High Court was less politically active. It tried to find intellectually satisfying reasons for decisions. The Gleeson Court is definitely a more conservative, black letter court. It's a Dawson-type court (7)." Daryl Dawson served on the Court from 1982 to 1997, during the heart of the Mason Court reforms, and frequently dissented. He was the sole dissenter in *Mabo*, concluding that native title rights do not exist outside of specific legislation that provides it and that absent this legislation there is no fiduciary duty for the government to recognize native title. He also departed from his colleagues in the implied rights cases. A Victoria judge concurred, "Ever since Gerry Brennan became the Chief Justice, he tended to draw back and I think under Murray Gleeson they're carrying on that way. I hate these terms, but [Gleeson] is what I would call—if you want to put him into a bracket—a black letter lawyer. Stick by the principles of the constitution (52:715)." When describing the transition from the Mason Court to the Brennan and Gleeson Courts, a Federal Court judge selected a single word: "Pendulum. That's the most accurate description. You've seen it go out the implied rights line of country and now you're seeing it go back. It's turned on its head (86:610)." The judge continued, "It's a very different High Court [today] from the one presided over by Mason in temper, outlook, [and] sense of the purpose of law....I obviously have a distinct lack of sympathy with what's been happening in recent times (86:700)." "The Gleeson Court is trying to go back to old forms of legal reasoning—the reasoning of the 1960s which was moving bits and pieces around," said a state appellate judge (103:10641). In rather blunt language, a Commonwealth attorney concluded, "[M]ost of the things the Mason Court did are being undone by the [Gleeson] Court (59:1215)."

At the time I interviewed most of my informants (1999–2000), they were quick to note that the implied rights jurisprudence was one area undergoing retrenchment. After first identifying in 1992 a constitutionally protected implied right to free political speech, the Mason Court gave this implication its broadest reading in *Theophanous* (1994), where it concluded that the implied right overrides the common law of defamation. The Brennan Court took a step to rein in this jurisprudence in its 1996 *McGinty* decision.[1] The case presented the Court with an opportunity to extend the implied rights jurisprudence to include a right to equality. McGinty argued that the presence of malapportioned legislative districts violated an equality right implicit in the constitutional requirement that parliamentarians be "directly chosen by the people." It was put to the Court that elections that occurred in malapportioned districts gave some voters more influence than others. A single voter had less potency in larger districts than smaller districts. The Brennan Court rejected this argument, however, effectively setting *Theophanous* as the outer boundary for the implication. A Commonwealth attorney said:

> We don't have a bill of rights, so people look for them by implication. The extreme example is *Theophanous* where the Mason Court said you've almost got a First Amendment right.... You've got the *Theophanous* cases which say you've got an implication of representative democracy.... Then someone asks how can you have representative democracy when one district has ten people in it and another has a million people in it—that's hardly representative democracy. The Court says you can't possibly draw that implication....It seems to me quite illogical to say you can draw these incredibly indirect ones on free speech, but you can't draw the most basic one—one vote, one value. What that shows us is that the Court does what it wants in these areas. I don't think this jurisprudence will go much further in the implied freedoms and rights. That's cut to the bone (59:3400).

The Brennan Court took a second step retrenching the implied rights jurisprudence in its 1997 *Kruger v. Commonwealth* decision.[2] The case questioned the constitutionality of the *Northern Territory's Aboriginal Ordinance 1918* that sanctioned the removal of Aboriginal children from their families and communities for the primary aim of assimilating them into white Australia. This practice had been widespread throughout the country and many states had comparable legislation. An estimated one in three to one in ten Aboriginal children, collectively referred to as the "stolen generation," were removed from their parental homes and sent to various missions and state facilities under this regime, which lasted from 1910 to 1970.[3] Alec Kruger argued that the law enabling his removal was unconstitutional on the grounds, *inter*

---

1. (1996) 136 CLR 140.
2. 146 ALR 126.
3. For more on the "stolen generation" see Healey (1998) and Wilson (1997).

alia, that it violated an implied constitutional right to free movement, equality, and association and the expressed freedom of religion, as well that it constituted an act of genocide.

Kruger was an important decision politically and symbolically because it raised the legality of a highly contentious indigenous policy and a controversial mode of constitutional interpretation. These would have been signal matters for the Mason Court. The Brennan Court ruled unanimously that the ordinance was valid and did not violate any expressed or implied constitutional freedoms. In the end, only two of six judges (Justices Toohey and Gaudron) agreed that the constitution contained an implied freedom of movement and association that ran counter to the ordinance. With *Kruger*, Mason's implied rights jurisprudence stalled. One informant recalled the day he argued the *Kruger* case:

> I argued the [*Kruger*] case in the High Court....If the case had come up three years before, I could have won the case. With the Court as constituted, I had no hope in hell. At one stage, I was the equivalent of on my hands and knees saying, "You can't disagree with this problem. This is so fundamental." It might have been Austin's or Dicey's saying that an uncontrolled Parliament can pass a law killing blue-eyed babies. I said, "Whatever you decide in this case, you can't agree with that. That is so outrageous and so unsustainable, that you have to at least agree with that. If that's the starting off premise, then it's not a long way to go to saying this particular piece of legislation is just as outrageous." I was pleading with them.... *Toohey half agreed and when he saw that the others wouldn't agree to it, he said to me, "It's a very lonely place here now." And everybody knew what he was talking about. I knew what he was talking about and I could feel that. The mood had gone—it had all changed* (emphasis added).

Oral arguments lasted four days and the transcript reveals how hard of a time Kruger had throughout. One can sense from the transcript just how skeptical the Court had become about implying rights from the constitution. Consider the following exchange with Mr. Kruger's attorney:

> MR FORSYTH: As to what was decided in *Leeth*, your Honour, we say that there was a majority for the view that the doctrine of legal equality is to be implied into the Constitution....There are obvious difficulties about—not so much difficulties, but room for discussion—about formulation of the boundaries. In our submission, this is not a borderline case and it is enough for us to say, as we do say,

that whatever else legal equality may forbid, the principle may forbid, it forbids the division of the one people and the one nation into a superior and an inferior category.

McHUGH J: But the Constitution, I am sorry to say, reeks of inequality in that sense. Take the Senate; take section 128 amending the Constitution—a vote of the smallest State is equal to the vote of the largest State; so the vote of a Tasmanian is 10 times more effective than the vote of somebody in New South Wales, both on terms of amending the Constitution or in terms of the Senate. Take other provisions: section 117 of the Constitution was drawn in the way it was so that Asians could be discriminated against; Aborigines were not counted; women were not given the vote under the Constitution.

Further evidence of the Court's mood change emerged when discussions turned to whether the rights that the constitution may imply even operate in Australia's territories.

DAWSON J: You may cover it in your submissions in relation to freedom of movement and association, but there is a more fundamental difficulty about any implied freedom of that sort in relation to the territories, is there not? If the freedom is derived from representative government, then the territories [are] not required to have representative government. Do you deal with that somewhere?

MR GRIFFITH: I am not sure we do specifically, your Honour.

DAWSON J: Nor are they required to be represented in the Parliament of the Commonwealth.

MR GRIFFITH: The point I make to freedoms which may affect the State and Territories is that one might say that on the issue of *Theophanous* and *Stephens* it may be that the same principle applies in the Northern Territory as it did in the States, for the reasons that the Court there …

DAWSON J: But it did not ever give any reasons; it did not ever turn its attention to the territories, but there is a fundamental difficulty, is there not?

MR GRIFFITH: I must say that I have been prepared to concede my friend's point about territory but, indeed, why should I?

DAWSON J: Representative government forms no part of the territory's constitutional guarantee.... When you get to a territory's law, there must be fundamental difficulties in drawing an implication of the sort that applies elsewhere when representative government forms no part of the constitutional requirements, not even in the sense of representative government within the territories or representative government in its form of the territories being represented in the Commonwealth Parliament. And when one considers the position of external territories it perhaps becomes even clearer.

GAUDRON J: Now that there is provision in the Constitution for territory senators and territory representation.

DAWSON J: That is a choice; that is not a constitutional requirement.[4]

Dawson was essentially arguing that the Commonwealth Constitution did not require representative governments in the territories; therefore, any constitutionally implied right to political speech based on representative government would extend only to the states and not the territories. Here Dawson went after the intellectual foundation of the implied rights jurisprudence: that rights can be implied if they are tethered to the constitutional requirement for representative government. He exposes the vulnerability of the tether holding the freedom of political speech—that it doesn't apply to the territories.

The Brennan Court took a third step to delimit the implied rights jurisprudence in its 1997 *Lange* decision. The reader will recall that *Lange* concerned how the constitutionally protected implied right of political speech was to be reconciled with defamation law. In a unanimous judgment, the Court concluded that the constitution's text and structure alone determine the concept of representative government and not by reference to political theories or principles.[5] The constitution's text and structure define the term to mean the following: 1) the legislature is chosen through elections by the people, 2) responsible ministerial government defines the relationship between the Executive and Legislative branches, and 3) constitutional amendments occur through popular referenda. The Brennan Court concluded that an implied right to political speech exists only to the extent that it promotes these governmental functions.[6] This interpretive strategy, relying on the constitution's

---

4. High Court Transcript. *Kruger & Ors v Commonwealth of Australia* M21/1995 (12–15 February 1996).

5. 189 CLR 520, 566–67.

6. Ibid., 560–61.

text and structure and eschewing broader principles or theories of government, stands in sharp contrast to the Mason Court's approach to constitutional interpretation. *Lange* is also significant because the Brennan Court preserved the implied freedom of speech but relied upon a common law protection—not constitutional—to resolve the case.

My informants placed great significance in *Lange*. "There is no doubt that *Lange* has limited the implied rights cases very, very severely," said a Commonwealth attorney. He continued, "The atmosphere is dead against that. That's something that's hard to find in the constitution. People like [Justice] McHugh would never accept that. There's one wonderful line in a case where he says, 'I've read right through the constitution and I can't find it. Where is it? Just show me which words again.' (59:1330)" Justice McHugh was not alone in questioning the scope of the implied speech protections, according to a South Australia judge. "The Court was worried about [its] own boundaries. They were concerned about how far they should go or should have gone. In *Lange*, you see the Court questioning the implied freedom....They thought perhaps we've gone too far and we've got to come back. Many people are concerned about using the constitution for these purposes (117: 3100)." Another judge thought the pullback was not surprising. "The High Court retreated from *Theophanous* to *Lange*....But that's not an unexpected development. One will often develop a general principle and then subsequent cases will demonstrate there is a need to qualify it (74:3400)."

Several informants thought the Court's approach to resolving *Lange*'s speech question involved a more orthodox stance. It could have relied upon the constitutionally implied freedom, but instead it had recourse to common law. A NSW judge explained that the Court's reliance on common law instead of constitutional law was strategic.

> In *Lange*...the Court said that its predecessors had gone too far. This was at a time when Mason had retired and Deane had become Governor General. They said there was a problem, but the solution to the problem was really to invent a new common law—qualified privilege—which simply means that it is reasonable to permit the media to comment on public figures, but it wasn't a constitutional right. It was just a piece of common law that no one had noticed before. The creation of new common law rights is perhaps less objectionable than trying to fiddle around with the constitution itself. This is the way a conservative would put it (103:1045)."

Some of my informants also thought the implied rights jurisprudence was unlikely to develop in the Gleeson Court (1998–present). "I don't think the High Court will go back on *Lange*," said a Commonwealth attorney. "They preserved the implication but it remains a relatively small implication. The [Gleeson] Court is not expanding it and there are no cases coming forward exploring the issue (66)."

These informants were prescient. Two recent cases illustrate the circumscribed approach the Gleeson Court takes to the implied rights methodology: *Coleman v. Power*[7] and *Mulholland v. Australian Electoral Commission* (2004).[8] The first case concerned Patrick Coleman, a Queensland law student, who was arrested for distributing pamphlets calling local police officials "corrupt" and "slimy." He was arrested and convicted of violating a section of Queensland's *Vagrants, Gaming and Other Offences Act* that deemed it an offense to insult someone in public. The law specifically said that "Any person who, in any public place...uses any threatening, abusive or insulting words to any person...shall be liable to a penalty of $100 or to imprisonment for 6 months." Coleman argued that this provision violated his implied constitutional freedom of political communication as defined in *Lange*. In a 4-3 decision, the Court concluded that the insulting words provision impermissibly impugned Coleman's implied freedom of political communication. Applying the *Lange* test, they said that the insulting words provision burdened this freedom and that it was not reasonably appropriate and adapted to serve a legitimate end.

The individual judgments in *Coleman* expose a fractured court. While no justice denied the existence of the implied freedom of political communication, there was significant disagreement between the majority and dissenting judgments about the type of speech that falls under it and how to balance this freedom against state interests. Chief Justice Gleeson, a dissenter, expressed concern about expanding the notion of "political speech" so much that it includes everything and means nothing.

> The facts of the case illustrate the vagueness of concepts such as "political debate."... Let it be accepted that [the appellant's] conduct was, in the broadest sense, "political." It was not party political, and it had nothing to do with any laws, or government policy.... [A]lmost any conduct of the kind prohibited by s 7, including indecency, obscenity, profanity, threats, abuse, insults, and offensiveness, is capable of occurring in a "political" context, especially if that term is given its most expansive application. Reconciling freedom of political expression with the reasonable requirements of public order becomes in-

7. 220 CLR 1.
8. 209 ALR 582.

creasingly difficult when one is operating at the margins of the term
"political."⁹

Other dissenting judges sought to delimit the implied freedom by underscor-
ing that the implied freedom protects speech that is "necessary for the effective operation of government"¹⁰ and certainly does not countenance insulting
words that "do not really express 'opinions' or enable the strengths and weak-
nesses of what genuinely are opinions to be identified." Justice Heydon said
that insults "form no part of criticism which rises above abuse. They reflect
the vices of intolerance rather than the virtues of tolerance. They can crush
individual autonomy rather than vindicating it."¹¹

Judges who formed the majority thought these concerns ill-founded. Justice
McHugh acknowledged the value judgments inherent in the *Lange* test, but criticized his colleagues who shied away from fulfilling this natural judicial function: "[T]here is nothing novel about courts making judgments when they are
asked *to apply* a principle or rule of law. Much of the daily work of courts requires them to make judgments as to whether a particular set of facts or circumstances is or is not within a rule or principle of law."¹² Protecting the implied freedom is the Court's constitutional obligation, according to Justice Kirby:

> [T]he principle expressed in *Lange* has been accepted by this court,
> and repeatedly applied.... This court should not cut back the consti-
> tutional freedom whilst pretending to apply it. That freedom is de-
> fensive of the core institutions established by our basic law. Repre-
> sentative democracy would be neutered in Australia if we had the
> buildings that house our parliaments and went through the forms of
> regular elections but restricted the robust free debates amongst citi-
> zens that are essential to breathe life into the accountability of par-
> liamentary government in Australia to the people who are sovereign.¹³

Justice Heydon's suggestion that civilized political discourse is really the sort
of communication that the constitution envisions as critical to representative
government came under acute scrutiny by Justice Kirby as well.

> Reading the description of civilised interchange about governmental
> and political matters in the reasons of Heydon J, I had difficulty in

9. *Coleman*, 30–1.
10. Ibid., 110.
11. Ibid., 126.
12. Ibid., 53.
13. Ibid., 82–3.

recognising the Australian political system as I know it. His Honour's chronicle appears more like a description of an intellectual salon where civility always (or usually) prevails. It is not, with respect, an accurate description of the Australian governmental and political system in action. One might wish for more rationality, less superficiality, diminished invective and increased logic and persuasion in political discourse. But those of that view must find another homeland. From its earliest history, Australian politics has regularly included insult and emotion, calumny and invective, in its armoury of persuasion. They are part and parcel of the struggle of ideas. Anyone in doubt should listen for an hour or two to the broadcasts that bring debates of the Federal Parliament to the living rooms of the nation.... [T]he Constitution addresses the nation's representative government as it is practised. It does not protect only the whispered civilities of intellectual discourse.[14]

What these excerpts illustrate is a divided court. All agree that the implied freedom is there in the constitution. They profoundly disagree over what its presence entails and how to define political speech. What can be said is that *Coleman* preserves the implied freedom as defined by *Lange*.

The *Mulholland* case also presented the Court with questions about the scope and potency of implied freedoms. Mulholland, the appellant, was a registered officer of the Democratic Labor Party (DLP), which split from the Australian Labor Party in the 1950s out of fear that communists had infiltrated the ALP. For the DLP to appear on the federal election ballots, the party had to register according to the federal election law, which states that any party without representation in Parliament must submit the names of 500 party members, none of whom may also be registered with other parties. Mulholland challenged the "500 rule" and the "no-overlap rule" as unconstitutionally violating the implied freedom of political communication, association, and privacy. He lost his claim on each ground. A unanimous court concluded that these particular provisions of the electoral act were consistent with the constitutional requirements that representatives be "directly chosen by the people." Five concluded that the rules did not burden the implied freedom of communication; indeed, the registration requirements seek to improve informed communication between political parties and voters. This case is significant for several reasons. First, the Court preserved the argument that a freedom of political communication is implied by the requirement that representatives be

---

14. Ibid., 91.

"directly chosen by the people." However, it did not heighten the threshold that the state must meet to infringe justifiably upon the implied freedom. It stuck to *Lange*'s conclusion that the freedom of political communication is not a free standing right; rather, it is tied inherently to the text and structure of the constitution and should be confined to protect "speech" that is required for representative government. A more adventuresome court could have extended these implied freedoms or heighten the requirements for the government to infringe upon them constitutionally. The Gleeson Court opted against doing that. In sum, the *Coleman* and *Mulholland* cases are but two in a long line of post-Mason Court decisions illustrating the retreat from the outer boundaries of the Mason Court's implied rights jurisprudence. The consolidation that has occurred in this area is emblematic of what has happened to many areas of private and public law.

Reconsidering the Politicized Judicial Role

My informants also perceived the Brennan and Gleeson Courts pulling back in their fidelity to the politicized role, most notably along the legal reasoning dimensions. The Gleeson Court has brought "a complete sea change in the overall legal and political stance of the Court," said a Commonwealth attorney. He continued, "It has moved to a much more conservative legal approach— much more black letter approach—from a more adventurous constitutional theory.... You've got a very strong group of what we might call in America originalists in one form or another. It looks like you've got five Scalia's there, but you haven't. You've certainly got a Court which is less willing to do adventurous things (59:345)." A Federal Court judge concluded, "There is this on the Gleeson Court: Gleeson himself is a minimalist. He says, 'I've got a dispute. What is the simplest...way to resolve it? What do I have to do to resolve it, because I don't want to do anything more than that.'...Gleeson is likely to try to produce a move back towards older forms of legal reasoning (103:10641)." In this judge's mind, the older forms mean a return to pre-Mason days.

Another Federal Court judge described the change in legal reasoning as follows: "[The Mason Court] opened the world up from what it had been under the British yoke.... It's inevitable that once you open things up then you have a reconsideration. I remember when Brennan was first appointed Chief Justice. He described his period as one...of consolidation of changes that had occurred. I don't know how Gleeson would describe his. I don't even think he would bother even to have an approach." The Gleeson Court distinguishes itself in that "Methodology assumes a greater significance than it might previously. There is far less interest in the inexorable movement in the internationalization of law. I don't think they're showing anything quite like the same interest that the previous Court did (86:2600)."

The Gleeson Court's emphasis on legal method means that it pays less attention to consequences of decisions. It was harshly criticized in this regard for its 1999 *Wakim* decision.[15] Indeed, if *Mabo* captured the Mason Court's esprit, *Wakim* does the same for the Gleeson Court. Before describing the appellate judges' reactions to *Wakim* and why they considered it a touchstone case, some background is warranted.

In 1987 the Commonwealth and state parliaments enacted cross-vesting legislation that enabled state courts to exercise Federal Court jurisdiction and vice versa.[16] Cross-vesting jurisdiction between the Federal Courts and state supreme courts, something both the Commonwealth and states endorsed, was lauded for the benefits it brought to litigants. It was thought to decrease delays, lower costs, and reduce the uncertainty because it enabled state courts to handle cases that raised state and federal questions. No longer was it necessary to farm out the federal questions.

In *Wakim*, the Court tackled a specific cross-vesting question: Could federal courts be vested with state and territory supreme court jurisdiction? The appellant, Wakim, was a creditor in a bankruptcy dispute who claimed that the bankruptcy trustee and its solicitors acted in a negligent manner for failing to take steps that could have increased the amount of money available to creditors from the bankrupt's estate. This negligence claim was filed in Federal Court. Negligence is a common law matter normally handled in state supreme courts, save for the cross-vesting jurisdiction. The solicitors sought relief from the Federal Court hearing the matter, arguing that the cross-vesting scheme was invalid.

The High Court agreed, concluding that the cross-vesting scheme did not validly confer jurisdiction on the Federal Court to hear the common law negligence claim. Neither the Commonwealth nor the states had the power to confer this jurisdiction. The states lacked the power because the only matters federal courts can handle are those falling under the jurisdiction outlined in Chapter III of the constitution. Chapter III forbids the states from adding to federal court jurisdiction.

Although the states disabused this power, could the Commonwealth Parliament grant state jurisdiction to federal courts? The constitution contains no ex-

---

15. *Re Wakim; Ex parte McNally* 198 CLR 511.
16. *Jurisdiction of Courts (Cross-Vesting) Act* 1987 (Cth).

plicit provision enabling it, so the conferral of state jurisdiction on federal courts can occur only if incidental to the Commonwealth's expressed power to confer federal jurisdiction on federal courts. The Court concluded that measures promoting the "effectiveness of federal jurisdiction" could be justified. It rejected, however, the argument that cross-vesting was incidental to an expressed power for the following reason: vesting federal courts with state jurisdiction makes the exercise of state jurisdiction more effective, but it does little to make the exercise of federal jurisdiction more effective. Indeed, when federal courts exercise state jurisdiction, they may become less effective in fulfilling their responsibilities.[17]

The critical point for purposes here is that the Court dismissed all arguments over cross-vesting's convenience and expediency. The Commonwealth and state parliaments all consented to the scheme. Federal and state judges welcomed the efficiency it provided. An official review conducted four years after cross-vesting was instigated concluded that it had "a profound and beneficial impact on the Australian judicial system" (Opeskin 1998, 28). The Court dismissed all such arguments. Justices Gummow and Hayne wrote, "The Court is entrusted with the preservation and application of constitutional distinctions. Were the court to disregard those distinctions, on the ground that at a particular time and to some minds they appear inconvenient or otherwise unsatisfactory, the court would not only fail in its task but would exceed its authority."[18] Chief Justice Gleeson wrote, "The cross-vesting legislation has been commended as an example of co-operation between the Parliaments of the Federation. Approval of the legislative policy is irrelevant to a judgment as to constitutional validity.... The [P]arliaments... cannot, by co-operation, amend the Constitution.... Its convenience has been determined by the Parliaments. The duty of the Court is to determine its legality."[19]

Several informants thought *Wakim* captured the Gleeson Court's penchant for more orthodox legal reasoning. A Federal Court judge remarked:

> *Wakim* is emblematic of an environment that's being created today about courts and dispute resolution. It's been created by the High Court. The Chief Justice of the High Court has said there is no need to have a uniform court system. [T]hat's an extraordinary observation. Almost none of them have had any significant trial experience....If you think about [*Wakim*], it has nothing to do with solving actual grievances within your community. They're saying you can solve grievances, but you can't go to that court to do it, even though

---

17. For an insightful summary of the cross-vesting cases, see Hill (1999).
18. *Re Wakin*, 569.
19. Ibid., 540.

it's the natural court to hear the substantive complaint.... I see *Wakim* as reasonably emblematic of how [the Gleeson Court] approaches a lot of matters. There is a far greater preoccupation with traditional technique... than the more open... approach you would get in a Mason or Deane environment.... I better watch what I say because I know the judges very well. *Wakim*... doesn't give a damn about consequences (86:1300).

The judge then assessed the judicial community's reaction to *Wakim*: "I think if you went around the Federal Court, there would be a certain level of disenchantment with the High Court, mainly because no one can understand why they would want to do what they've done in relation to the [Federal Court].... Why it happened God only knows. No one has given me a convincing reason, least of all the judges of the High Court (86:1700)." *Wakim* fostered strong reactions among informants. "*Wakim* is a f***ing outrage," said a Federal Court judge. "The real justification for *Wakim*—the one they will never articulate—is that the Federal Court pinched all the good work from the state courts and left the state supreme courts languishing." The judge continued:

> In Victoria people paid money not to go to the Supreme Court but to go to the Federal Court—better, more efficient justice. Even if you had a two-Bob company claim, people would pay the $3000 fee instead of the $300 fee to take it into the Federal Court.... [T]he High Court... had Ken Hayne from the Court of Appeal in Victoria, Michael McHugh from the Court of Appeal in NSW, Mary Gaudron, the [former] Solicitor-General [of] NSW, and Gleeson was Chief Justice of NSW. There is no constitutional imperative for *Wakim* to be decided the way it was except that it protects the supreme courts of the states.... That's the justification for the decision, but you won't read that anywhere in the judgment (86:3100).

One can only speculate on ulterior motives. Nothing from the High Court indicates that its real motivation in *Wakim* was anything other than to prevent parliaments from treading on Chapter III of the Constitution. Regardless, *Wakim* emblematizes the Gleeson Court's general conception of the judicial role. It sees itself less as a policy making institution and gives, therefore, less consideration to the consequences that stem from decisions. In *Wakim*, it was willing to overturn a federal statute that fostered a workable solution to jurisdictional disputes within a federated judicial system.

What is most telling is that my informants saw the Gleeson Court promoting no meaningful political value or constitutional principle in striking down cross-vesting. The Court claims that preserving Chapter III jurisdictional purity qualifies, but several judges found that unconvincing. A South Australia judge remarked, "Cross-vesting was working well. As a practical measure it was a good way to come to terms with the federal structure—not to disadvantage the parties (117:10130)." A Western Australia judge suggested the absence of any significant principle: "All the lawyers and judges would think, bar the six majority judges on the High Court, that the *Wakim* decision, and subsequent decisions, are really not preserving any great public virtue and have made for a less cooperative federalism and a duplication between federal and state that is highly undesirable (11:5845)." A Commonwealth attorney confided, "My main criticism is that the *Wakim* decision... doesn't seem to be preserving or protecting any real constitutional value. No constitutional values were at stake. The states liked it. There were no constitutional values lying behind the outcome. In [the Mason] days we would have gotten an articulated constitutional value (59:2600)." A Federal Court judge concurred, "Why, with a state of affairs which is positive and beneficial to the operation of the federation and also facilitates orderly dispute resolution when there is no positive constitutional impairment to it, would [the Court] take such an extraordinary step? It's created chaos (86:445)."

To summarize the chapter thus far, a strong consensus emerged from my interviews that the post-Mason Courts, particularly the Gleeson Court, underwent a consolidation on at least two fronts. First, the contemporary Court has pulled back from some of the more controversial doctrinal innovations that marked the Mason era. Second, it has abandoned the politicized role and retreated in some measure toward the orthodoxy. This section illustrated the pullback in substantive law by exploring developments in the implied rights doctrine. It also illustrated the shift toward the orthodoxy by examining the legal reasoning employed in the cross-vesting case. Why consolidation occurred on these fronts is explored below.

POLITICAL FACTORS THAT CONTRIBUTED TO RETRENCHMENT

In his seminal work, *The American Supreme Court*, Robert McCloskey argues that the U.S. Supreme Court secured its greatest institutional successes not when it plunged headlong into the nation's most profoundly divisive issues to answer them boldly. When the Court "tried to goad the nation faster toward Utopia," to borrow McCloskey's phrase, it proved most effective when it took "slow and gingerly steps" instead of "leaps and bounds (1994, 209–11)." McCloskey concludes that the Court is most effective when it operates "at the margins" of political controversies and not at the epicenters because it can guard its institutional power and legitimacy. Forbearance is the best method for sustaining power and legitimacy. McCloskey's thesis goes some way to explain the post-Mason Courts' retreat toward the orthodoxy. If he surveyed the High Court's record during the 1980s and 1990s, McCloskey would no doubt observe that the Mason Court took anything but "slow and gingerly steps" in goading Australia. The Mason era clearly was a time when the Court extended itself into the political system in a manner and to an extent previously unknown. As evidenced in previous chapters, the Mason Court did more than tweak substantive law here and there. Likewise, the changes it introduced to legal reasoning were more than modest. Indeed, its activism was so sweeping that one can speak of a wholesale transformation in its role. This transformation occurred not with the Court staying at the margins of political controversies; the Court became the controversy.

Criticisms of the High Court as an institution and of its judges were more potent in the 1990s than at any previous time. The Mason Court certainly did the most to engender criticism, but the manifestation of this criticism seemed to lag. It took some time for observers to appreciate fully the Mason Court's agenda and the consequences of its decisions and legal reasoning. Others reserved judgment, not knowing the extent of reforms to come. For others, it took the cumulative effect of the Mason era to exhaust the surplus legitimacy that many extended to the Court. In the end, the most white-hot criticism from political and legal circles was dumped on the Brennan Court, specifically its *Wik* decision. The reader will recall that *Wik* addressed whether pastoral leases could co-exist or extinguish native title. Roughly 42 percent of the Australian landmass (mostly interior) is managed under pastoral leases. A High Court judge summarized the reaction:

> I don't think *Mabo* got that much controversy. It came down. Everything was relatively quiet. When the controversy started was when the claim was made for *Wik* when grazers' interests were at stake. Their political clout in this country has always been as significant as their counterparts in [the U.S.] who refuse to allow free trade with respect to meat. They've always been a significant political force.... A large part of the controversy was made by the politicians rather than by the public at large. The politicians generated it and pro-

moted it for their own political ends.... It was simply the occasion for people to beat some drums that were thought to have political mileage (92:20145).

It should come as little surprise that *Wik*, which impacted so much land and such powerful political interests, precipitated a nationwide political debate on the High Court's role years after the Mason Court took its first steps to effectuate the politicized role. Critics looked to *Wik* as only one example of many where the Court usurped parliamentary power and approbated rogue interpretations to the constitution, statutes, and common law.

The Court concluded in *Wik* by a 4–3 majority (Justices Toohey, Kirby, Gummow, and Gaudron) that native title and pastoral leases could co-exist. Native title was extinguished only with a written act where the government made the extinguishment explicit.

Queensland, Western Australia, and the Northern Territory—the three regions most impacted by *Wik*—called for Commonwealth legislation to overturn the decision shortly after it was handed down. In 1997, Queensland Premier Bob Borbidge took the lead attacking the *Wik* decision and the High Court, which was not surprising given that 85 percent of Queensland was subject to native title claims. Recognizing the political firestorm that *Wik* generated, Prime Minister Howard organized a conference of national and state officials in January 1997 to explore a response. No formal action came from that conference, but Howard indicated that reforms to the *Native Title Act* (passed in 1993 after the High Court handed down *Mabo*) would be required, but he would not overturn *Wik* through legislation. Borbidge began in February a multi-month attack on the High Court and its judges. His rhetoric transcended the native title cases and really addressed the High Court's role. For example, he told an audience in February 1997, "If the High Court is going to change its role, and that's what it has signaled—it's going to start to make the laws and not interpret them—then like every other institution in Australia, that comes at a price and the price is accountability." Further, "If the High Court is embarking on a course of judicial activism, the High Court itself has discarded the principle of the doctrine of the separation of powers."[20]

It is important to recall that Howard's Liberal Party had formed a coalition government following the 1996 federal election with Tim Fischer and his National Party, a party that mainly represents farming and rural interests. Fischer, who became Deputy Prime Minister in the Coalition Government, cas-

---

20. Gervase Greene. February 11, 1997. "Court Warned to Keep Out of Politics," *The Age*, p. 6.

tigated *Wik* as "judicial activism writ awful."[21] Queensland's Borbidge was also a National Party member, so with Borbidge and Fischer attacking the Court, Howard had to respond in some fashion. His Attorney-General, Daryl Williams, did not want to disappoint National Party colleagues so he offered muted criticism in February 1997. "Limits on the judicial function stem directly from the place of the judiciary in the careful balancing of the separation of powers.... Judges must, to act legitimately, refrain from trespassing on the proper role of the legislature."[22] Howard himself joined the attack a few weeks later: "One of the problems is that the perception had developed that some judges believe it is their role to give the Parliament a hurry-on and do things that they think the Parliament should have done."[23]

Borbidge and the other premiers coupled their verbal attacks with proposals to alter radically the High Court. Their proposals included,

- a constitutional amendment to enable Australian voters to select and terminate High Court judges,

- shorter tenure for High Court judges,

- granting state parliaments the power to veto judicial appointments,

- giving states the power to fill every second High Court vacancy,

- establishing a separate appointment apparatus that would enable greater state participation, and,

- creating a new Federal Constitutional Appeals Court, composed of the six state supreme court chief justices and three other state appointed judges, that would review High Court decisions.[24]

The Opposition in Canberra provided some cover for the High Court. In rather colorful prose, for instance, Deputy Opposition Leader Gareth Evans characterized Borbidge as a "sloping forehead, knuckles dragging on the ground, constitutional primitive."[25] Borbidge may have been a constitutional primitive, but it was the survival of the fittest in the political world that mo-

21. John Short and Scott Emerson, February 8, 1997, "Wipe out native title, says Fischer," *The Australian*, p. 1.

22. Ibid.

23. Ross Peake, March 1, 1997, "Howard Joins Court Attack," *Canberra Times*, p. 1.

24. Michael Millett, February 19, 1997, "*Wik* Anger: Premiers Seek Veto on High Court Judges," *Sydney Morning Herald*, p. 1.

25. Ibid.

tivated Borbidge. Many observers thought he was trying to shore up additional support for the National Party Government in Queensland to call an early election and win an outright majority. He had formed a minority government with the help of an independent.

Responding to these criticisms and threats from leading politicians, the judiciary fired a surprising shot across their bow. In April 1997, eight chief justices of the state and territorial supreme courts issued a Declaration of Judicial Independence that stressed the importance of public confidence in the judiciary and its impartiality. The declaration, drawn from a similar statement of principles from the International Commission of Jurists, addresses the tenure of judges and the importance of judicial independence from the executive government.[26] In late September, Chief Justice Brennan joined the fray by warning that any erosion of judicial independence would threaten the rule of law in Australia. That chief justices felt compelled to defend the courts publicly was not unprecedented, but for them to do so in such a collective and outspoken way was probably without precedent, and it sharply illustrated the politically embattled situation in which the High Court found itself in the late 1990s.

As state and federal leaders joined the chorus of High Court critics, Chief Justice Brennan and others became alarmed at the possible erosion of judicial legitimacy. One could appreciate his concern given the editorials that regularly appeared in major newspapers. *The Age* ran an editorial, for instance, with this opening paragraph:

> Will democracy in Australia survive the 21st century? Perhaps not, if the courts and legal thinking continue on their present paths. The joint statement by the Chief Justices of the states and territories this week, subsequently endorsed by the Chief Justice of the High Court, represents a bid for power in our constitutional system equivalent to the manner in which Parliament wrested control of spending from the Crown in 17th century England.[27]

Brennan wrote privately to Fischer to ask him to call off the dogs and avoid irrevocable damage to the Court. He then found occasion to respond publicly to critics during the oral arguments for the *Lange* defamation case. "Two

---

26. See http://wwwlaw.murdoch.edu.au/icjwa/ausprin.htm (accessed May 19, 2002) for copy of declaration.

27. Padraic McGuinness, April 16, 1997, "Power-Hungry Judges Push Too Far," *The Age*, p. 13.

things must be remembered. First, that a court has no agenda of its own. It is there to decide cases between parties and the issues for its determination are those which the parties plead. Secondly, that once the parties have brought an issue to the court, the court has no option but to determine the issues so brought. In doing so, it must apply the law as best it sees it."[28] In May 1997 the Howard Government rejected all proposals to reform the High Court appointment process. It promised greater consultation with state governments but assured them that appointment powers would remain in the federal cabinet. The controversy spiraled on for the year.

Another High Court rejoinder came in a well publicized speech that Justice Kirby delivered to the American Bar Association in January 1998 titled, "Attack on Judges—A Universal Phenomena." Kirby surveyed politicians' attacks on courts in Britain and New Zealand, concluding they are "genteel by comparison to those that have engaged the Australian judiciary." He then cataloged some of the derogatory monikers lobbed at the Court:

> "Bogus," "pusillanimous and evasive," guilty of "plunging Australia into the abyss," a "pathetic...self-appointed [group of] Kings and Queens," a group of "basket-weavers," "gripped...in a mania for progressivism," purveyors of "intellectual dishonesty," unaware of "its place," "adventurous," needing...a sentence to "life on the streets," an "unfaithful servant of the Constitution," "undermining democracy," a body "packed with feral judges," "a professional labor cartel." There were many more epithets of a like character, many stronger.[29]

Kirby's explicit response to the criticism and name calling, as Brennan did the year before, may have struck his audience of American judges and lawyers as refreshingly quaint. How ubiquitous the judicial rejoinders would be if a U.S. Supreme Court judge responded to every tide of criticism. Regardless of the American audience's reaction, 1997 was significant for the sustained criticism directed at the High Court. By all indications, the attacks took their toll. The political firestorm left its mark. A Victoria judge offered: "You probably find

28. *Lange v. The Australian Broadcasting Corporation* S109/1996 (4 March 1997). Transcript of proceedings at Canberra on Tuesday, 4 March 1997 at 10:23 a.m.

29. Justice Michael Kirby, January 5, 1998, "Attacks on Judges—A Universal Phenomena." Speech delivered at the American Bar Association, Section on Litigation, Winter Leadership Meeting, Maui, Hawaii. See http://www.hcourt.gov.au/speeches/kirbyj/kirbyj_maui.htm (accessed on May 19, 2002).

that after Tony Mason went, Gerry Brennan was a bit concerned about the vitriol that had been directed at the High Court and tended to react to it....I
think what Gerry Brennan sought to do was try to reassure the public that
they weren't in politics. Therefore, they drew in their horns a bit (52:2430)."
A High Court judge said:

> The Gleeson Court has tended to revert to the earlier mode of rea-
> soning....I don't suppose members of the Court would say they were
> reacting to the criticism, because judges rarely say that. I don't know
> whether they were in fact reacting to it. But there is often a reaction
> in various fields of thought. One goes to an extreme and then recoils
> from it. I think the Court went to an extreme and it has recoiled from
> it (94:2230).

The year 1997 was a year unlike any other in High Court history. It began
with newspapers running stories shortly after the holidays about a revolutionary High Court decision that appeared to throw the land system into
utter chaos. Those interests who stood to lose the most under *Wik* allied with
state and federal politicians who gladly amplified the passionate objections
to *Wik* and disdain for those who reached it. The High Court was assailed as
activist and illegitimate to an extent previously unseen. Select judges attempted to defend the judiciary, but these efforts were less effective than a
prompt and deliberate exit from center stage. This section has shown that a
retrenchment occurred partly in response to the sustained criticism coming
from political circles. The next section identifies institutional variables that
contributed.

INSTITUTIONAL CONDITIONS
ENCOURAGING RETRENCHMENT

This section explores institutional conditions that encouraged the aban-
donment of the politicized role. Again, the notion of an "institution" is defined in broad terms to include tangible structures such as parliaments, constitutions, courts, as well as more informal institutions such legal doctrines,
norms and conventions, or what Rogers Smith calls "cognitive structures" that
form cultures and social patterns within communities (1995, 91). Using this
definition, the interview data point to three institutional conditions that encouraged the post-Mason Court to shy away from the politicized role: the
dearth of support within the judicial community for the politicized role, in-

sufficient constitutional infrastructures to support and justify it, and the turnover in Court membership due to the retirement provision.

How the Transformation Played within the Broader Judicial Community

Jack Peltason's *Fifty-Eight Lonely Men* explored the challenges confronting southern federal district judges in carrying out the U.S. Supreme Court's desegregation mandate. Peltason aptly captured the difficult position that the *Brown v. Board of Education* decision placed them in as members of two communities— a judicial community whose top court deemed segregation unconstitutional and a local political community often opposed to integration. Some judges bucked local pressures and recalcitrant political leaders and moved as the *Brown* II decision required "with all deliberate speed" in issuing desegregation orders and requiring police protection for civil rights marches. Other judges proved more complicit, sometimes enabling school boards to delay desegregation. Whether the Court proved efficacious with regard to *Brown* depended often on the local political landscapes and the individual dispositions of southern federal district judges. Unless they were willing to apply *Brown*'s dictate to local situations and cases, the history of desegregating the south would look profoundly different.

Peltason's account underscores the significant role that lower court judges often have implementing higher court decisions. Drawing upon his insights about vertical relationships within judicial communities, I assert that the transformation's long-term success or failure rested in some measure on how intermediate appellate court judges reacted to the reforms. These intermediate appellate judges (the state supreme court judges and Federal Court judges) were not placed in the same position as southern U.S. federal judges were: called to implement a higher court directive in an often hostile local community. However, the High Court judges were members of the same (comparatively small) judicial community as the intermediate appellate judges. One feature to this community is how well they know each other. I became acutely aware of this when conducting my interviews. Judges in one state or city talked about judges in other states and cities in surprisingly informative detail. Nearly all informants spoke about their High Court colleagues with notable confidence and authoritativeness. Moreover, High Court judges demonstrated a familiarity with the intermediate courts—their composition, recent cases decided, pending cases, and jurisprudential leanings. The relatively small number of judges who exercise appellate jurisdiction and consider themselves members of this community explains this familiarity. They went to the same law schools, practiced at the bar together, and as judges they now read each other's work, monitor developments in each other's jurisdictions, and attend the same professional conferences.

My interview data suggest this judicial community has its own culture, norms, and expectations that animate and constrain its members, including High Court judges. It is my contention that the politicized role's ability to out-live those Mason Court judges who most supported it demanded a certain level of diffuse support within this broader judicial community. It never gained this. Australia's intermediate appellate judges were (and still are) divided over the politicized role. This dearth of support may be attributed to the inability of Mason Court judges to cultivate through their judgments and extra-legal writ-ings and other communications support for the politicized role. I found pock-ets of support among intermediate appellate judges for particular High Court decisions or doctrinal developments, but absent from my interviews were broad endorsements for the role transformation. Just what level of diffuse support would have encouraged the Mason Court reforms to outlive the Mason Court itself is difficult to pinpoint. Just where was the tipping point? This is a pro-foundly complex question to which the data I gathered say little, except for what might come off as bromides. The data point to two facts. First, no consensus emerged from this larger judicial community around the idea that the post-Mason Court should continue to advance the politicized role. I confronted in-termediate judges across the country who responded to the Mason Court with tepid enthusiasm and others with significant apprehension. Second, the Mason Court judges' efforts to convince this community as to the politicized role's value insufficiently buttressed their enthusiasm and ameliorated their apprehensions.

The best evidence for the Mason Court's failure on this front is seen in ear-lier chapters, where current members of the appellate judiciary spoke in support of the orthodox and politicized roles. If one conclusion emerges from the inter-views, it is that Australia's appellate bench was passionately divided at the time of the interviews (and still is) over the politicized role. This division goes far deeper than a few renegades, contrarians, or curmudgeons. Australia's judicial community finds itself at that foggy yet definitive moment where two visions for the High Court are competing for ascendance within the intermediate judicial ranks. The judges now know and have witnessed the character and consequences of these competing visions. Yet, this judicial community has not embraced one and rejected the other. The Gleeson Court has retreated from several intellectual outposts that the Mason Court constructed, but there is a difference between re-treat and outright rejection. This retreat continues apace, in part, because the judicial community remains skeptical. The Mason Court failed to build enough consensus within the judicial community for the reforms to carry on uninter-rupted.

Not only were significant segments of the appellate bench skeptical, so too was much of the legal bar. "There is a large component of the bar in [Victoria] and NSW which reacted with hostility to the new method of reasoning. They don't feel comfortable with it. They feel judges have been treading into public policy areas and making legislative decisions rather than doing what they should be doing, which is essentially declaring the law. I have no doubt at all that a substantial percentage of the bar in this state would hold that view (44:330)." The same judge conveyed the challenges he faced as a barrister employing Mason Court principles before intermediate appellate judges.

> I can tell you when you try to invoke the implied rights doctrine in the lower courts in this country, the traditional judge reacts strongly against it. They might feel themselves compelled—dragged unwillingly—to follow those cases and apply them in particular cases, but I tried in the Full Federal Court, for example, and got absolutely nowhere. They read it down. They said, "We of course know what you're saying and we understand the High Court said that but that case is different." The traditional technique of distinguishing a case is used to avoid the consequences of applying those sorts of principles. *We have a fair distance between the judges on the High Court, in terms of their approach, and judges who sit at levels below them—a philosophical divide which makes it quite difficult to work with High Court authority in the lower courts* (44:900) (emphasis added).

Why then was the Mason Court unable to sway the judicial community? I advance that a primary reason for the lack of converts is, to continue with the religious metaphor, that the Mason Court asked judges to adopt a religion they did not know and could not practice.

To develop this point, a comparison must first be drawn between how U.S. and Australian courts handle constitutional questions. U.S. Federal District Courts today are vested with *original jurisdiction* over cases arising under the constitution. This means that under most circumstances if a litigant raises a constitutional question, the U.S. district court judge makes a determination on it. This decision may be appealed. It may be reversed. But they have the authority to make it (Richardson and Vines 1970; Wright 1994; Rowland and Carp 1996; Lyles 1997).[30] The Australian procedures for handling constitu-

---

30. This was not always the case. Federal district courts exercised a much more limited jurisdiction from their creation in 1789 until Congress brought sweeping reforms under the Judiciary Act in 1875. These reforms established federal district courts as general courts of first instance in federal matters, including constitutional disputes.

tional questions are altogether different. Rather than vesting the Federal Court with original jurisdiction over constitutional matters, the Commonwealth Constitution gives that jurisdiction to the High Court. As described in an earlier chapter, anytime a constitutional question emerges in a state or federal trial court, the issue may be removed to the High Court for consideration. All attorneys-general are notified and given the option to intervene in the proceedings (*Judiciary Act* s. 78A,B). Parliament enacted these reforms in 1976.[31] Once a constitutional question is removed to the High Court, proceedings in the trial court may be stayed until the question is resolved. The *Judiciary Act*'s removal requirement elevates constitutional discourse and deliberation out of trial courts and into the High Court. The upside to this approach is the fast resolution of constitutional questions. The political and legal systems do not have to wait for the case to meander through the lower and intermediate courts. One potential downside is that it excludes lower court judges from participating in constitutional deliberation.

If Australia's judicial community perceives constitutional deliberation as something reserved for the High Court, if the *Judiciary Act* discourages federal court judges from grappling with constitutional issues themselves, then the removal provision could impact how lower court judges perceive revolutionary constitutional reform occurring in the High Court. It means that Australia's Federal Court and state Supreme Court judges are not participating in their country's constitutional deliberations. They become observers and consumers rather than participants. A Federal Court judge described his experience with constitutional litigation as follows: "The Federal Court is not directly concerned with the powers of Parliament. That's essentially a matter for the High Court, in the sense that the only way the powers of Parliament could be checked is by a challenge to the constitutionality of legislation—by and large we're not concerned with that.... *When constitutional questions arise, the sole arbiter of those is the High Court* (28:1900) (emphasis added)."

State supreme courts have even less exposure to constitutional litigation. These courts regularly exercise judicial review powers, but mostly over executive and administrative decisions. Notwithstanding the tradition of parliamentary sovereignty, state supreme courts were intended to have legislative review powers as well, but conventions discourage this practice (Lumb 1977,

---

31. The *Judiciary Act* provides, "Section 40(1) Any cause or part of a cause arising under the Constitution or involving its interpretation that is at any time pending in a federal court...or in a court of a state or territory may, at any stage...be removed into the High Court under an order of the High Court, which may, upon application of a party for sufficient cause shown, be made on such terms as the Court thinks fit."

p. 113). A South Australia judge explained: "[State] constitutional review does not tend to arise in state jurisdictions really. I can't remember when such a situation arose. From time to time we have had to look at the legality of subordinate legislation...whether that was within or without power. Judicial review as you contemplate really only arises in the federal arena, because all of the state parliaments are sovereign within their own areas of legislative power (14:1600)." A Queensland appellate judge offered a similar assessment for his state's judiciary:

> Under our system in the states, parliament is supreme....It's worse in Queensland than elsewhere because there is no upper house. The Commonwealth is different. Its powers are somewhat controlled and the High Court controls the interpretation of that....We've got no power to place limits on the state assembly. We're like the judges in England. If a constitutional question arises (and it usually arises at the boundary of state and federal power) what we have to do under the procedures...from the Commonwealth is...to say this raises a constitutional question. All the attorneys-general for the states and Commonwealth must be advised. Once they know, they can come in and say we want that removed into the High Court. So, the High Court decides these things. If they don't, then it's a matter they don't care about and it stays here. But we don't very often get to look at constitutional questions in the state courts (2:3500).

A final noteworthy component to this removal provision is that state and Commonwealth attorneys-general exercise the exclusive right to remove cases to the High Court. A consequence to this arrangement is that constitutional litigation (thereby deliberation as well) is a government dominated activity. Attorneys-general intervene far more regularly than private interests precisely because of the removal rules. If excluding state and federal court judges from the constitutional dialogue had a deleterious effect on the politicized role's success, then granting exclusive power to attorneys-general to remove matters only excludes more voices from deliberation. The justifications for this exclusive removal power are reasonable enough: Because Australia lacks a constitutional bill of rights, the constitution deals primarily with distributing power between the federal and state governments and between the federal branches. This inclines constitutional dialogue toward issues germane to state and national governments. Non-governmental participants enter the dialogue only after the attorneys-general initiate the removal.

What I advance is that the removal requirement itself negatively impacted the transformation's long term success. The Mason Court promoted the politicized role, with all of its implications and controversies, in a judicial system that excluded, for the most part, Federal Court and state supreme court judges. The Mason Court reforms did not fall on deaf ears; rather, the decisions arrived in a constitutional language with which the judges were unfamiliar. The support base for the Mason Court's reforms was further limited by the rule that only governmental entities can remove constitutional questions from trial courts to the High Court. Nongovernmental entities remain active in constitutional litigation, but they are not as involved as they could be given the removal rule. Any revolution from the top requires some foot soldiers in the street. The Mason Court had few, which made its revolution all the more tenuous.

The Constitutional Infrastructure

A second institutional factor that contributed to the retrenchment in the post-Mason era was the absence of a sufficient constitutional infrastructure to legitimize some of the critical reform efforts. Included within this concept of a "constitutional infrastructure" are the powers and duties formally prescribed to the High Court. My informants indicated that the Mason Court built some of its jurisprudence on an ill-matched constitutional infrastructure. Sheer judicial will can patch over gaps in a constitutional framework—those features of the constitution that do not readily support a certain exercise of power. Over the longer term, however, that constitutional infrastructure cannot be ignored.

The importance of constitutional infrastructure to judicial role transformations is well illustrated in recent Canadian Supreme Court history. The 1982 Charter of Rights and Freedoms has garnered much attention in legal and political circles, in large measure because it profoundly altered the Supreme Court's institutional role in the political system.[32] Before the Charter, however, the Court lacked sufficient constitutional infrastructure to advance any significant rights jurisprudence. Canada's Supreme Court experimented with its own implied rights jurisprudence as far back as the 1930s. Its fullest articulation came in the 1957 *Switzman* v. *Elbling* decision,[33] where the Court concluded that Canada's constitution contained an implied freedom of political speech. The Court first justified the implication on grounds that the constitution's preamble, which called for a "constitution similar in principle

---

32. See Monahan (1987); Russell (1992); Manfredi (2001); Mandel (1994); Morton et al. (2000).
33. [1957] SCR 285.

to that of the United Kingdom," implied that Canadians enjoyed whatever rights and freedoms were extant in Britain in 1867 when the constitution was ratified. Second, it based the implication on the importance of political speech in a representative democracy. After *Switzman*, the implied rights doctrine slowly withered.

Three years after *Switzman*, Parliament enacted a statutory Bill of Rights, which recognized, *inter alia*, an individual's right to life, liberty, due process, freedom of religion, speech, assembly, and equality. Canadian scholars have noted how little the Bill of Rights (1960) changed the exercise of judicial review, and therefore, the Supreme Court's role. Its application was limited to the federal government, but most important, as a statute lacking constitutional status it was technically no different from statutes governing dog catchers. The Supreme Court balked at giving life to this new statement of rights and freedoms, not because these hurdles were insurmountable, but because the Court chose to see them as insurmountable (Manfredi 2001). The Court signaled its conservative approach toward the Bill of Rights (1960) shortly after its enactment, and from 1960 to 1982 its reliance on the statute was paltry. Peter Russell reports that a mere five out of thirty-four cases based on the bill succeeded (1987, 343). It was not until rights protection measures went from the statute books to the constitution itself that the Canadian Supreme Court's transformation was possible (Knopff and Morton 1992, 4).[34] The change in infrastructure—from statutory to constitutional—was critical in providing the Court institutional support for Canada's rights revolution.

The Canadian experience is instructive for understanding the post-Mason era. It demonstrates the importance of adequate constitutional infrastructure to support whatever role courts assume in the political system. Just as Canada's constitutional infrastructure before the Charter provided inadequate support for major reform on the civil rights front, so too Australia's constitutional infrastructure proved inadequate for the Mason Court reforms.

An oft-mentioned example where the Mason Court proceeded on tenuous grounds was in its protection of rights through implication. Although the Court was known to draw implications in other areas of law, inferring rights from the constitution was precarious. Consider the following from a Commonwealth attorney:

> The problem is you've got a constitution with no bill of rights. The only rights contained in it aren't really rights. Section 117 was just

---

34. Yet see Epp (1998) who argues that the litigation support structure put in place before the Charter was also important.

states rights—you can't discriminate against residents of other states. Hardly a charter of rights and freedoms. Section 116 on religion was not freedom of religion. It was just that you couldn't have an established church in Australia. Even Section 51(xxxi), the acquisition of property on just terms, was really just defense of propertied classes if anything. Because there is no bill of rights some people try to get one through implication (59:3400).

Another Commonwealth attorney thought the implied rights cases overextended the Court. "My own view is that the principles which are articulated do not have constitutional support. Well meaning judges who went along with the…approach I think left themselves exposed. They were at the point of self-levitation (127)." A Federal Court judge remarked, "The materials that led to that conclusion are so exiguous that you must wonder about the lack of logic or validity in the process (103:5000)." A Queensland judge offered a like assessment:

> One difficulty with the Court using progressive methods to build some of those fundamental values into our system is that it requires a degree of legal artificiality, which is not only limiting but coercive for the future because it's easy to overthrow. That's what has happened to some of the Mason developments. The free speech [jurisprudence], which was moving forward so effectively, has been taken back by the post-Mason court. It had no solid foundation except in some notion of implications in the constitution related to representative government.… *It had no formal basis there where you could actually look and see it. So the critics who want to move back into majority will are able to say the Court's acting illegitimately. It makes it much more difficult establishing that the Court is acting legitimately.… We don't have a formal structure that lets the Court play this balancing role* (87:2600) (emphasis added).

The implied rights jurisprudence failed to develop beyond *Theophanous* because the Court lacked adequate constitutional infrastructures for it to do so persuasively and while retaining legitimacy. Much was missing. The Court obviously lacked a constitutional or statutory statement of rights that would provide a valuable textual hook on which to hang its rights jurisprudence. The Court also lacked a legacy of identifying and protecting civil and political rights. Previous Courts had protected economic rights, but it was never seen as a major fount for civil liberties and freedoms. As discussed earlier, this is due in part to a faith in the adequacy of common law and parliamentary statutes. These are just two conditions that discouraged further development of the implied rights jurisprudence.

The fate of the implied rights jurisprudence in the post-Mason era may also explain why a pullback has occurred in the broader role transformation. The High Court's power and legitimacy are not secured using the purse or sword, but rather through persuasion. Courts are persuasive when their decisions are not capricious or arbitrary and when based on *a priori* rules or principles that transcend the whims and proclivities of individual judges. Courts are also persuasive when they demonstrate that their decisions are reasonable given the powers, duties, and remedies available through the constitution, statutes, common law, conventions, and customs. What the Brennan and Gleeson Courts lacked was a capacity to justify persuasively the politicized role on institutional grounds. They were unable to employ the argument that could have provided significant cover: that by further promoting the politicized role they were simply fulfilling their prescribed constitutional obligations. Had that infrastructure existed, and had a sufficient number of Brennan and Gleeson Court judges favored the politicized role, they could have quelled some of the challenges and legitimized the politicized role, had they wanted. Similarly, if Australia's constitutional infrastructure better accommodated the politicized role, it is conceivable that reforms could have outlived the Mason Court. Had this infrastructure existed even hesitant Brennan or Gleeson Court judges might have felt the weight of institutional obligation. Alas, that infrastructure was absent.

Mandatory Retirement and the Chief Justiceship

The third institutional feature that contributed to the retreat, ironically, is a factor that contributed to its genesis: the mandatory retirement law. The reader will recall from previous chapters that in 1977 Australians amended their constitution to require mandatory retirement at age seventy for all federal judges. The provision did not apply to judges appointed before the constitutional amendment was ratified, with one exception. Judges appointed before the amendment but promoted after to chief justiceships fell under the rule. That exclusion contributed to the onset of the transformation, with Harry Gibbs having to retire from the chief justiceship in 1981 at age 70, after only six years at the helm. It similarly facilitated the retreat.

Two High Court chief justices faced mandatory retirement in the late 1990s, and their replacements were less sympathetic to the politicized role. Those two retirements were Chief Justices Mason and Brennan in 1995 and 1998, respectively. Mason retired the year before Prime Minister Keating and the Labor Party lost in federal elections to John Howard's Liberal Party. Before leaving office, however, Keating promoted Gerard Brennan to the top job and filled the puisne judicial vacancy with William Gummow from the Federal Court in Sydney.

A Labor appointee, Justice Gummow is something of an enigma. It is difficult classifying him in broad terms as a proponent of either the orthodox or politicized role. His judicial philosophy has proven more conservative than other Labor appointees. As one judge remarked, "Gummow is a Labor appointee, but he is not an obvious Labor judge (67)." My informants described him as a "black letter lawyer" and "a legalistic judge who came up the legal track," meaning his professional experience was at the bar rather than politics (32:915). Others described him as a "conservative," "an outstanding conservative lawyer (77:1500)," "a legal scholar (67)," "eccentric (85:700)," "an influential technician and a lawyer's lawyer (66)." Several informants were quick to distinguish Gummow from Mason. "The influence of Gummow…is fairly conservative—a black letter lawyer. He's a very good technical lawyer, and I think it's the technicalities that attract him rather than broad sweeps of creative principle.…Gummow favors the discipline of words first (89:1600)," said a Federal Court judge. Another suggested, "You have a very classically learned judge…in Gummow. If it's in Chancellor, Kent, or Story, he'll have it all out. His mind takes him to a certain type of methodology (86:2600)." A Commonwealth attorney said Gummow "addresses things through the legal lens. [He] prefers change that is incremental and detached (66)."

The appointment of a more conservative judge following the Mason Court controversies is not surprising, even from a Labor Government. One informant suggested that Gummow was a "compromise appointment" between the Labor Party and the Opposition. The High Court's activism could no longer be tolerated so a middle of the road appointment was made. A Commonwealth attorney admitted, "Several of us asked, 'Why are you appointing this technician?' Gummow was the dark horse appointment who appealed to the center (66)." An *Australian Financial Review* editorial expressed relief yet wonderment at Gummow's appointment: "Considering some of the monstrous elevations that this Government could have made, and which would have debauched the court, Mr. Justice Gummow comes as an enormous relief. How he came to have some political admirers in Canberra is a mystery. This quiet, learned bachelor, who lives alone in the tranquility of the lower North Shore of Sydney, would never dream of lobbying or attracting a political sponsor."[35]

---

35. Richard Ackland, March 29, 1995, "Canberra picks a winner to fill High Court vacancy," *Australian Financial Review*, p. 20.

Although many informants shared this reporter's assessment and perhaps relief with Gummow's appointment, at least one judge thought that under Gummow's legalistic, technical veneer is a closet reformer.

> Gummow gives the appearance of working it out from first principles but really coming up with something entirely novel. You find a footnote to the *Yale Law Journal* there, you find what Fonblanque said on equity in 1833 there, you find what some judge in the eighteenth century said there, and lo and behold, there's a new thing....The result that he gets is the result that he wants. The process of getting it is a process of disguise—not subterfuge—but concealment. The Mason/Deane approach is franker because it purports to be based on effects on the economy, society, morals, emotions, which on the face of it aren't taken into account with the Gummow approach (103:5000).

The extent to which Gummow's legal reasoning harkens back to a Dixonian approach is an important question, for it reminds one of the capacity for reform even with orthodox legal reasoning. The point to be drawn from this cursory description of Gummow is that Mason's retirement gave way to a more conservative judge, notwithstanding the fact that Mason was a Liberal Government appointee and Gummow a Labor Government appointee.

Gerard Brennan's required retirement as chief justice in 1998 only retrenched the politicized role further. Although he was not the strongest proponent of the Mason Court reforms, many times dissenting from the reform-minded majority, his retirement was consequential. The task of finding Brennan's replacement in 1998 fell to the Howard Government. That year the Prime Minister found himself in the rather fortuitous position of making his third High Court appointment in as many years. Brennan's successor and the current Chief Justice, Murray Gleeson, came to the Court in 1998 after serving as the NSW Supreme Court's Chief Justice. His appointment to the top spot marked a further setback for the politicized role. My informants generally regarded Gleeson as a conservative judge disinclined to promote the politicized role. Creative reasoning and political controversy are two things Gleeson avoids. One Federal Court judge remarked, "Gleeson is different from Mason in temper, outlook, and his sense of the purpose of law. Langdell and the science of law would be at home [in the present court] (86:500)." Another judge concurred: "Gleeson gets us back to law and not sociology. Gleeson doesn't have a heart so there is no danger in him being overly smuffy to anyone. He'll apply the rules—bang, bang, bang. That's it (3:2000)." One can only speculate how long the tenures of Chief Justices Mason and Brennan would have gone beyond age 70 without the mandatory retirement law in effect. What is not speculative is the law clearly brought two justices with more conservative philosophies to the Court.

Recent Howard Government Appointments: Reinforcing the Retreat

As suggested earlier in this chapter, politics played an important part in the politicized role's failure to outlive the Mason Court. The elected branches became beleaguered from the break-neck reforms—substantive and stylistic—under Mason and to a lesser extent under Brennan. Gummow's appointment in 1995 sent an important signal. The Keating Government theoretically could have replaced Mason with an equally strident reformer. Such judges occupy the appellate judiciary's ranks. Many I interviewed. Gummow's appointment signaled, however, that even the Labor Government had reached its limits, or alternatively, that it was unwilling to expend political capital defending a more reform-minded appointee. Gummow's appointment appeared less about party politics and more about the elected branches putting the brakes on the Court.

Since the Howard Government came to power in 1996, it has made five appointments to the Court. Gleeson's appointment as Chief Justice has been canvassed. The four other appointments were Kenneth Hayne in 1997 (who replaced Daryl Dawson), Ian Callinan in 1998 (who replaced John Toohey), Dyson Heydon (who replaced Mary Gaudron), and Susan Crennan in 2005 (who replaced Michael McHugh). All four ensured that the transformation proceeded no further.

Dawson served throughout the Mason Court as one of the more conservative judges, dissenting from the Mason majority in several banner decisions, including *Mabo, Dietrich, Australian Capital Television,* and *Langer.* Hayne represented an ideological swap with Dawson, so his appointment had less consequence on the balance of power on the Court. Both came from the traditionally more conservative Victoria bench and bar. Dawson had been the state's Solicitor-General from 1974 to 1982 before joining the Court. Hayne served on Victoria's Supreme Court (1992–1995) and Court of Appeal (1995–1997). Informants described Hayne as "a conservative lawyer (77)," "someone who prefers change that is slow and incremental (66)," and a "black letter lawyer (90)."

Howard's next appointment, Ian Callinan, replaced John Toohey in 1998 who left the Court two years short of mandatory retirement age. Callinan's appointment was more crucial than Hayne's given who he replaced. Toohey had been a strong proponent of the politicized role while Callinan is not.

Toohey was in the majority in *Dietrich*, *Mabo*, and *Wik*. He joined Gaudron in *Kruger*, concluding that members of the "stolen generation" might have an implied constitutional right to freedom of movement and religion. Toohey was one of only two judges—Deane the other—who concluded in *Leeth* (1992) that the constitution implies a right to equality.

Callinan, on the other hand, was as one informant put it, "appointed because he was conservative." The judge continued, "I don't think anyone who knew the work of the High Court would have considered Callinan as an acceptable appointee to the High Court, in terms of experience or ability. He was a very good trial advocate. That's what he was—the beginning and end of it I think. He wouldn't have appeared in the High Court more than a half-dozen times in his life. He was a surprise appointment and he was appointed for that reason (77:900)." Another judge said, "Callinan is a Queenslander. Most of them have decentralized notions of Australia and the preservation of the states (60:930)." An author and playwright as well as a lawyer, Callinan came straight from the Queensland bar in 1998. Whatever creative license he takes in his fictional writing does not carry over into his legal writing. He is an orthodox judge throughout. As a barrister he openly criticized *Mabo*, considering it an illegitimate extension of the judiciary into a realm better left to parliaments, and spoke out against the implied rights decisions. In an infamous speech before the conservative Samuel Griffith Society, Callinan disclosed a host of conservative leanings. He advocated reinstituting the right of appeal to the High Court and abolishing the Court's capacity through special leave applications to decide which cases to hear. "In defining the jurisdiction of the Court it is unlikely that the Founders would have imagined that the Court would in its unfettered discretion ever be permitted to pick and choose the cases that it might put aside or hear," he stated. He then asked rhetorically, "If war is too important to be left to the generals, should the definition of a Court's jurisdiction be left effectively, exclusively to the Court? I would have thought not." Callinan also cautioned against implying rights from the constitution given the uncertainty that it creates and wondered aloud whether the Mason Court was "anxious to make its mark as an innovator."[36]

After serving on the Court for fifteen years and successfully battling cancer, Mary Gaudron announced in June 2002 her intent to retire that next February. The vacancy that her retirement would create was infused with significance. She was the first female High Court judge, so much conversation

---

36. Ian Callinan QC (1994). "An Over-Mighty Court?" *Upholding the Australian Constitution: Proceedings of the Conference of the Samuel Griffith Society*, vol. 4, pp. 57–62.

swirled around whether Howard would appointment another woman. Her departure marked the exodus of another key participant in the role transformation, leaving only one Mason era judge on the Court, Michael McHugh. The vacancy also raised the question of whether Howard would tap someone from outside Victoria or New South Wales, whence the bulk of appointees come. Not a single appointment has come, for example, from the South Australia bar or bench in all the Court's history, much to that state's chagrin. Finally, Gaudron's departure provided the Howard Government with its fourth appointment. In the turbulent world of parliamentary government, it is no easy feat for a prime minister to stay in power long enough to appoint a majority of the Court, which Gaudron's vacancy occasioned. Only four other prime ministers boast this opportunity: Alfred Deakin (1905–1908), Robert Menzies (1949–1966), and Robert Hawke (1983–1991). The significance was not lost on the Howard Government, which stressed in press coverage how far-reaching and collaborative their consultations and deliberations were. State attorneys-general, prominent lawyers, and judges were consulted.

It was reported that cabinet discussions pitted Queensland's Federal Court Judge Susan Kiefel against NSW Court of Appeal Judge Dyson Heydon. Heydon got the nod. No one doubted his qualifications: a Rhodes Scholar, appointed the youngest dean of Sydney Law School, prolific legal scholar, and two years experience on the highest NSW court. If Howard or any cabinet member questioned his jurisprudential leanings, those Heydon put to rest in an October 2002 speech delivered at a gathering organized by the conservative magazine, *Quadrant*. Although Heydon would not receive the appointment for another month, legal scholars informally refer to this as Heydon's "acceptance speech." In it he decried judicial activism and launched a full-scale assault on the Mason Court. A few choice paragraphs will illustrate:

> [A] fundamental change in the judiciary has taken place which has caused two new types of pressure on probity. The fundamental change is that it has a different character from that of a generation ago. There is within its increased ranks a large segment of ambitious, vigorous, energetic and proud judges. Ambition, vigour, energy and pride can each be virtues. But together they can be an explosive compound. Rightly or wrongly, many modern judges think that they can not only right every social wrong, but achieve some form of immortality in doing so....

> Here the delusion of judicial immortality takes its most pathetic form, blind to vanity and vexation of spirit. In all, the words Gladstone used about the annexation of the Transvaal in 1879 might be applied to the new judicial class: "See how powerful and deadly are the fascina-

tions of passion and of pride." John Gava has rightly described the judges so affected as "hero judges" (Heydon 2003).

This new type of judge, or in this book's language the new judicial role, emerged from the confluence of several factors.

> The new class arose partly because almost all modern judges were ed-ucated in law schools staffed by professional law teachers as distinct from practitioners teaching part-time, and a critical analysis of the merits of legal rules was a significant aspect of that education. It arose partly because of a wider interest in United States law, where some authority somewhere can usually be found to support any proposi-tion, and where constantly changing majorities in the Supreme Court tend to generate changing jurisprudence in constitutional cases on the Bill of Rights. It arose partly because Law Reform Commissions have in the last forty years become a common feature of life here and else-where. And it arose partly because since the early 1960s the fashion has been for legal intellectuals to be *quarante-huitard*, to be dismis-sive of what they do not fully understand and to think like an edito-rial in the *Guardian* (Ibid.).

This speech was a stunning piece of judicial rhetoric that called into question the politicized role. It provides a thoroughgoing synthesis of how orthodox judges reacted to the Mason Court. Whether this speech influenced the Howard Government's thinking on Gaudron's replacement or just affirmed their decision is beside the point. With Heydon's appointment, Howard se-cured another conservative judge, one openly hostile toward the Mason Court and its politicized role.

In 2005, Michael McHugh announced his retirement from the Court, the last of the current justices to serve during the Mason era. The Howard Gov-ernment filled its fifth vacancy in November 2005, appointing Susan Crennan from the Federal Court. The first female president of the Australian Bar As-sociation and long-time Victoria barrister, Crennan arrived in Canberra after two years on the Federal Court. Her short tenure there makes it difficult to assess her likely impact on High Court jurisprudence—she handed down only 76 judgments and over half of those concerned refugee or immigration mat-ters. She comes from a working class upbringing and the ALP endorsed her, but it's too early to read the tea leaves.

Howard's quintuple (Chief Justice Gleeson and Justices Callinan, Hayne, Heydon, and Crennan) definitely has fostered a Court less sympathetic to the politicized role. These appointments confirm the Mason Court's failure to convince the political branches (irrespective of party politics) on the politicized role's merits and the need for transformation-sustaining appointees. The Howard Government has successfully put the genie back into the bottle.

When asked about why the Mason Court reforms sputtered, my informants frequently pointed to Howard's appointments. A Victoria judge commented, "In the 1980s when the High Court starting implying things in the constitution, it upset many parliamentarians. There was a huge call for the appointment of that chap from Queensland. The Premier wanted a capital-C conservative and they put Callinan on. That was a bit of horse trading between the political parties that made up the coalition (77:830)." A Queensland judge offered his own assessment:

> Virtually at the same time Deane retired, Mason and Toohey also retired. So you had three of the majority of four going at almost the same time.... [B]oth sides of politics, Labor and conservative, were concerned about the way the High Court was going, not so much with Aboriginal rights from the Labor point of view, but with the implied rights area. Particularly so far as it might affect politicians' role. I think they wanted that reined back a bit, so they were looking for appointees who would be conservative (77:1130).

A Commonwealth attorney suggested:

> The two most polarized people in that Parliament are Nick Bolkus and [Bronwyn] Bishop. She's the extreme right of the Liberal Party, he's the extreme left of the Labor Party. One thing they would agree on is that the most important person to get on the High Court is a centrist. I think that's interesting because although we have a very polarized political system, there are some issues which many federal politicians see as more important than their political views (59).

The Howard Government's desire for a more conservative Court was realized with the appointment of Gleeson, Callinan, Hayne, Heydon, and Crennan. A Commonwealth attorney remarked, "These appointments have totally changed the Court—a total change. I think there were four or five appointments within a very short number of years. You get a high level of appointments in a small number of years. It's one of the most dramatic of all changes in High Court history.... The consequence has been a complete sea change in the legal and political stance of the Court (59:345)." These appointments have brought, according to a NSW judge, "a slight swing to the right. Toohey was a terrible communist. Brennan wasn't much better (3:4400)."

These appointments cemented in place for the short-term a High Court generally hostile toward the politicized role. This chapter has demonstrated how the interplay of institutional, individual, and political factors is responsible for the retrenchment that has occurred in the post-Mason era. The final chapter explores the longer-term consequences to the transformation and what it reveals about the broader judicial role transformation phenomena.

8

CONCLUSIONS

I begin this final chapter with an assessment of Australia's judicial role transformation, paying particular attention to its prospects given the Court's current composition and Australia's political climate. I then evaluate the politicized role's longer-term durability in the High Court and broader judicial community and conclude by asking what public law scholars might learn from the High Court's transformation under Chief Justice Mason and retreat under Chief Justice Gleeson. What generalizations can be reached about judicial role transformations and what conditions make their genesis and viability more likely?

THE FUTURE OF THE HIGH COURT'S JUDICIAL ROLE TRANSFORMATION

The Mason Court no doubt successfully infused within Australia's legal and political systems a new institutional vision for the High Court. For several years in the early 1990s, a majority on the Court was keen to promote the politicized judicial role. The numbers were there, the intellectual leadership was in place, and at least until *Wik* the reforms did not generate paralyzing criticism from politicians or the public. Then came the revenge of institutional and political factors that stymied further advancement of the politicized role. Within a few short years, the Howard Government was able to change the Court's composition to an extent that would make even Franklin Roosevelt blush. Not one of today's High Court justices served during the Mason era. Justice Michael Kirby, appointed during Chief Justice Brennan's tenure, is the only current justice somewhat amenable to the Mason Court reforms, yet his support for the politicized role is not unqualified. The presently constituted Court seems content with the retrenchment that has occurred in the post-Mason era; indeed, Prime Minister John Howard appointed Chief Justice Gleeson and Justices Hayne, Callinan, and Heydon with that expectation in mind. One would be hard pressed to expect a volte-face or gradual slide toward the politicized role. The Gleeson Court may reach an occasional decision or maintain a legal doctrine that comports with the politicized role—the post-Mason treatment of the implied rights doctrine comes to mind—but its institutional *raison d'être* will align more with the orthodox than the politicized role. Nor do I see Justice Kirby or others exerting the intellectual leadership that could compel partial or complete conversions among his colleagues. Justice Kirby is something of a pariah to many in the judicial and political communities and his decisions seem increasingly distanced from his colleagues' judgments. Since Gleeson became Chief Justice, Kirby has taken on a Holmesian-like role of being the Court's great dissenter.

The High Court then has entered a time of relative role stability, for better or worse, given its current composition. Recognizing that conversions could occur—no one foresaw in 1972 "Mason-II," as one informant described Sir Anthony Mason after his "conversion"—but are unlikely, the politicized role will gain no ground absent new appointments. The judges are under no obligation obviously to remain on the Court until age 70, but if we assume that the current judges stay until mandatory retirement, some longer-term assessment become possible. How does the tenure clock look for the current justices? Howard faced a fifth appointment opportunity in late 2005 with Justice McHugh's retirement. Susan Crennan filled that spot. The length of term remaining for the judges follows: Chief Justice Gleeson (three years), Justice Gummow (seven years), Justice Kirby (four years), Justice Hayne (ten years), Justice Callinan (two years), Justice Heydon (nine years), and Justice Crennan (ten years).[1] If all judges serve their maximum terms, the High Court for at least the next ten years will be a court that John Howard and the Liberal Party built. In the 2004 federal elections, Australians returned Howard and his Liberal Party to a historic fourth term. The next federal election will occur in 2007. Depending upon the election's timing, Howard may get a sixth appointment. Justice Callinan turns 70 in 2007. If Howard appoints Callinan's replacement before the election or wins the election, the Court will be comprised of five Howard appointees and two Keating (Labor) appointees. If the appointment falls to the 2007 victor, the Court's composition looks a bit less certain.

Despite some chatter within his party that it is time for Howard to pass the leadership reins to his deputy, Peter Costello, Howard has indicated a desire to lead the party through the next election in 2007. This contest will be critical to the Court's composition and will profoundly impact its role orientation for the next decade. Much is at stake. Whoever wins the 2007 election will

---

1. These figures are based on the length of service remaining at the end of 2005.

confront two vacancies in addition to Justice Callinan's: Chief Justice Gleeson in 2008 and Justice Kirby in 2009. If the Liberal Party wins in 2007, six out of seven justices would be Liberal Party appointees. Justice Gummow would be the lone Labor Party appointment. The Court could look far different if Labor wrestled a victory from Howard in 2007. Two scenarios could play out with a Labor victory. If Howard fills Justice Callinan's spot before losing the 2007 election, the Court would have a 4-3 split favoring Howard appointees. If the spot is filled after a Labor victory in 2007, the Court would have a 4-3 split favoring Labor appointees. The Court's trajectory over the next five years, then, will go in one of three directions: first, Labor appointees will forge a slim majority if Labor wins the 2007 election and also appoints Callinan's replacement; second, Labor wins the 2007 election but Howard appoints Callinan's replacement beforehand, giving the Liberals a 4-3 majority; third, Howard wins the 2007 election and will have appointed six of the seven judges. To state the obvious, then, the politicized role's future depends, in part, on federal politics. If Labor wins in 2007, proponents of the politicized role have a bright spot. If not, the orthodoxy will gain ascendance and the Mason Court revolution will look more and more distant. Casting it in these terms does not mean that the politicized role has no chance of advancing with Liberal appointees. It just seems less likely.

Absent the political constellations aligning themselves at just the right time for transformation-friendly appointees, the next best hope for the politicized role is some sort of significant political or constitutional reform that compels the Court to take new jurisdictions or duties. If Australia adopted, for example, a statutory or constitutional bill of rights, the politicized role might find some new life even among the Court's current members. The Canadian experience with the Charter shows the power of this sort of institutional reform.

The bill of rights option is not out of the question. Proposals have been considered in Parliament and law reform commissions for decades. Labor Governments are generally more supportive of the idea than Liberal Governments (Alston 1994; Williams 2000b). I would be more sanguine about the chances for a bill of rights had Australians approved the republic referendum in 1999. Becoming a republic could have overcome the obvious inertia against significant constitutional reform. Several informants thought that becoming a republic would have been a first and necessary step toward adopting a bill of rights. I found strong support among Australia's appellate judges for a bill of rights, particularly Federal Court judges. This sort of reform must come from the elected branches, however, and if history is any indictor, both major parties would have to support such a measure for Australians to approve it. One thing can be said about contemporary Australia: The polity and politicians are not averse to exploring, debating, and voting on constitutional reform. In 2004, the Australian Capital Territory, in fact, adopted a statutory bill of rights. While its impact has yet to be determined in practical terms, some observers think that such efforts at the state and territory levels may soften the ground for similar steps at the national level.

A bill of rights would provide an important cornerstone to the constitutional infrastructure upon which the Court could advance the politicized role. Even if it was never realized, other institutional features that encouraged the transformation during the Mason Court are still in place, including the special leave process. Informal institutional features could also facilitate the politicized role, including the increasing practice of third-party intervention and amici participation in High Court litigation. These institutional features bode well for the politicized role.

As important to advancing the politicized role as any of these formal or informal institutional conditions, however, is the presence of legal realism in the judicial and political communities. Judges disagree about the purposes of appellate litigation, the preferred modes of constitutional interpretation, and the normative relationship between courts and politics, but this can be said: the Mason Court's legacy is extant. The politicized role, now imbedded in High Court history, can be discounted, ignored, and abandoned by future judges. Its existence—this period in High Court history—cannot be denied. It may lay dormant in the near term, but it is now available as an intellectual fount and reference point for future lawyers and judges.

The Mason Court's most significant reform was that it ushered the legal and political systems from a pre-legal realist stance to a legal realist stance. This voyage was one that occurred in the U.S. decades ago, but the institutional, individual, and political factors outlined in chapters 2 and 3 gave the orthodox role longevity and delayed this voyage in Australia. It is my contention that this shift to legal realism represents a point of no return. To suggest today that judges exercise no choice or that the Court and its members are not part of the political system is untenable after the Mason Court. Any future Court that wishes to advance the politicized role would no longer have to contest seriously with pre-legal realist rhetoric in the legal and political communities.

Perspectives Gained from the High Court's Transformation

Although this book gives a close, rich retrospective on the High Court's transformation, I hope it also speaks to broader issues in political science and law. What does this period of High Court history tell us about supreme courts as institutions, the individuals who fill their ranks, and the roles that they assume in political systems?

First, in detailing the events that befell Australia's High Court in the 1980s and 1990s and in providing first hand descriptions from judges, this book confirms that Australian jurists think in role terms. By that I mean that judges individually hold prescriptive ideas about their institution's mission and that they see themselves as "stewards of that mission," to paraphrase Howard Gillman (1999). The interview data confirm time and again that these prescriptive "bundles of ideas" actually matter. Judges think in role terms and their decisions and behaviors are shaped by their role conceptions.

A second thing that emerges from the interview data is that these role conceptions are not simply reflections of individual policy preferences. Ideas, norms, duties, traditions, principles, and political and legal theories are but some of the components that go into a judicial role conception. If one thing came through in my interviews, it was how little Australian judges talked about policy preferences. Not only did judges rarely speak about personal policy preferences in framing their role conceptions, informants rarely employed "preference maximizing" language when describing other judges' motivations. Rather, ideas about the duties and capacities of courts—not just base policy preferences—framed how informants spoke about the High Court's transformation. There was much talk about "preferences," but these were preferences for the Court pursuing one institutional role over another, not personal policy preferences or attitudes. To the extent this book succeeds in demonstrating the importance of institutions and ideas over raw policy preferences in framing judicial role conceptions, it challenges several fundamental premises that dominate American court scholarship: first, that judges are simply preference maximizing actors; second, that laws and institutional powers are used by these actors to promote desired political outcomes; and third, that legal reasoning is simply rhetoric to rationalize actions. Attitudinalists would look to the High Court's transformation as simply a retooling of the rhetoric used to secure policy preferences. My interview data confirm either the exact opposite or that Australian appellate judges are completely deluding themselves (and those who interview them) about their thought processes.

This book addresses more than how individual judges perceive their roles. Its central argument is institutional: that the High Court in the 1980s and 1990s departed from a long established orthodox role in pursuit of an alternative institutional vision. To suggest that an institution such as the High Court could pursue different roles at different times in its history, all the while fulfilling its constitutional duties, is hardly controversial. That institutional role transformations occur is not surprising. The more compelling questions are why the transformation occurred when it did, what factors facilitated it, and how does one account for its success or failure? This book concludes that the interplay of individual, institutional, and political factors precipitated the High Court's transformation. In advancing the interplay thesis, it denies the ascendance of a single theory to explain the transformation's genesis and retrenchment.

Putting the High Court's Transformation in Comparative Perspective

When one compares the High Court's role transformation with the role changes that have occurred in the last twenty years or so in other judiciaries, Australia's stands out. Put simply, Australia's transformation was endogenous to the High Court to an extent not true elsewhere. The High Court under Mason's leadership abandoned the orthodoxy not out of statutory or constitutional obligation, not because it was suddenly vested with new judicial review powers, but because the individual judges on the Court held role conceptions that compelled them to pursue the politicized role. Judicial role transformations in Canada and New Zealand, for example, have the common component that change came after the enactment of new rights-protecting laws—a constitutional bill of rights in Canada and a statutory bill of rights in New Zealand.

The High Court's transformation occurred absent institutional precipitants of this magnnitude; rather than compelling a transformation by mandating the Court to embark on new jurisprudence (such that might come with a constitutionally entrenched bill of rights) institutional reforms in the High Court simply made conditions more hospitable. There is nothing in the mandatory retirement provision, the special leave process, or abolition of Privy Council appeals that necessitates a role transformation. These institutional precipitants created an environment in which judges' role conceptions could play themselves out.

Recognizing this difference between Australia's institutional precipitants and Canada's or New Zealand's makes the Mason Court all the more remarkable. It promoted the politicized role (and the substantive legal changes that accompanied it) absent strong institutional support outside the Court. Which court expended more institutional capital and risked more institutional legitimacy: the U.S. Supreme Court extending First Amendment speech protection to include symbolic speech or the High Court crafting speech protections, absent a First Amendment, through constitutional implication (e.g. *ACT v. Commonwealth*)? The answer is at least debatable.

What might the Australian case then tell political scientists about judicial role transformations in general? First, it illustrates that transformations can begin from within; that is, shifts in a judicial institution's role are possible if the numbers are there. Chief Justice Mason enjoyed consistent support from Justices Deane, Toohey, and Gaudron. They had the numbers to speak for the High Court as an institution. The Australian case also demonstrates how susceptible internally driven transformations are to collapse. Lacking sufficient institutional and political support, the High Court's transformation remained viable as long as the numbers were there to sustain it. The politicized role advanced from the late 1980s until the mid-1990s when mandatory retirements created vacancies that were filled by appointees skeptical about the transformation.

The Australian case also demonstrates the centrality of formal and informal institutions in starting and sustaining role transformations. The institutional features that encouraged the transformation were mentioned previously. Institutions played a significant part with the pullback as well, including the mandatory retirement provision, insufficient constitutional infrastructures to legitimize the reforms, and inadequate support for the politicized role among intermediate appellate judges. A clear conclusion to be drawn is that transformations are untenable in the long-term without exogenous support. This support from outside the Court may include transformation-sustaining judicial appointments, legislation that endorses or supports the reforms, and diffuse support within the judicial and political communities. Without exogenous support for the Mason Court's reforms, it just became a matter of time for the institutional restraints and political criticisms to exact their toll.

The book also confirmed time and again that public law scholars must continue to heed Herman Pritchett's advice to keep the "jurisprudence" in political jurisprudence. Judges talk and think about law. Those thoughts are not simply shell games to cover up policy preferences. Law matters. Not only do judges talk and think about law, they tend to talk and think about private law much of the time. Too often American political scientists studying courts fixate on public law matters and overlook significant developments in private law. One can hardly fault the discipline. Intellectual curiosities begin with what is familiar and known. Ignoring the politics and political implications of private law developments on courts is a mistake. Bloody revolutions may be underway in contract or estoppel law and too often political scientists are glued to saber rattling in constitutional matters. This book strived to incorporate public and private law developments in its analyses. Given my interview data, I would be remiss to do otherwise. It became clear early on in the project that many informants spent more time thinking and writing about private law than public law matters. Those who study courts and judges as political institutions and political actors do themselves and the profession a disservice, in my opinion, by focusing on familiar slivers and ignoring unfamiliar planks. I do not belie the challenges this may present for political scientists, nor do I pretend to think that political scientists can do lawyers' work with the same aptitude. Res judicata and collateral estoppel are conceptually more opaque to political scientists (this author included) than separation of powers or the Second Amendment. These challenges should not dissuade political scientists. We must be able to talk about what the judges are talking about, not what we wish they would spend more time talking about, if we really what to understand them as political actors.

Another theme that this book advanced was the symbiotic relationship between jurisprudence and politics. Academic lawyers tend to ignore "the political" in the law. Political scientists tend to ignore "the legal" in the law. When accounting for jurisprudential development, some legal academics focus myopically on the courts and neglect the impact of *realpolitik*. Some political scientists are guilty of the inverse—too quick to dismiss the role of "the law" in jurisprudential development. This is due in large measure to the ascendance of behavioralism within political science and attitudinalism and strategic-voting theories within public law research. Here scholars neglect the real ways in which institutions, precedent, and legal rules shape and constrain case law and doctrinal developments. This book strived to operate between these extremes. Law absolutely matters. Politics absolutely matters. The collusion of law and politics offers the best explanation for the High Court's role transformation.

APPENDIX A

LIST OF PARTICIPANTS

High Court of Australia

Chief Justice Murray Gleeson
Justice Kenneth Hayne (interviewed while on Supreme Court of Victoria)
Justice Dyson Heydon (interviewed while on NSW Court of Appeal)
Justice Michael Kirby

(Retired)

Chief Justice Sir Gerard Brennan
Chief Justice Sir Anthony Mason
Chief Justice Sir Harry Gibbs
Justice Daryl Dawson
Justice Mary Gaudron (interviewed while on High Court)
Justice Sir Ninian Stephen

Federal Court of Australia

Justice Bryan Beaumont
Justice Arthur Emmett
Justice John Dowsett
Justice D.P. Drummond
Justice R. Finkelstein
Justice Paul Finn
Justice Robert French
Justice A.H. Goldberg
Justice Roger Gyles
Justice P. Heerey
Justice Terence Higgins
Justice Leslie Katz

Justice Susan Kenny
Justice M. Lee
Justice Kevin Lindgren
Justice R. Merkel
Justice Jeffrey Miles
Justice R. Nicholson
Justice Anthony North
Justice Donnell Ryan
Justice Ronald Sackville
Justice Jeffrey Spender
Justice Margaret Stone
Justice Mark Weinberg

Supreme Court of New South Wales

Court of Appeal

President, Justice Keith Mason

Justice Margaret Beazley
Justice Gerald Fitzgerald
Justice Roger Giles
Justice Kenneth R. Handley
Justice Roderick P. Meagher
Justice Lancelot Priestley
Justice Charles Sheller
Justice Paul Stein

Trial Division

Justice Wm. Windeyer
Justice Geza F.K. Santow

Queensland Court of Appeal

Chief Justice Paul de Jersey
President, Justice M.A. McMurdo
Justice G.L. Davies
Justice B. McPherson

South Australia Supreme Court

Chief Justice John Doyle
Justice David Bleby
Justice Bruce Debelle
Justice Bruce Lander
Justice Brian Martin
Justice Edward Mullighan

Justice Graham Prior
Justice Horton Williams
Justice Leslie Olsson
Justice John Perry
Justice David Wicks

Victoria Court of Appeal

Justice John Winneke, President
Justice John Batt
Justice Peter Buchanan
Justice Frank Hortin Callaway
Justice Stephen P. Charles
Justice Alex Chernov

Western Australia Supreme Court

Northern Territory Supreme Court

Chief Justice David Malcolm
Justice Robert Anderson
Justice Desmond Heenan
Justice David Ipp
Justice Geoffrey Kennedy
Justice John McKechnie
Justice Michael Murray
Justice Kevin Parker
Justice Leonard Roberts-Smith
Justice Graeme Scott
Justice Anthony Templeman
Justice Henry Wallwork
Justice Christine Wheeler

Chief Justice David Martin
Justice Dean Mildren

Australian Capital Territory Supreme Court

Chief Justice Jeffrey Miles
Justice Kenneth Crispin
Justice Terence Higgins

Supreme Court of Tasmania

Justice P.W. Slicer

Government Officials / Barristers

Hon. Daryl Williams AM QC MP, Commonwealth Attorney-General
Mr. D.M. Bennett QC, Commonwealth Solicitor-General
Dr. Gavan Griffith, Former Commonwealth Solicitor-General
Mr. H.C. Burmester, Chief General Counsel, Australian Govt. Solicitor
Mr. P.A. Keane QC, Queensland Solicitor General

Mr. Alan Rose, President Australian Law Reform Commission
Dr. Kathryn Cronin, Law Reform Commission

Mr. Berard Bongiorno QC
Mr. A.R. Castan QC
Mr. David Jackson QC
Mr. James Merralls QC
Mr. B.J. Shaw QC

Justifications and Strategies for Interviewing Australia's Legal Elite[1]

Social scientists have employed interviews to study a wide range of social and political actors. One stocktaking concludes that 90 percent of all social science investigations use some kind of interview data (Brenner, Brown et al. 1985). In political science, popular works such as Richard Fenno's *Home Style* (1978) have shown that "soaking and poking" through personal interviews can produce insights that are otherwise unavailable, yet political scientists are generally less amenable to employing interviewing methods than anthropologists and sociologists. In particular, political scientists who study courts and judicial processes have doubted the feasibility and utility of using interviews in their research. This book suggests otherwise. This appendix outlines stratagems and techniques that can be useful for interview research on judicial and other elites.

If politics is about "who gets what, when, and how?" then the judiciary's function is political in a basic sense. Judges choose winners and losers, as the U.S. Supreme Court showed so dramatically in America's 2000 electoral struggle. It is surprising, then, how few political scientists ever sit down and talk with judges. One might expect national elite surveys—in which political, business, trade union, and many other elites are interviewed—to include judges regularly. But this is not so. Though judges have been interviewed in a few such surveys (mainly in Germany—see Wildenmann et al. 1982; Hoffmann-Lange 1992), most elite surveys have not done so—not in America (Moore 1979), Australia (Higley et al. 1979), Canada (Presthus 1973), Brazil (McDonough 1981), Britain and Italy (Putnam 1973), Yugoslavia (Barton et

---

1. An earlier version of this appeared as "Interviewing Australia's Senior Judiciary: A Research Note," *Australian Journal of Political Science*, vol. 37, n. 1 (March 2002), pp. 131–42.

al. 1973), or Taiwan (Czudnowski 1987). Judges are conspicuous by their absence from the European Commission's Top Decision Makers Survey (Spence 2000), even though some 3,700 elites in the fifteen member states were interviewed.

Only a handful of American public law studies have employed interviews (Vose 1959, 1972; Heumann 1977; O'Connor and Epstein 1982; Perry 1991; McGuire 1993; Schwartz 1996; Epp 1998), and most of these relied on interviewing as a secondary research tool to identify variables and frame hypotheses. Even fewer scholars have used interview data to study Australian courts and judges (e.g., Thomson 1987; Sturgess and Chubb 1988). Written judgments, speeches, biographies, newspapers, *Who's Who* publications, and similar print sources are more commonly used to gather judicial data in Australia.[2]

It is widely believed that judges are extremely reluctant to grant interviews and that even if they can be persuaded to do so they will say little of consequence. Norms and expectations about the judiciary's role do inhibit judges' readiness to grant scholars interviews. Some hesitate because they believe (or say they believe) in a mechanistic model of judicial decision-making: ascertain the facts, find the relevant law, and apply it to the facts. The judge simply pulls legal levers. Consequently, talking to judges about their decisions and processes is a waste of time because the law—not the judge—shapes outcomes. The belief that they must remain neutral and above politics also explains why judges often refuse interview requests. Interviewers' probings might jeopardize their non-political, neutral stance. Finally, judges may not grant interviews because they fear that what they say could bring unfavorable or sensationalized attention. In the United States, books such as *The Brethren* by Washington Post reporters Bob Woodward and Scott Armstrong (1981) and *Closed Chambers* by Edward Lazarus (1998) that expose the inner workings of courts in a warts-and-all manner have lent evidence to this concern.

Political scientists have their reservations about interviewing judges. In an earlier era, many political scientists viewed the judiciary more as a legal than a political institution and they left the study of courts to lawyers and legal scholars. Few political scientists any longer subscribe to this view. Nevertheless, the perception remains that it is difficult to gain entrée to judges (Johnson 1989). Moreover, soaking and poking the judiciary is time-consuming and expensive. Political scientists who think about interviewing judges also face their own variant of *The Brethren* factor. Given the discipline's strong emphasis on quantitative and rigorous research methods, many scholars fear that data

---

2. See Neumann (1973); Galligan (1987); Fricke (1988); and Blackshield et al. (2001).

gained through personal interviews with judges will be dismissed as anecdotal and journalistic (Epstein 1989/1990; King, Keohane et al. 1994). Still others conclude that their research questions cannot be answered effectively with interview data. In-depth interviewing adds little, for example, to studying correlations between judges' social backgrounds and sentencing patterns in criminal cases. Despite all this, I want to show how interviews with judges can be an effective research strategy.

OBTAINING INTERVIEWS

I sought interviews with the most senior appellate judges. On the Commonwealth bench this meant, at the time, the seven current and nine retired High Court justices, together with a sample of the 50 Federal Court judges. I also pursued 78 appellate judges in the state and territory Supreme Courts.[3] I wanted to interview as many of these 135 judges as time, funds, and their cooperation allowed.

Gaining access to senior jurists who are unaccustomed to being interviewed, much less to participating in social science research, is difficult. I made initial contact with them through a brief letter. Because judges have an inordinate amount of paper crossing their desks and very hectic schedules, my letter was succinct. To show my bona fides, I attached my credentials and, after the first dozen interviews were completed, a list of previous participants. This ever-growing list gave recipients some assurance about my project's legitimacy and significance. These items were mailed or faxed, depending on how quickly the material needed to reach a judge. I feared initially that faxing this material would negatively influence participation rates because it would appear too informal and hurried. This proved not so. I soon discovered that phoning a judge's chambers to obtain fax and other contact details enabled me to introduce myself to the judge's staff, which proved crucial to gaining many interviews.

Scholars who interview elites stress the importance of outlining their projects only very generally when first contacting respondents (Dexter 1970). Accordingly, I limited my project description to a few sentences. Uncertain if

---

3. In states that maintain separate Courts of Appeal within the judicial system (New South Wales, Victoria, and Queensland), I sought interviews only from Court of Appeal judges. South Australia, Western Australia, Tasmania, and the two federal territories do not have separate appellate courts. They empanel Supreme Court judges to sit in appellate capacity when necessary. Where no permanent appellate bench exists, I invited all Supreme Court judges to participate.

judges would read my entire letter, the first paragraph ended with a request to speak to them about my project. I deliberately avoided the word "interview" until much later in the letter, in case images of a formal, on-the-record interrogation might scare off some judges. Subsequent paragraphs told more about my project and credentials and then promised complete anonymity and confidentiality. This promise was critical to securing several judges' participation. It turned out that while all judges who participated were willing to be listed as participants in the research, 70 percent insisted that their comments remain anonymous.

Forty percent of the judges answered my letter before I could make a follow-up phone call. I phoned the others four or five days after sending my letter. Judges' staffs served as gatekeepers, facilitating or thwarting access. In most instances, not surprisingly, secretaries and clerks reviewed my letter, but participation rates were not significantly affected by this screening. In a handful of cases, staff threw out my letter, so that when I placed my follow-up call I was either asked for another copy or connected directly to the judge and asked to summarize my project. In most cases, my follow-up call prompted a decision one way or the other. My sense was that some judges were nudged into participating simply because I was waiting on the phone for an answer. Others used my call as a quick and convenient opportunity to decline.

PARTICIPATION RATES

I conducted a total of 82 in-depth interviews.[4] From the universe of 66 Commonwealth judges, I interviewed 34 and from the universe of 78 state and territory Supreme Court judges I interviewed 48. Four of the seven current High Court justices and six of the nine retired High Court justices participated. I interviewed 19 of the 29 judges who sit on separate state Courts of Appeal (New South Wales, Victoria, Queensland). The overall participation rate was 66 percent.[5]

What contributed to this successful participation rate? First, there was novelty in an American political scientist studying the Australian judiciary. Second, because very few Australian scholars have interviewed members of the

---

4. Rounds of interviews were conducted intermittently between 1997 and 2001, with the bulk occurring from October 1999 to May 2000.

5. This participation rate is calculated by dividing the number of interviews conducted by the number of judges actually approached for interviews. Due to time and travel limitations, I asked only a sample (30 out of 50) of Federal Court judges for interviews.

judiciary—none in a systematic manner, so far as I am aware—I was not elbowing past others for interviews. Third, very few judges expressed familiarity with the more polemical themes and methodologies in contemporary American public law research. They might have hesitated if they had thought (incorrectly) that I was bent on reducing their decision-making to what they had for breakfast. Fourth, some judges participated because of commonalities between the American and Australian legal systems (see Dixon 1965b; Rich 1993; Thomson 1997). The two countries' common law heritage and similar constitutional structures provided valuable comparisons and contrasts during many of my interviews.

It is also likely that a foreign scholar has the advantage, *ceteris paribus*, of not belonging to one camp or another in local legal, political, or academic circles. While a foreigner may have difficulty gaining access in some situations, he or she is not usually regarded as a threat. For example, many Australian academic colleagues thought that my foreign status freed judges from giving overly guarded responses. In addition, more than a few of the judges I interviewed had attended American universities as students or as visiting jurists, or they had children who studied in the United States. A half-dozen judges had held or had children who held the same Fulbright Fellowship that supported my research. Still others had genuine intellectual interests in American history and law and were quick to demonstrate their knowledge of American politics and recount their interactions with American judges and lawyers.

Participation was bolstered by my "quasi-snowballing" strategy in which, at the end of most interviews, I asked for names of other judges whom I should contact. When writing those judges subsequently, I mentioned in the first paragraph that judge so and so recommended them. This was "quasi-snowballing" because my respondent pool did not depend on respondents identifying additional participants. The population of potential respondents was known in advance, but the personal recommendations I obtained certainly increased the participation rate. Finally, I took pains to allay concerns about an adversarial interview, describing it as a "dialogue" and a "conversation."

The most effective strategy for boosting participation, particularly in the state appellate courts, was to secure the chief justices' cooperation at the outset. I asked the chief justices for permission to contact their colleagues and encouraged them to promote my project if an appropriate occasion arose. The risk was that the chief justice might block access or discourage colleagues from participating, but this did not happen. On the contrary, gaining the chief justices' cooperation elevated the project's legitimacy and motivated others to participate. It enabled me to inform the puisne judges that their chief justice was aware that I was writing them and that, in several instances, he or she had already participated.

Why did some judges choose not to participate? Most claimed they were too busy. Indeed, written or verbal refusals were not always received directly from the judges but, rather, from their staffs. It is impossible to know if judges offered the real reason for declining or were just polite when citing lack of time. Some doubtlessly declined because they feared jeopardizing the public's belief in their impartiality, because they wanted to remain out of public view, or because they disapproved of my research.

Does interview-driven research bias participation? It is possible that activist judges are more inclined to participate than conservative judges, but I did not find this so. My interview data are distributed fairly evenly across the spectrum of judicial opinion. No doubt some judges granted an interview because it was consistent with their vision of a more activist, visible judiciary. However, many conservative judges anticipated their activist colleagues and, in turn, granted an interview to prevent bias. Some relished this counterbalancing role, remarking, "You probably have not heard this from many of my colleagues!" or "I bet this is not what you expected to hear!"

One might expect that the political firestorm surrounding the High Court in the 1990s would have discouraged judges from participating. What better way to avoid further criticism than to batten down the hatches? I believe that the controversies had a mixed effect on participation. Australia inherited the British convention whereby the Attorney-General, as the country's first law officer, is traditionally responsible for defending the courts from criticism and attack (King 2000). When, in light of the High Court's controversial native title decisions, a former Commonwealth Attorney-General refused to fulfill this role, it fell to the judiciary to defend itself (see Mason 1997; Williams 1998; Brennan 1998). Bucking tradition, several High Court justices consented to media interviews in order to explain their decisions and the judiciary's role in the political system.[6]

I suspect some judges granted my interview request because of these earlier instances where select High Court members engaged the media themselves. Most judges, however, thought the best way to maintain the public's confidence was to confine their views to their written judgments. A din of criticism, in fact, was voiced in my interviews toward those judges who regularly speak in public. Many said that such judges violate expectations of neu-

---

6. See *The Chief Justice*, Four Corners, Australian Broadcasting Corporation (ABC), 3 April 1995; *Matters of Judgment*, Lateline, ABC, 15 July 1997; *The Brennan Way*, Lateline, ABC, 21 May 1998; and *The Highest Court*, Inside Stories, ABC, 26 May 1998.

trality and a constitutional mandate for courts to remain above politics.[7] Even among those not hostile to judges appearing in the media, many thought that only chief justices should do so. In sum, the judiciary's perceived reluctance toward granting interviews is real, but scholars can do much to mitigate these reservations.

Conducting Interviews

Because I wanted to tap judges' unrehearsed perceptions and opinions about their judicial roles, I usually did not provide interview questions in advance. Only when a judge's participation was conditioned on first viewing the questions did I send a brief sketch of the interview schedule. Seven respondents made this a condition; the rest were content to know in advance only what general topics would be canvassed.

The interviews averaged approximately an hour. The shortest was sixteen minutes when staff interrupted to announce an unexpected commitment needing urgent attention. The longest lasted more than three hours. The interviews were semi-structured, meaning that I covered a core set of topics in each. A combination of open-ended and more circumscribed questions was prepared in advance to explore each topic. I closely tracked my interview guide in many interviews, covering topics and asking questions in the prearranged order. But it was sometimes necessary to reorder or reword questions as the interview unfolded in order to maintain a natural, logical conversation. Open-ended questions encouraged complex and lengthy answers and gave respondents freedom to disclose the relative importance of phenomena. Most judges comfortably fielded the open-ended questions. For example, "What are we to make of the High Court in the 1990s?" was effective for garnering many frank evaluations of the High Court. More narrowly tailored questions were necessary to draw out judges who were less at ease with open-ended ones. State appellate judges ably handled questions regarding High Court doctrine and cases, even in areas of law where they infrequently exercise jurisdiction, such as Commonwealth constitutional law.

Several features of the interview design tested the data's validity. The in-depth nature of the interviews enabled me to probe for internal consistency and resolve any apparent inconsistencies. Asking respondents to define terms and concepts and offer examples and illustrations lent additional precision to

---

7. See *Wilson v. Minister for Aboriginal & Torres Strait Islander Affairs* (1996) 189 CLR 1.

the data. Addressing the core issues of my research in all interviews allowed me to compare, group, and categorize judges' responses with confidence. Moreover, interviewing such a large cross-section of the senior appellate bench tapped the diversity of opinion within and between various state and federal courts. Finally, interviewing judges from each state and territory made conclusions about the judiciary as a whole all the more reliable and decreased the chance of missing important regional perspectives due to the large Sydney and Melbourne benches.

Some questions or words tended to act as blocks in the conversation. Respondents objected, for instance, to questions about their court's agenda. While I used the term to mean the collection of cases that a court handles, many respondents thought I was suggesting that judges use their caseloads to advance personal policy preferences. Some respondents were hesitant to talk about particular judges by name. I effectively skirted this by posing more generic questions about the judge's argument rather than about the judge. I also found it sensible to delay controversial normative questions until near the end of interviews, once rapport was firmly evidenced. To begin with brash questions would have been foolhardy, particularly with judges who had never before been interviewed by an academic.

How to record interview data is a problem. Should one depend on a recording device or written notes? Both have been used successfully, but each has advantages and drawbacks (see Gorden 1969; Patton 1980; Lummis 1987; Jones 1991). My decision to use a recording device stemmed from several unique aspects of my interviews. First and as noted, the answers I obtained were complex and lengthy, often laced with caveats and qualifications. A recording device was, therefore, essential. Second, the device facilitated a conversational interview style. It allowed me to concentrate on what was being said, instead of juggling the conversation while trying to take complete notes. Third, it gave me verbatim transcripts so that I could accurately report the data, and at the same time, make it difficult for respondents to deny statements.[8] In principle, at least, recorded interviews can also enable other researchers to verify the primary researcher's conclusions and interpretations. Fourth, while some scholars worry that recording equipment stultifies interviews, this was not apparent, perhaps because judges are accustomed to having their every word recorded in court transcripts.

I sought, nonetheless, to make the recording unobtrusive. At the outset I asked permission to use a recorder and all but 5 percent consented. I also re-

---

8. Many judges shared my concern for accuracy, secretly recording the interviews for their own protection, so I learned from several judges' associates.

peated my promise of confidentiality and anonymity and said I would gladly turn off the recorder whenever necessary. Several judges instructed me to do so at various points. I used a portable digital audio recording deck with an external, flat, omni-directional microphone. The recorder stayed in my briefcase during each interview, with the cassette-size microphone placed on a desk or table near the respondent. A more conventional handheld micro-cassette recorder with an internal microphone would have been inadequate in many interviews. Street noises, air conditioning, and the clipped cadences and quiet voices of many judges made a sensitive recorder imperative.

Most judges were willing to speak to me on days they were sitting in court, but this meant early morning or late afternoon interviews that were too short. It was preferable to schedule interviews on days when judges were in chambers or not in court, so that courtroom commitments did not interfere. In-depth interviewing requires such attentive listening that I found myself less effective if I conducted more than two interviews per day. Scheduling problems required four and five interviews on a few days, but this was far from desirable.

My experience was consistent with the view that elite respondents must not feel that their time is being wasted (Zuckerman 1972). Elites may use any number of exit strategies once they perceive that an interviewer is ill prepared, uninformed, hostile in tone, or otherwise wasting their time. To avoid this, substantial preparation is necessary for each interview. In my research, this involved being thoroughly familiar with each judge's professional background, reading his or her published articles and speeches, and reviewing a sample of the judge's opinions in recent or well-known cases. I also read any available biographies. This preparation proved critical because it enabled me to tailor the wording of questions, provided valuable reference points, and prompted the thorough exploration of illustrations, caveats, qualifications and themes in answers.

My experience also confirmed the observation that if judges discover that an interviewer is familiar with their judicial writings and opinions and previous professional lives they are much less inclined to give perfunctory responses (Heumann 1989/1990). Indeed, on several occasions I found it necessary to show that I had done my homework before judges would invest any meaningful time or thought in the interview. For example, some judges first sized up my knowledge of Australian courts and law before answering any questions. One High Court justice said at the outset, "Let me turn the tables and ask you a few questions before you ask me anything. Who have you met on the Federal Court and how would you compare their judicial philosophies?"[9]

---

9. Interview with High Court Justice.

When I later mentioned this gambit to a former High Court associate, he replied, "That sounds just like Justice X. He was testing you to see if he should invest his time."

Despite my preparation, there were occasions (more often in the earlier interviews) when judges referred to a case, person, political event, or legal doctrine with which I was unfamiliar. What to do in such situations? The choice is between admitting ignorance and asking for clarification or feigning familiarity and continuing the interview. The obvious advantage to admitting ignorance and getting clarification is a gain in understanding. But the downside is interrupting and sidetracking the judge's train of thought. If the issue seemed inconsequential, it was better to feign familiarity and let the judge continue.

The ability to sit comfortably in silence is also important for successful interviews. At least when dealing with judges, one must relish silences or pauses in their ruminations and fight the urge to fill them with further questions or comments. Many times a pause or silence meant a judge was thinking further about the question, formulating an answer before speaking, or evaluating the answer he or she just provided. More than a few questions elicited as a first response something like, "I haven't thought about that before," requiring me to sit quietly while the judge considered the matter. On other occasions, pauses or silences signaled a hedged answer. The challenge then became waiting patiently to see if the judge would flesh out the hedged response after enough silence. A technique I employed frequently was to maintain eye contact and stay silent or turn my attention to my notes after a preliminary response. A "standoff" then ensued, won by whoever was more comfortable with the silence. My comfort level grew as the project progressed, so I usually won these standoffs. Winning them can be uncomfortable and a potential irritant, but many of the supplemental answers forced by standoffs are real gems. On the whole, I believe judges perceived my silence as an indication of respect and deference, not an irritant.

The Value of Interviewing

The interviews provided respondents the unique opportunity to discuss, outside of an actual legal dispute, the judicial process and their decision-making. Feeling little pressure to couch responses in legalese, many judges were quick to disclose personal attitudes and values. Conducting anonymous interviews provided lower court judges the opportunity to assess candidly their High Court colleagues. The judicial hierarchy typically discourages judges from voicing such critiques. Securing such candid assessments was critical for my project. One would be hard pressed to find the same level of candor in written judgments or public speeches as I secured through interviews.

Interviewing is also remarkably efficient. One aim of my research was to gather data about judges' general outlooks on legal reasoning. I could have read, of course, judgment after judgment for implicit or explicit comments on legal reasoning to assemble these data—a cumbersome and time-consuming process. Asking the judges directly about their judicial philosophies proved far more efficient. Interviewing is also highly adaptive because it obviously allows dialogue between the researcher and respondents. Researchers can observe how respondents interpret questions and clarify or modify them as necessary. Having the ability to respond to these interpretations is generally unavailable with other survey instruments, such as mailed questionnaires. It can make all the difference in comparative research, however, where words frequently carry different meanings and respondents bring new interpretations to questions.

BIBLIOGRAPHY

Abraham, Henry. 1997. "Reflections on the Contemporary Status of Our Civil Rights and Liberties and the Bill of Rights." *Journal of Law and Politics* 13: 7–20.

Allen, T. and B. Anderson. 1994. "The Use of Comparative Law by Common Law Judges." *Anglo-American Law Review* 23(4): 435–59.

Alston, Philip. 1994. *Towards an Australian Bill of Rights.* Canberra, Sydney: Centre for International and Public Law, Australian National University and the Human Rights and Equal Opportunity Commission.

Ashcroft, Paul, Bryan Gibson, et al. 1999. *Human Rights and the Courts: Bringing Justice Home.* Winchester, England: Waterside Press.

Austin, John. 1885. *Lectures on Jurisprudence: The Philosophy of Positive Law.* London: J. Murray.

Australian Law Reform Commission. 2001. *The Judicial Power of the Commonwealth Report: A Review of the Judiciary Act 1903 and Related Legislation.* Sydney: The Commission.

Baaklini, Abdo I. and Helen Desfosses. 1997. *Designs for Democratic Stability: Studies in Viable Constitutionalism.* Armonk, N.Y.: M.E. Sharpe.

Baas, L.R. 1971. "Judicial Role Perceptions: A Q-Technique Study of Ohio Judges." *Law and Society Review* 6: 343–66.

Barton, Allen H., Bogdan Denis Denitch, et al. 1973. *Opinion-Making Elites in Yugoslavia.* New York: Praeger.

Barwick, G. 1995. *A Radical Tory: Garfield Barwick's Reflections And Recollections.* Leichhardt, N.S.W.: Federation Press.

Beasley, F.R. June 1955. "Appeals to the Judicial Committee: A Case for Abolition." *Res Judicatae* 7(1): 399–414.

Beaumont, B. 1999. "Contemporary Judgment Writing: The Problem Restated." *Australian Law Journal* 73(10): 743–48.

Becker, Theodore Lewis. 1964. *Political Behavioralism and Modern Jurisprudence: A Working Theory and Study in Judicial Decision-Making.* Chicago: Rand McNally.

———. 1966. "A Survey of Hawaiian Judges: The Effect on Decisions of Judicial Role Variations." *American Political Science Review* 60: 677–80.

Berry, Marvin Payne. 1974. "A Study of Judicial Role Orientations in Fifteen Western States." Ph.D. Diss., Washington State University.

Beth, Loren. 1975. "The Judicial Committee: Its Development, Organisation and Procedure." *Public Law* 3(4): 219–41.

Betten, Lammy. 1999. *The Human Rights Act 1998: What It Means: The Incorporation of the European Convention on Human Rights into the Legal Order of the United Kingdom.* The Hague: M. Nijhoff Publishers.

Bickel, Alexander M. 1986. *The Least Dangerous Branch: The Supreme Court at the Bar of Politics.* New Haven: Yale University Press.

Biddle, Bruce J. 1979. *Role Theory: Expectations, Identities, and Behaviors.* New York: Academic Press.

Biddle, Bruce J. and Edwin J. Thomas. 1966. *Role Theory: Concepts and Research.* New York: Wiley.

Blackshield, Tony, Michael Coper, and George Williams. 2001. *The Oxford Companion to the High Court of Australia.* Melbourne: Oxford University Press.

Blackshield, Tony. 1978. "X/Y/Z/N Scales: The High Court of Australia, 1972–1976." In *Understanding Lawyers: Perspectives on the Legal Profession in Australia*, Roman Tomasic (ed.), Sydney: Law Foundation of New South Wales, 133–77.

Blainey, Geoffrey. 1968. *The Tyranny of Distance: How Distance Shaped Australia's History.* Melbourne: Macmillan.

Bone, Robert G. 1995. "Lon Fuller's Theory of Adjudication and the False Dichotomy Between Dispute Resolution and Public Law Models of Litigation." *Boston University Law Review* 75(5): 1273–1324.

Brennan, G. January 1998. "The State of the Judicature." *Australian Law Journal* 72(1): 33–46.

———. April 21, 1995. Speech on Swearing in as Chief Justice. Canberra. Http://www.hcourt.gov.au/speeches/brennanj/brennanj_swearing.htm. Last accessed May 10, 2005.

Brenner, Michael, Jennifer Brown, et al. 1985. *The Research Interview, Uses and Approaches.* London, Orlando: Academic Press.

Brewer Carias, Allan-Randolph. 1989. *Judicial Review in Comparative Law*. Cambridge, New York: Cambridge University Press.

Brigham, John. 1987. *The Cult of the Court*. Philadelphia: Temple University Press.

Brodie, Ian. 2002. *Friends of the Court: The Privileging of Interest Group Litigants in Canada*. Albany: State University of New York Press.

Burgess, Susan. 1993. "Beyond Instrumental Politics: The New Institutionalism, Legal Rhetoric, and Judicial Supremacy." *Polity* 24: 445–59.

Butler, Andrew. 2000. "Judicial Indications of Inconsistency—a New Weapon in the Bill of Rights." *New Zealand Law Review*, Part 1: 43–60.

Butler, Frances. 2000. *Human Rights for the New Millennium*. The Hague: Kluwer Law International.

Caldeira, Gregory A. and John R. Wright. 1988. "Organized Interests and Agenda Setting in the U S Supreme Court." *American Political Science Review* 82: 1109–27.

Campbell, Enid. 2003. "Reasons for Judgment: Some Consumer Perpsectives." *Australian Law Journal* 77(1): 62–71.

———. 1965. "Colonial Legislation and the Laws of England." *Tasmanian University Law Review* 2: 148–175.

———. 1998. "Intervention in Constitutional Cases." *Public Law Review* 9: 225–36.

Castles, Alex C. 1963. "The Reception and Status of English Law in Australia." *Adelaide Law Review* 2:1–29.

———. 1971. *An Introduction to Australian Legal History*. Sydney: Law Book Co.

Charlesworth, Hilary. 1994. "The Australian Reluctance About Rights." In *Towards an Australian Bill of Rights*, Philip Alston (ed.), Canberra: Centre for International and Public Law, Australian National University and the Human Rights and Equal Opportunity Commission, 21–54.

Chayes, Abram. 1976. "The Role of the Judge in Public Law Litigation." *Harvard Law Review* 89: 1281–84.

Cheney, Deborah. 1999. *Criminal Justice and the Human Rights Act 1998*. Bristol, England: Jordan Pub.

Childers, H.R.E. 1901. "What Court of Appeal Will Satisfy Australia?" *Nineteenth Century*: 157–58.

Clayton, Cornell and Howard Gillman. 1999. *Supreme Court Decision-Making: New Institutionalist Approaches.* Chicago: The University of Chicago Press.

Clayton, Richard and Hugh Tomlinson. 2001. *Privacy and Freedom of Expression.* Oxford: Oxford University Press.

Cooke, Elizabeth. 2000. *The Modern Law of Estoppel.* New York: Oxford University Press.

Corwin, Edward Samuel. 1936. "The Constitution as Instrument and Symbol." *American Political Science Review* 30: 1071–85.

———. 1940. *The President, Office and Powers; History and Analysis of Practice and Opinion.* New York: New York University Press.

Cowen, Zelman and Leslie Zines. 1978. *Federal Jurisdiction in Australia.* Melbourne: Oxford University Press.

Crawford, James. 1982. *Australian Courts of Law.* Melbourne: Oxford University Press.

Craven, Gregory (ed.). 1986. *Official Record of the Debates of the Australasian Federal Convention.* Sydney: Legal Books.

Czudnowski, M. 1987. "Interviewing Political Elites in Taiwan." In *Research Methods for Elite Studies,* G. Moyser and Margaret Wagstaffe (eds.), London: Allen & Unwin, 232–50.

Dahl, Robert. 1957. "Decision-Making in a Democracy: The Supreme Court as a National Policy-Maker." *Journal of Public Law* 6: 279–95.

Davenport, Christian. 1996. "'Constitutional Promises' and Repressive Reality: A Cross-National Time-Series Investigation of Why Political and Civil Liberties Are Suppressed." *Journal of Politics* 58: 627–54.

Davies, Margaret. 1996. *Delimiting the Law: Postmodernism and the Politics of Law.* London: Pluto Press.

Deakin, Alfred. 1963. *The Federal Story: The Inner History of the Federal Cause, 1880–1900.* Parkville, Victoria: Melbourne University Press.

Dexter, Lewis Anthony. 1970. *Elite and Specialized Interviewing.* Evanston, Ill.: Northwestern University Press.

Diamond, Larry Jay. 1997. *Consolidating the Third Wave Democracies.* Baltimore: Johns Hopkins University Press.

Dias, Reginald and Walter Michael. 1976. *Jurisprudence.* London: Butterworth.

Dicey, Albert V. 1982. *An Introduction to the Study of the Law of the Constitution (8th Edition).* Indianapolis: Liberty Fund.

Dixon, Sir Owen. 1965a. "The Law and the Constitution." In *Jesting Pilate and Other Papers and Addresses,* Sydney: Law Book Company, 38–60.

———. 1965b. "Two Constitutions Compared." In *Jesting Pilate and Other Papers and Addresses,* Sydney: Law Book Company, 100–12.

———. 1965c. "Common Law as Ultimate Constitutional Foundation." In *Jesting Pilate and Other Papers and Addresses.* Sydney, Law Book Company, 203–13.

Dolbeare, Kenneth. 1967. *Trial Courts in Urban Politics: State Court Policy Impact and Functions in a Local Political System.* New York: Wiley.

Douglas, Roger. 1969. "Judges and Policy on the Latham Court." *Politics* 4: 20–41.

Doyle, J. 1999. "Judgment Writing: Are There Needs For Change?" *Australian Law Journal* 73(10): 737–42.

———. 2001. "Judging Democracy: The New Politics of the High Court of Australia by Patapan." *Australian Journal of Political Science* 36(2): 389–90.

Dworkin, R. M. 1996. *Freedom's Law: The Moral Reading of the American Constitution.* Cambridge, Mass.: Harvard University Press.

———. 1997. "Order of the Coif Lecture: In Praise of Theory." *Arizona State Law Journal* 29: 353–76.

Edwards, J. 1964. *Law Officers of the Crown.* London: Sweet & Maxwell.

Elster, Jon and Rune Slagstad. 1988. *Constitutionalism and Democracy.* Cambridge: Cambridge University Press.

Ely, John Hart. 1980. *Democracy and Distrust: A Theory of Judicial Review.* Cambridge: Harvard University Press.

Epp, Charles R. 1998. *The Rights Revolution: Lawyers, Activists, and Supreme Courts in Comparative Perspective.* Chicago: University of Chicago Press.

Epstein, Lee and Jack Knight. 1997. "The New Institutionalism, Part II." *Law and Courts* 7(2): 4–9.

Epstein, Lee. 1991. "Courts and Interest Groups." In *The American Courts: A Critical Assessment,* John Gates and Charles Johnson (eds.), Washington, D.C.: CQ Press, 335–45.

———. 1996. *The Supreme Court Compendium: Data, Decisions, and Developments.* Washington, D.C.: Congressional Quarterly.

———. December 1989 / January 1990. "Interviewing U.S. Supreme Court Justices and Interest Group Attorneys." *Judicature* 73: 196–202.

Fenno, R. F. 1978. *Home Style: House Members in Their Districts.* Boston: Little Brown.

Fischer, Gerhard. 1989. *Enemy Aliens: Internment and the Homefront Experience in Australia, 1914–1920.* St Lucia (Qld): University of Queensland Press.

Fiss, Owen M. 1979. "Foreword: The Forms of Justice." *Harvard Law Review* 93: 39–44.

———. 1982. "The Social and Political Foundations of Adjudication." *Law and Human Behavior* 6: 121–28.

Flango, Victor E., Lettie McSpadden Wenner, Manfred Wenner. 1975. "The Concept of Judicial Role: A Methodological Note." *American Journal of Political Science* 19: 277–89.

Freund, Paul Abraham. 1961. *The Supreme Court of the United States: Its Business, Purposes and Performance.* Cleveland: World Pub. Co.

Fricke, G. 1986. *Judges of the High Court.* Hawthorn, Victoria: Hutchinson of Australia.

Fuller, Lon. 1978. "Forms and Limits of Adjudication." *Harvard Law Review* 92: 353–409.

Funston, Richard. 1975. "The Supreme Court and Critical Elections." *American Political Science Review* 69: 795–811.

Galligan, Brian. 1987. *Politics of the High Court: A Study of the Judicial Branch of Government in Australia.* St. Lucia; New York: University of Queensland Press.

Gibson, James. 1981. "The Role Concept in Judicial Research." *Law and Policy Quarterly*: 3: 291–311.

———. 1983. "From Simplicity to Complexity: The Development of Theory in the Study of Judicial Behavior." *Political Behavior* 5: 7–49.

Gillman, Howard. 1993. *The Constitution Besieged: The Rise and Demise of Lochner Era Police Powers Jurisprudence.* Durham: Duke University Press.

———. 1999. "The Court as an Idea." In *Supreme Court Decision-Making: New Institutionalist Approaches,* Cornell Clayton and Howard Gillman (eds.), Chicago: The University of Chicago Press, 65–90.

Glendon, Mary Ann. 1993. *Rights Talk: The Impoverishment of Political Discourse.* New York: Free Press.

Glick, Henry and Kenneth Vines. 1969. "Law-Making in the State Judiciary: A Comparative Study of Judicial Behavior." *Political Behavior* 5: 7–49.

Goldman, Sheldon. 1982. *Constitutional Law and Supreme Court Decision-Making: Cases and Essays*. New York: Harper & Row.

Gorden, Raymond L. 1969. *Interviewing: Strategy, Techniques, and Tactics*. Homewood, Ill.: Dorsey Press.

Graber, Mark. 1993. "The Nonmajoritarian Difficulty: Legislative Deference to the Judiciary." *Studies in American Political Development* 7: 35–73.

Gross, Neal Crasilneck. 1958. *Explorations in Role Analysis: Studies of the School Superintendency Role*. New York: Wiley.

Groves, M. and R. Smyth. 2004. "A Century of Judicial Style: Changing Patters in Judgment Writing on the High Court." *Federal Law Review* 32: 255–80.

Haines, Charles and Foster H. Sherwood. 1944. *The Role of the Supreme Court in American Government and Politics*. Berkeley: University of California Press.

Hand, Learned. 1958. *The Bill of Rights*. Cambridge: Harvard University Press.

Hart, Henry Melvin and Albert M. Sacks. 1958. *The Legal Process: Basic Problems in the Making and Application of Law*. Cambridge: Harvard University Press.

Healey, Kaye. 1998. *The Stolen Generation*. Balmain, N.S.W.: Spinney Press.

Heumann, M. 1977. *Plea Bargaining*. Chicago: University of Chicago Press.

———. December 1989 / January 1990. "Interviewing Trial Judges." *Judicature* 73: 200–2.

Heydon, D. 2003. "Judicial Activism and the Death of the Rule of Law." *Quadrant* 47(1): 9–22.

Higley, John, Desley Deacon, et al. 1979. *Elites in Australia*. London, Boston: Routledge & K. Paul.

Hill, Graeme. 1999. "The Demise of Cross-Vesting." *Federal Law Review* 27: 547–75.

Hoffman, David and John Rowe. 2003. *Human Rights in the U.K.: A General Introduction to the Human Rights Act 1998*. Harlow, England: Pearson/Longman.

Hoffman-Lange, U. 1992. "Eliten, Macht Und Konflikt in Der Bundesrepublik." *Opladen* 1: 409–38.

Holland, Kenneth M. 1991. *Judicial Activism in Comparative Perspective*. New York, NY: St. Martin's Press.

Holmes, Oliver Wendell. 1897. "The Path of the Law." *Harvard Law Review* 10: 457–78.

Howard, J. Woodford. 1977. "Role Perceptions and Behavior in Three U.S. Courts of Appeals." *Journal of Politics* 39: 916–38.

Hutley, F.C. 1981. "The Legal Traditions of Australia as Contrasted with Those of the United States." *Australian Law Journal* 55: 63–70.

Irving, Helen. 1999. *To Constitute a Nation*. Cambridge, U.K.: Cambridge University Press.

Jackson, David. 1997. "Practice in the High Court of Australia." *Australian Bar Review* 15: 1–60.

Jackson, Donald Wilson and C. Neal Tate. 1992. *Comparative Judicial Review and Public Policy*. Westport, Conn.: Greenwood Press.

Jackson, Donald Wilson. 1997. *The United Kingdom Confronts the European Convention on Human Rights*. Gainesville: University Press of Florida.

Jaensch, Dean. 1986. *Getting Our Houses in Order: Australia's Parliament, How It Works and the Need for Reform*. Ringwood, Vic.: Penguin.

———. 1991. *Parliament, Parties and People: Australian Politics Today*. Melbourne: Longman Cheshire.

Jaffe, Louis Leventhal. 1965. *Judicial Control of Administrative Action*. Boston: Little Brown.

Johnson, Charles W. 1989. "Strategies for Judicial Research: Soaking and Poking in the Judiciary." *Judicature* 73: 192–93.

Jones, Carol. 1991. "Qualitative Interviewing." In *Handbook for Research Students in the Social Sciences*, Graham Allan and Chris Skinner (eds.), London: The Falmer Press, 203–14.

Joseph, Philip. 1996. "The New Zealand Bill of Rights Act 1990." *Public Law Review* 7: 76–92.

Kearney, Joseph D. and Thomas W. Merrill. 2000. "The Influence of Amicus Curiae Briefs on the Supreme Court." *University of Pennsylvania Law Review* 148(3): 743–855.

Kelly, James. 1999. "The Charter of Rights and Freedoms and the Rebalancing of Liberal Constitutionalism in Canada, 1982–1997." *Osgoode Hall Law Journal* 37: 625–94.

———. 2005. *Governing with the Charter: Legislative and Judicial Activsm and Framers' Intent*. Vancouver: UBC Press.

King, Gary, Robert O. Keohane, et al. 1994. *Designing Social Inquiry: Scientific Inference in Qualitative Research*. Princeton, N.J.: Princeton University Press.

King, L. July 2000. "The Attorney-General, Politics, and the Judiciary." *Australian Law Journal* 74(7): 444–60.

Kirchheimer, Otto. 1980. *Political Justice: The Use of Legal Procedure for Political Ends*. Westport, Conn.: Greenwood Press.

Knopff, Rainer and F. L. Morton. 1992. *Charter Politics*. Scarborough, Ont.: Nelson Canada.

Koelble, Thomas. 1995. "The New Institutionalism in Political Science and Sociology." *Comparative Politics* 27(1): 231–43.

La Nauze, John Andrew. 1972. *The Making of the Australian Constitution*. Carlton, Victoria: Melbourne University Press.

Lamer, Antonio. 1992. "How the Charter Changes Justice." *Globe and Mail* (Toronto), 11.

Lane, Jan-Erik. 1996. *Constitutions and Political Theory*. Manchester; New York: Manchester University Press.

Lasser, William. 1985. "The Supreme Court in Periods of Critical Realignment." *Journal of Politics* 47: 1174–87.

Lawrence, Susan E. 1990. *The Poor in Court: The Legal Services Program and Supreme Court Decision Making*. Princeton, N.J.: Princeton University Press.

Lazarus, Edward. 1998. *Closed Chambers: The First Eyewitness Account of the Epic Struggles Inside the Supreme Court*. New York: Times Books/Random House.

Lijphart, Arend and Carlos H. Waisman. 1996. *Institutional Design in New Democracies: Eastern Europe and Latin America*. Boulder, Colo.: Westview Press.

Llewellyn, Karl N. 1996. *The Common Law Tradition: Deciding Appeals*. Buffalo, N.Y.: W.S. Hein.

Lumb, R. D. 1977. *The Constitutions of the Australian States*. St. Lucia, Queensland: University of Queensland Press.

Lummis, Trevor. 1987. *Listening to History: The Authenticity of Oral Evidence*. London: Hutchinson Education.

Lyles, Kevin L. 1997. *The Gatekeepers: Federal District Courts in the Political Process*. Westport, Conn.: Praeger.

Maltzman, Forrest, James Spriggs II, Paul Wahlbeck. 1999. "Strategy and Judicial Choice: New Institutionalist Approaches to Supreme Court Decision-Making." In *Supreme Court Decision-Making: New Institutionalist Approaches*, Cornell Clayton and Howard Gillman (eds.), Chicago: The University of Chicago Press, 43–63.

Mandel, Michael. 1994. *The Charter of Rights & the Legalization of Politics in Canada*. Toronto: Thompson Educational Publishing.

Manfredi, Christopher P. 2001. *Judicial Power and the Charter: Canada and the Paradox of Liberal Constitutionalism* (2 ed.). New York: Oxford University Press.

March, James G. and Johan P. Olsen. 1989. *Rediscovering Institutions: The Organizational Basis of Politics*. New York: Free Press.

Mason, A. F. 1987. "The State of the Australian Judicature." *Law Institute Journal* 61: 1120–23.

———. 1996. "The Regulation of Appeals to the High Court of Australia." *University of Tasmania Law Review* 15(1): 1–21.

———. 1997. "No Place in a Modern Democratic Society for a Supine Judiciary." *Law Society Journal* 35(11): 51–55.

———. 2000. "The Evolving Role and Function of the High Court." In *The Australian Federal Judicial System*, Brian Opeskin and Fiona Wheeler (eds.), Carlton South, Vic.: Melbourne University Press, 95–122.

Mason, Anthony and Cheryl Saunders. 1996. *Courts of Final Jurisdiction: The Mason Court in Australia*. Annandale, NSW: Federation Press.

McCloskey, Robert G. and Sanford Levinson. 1994. *The American Supreme Court*. Chicago: University of Chicago Press.

McCubbins, Mathew D. and Thomas Schwartz. 1984. "Congressional Oversight Overlooked: Police Patrols Versus Fire Alarms." *American Journal of Political Science* 28: 165–79.

McDonough, P. 1981. *Power and Ideology in Brazil*. Princeton: Princeton Univ. Press.

McGuire, Kevin T. 1993. *The Supreme Court Bar: Legal Elites in the Washington Community*. Charlottesville, Va.: University Press of Virginia.

McLachlan, Noel. 1989. *Waiting for the Revolution: A History of Australian Nationalism*. Ringwood, Vic.: Penguin.

McPherson, B. H. 1989. *The Supreme Court of Queensland, 1859–1960: History, Jurisdiction, Procedure*. Sydney: Butterworths.

Meese, Edwin. 1985. "The Attorney General's View of the Supreme Court: To-ward a Jurisprudence of Original Intention." *Public Administration Review* 45: 701–4.

Monahan, Patrick. 1987. *Politics and the Constitution: The Charter, Federalism, and the Supreme Court of Canada.* Toronto: Carswell.

Moore, G. 1979. "The Structure of a National Elite Network." *American Sociological Review* 44(5): 673–92.

Morton, F. L. and Rainer Knopff. 2000. *The Charter Revolution and the Court Party.* Peterborough, Ont.: Broadview Press.

Morton, F. L., P.H. Russell, and T. Riddell. 1994. "The Canadian Charter of Rights and Freedoms: A Descriptive Analysis of the First Decade, 1982–1992," *National Journal of Constitutional Law* 5: 1–60.

Murphy, Walter F. 1964. *Elements of Judicial Strategy.* Chicago: University of Chicago Press.

Neumann, E. 1973. *The High Court of Australia: A Collective Portrait, 1903–1972.* Sydney: University of Sydney, Dept. of Government and Public Administration.

North, Douglass C., Barry R. Weingast, et al. 1989. "Constitutions and Commitment: The Evolution of Institutions Governing Public Choice in Seventeenth-Century England." *Journal of Economic History* 49: 803–32.

O'Connor, Karen and Lee Epstein. 1982. "The Importance of Interest Group Involvement in Employment Discrimination Litigation." *Black Law Journal* 7(3): 411–26.

Olson, Mancur. 1993. "Dictatorship, Democracy, and Development." *American Political Science Review* 87: 567–76.

Olson, Susan M. 1990. "Interest-Group Litigation in Federal District Court: Beyond the Political Disadvantage Theory." *Journal of Politics* 52(3): 854–82.

Opeskin, Brian R. 1998. "The Rise and Fall of Cross-Vesting of Jurisdiction." *Constitutional Law & Policy Review* 1(2): 28–34.

Opeskin, Brian and Fiona Wheeler. 2000. *The Australian Federal Judicial System.* Carlton South, Vic.: Melbourne University Press.

Pacelle, Richard L. 1991. *The Transformation of the Supreme Court's Agenda: From the New Deal to the Reagan Administration.* Boulder: Westview Press.

Palmer, Andrew. 2000. "Legal Professional Privilege: The Demise of the Sole Purpose Test." *Law Institute Journal* 74(3): 50–2.

Palfreeman, A. C. 1967. *The Administration of the White Australia Policy*. Melbourne: Melbourne University Press & Cambridge University Press.

Parkinson, Patrick. 1994. *Tradition and Change in Australian Law*. Sydney: Law Book Co.

Patapan, Haig. 1996. "Rewriting Australian Liberalism: The High Court's Jurisprudence of Rights." *Australian Journal of Political Science* 31(2): 225–42.

———. 1999. "Separation of Powers in Australia." *Australian Journal of Political Science* 34(3): 391–405.

———. 2000. *Judging Democracy: The New Politics of the High Court of Australia*. Oakleigh, Vic.: Cambridge University Press.

———. 2002. "High Court Review 2001: Politics, Legalism, and the Gleeson Court." *Australian Journal of Political Science* 37(2): 241–53.

Paterson, Alan. 1982. *The Law Lords*. London: Macmillan.

Patton, Michael Quinn. 1980. *Qualitative Evaluation Methods*. Beverly Hills: Sage Publications.

Perry, H. W. 1991. *Deciding to Decide: Agenda Setting in the United States Supreme Court*. Cambridge, Mass.: Harvard University Press.

Perry, Michael J. 1982. *The Constitution, the Courts, and Human Rights: An Inquiry into the Legitimacy of Constitutional Policymaking by the Judiciary*. New Haven: Yale University Press.

Pierce, Jason L. 2002. "Interviewing Australia's Senior Judiciary." *Australian Journal of Political Science* 37(1): 131–42.

Plehwe, R. 1980. "The Attorney-General and Cabinet: Some Australian Precedents." *Federal Law Review* 11: 1–18.

Pound, Roscoe. 1959. *An Introduction to the Philosophy of Law*. New Haven: Yale University Press.

Powell, H. Jefferson. 1985. "The Original Understanding of Original Intent." *Harvard Law Review* 98(5): 885–948.

Presthus, Robert Vance. 1973. *Elite Accommodation in Canadian Politics*. Cambridge, England: University Press.

Priest, Joan. 1995. *Sir Harry Gibbs: Without Fear or Favour*. Mudgeeraba, Qld: Scribblers Pub.

Principe, Michael. 1993. "The Demise of Parliamentary Supremacy? Canadian and American Influences Upon the New Zealand Judiciary's Interpretations of the Bill of Rights Act of 1990." *Loyola of Los Angeles International and Comparative Law Journal* 16: 167–200.

Provine, Doris Marie. 1980. *Case Selection in the United States Supreme Court.* Chicago: University of Chicago Press.

Putnam, Robert D. 1973. *The Beliefs of Politicians: Ideology, Conflict, and Democracy in Britain and Italy.* New Haven: Yale University Press.

Quick, John and Robert Randolph Garran. 1976. *The Annotated Constitution of the Australian Commonwealth.* Sydney: Legal Books.

Ramseyer, Mark. 1994. "The Puzzling (in)Dependence of Courts: A Comparative Approach." *Journal of Legal Studies* 23: 721–47.

Rich, William. 1993. "Converging Constitutions: A Comparative Analysis of Constitutional Law in the United States and Australia." *Federal Law Review* 21: 202–27.

Richardson, Ivor. 1995. "Rights Jurisprudence—Justice for All?" In *Essays on the Constitution*, Philip Joseph (ed.), Wellington, New Zealand: Brooker's, 61–83.

Richardson, Richard J. and Kenneth Nelson Vines. 1970. *The Politics of Federal Courts: Lower Courts in the United States.* Boston: Little Brown.

Rishworth, Paul. 1997. "Human Rights and the Bill of Rights." *New Zealand Law Review* 1: 349–73.

Rishworth, Paul and Grant Huscroft, et al. 2003. *The New Zealand Bill of Rights.* South Melbourne, VIC: Oxford University Press.

Rohde, David W. and Harold J. Spaeth. 1976. *Supreme Court Decision Making.* San Francisco: W. H. Freeman.

Rowland, C. K. and Robert A. Carp. 1996. *Politics and Judgment in Federal District Courts.* Lawrence, Kan.: University Press of Kansas.

Russell, Peter H. 1987. *The Judiciary in Canada: The Third Branch of Government.* Toronto: McGraw-Hill Ryerson.

———. 1992. "The Supreme Court in the 1980s: A Commentary on the S.C.R. Statistics." *Osgoode Hall Law Journal* 30: 771–95.

———. 2000. "The Political High Court: How the High Court Shapes Politics by David Solomon." *Australian Journal of Political Science* 35(3): 542.

Saunders, Kay and Roger Daniels. 2000. *Alien Justice: Wartime Internment in Australia and North America.* St. Lucia, Queensland: University of Queensland Press.

Sawer, Geoffrey. 1967. *Australian Federalism in the Courts.* Melbourne: Melbourne University Press.

Scheb, John and Thomas Ungs. 1987. "Competing Orientations to the Judicial Role: The Case of Tennessee Judges." *Tennessee Law Review* 54: 391–411.

Scheb, John M., II, Thomas D. Ungs, et al. 1989. "Judicial Role Orientations, Attitudes and Decision Making: A Research Note." *Western Political Quarterly* 42: 427–35.

Schubert, Glendon A. 1974. *The Judicial Mind Revisited: Psychometric Analysis of Supreme Court Ideology*. New York: Oxford University Press.

Schubert, Glendon. 1969. "Judicial Attitudes and Policy-Making in the Dixon Court." *Osgoode Hall Law Journal* 7(1): 1–29.

Schwartz, B. 1996. *Decision: How the Supreme Court Decides Cases*. New York: Oxford University Press.

Segal, Jeffrey and Harold J. Spaeth. 1993. *The Supreme Court and the Attitudinal Model*. New York: Cambridge University Press.

Selway, B. M. 2003. "Methodologies of Constitutional Interpretation in the High Court of Australia." *Public Law Review* 14(4): 234–50.

Shapiro, Martin M. 1981. *Courts: A Comparative and Political Analysis*. Chicago: University of Chicago Press.

Shapiro, M. and Alec Stone Sweet. 2002. *On Law, Politics, and Judicialization*. Oxford: Oxford University Press.

Skowronek, Stephen. 1995. "Order and Change." *Polity* 28: 91–96.

Smith, Rogers M. 1985. *Liberalism and American Constitutional Law*. Cambridge, Mass.: Harvard University Press.

———. 1988. "Political Jurisprudence, the 'New Institutionalism,' and the Future of Public Law." *American Political Science Review* 82: 89–108.

———. 1995. "Ideas, Institutions, and Strategic Choice." *Polity* 28: 135–40.

Smyth, R. 2000. "The 'Haves' and the 'Have Nots': An Empirical Study of the Rational Actor and Party Capability Hypotheses in the High Court 1948–99." *Australian Journal of Political Science* 35(2): 255–74.

———. 2001. "Judicial Interaction on the Latham Court: A Quantitative Study of Voting Patterns on the High Court, 1935–1950." *Australian Journal of Politics and History* 47(3): 330-50.

———. 2002. "Historical and Consensual Norms in the High Court." *Australian Journal of Political Science* 37(2): 255–66.

———. 2003. "Explaining Historical Dissent Rates in the High Court of Australia." *Commonwealth and Comparative Politics* 41(2): 83–114.

Smyth, Russell and Mita Bhattacharya. 2001. "The Determinants of Judicial Prestige and Influence: Some Empirical Evidence from the High Court." *Journal of Legal Studies* 30(1): 223–52.

Spaeth, Harold J. 1961. "An Approach to the Study of Attitudinal Differences as an Aspect of Judicial Behavior." *Midwest Journal of Political Science* 5: 165–80.

Spence, J. 2000. *The European Union: A View from the Top, Top Decision Makers and the European Union.* EOS Gallop Europe. URL: <http://europa.eu.int/ comm/dg10/epo/eb-top/en.html>. Consulted 6 March 2001.

Spence, Michael. 1999. *Protecting Reliance: The Emergent Doctrine of Equitable Estoppel.* Oxford: Hart.

Stepan, Alfred C. and Cindy Skach. 1993. "Constitutional Frameworks and Democratic Consolidation: Parliamentarianism Versus Presidentialism." *World Politics* 46: 1–22.

Sterett, Susan. 1993. "Judicial Review in Britain: Part of a Special Issue on the New Constitutional Politics of Europe." *Comparative Political Studies* 26: 421–42.

Stone, Julius. 1964. *Legal System and Lawyers' Reasonings.* Stanford, Calif.: Stanford University Press.

Stone Sweet, Alec. 2000. *Governing with Judges: Constitutional Politics in Europe.* Oxford: Oxford University Press.

Sturgess, G. and P. Chubb. 1988. *Judging the World: Law and Politics in the World's Leading Courts.* Sydney: Butterworths.

Sunkin, Maurice. 1994. "Judicialization of Politics in the United Kingdom: Part of a Symposium on the Judicialization of Politics." *International Political Science Review* 15: 125–33.

Swinfen, David B. 1975. "Henry Brougham and the Judicial Committee of the Privy Council." *Law Quarterly Review* 90: 396–465.

Swinfen, David B. 1987. *Imperial Appeal: The Debate on the Appeal to the Privy Council, 1833–1986.* Manchester, U.K.: Manchester University Press.

Tanenhaus, Joseph, Marvin Schick, et al. 1963. "The Supreme Court's Certiorari Jurisdiction: A Cue Theory." In *Judicial Decision-Making*, Glendon Schubert (ed.), New York: The Free Press, 111–32.

Tate, C. Neal and Torbjörn Vallinder. 1995. *The Global Expansion of Judicial Power.* New York: New York University Press.

Thompson, Elaine. 1980. "The Washminster Mutation." In *Responsible Government in Australia,* Patrick Moray Weller and Dean Jaensch (eds.), Richmond, Vic.: Australasian Political Studies Association, 32–40.

———. 2001. "The Constitution and the Australian System of Limited Government, Responsible Government, and Representative Democracy: Revisiting the Washminster Mutation." *University of New South Wales Law Journal* 24(3): 657–69.

Thomson, James A. 1997. "American and Australian Constitutions: Continuing Adventures in Comparative Constitutional Law." *John Marshall Law Review* 30: 627–41.

Thomson, R. 1987. *The Judges: A Portrait of the Australian Judiciary.* Sydney: Allen & Unwin.

Topperwien, Bruce. 2001. "Foreign Precedent." In *Oxford Companion to the High Court of Australia,* Anthony Blackshield et al. (eds.). Melbourne, VIC: Oxford University Press.

Uhr, John. 1998. *Deliberative Democracy in Australia: The Changing Place of Parliament.* Cambridge, U.K.: Cambridge University Press.

Ulmer, S. Sidney, William Hintze, and Louise Kirklosky. 1972. "The Decision to Grant or Deny Certiorari: Further Consideration of Cue Theory." *Law and Society Review* 6: 637–43.

Vallinder, Torbjörn. 1994. "The Judicialization of Politics: A Worldwide Phenomenon—Introduction." *International Political Science Review* 15: 91–100.

Vose, Clement E. 1959. *Caucasians Only: The Supreme Court, the NAACP, and the Restrictive Covenant Cases.* Berkeley: University of California Press.

———. 1972. *Constitutional Change: Amendment Politics and Supreme Court Litigation Since 1900.* Lexington, Mass.: Lexington Books.

Wahlke, John C. 1962. *The Legislative System: Explorations in Legislative Behavior.* New York: Wiley.

Waltman, Jerold L. and Kenneth M. Holland. 1988. *The Political Role of Law Courts in Modern Democracies.* New York: St. Martin's Press.

Warden, James, M. G. Haward, et al. 1995. *An Australian Democrat: The Life, Work, and Consequences of Andrew Inglis Clark.* Hobart: Centre for Tasmanian Historical Studies, University of Tasmania.

Warden, James. 1992. "Federalism and the Design of the Australian Constitution." *Australian Journal of Political Science* 27(Special Issue): 143–58.

Weaver, R. Kent and Bert A. Rockman. 1993. *Do Institutions Matter? Government Capabilities in the United States and Abroad*. Washington, D.C.: The Brookings Institution.

Wechsler, Herbert. 1959. "Toward Neutral Principles." *Harvard Law Review* 73: 1–35.

Weingast, Barry R. 1993. "Constitutions as Governance Structures: The Political Foundations of Secure Markets." *Journal of Institutional and Theoretical Economics* 149(1): 286–311.

Weisbrot, David. 1990. *Australian Lawyers*. Melbourne: Longman Cheshire.

Wildenmann, R., Max Kaase, et al. 1982. *Fuhrungsschicht in Der Bundesrepublik Deutschland 1981*. Mannheim: Universitat Mannheim.

Williams, D. April 1998. "Judicial Independence." *Law Society Journal* 36(3): 50–51.

Williams, George. 1999. *Human Rights under the Australian Constitution*. South Melbourne: Oxford University Press.

Williams, George. 2000a. "The Amicus Curiae and Intervener in the High Court of Australia: A Comparative Analysis." *Federal Law Review* 28: 365–402.

Williams, George. 2000b. *A Bill of Rights for Australia*. Sydney: University of New South Wales Press.

Williams, George and Adrienne Stone. 2000. *The High Court at the Crossroads*. Leichhardt, NSW: Federation Press.

Wilson, Ronald et al. 1997. *Bringing Them Home: A Guide to the Findings and Recommendations of the National Inquiry into the Separation of Aboriginal and Torres Strait Islander Children from Their Families*. Sydney: Human Rights and Equal Opportunity Commission.

Wold, John T. 1974. "Political Orientations, Social Backgrounds and Role Perceptions of State Supreme Court Judges." *Western Political Quarterly* 29(2): 239–48.

Woodward, Bob and Scott Armstrong. 1981. *The Brethren: Inside the Supreme Court*. New York: Avon Books.

Wright, Charles Alan. 1994. *The Law of Federal Courts*. St. Paul, Minn.: West Pub. Co.

Zander, Michael. 1997. "A Bill of Rights for the United Kingdom — Now." *Texas International Law Journal* 32(3): 441–49.

Zines, L. 1986. "The Federal Balance and the Position of the States." In *Official Record of the Debates of the Australasian Federal Convention: The Convention Debates 1891–1898: Commentaries, Indices and Guide*, Gregory Craven (ed.), Sydney: Legal Books 6: 75–87.

———. 2002. "Legalism, Realism and Judicial Rhetoric in Constitutional Law." *Constitutional Law & Policy Review* 5(2): 21–30.

Zuckerman, Harriet. 1972. "Interviewing an Ultra-Elite." *Public Opinion Quarterly* 36(2): 159–75.

Index